CATECHISM STORIES

A Teachers' Aid-book in five parts

with references to the

Revised Baltimore Catechism No. 2

By

REV. F. H. DRINKWATER

Catholic Authors Press
www.CatholicAuthors.com

NIHIL OBSTAT:
PATRITIUS MORRIS, S.Th.D., L.S.S.
Censor deputatus.

IMPRIMATUR:
LEONELLUS CAN. EVANS,
Vic. Gen.

WESTMONASTERII,
die 23a Februarii 1939.

First published 1939
Reprinted 2007 Catholic Authors Press

ISBN: 978-0-9782985-3-1

Catholic Authors Press

www.CatholicAuthors.org

PREFACE

THIS book is meant to be used with the Abbreviated Catechism, which forms the catechism-course for ' senior ' children (elementary schools) in the Diocese of Birmingham. It is, of course, no substitute for the doctrinal aid-book covering the same ground. Both books are needed, and if it had been practicable they might have been better united into a single aid-book. For these stories (it is hoped) will not be merely decorative, a sort of pleasant interlude during the religious lesson, but will have a true structural function in building up and explaining the Catechism answers.

Consequently I trust that teachers of junior children will resist the temptation to use this book. The juniors, as much as the seniors and more, need doctrine in story form, but their less critical minds can often be satisfied with simple narratives of the ' One-day-Johnny-met-the-priest ' kind. Father Raemers, C.SS.R., shows us excellently how to do it in the booklets of his ' King Series ' (Sands & Co.), numbers one to twelve.

We must remember that stories which to us are over-familiar are still new to the young, and therefore in this book there are many old favourites and also material adapted from previous collections ; the best of the latter being Spirago-Baxter & Chisholm, both however labouring under disadvantages of expensiveness and old-fashioned taste.

Some of our stories are evidently more for boys and some more for girls, but most, perhaps, will serve for both and thus be useful even in those ' senior mixed ' classes for whose teachers I must say I always feel rather sorry.

Grateful thanks are due to several helpers, but especially to Miss V. C. Barclay and Miss M. M. Davitt.

So now may this book and those who use it have the blessing and assistance of Our Lord Himself, who had such effective stories for His different hearers, and without stories did not speak to them; and of His Holy Mother also, who perhaps had contributed something of her own to that Gift.

F. H. D.

NOTE TO AMERICAN EDITION

The stories in this book were arranged to fit an abbreviated form of the English Catechism. It has been thought best to leave the English answers in their place, as they will sometimes throw light on the point of a story. But at the head of each story, or group of stories, will be found the appropriate reference to *The Revised Baltimore Catechism No. 2*.

By glancing through the Table of Contents, the American reader should easily find the stories (if any) which are suitable for a given answer in the American Catechism.

CONTENTS

PREFACE

Part I: The Creed

BALTIMORE 1, 2, 48-50
ENGLISH CATECHISM 1
1. We did not make ourselves. *(The astronomer's model)*
2. 'Blessed be Thou for creating me!' *(St. Clare)*.
3. Since God made us, we belong to Him. *(Sand competition)*
4. The soul is an immortal spirit, in God's likeness. *(The infidel prince)*
5. God upholds us in existence. *(St. Kevin and the blackbird)*

BALTIMORE 3-4
ENGLISH CATECHISM 2
6. God wants to share His happiness. *(The adopted foundling)*
7. God made me to love Him. *(Curé of Ars)*.
8. 'Thou hast made us for Thyself.' *(St. Augustine)*
9. Where are we bound for? *(Two girl emigrants)*.

BALTIMORE 4, 50
ENGLISH CATECHISM 7
10. The Soul is the highest part of man. *(St. Anselm)*
11. 'What doth it profit a man?' *(Matt. xvi, 23)*
12. This night they require thy soul. *(Luke xii, 16)*.
13. Taking most care of his guinea-pig! *(A boy and his pet)*
14. The one thing necessary. *(St. Philip)*.
15. We make our own eternity. *(Building a house)*.
16. This life is nothing compared with Eternity. *(Madman in a shipwreck)*.

BALTIMORE 120-124, 200-203
ENGLISH CATECHISM 8
17. The Three Theological Virtues. *(Jumping into the cellar)*.
18. Our need of Revelation. *(The Eastern king)*

vii

viii CONTENTS

P

19. We need correct information. *(In the wrong train)* .
20. The gift of Faith. *(St. Paulinus)* .
21. Hope in God's promises. *(The stamp-collection)*
22. Trust in God only. *(Ezechias and Sennacherib)*
23. How God keeps His word. *(Holy Simeon)* .
24. The virtue of Charity. *(St. Teresa)* .

BALTIMORE 6-7
ENGLISH CATECHISM 14

25. Devotion to the Creed. *(St. Peter Martyr)* .

BALTIMORE 8-11
ENGLISH CATECHISM 17

26. 'Alone exists of Himself.' *(God tells His Name to Moses)* .
27. Infinite in all perfections. *(Eithne and Fedelm)* .
28. The Footprints of Allah. *(The Bedouin and the atheist)* .
29. Infinite Beauty. *(Rabbi Joshua)* .

BALTIMORE 12-23
ENGLISH CATECHISM 20-23

30. Our Knowledge of God. *('They'll know now')* .
31. We know God by our reason . *('My dog and cat')* .
32. The Unbeginning. *('Who made God?')* .
33. From eternity to eternity Thou art God! *(Grains of sand)* .
34. God is Spirit, present everywhere, all-mighty. *(St. Paul at Athens)* .
35. God knows and sees all things. *(Mother M. Hallahan)*

BALTIMORE 35-37
ENGLISH CATECHISM 19

36. Creator of Heaven and Earth. *(The old Spanish woman)* .
37. Creator of life. *(Protoplasm)* .
38. Creator of all things, visible and invisible. *(St. Anthony and the fishes)* .
39. God's Providence guides all His Creation. *(The treasure-hunt)* .

BALTIMORE 24-34
ENGLISH CATECHISM 25-26

40. The Mystery of the One and the Three. *(St. Augustine and the boy)* .
41. Three Persons in God. *(The Shamrock)* .
42. God is above our finite minds. *(St. Thomas Aquinas)*

CONTENTS ix

BALTIMORE 77-79
ENGLISH CATECHISM 32
    43. The Son of the living God. *(Confession of Peter)* . 28
    44. God so loved the world. *(Nicodemus)* . . . 29
    45. Made man for us. *(Luke* xv, 1-10) 30
    46. What manner of Man is this? *(Mark* iv, 36-40) . 31

BALTIMORE 80
ENGLISH CATECHISM 34
    47. True God of true God. *(Council of Nicaea)* . . 31
    48. Consubstantialem Patri. *(John* viii, 51, etc.) . . 32
    49. 'Indeed the Son of God.' *(The centurion)* . . 32
    50. 'Before the day-star have I begotten Thee.' *(Ps.* cix, etc.) 32

BALTIMORE 81
ENGLISH CATECHISM 38
    51. Our Lord has the nature of man. *(Gethsemane)* . 33
    52. 'He emptied Himself.' *(St. Paulinus of Nola)* . 33
    53. Christ is our Elder Brother. *('He's my brother!')* . 34
    54. In all things like as we are. *(Father Damien)* . . 34

BALTIMORE 82-86
ENGLISH CATECHISM 40
    55. Descendit de coelis. *(The king in disguise)* . . 35
    56. Christ the Bridge. *(Gen.* xxviii, 10, etc.) . . . 36
    57. The Spirit of Christmas. *(In Flanders,* 1914) . . 36

BALTIMORE 84 and 103
ENGLISH CATECHISM 46
    58. 'As God, Jesus Christ is everywhere.' *(St. Edmund and the Boy)* 38
    59. 'As God made man, He is in heaven.' *(St. Stephen)* . 39
    60. Alpha and Omega. *(Apoc.* i, 10, etc.) . . . 40
    61. 'And in the Blessed Sacrament.' *(St. Paschal Baylon)* 40

BALTIMORE 85-87
ENGLISH CATECHISM 48
    62. Ave gratia plena. *(Luke* i, 26, etc.) 41
    63. Mary's place in the Creed. *(The orphan and the clergyman)* 41
    64. Mother of Christ. *(B. Angela of Foligno)* . . 41

BALTIMORE 88
ENGLISH CATECHISM 49
    65. Guardian of Jesus and Mary. *(Matt.* i, 18, etc.) . 42
    66. St. Joseph's power with God. *(St. Teresa)* . . 42

CONTENTS

PAGE

BALTIMORE 90-94
ENGLISH CATECHISM 55

67. 'Our Saviour suffered.' *(Luke xxiv, 18, etc.)*	43
68. Saviour of Mankind. *(Legend of Calvary)*	44
69. 'He shall save His people from their sins.' *(Picture of Perpetual Succour)*	44
70. 'He died for me.' *(The Illinois farmer)*	44
71. 'I, if I be lifted up.' *(St. John Gualbert)*	45
72. 'Greater love than this.' *(Night patrol)*	46
73. Dux vitae mortuus. *(Arnold von Winkelried)*	46
74. A Ransom for many. *(Matt. xx, 20, etc.)*	46
75. 'You are bought with a price.' *(The slave-girl)*	47
76. The price by which we were ransomed. *(The old picture)*	47

BALTIMORE 487-689
ENGLISH CATECHISM 59

77. How to make the Sign of the Cross. *(St. Bernadette)*	48
78. Strength from the Crucifix. *(St. Joseph of Leonissa)*	50
79. Welcoming the Cross. *(B. Osanna of Mantua)*	50
80. The joy of suffering with Christ. *(St. Ignatius of Antioch)*	51

BALTIMORE 95-97
ENGLISH CATECHISM 63-64

81. 'He descended into hell.' *(Second Adam meets the First)*	52

BALTIMORE 98-99
ENGLISH CATECHISM 66

82. 'Resurrexit sicut dixit.' *(Easter Sunday)*	53
83. Witnesses of His Resurrection. *(St. Peter's first sermon)*	54
84. 'He raised His Blessed Body to life again.' *('Destroy this temple')*	54
85. A sign from God. *(Voltaire's advice)*	55
86. 'My Lord and my God!' *(St. Marina)*	55
87. The Sign of Jonas the prophet. *(Matt. xii, 38, etc.)*	56

BALTIMORE 101-102
ENGLISH CATECHISM 69

88. The Ascension. *(Acts i, 9, etc.)*	57
89. Christ the King. *(St. Martin's vision)*	58

BALTIMORE 103
ENGLISH CATECHISM 70

90. 'Viva Cristo Rey!' *(Mexican persecution)*	58

CONTENTS

BALTIMORE 104, 180, 182
ENGLISH CATECHISM 72
   91. The Day of Reckoning. *(Matt.* xiii, 24, etc.)
   92. Fair warning. *(Matt.* xxv, 31, etc.)
   93. 'To judge the living and the dead.' *(St. Methodius)*

BALTIMORE 181
ENGLISH CATECHISM 76
   94. Everyone will be judged at death. *(A newspaper cutting)*
   95. 'The first five minutes after death.' *(Scottish explorer)*

BALTIMORE 181
ENGLISH CATECHISM 73
   96. Our conscience will supply the evidence. *(Skating accident)*
   97. 'Be not to me a Judge but a Saviour.' *(The youth in the train)*

BALTIMORE 105-107
ENGLISH CATECHISM 80
   98. The Holy Ghost equal to Father and to Son. *(St. Edmund)*

BALTIMORE 108, 140-143
ENGLISH CATECHISM 82
   99. 'To enable them to found the Church.' *(Acts* ii, 1, etc.)

BALTIMORE 136, 139
ENGLISH CATECHISM 84-85
   100. Union of all the faithful. *('I am the Vine')*
   101. 'If I forgot thee, O Jerusalem!' *(A story from Korea)*
   102. Christ the Head of the Church. *(Letter from St. Paul)*

BALTIMORE 137, 144-145, 162, 165
ENGLISH CATECHISM 12
   103. 'Teach all nations.' *(Matt.* xxviii, 18, etc.)

BALTIMORE 162-165
ENGLISH CATECHISM 101
   104. Christ's promises to the Church. *(Matt.* xvi, 17, etc.)
   105. The Church cannot err in matters of Faith. *(Galileo)*

BALTIMORE 136, 147, 156
ENGLISH CATECHISM 86
   106. Any Society needs a head. *(The new club)*
   107. Head of the Church on earth. *(B. Cuthbert Mayne)*

CONTENTS

PAGE

BALTIMORE 147-148
ENGLISH CATECHISM 87

    108. The First Pope. *(Story of St. Peter)* . . . 71
    109. Successor of St. Peter. *(St. Catherine of Avignon)* . 72

BALTIMORE 148
ENGLISH CATECHISM 89-90

    110. Father of all Christians. *(Nicholas Breakspeare)* . 74

BALTIMORE 164
ENGLISH CATECHISM 93

    111. Shepherd and Teacher of all Christians. *(Vatican Council)* 75

BALTIMORE 152-160
ENGLISH CATECHISM 94-97

    112. 'Four marks by which we may know her.' *(Lost umbrella)* 77
    113. What Our Lord said about His Church. *(John xvii, 11, etc.)* 78
    114. One Lord, one faith, one baptism. *(B. Edward Morgan)* 78
    115. The Church makes people holy. *(The medicine)* . 79
    116. The Church produces the saints. *(Innocent III's dream)* 79
    117. Unworthy Christians. *(Matt. xiii, 24, etc.)* . . 80
    118. Catholic in place and time. *(B. Peter Wright)* . . 80
    119. The Church of all nations. *(Acts x, 9, etc.)* . . 81
    120. Catholic means Universal. *(Two friends in 1918)* . 82
    121. The true Church must be 'Apostolic.' *(The Twelve)* 83

BALTIMORE 170-174
ENGLISH CATECHISM 102

    122. 'In communion with each other. *(The Irish laybrother)* 84
    123. Our prayer can bring grace to others. *(St. Thérèse and the criminal)* 85
    124. How the saints help us. *(Nuns in Malaya)* . . 85
    125. Praying to St. Anthony. *(Man overboard)* . . 86
    126. We can help the souls of the dead. *(St. Malachy's sister)*. 87

BALTIMORE 173-184
ENGLISH CATECHISM 106

    127. The necessity of Purgatory. *(Machabeus and the slain)* 87
    128. 'A place where souls suffer for a time.' *(Dante's Purgatorio)* 88
    129. 'On account of their sins.' *(Wash and brush-up first)* 91

CONTENTS

BALTIMORE 175
ENGLISH CATECHISM 111-112

   130. Christ's power over sins left to His Church. *(John xx, 20, etc.)*

   131. 'Whose sins you shall retain.' *(St. Ambrose and Theodosius)*

BALTIMORE 51-61
ENGLISH CATECHISM 115

   132. Our share in the sin of Adam. *(The traitor prince)*

BALTIMORE 62
ENGLISH CATECHISM 117-118

   133. 'I am the Immaculate Conception.' *(St. Bernadette)*

BALTIMORE 64
ENGLISH CATECHISM 113

   134. Offending God: the only real evil. *(St. John Chrysostom)*

   135. 'Against the law of God.' *(Lee of Virginia)*

   136. How we know the law of God. *(A mountain track)*

BALTIMORE 66-69
ENGLISH CATECHISM 121-125

   137. Mortal sin, greatest of all evils. *(St. Louis)*

   138. Three conditions to make a Mortal Sin. *(Missing prayers)*

   139. Mortal sin kills the soul. *(Leonardo's model)*

   140. They who die in mortal sin. *(The dead tree)*

   141. 'Hell for all eternity.' *(A dream about Satan)*

   142. Men make their own hell. *(Dante's Inferno)*

BALTIMORE 70-72
ENGLISH CATECHISM 126

   143. Venial sin displeases God. *(St. Philip and the boys)*

   144. The greatest evil after mortal sin. *(St. Frances of Rome)*

   145. Avoiding venial sin. *(Margaret Sinclair)*

   146. 'Often leads to mortal sin.' *(Arthur and the Dwarf)*

BALTIMORE 176-179
ENGLISH CATECHISM 129

   147. 'We shall rise again at the Day of Judgement.' *(Luke xx, 27-38)*

   148. 'We shall rise again with the same bodies.' *(The Silver cup)*

BALTIMORE 186
ENGLISH CATECHISM 131

    149. 'The good shall live for ever.' *(St. Cuthbert and St. Aidan)* 104
    150. Eternal Bliss. *(The monk Felix)* . . . 104
    151. Look forward to Paradise. *(St. Dorothy)* . . 105

BALTIMORE 186
ENGLISH CATECHISM 132

    152. 'The Glory and Happiness of Heaven.' *(Dante in the Tenth Heaven)* 107
    153. 'Eye hath not seen . . .' *(Time for Sunday school)* . 108
    154. Where the true joys are. *(Ven. Roger Warren)* . 108

Part II: The 'Our Father'

BALTIMORE 475, 477-485
ENGLISH CATECHISM 141

    155. Our duty of prayer, as creatures. *(The absent piccolo)* 113
    156. 'We will never leave off praying.' *(Uganda Martyrs)* 113
    157. We have need of prayer. *(Marshal Foch)* . . 115
    158. 'We have kept up our prayers.' *(Lost hikers)* . . 115
    159. 'Prayers give power to action.' *(Moses against Amalek)* 116
    160. Prayer helps our work. *(John Wesley)* . . 117
    161. 'The raising up of the mind and heart.' *(Farm-labourer of Ars)* 117
    162. We cannot pray by proxy. *(The new young monk)* . 118
    163. Prayer must be interior. *(St. Bernard)* . . 118
    164. Praying like a parrot. *(A parrot that could pray)* . 119
    165. Distractions sure to come. *(St. Benedict and the peasant)* 120
    166. Wilful distractions. *(A nun's dream)* . . 120
    167. Raising our heart. *(Joyce Kilmer)* . . . 121

BALTIMORE 476
ENGLISH CATECHISM 142

    168. 'By thinking of God.' *(Shooting a lion)* . . 121
    169. The Prayer of Adoration. *(The two seraphim)* . 122
    170. The Prayer of Praise. *(Operation on tongue)* . 122
    171. The Prayer of Thanks. *(Two Angels)* . . 123
    172. Brother Deo Gratias! *(St. Felix of Cantalice)* . 123
    173. 'And by begging of Him all blessings.' *(Lend me three loaves)* 124
    174. The Prayer of Contrition. *(In Christ's parables)* . 124
    175. 'Blessings for soul.' *(Wounded German officer)* . 124
    176. 'Blessings for body.' *(The Canaanite woman)* . 125

CONTENTS

BALTIMORE 490
ENGLISH CATECHISM 145

   177. 'The Lord's Prayer.' *(Teaching the Apostles)* . . 125

BALTIMORE 492
ENGLISH CATECHISM 148-149

   178. God is Father of men in two ways. *(Genesis)* . . 126
   179. 'Father of all mankind.' *(A French Archbishop)* . 127
   180. Men are all One Family. *(Pope Pius XII)* . . 128
   181. The true equality of man. *(Pennies)* . . . 129
   182. 'Loves and preserves them all.' *(Boy and snail)* . 130
   183. We are God's children by adoption. *(Two orphans in Moscow)* 130
   184. Our Father's home is heaven. *(St. Cyril of Cappadocia)* 132

BALTIMORE 491
ENGLISH CATECHISM 150

   185. 'Our Father.' and not 'My Father.' *(St. Oswald)* . 133

BALTIMORE 493
ENGLISH CATECHISM 151

   186. God tells His Name to Moses. *(The ineffable Name)* 134
   187. We are made to give glory to God. *(The old Chinaman)* 134
   188. 'We pray that God may be known.' *(King Prempeh)* 135
   189. 'By all His creatures.' *(The big flat stone)* . . 136
   190. Seed of the Church. *(Chinese martyrs)* . . . 136

BALTIMORE 494
ENGLISH CATECHISM 152

   191. 'Thy Kingdom Come!' *(The Monk Cassianus)* . . 138
   192. God's grace is precious beyond all else. *(Hidden treasure)* 139
   193. The State of Grace. *(Medical inspection)* . . 140
   194. The Militant Kingdom of God. *(King Michael)* . 140

BALTIMORE 495
ENGLISH CATECHISM 153

   195. 'That God may enable us by His grace.' *(Old violin)* 142
   196. His Will, not our own will. *(Two mothers)* . . 143
   197. On earth or in heaven, God's Will. *(St. Ignatius)* . 143
   198. 'As the Blessed do in heaven.' *(In His Will is our Peace)* 144
   199. Our troubles are permitted by God's Will. *(A grumbler)* 145

CONTENTS

BALTIMORE 496
ENGLISH CATECHISM 154

200. 'Give us this day our daily bread.' *(Stone and serpent)*
201. 'Give us,' not 'give me.' *(Lady Jane Grey)*
202. The prayer of Faith. *(St. Brigid and the butter)*
203. Praying for rain. *(Thundering Legion)*
204. Answering in a different way. *(Naval officer)*
205. Refusal is an answer too. *(Little girl in train)*

BALTIMORE 497
ENGLISH CATECHISM 155

206. 'As we forgive them that trespass against us.' *(Red Indian Chief)*
207. The necessity of forgiving. *(Martyr turned coward)*
208. Forgiving our enemies generously. *(James Connolly)*

BALTIMORE 498, 46-47
ENGLISH CATECHISM 156

209. Keep out of temptation! *(A parable by St. Anthony)*
210. Don't argue with temptations. *(Epictetus)*
211. Making temptation remote. *(Odysseus and sirens)*
212. Temptations resisted bring strength. *(St. Aquinas)*

BALTIMORE 499
ENGLISH CATECHISM 157

213. 'Deliver us from evil.' *(Casting out spirits)*
214. 'From all evil, past, present, and to come.' *(St. Joan)*
215. God can set us free. *(St. Peter's deliverance from prison)*
216. God's protection can work through natural means. *(A farm-house in 1812)*

BALTIMORE 86-87
ENGLISH CATECHISM 160-164

217. The making of the 'Hail Mary.' *(St. Ildephonsus, etc.)*
218. The power of the 'Hail Mary.' *(In the condemned cell)*
219. 'And at the hour of our death.' *(Hospital story)*
220. 'To honour Our blessed Lady.' *(Our Lady's Tumbler)*
221. Devotion to Our Lady. *(St. Crispin of Viterbo)*
222. Our Lady answers a Novena. *(At Arras)*
223. Our Lady's power. *(A cure at Boulogne)*
224. 'Ask Our Lady for everything.' *(John Traynor)*

BALTIMORE 85
ENGLISH CATECHISM 167

225. All women are honoured in God's Mother. *(Chinese girl)*

CONTENTS xvii

BALTIMORE 171, 172, 215-218
ENGLISH CATECHISM 158

226. 'We should ask the Angels and Saints to pray for us.' *(St. Lucy)* 165
227. The Saints are 'our friends and brethren.' *(St. Ignatius)* 165

Part III: The Commandments

BALTIMORE 195
ENGLISH CATECHISM 174

228. 'God gave the Ten Commandments to Moses' *(from Exodus)* 169
229. 'Christ confirmed them in the New Law.' *(Matt. xix, etc.)* 169

BALTIMORE 200-203
ENGLISH CATECHISM 176

230. 'To worship the one, true, and living God.' *(Painting out the lamp)* 170

BALTIMORE 204-206
ENGLISH CATECHISM 177

231. Professing our Faith openly. *(Pavlov)* . . 171
232. Refusal to deny the Faith. *(Mandarin's order)* . 171
233. Zeal for the Faith. *(B. Nicholas Garlick)* . . 172
234. Avoiding 'all false religions.' *(Venerable R. Milner)* 172
235. Taking part in a false religion. *(With a non-Catholic friend)* 173
236. Reading bad books. *(Two ways of acting)* . . 174
237. Heresy to be hated, but not heretics. *(St. Hilary)* . 174
238. Patience with unbelievers. *(Legend of Abraham)* . 175
239. 'Culpable ignorance.' *(St. Aldhelm)* . . . 175

BALTIMORE 207-209
ENGLISH CATECHISM 179

240. The virtue of Hope. *(St. Martin and the tree)* . 175
241. 'The lovely virtue of Courage.' *(St. Genevieve)* . 176
242. Despair. *(Judas)* 177
243. Over-confidence. *(Pachomius and the monk)* . 177

BALTIMORE 189-190
ENGLISH CATECHISM 320

244. 'Thou shalt love the Lord thy God.' *(Chained to his cave)* 177
245. 'Love is the fulfilling of the Law.' *(The beloved disciple)* 178

CONTENTS

PAGE

246. 'Thou shalt love thy neighbour.' *(Good Samaritan)* 178
247. Loving our neighbour as ourself. *(The water-bottle)* 178
248. Heroic charity. *(Wreck of the 'Birkenhead')* . . 179
249. 'Where Love is, God is.' *(Tolstoy's story)* . . . 179

BALTIMORE 212-223
ENGLISH CATECHISM 180

250. 'Thou shalt not have strange gods before Me.' *(Elias)* 180
251. The virtue of 'Religion.' *(Five-finger exercise)* . 181
252. 'The honour that belongs to God alone. *(Theban Legion)* 181
253. Superstition. *(The wrong horoscope)* . . . 182
254. 'Superstitious practices.' *(The broken tumblers)* . 183

BALTIMORE 224-235
ENGLISH CATECHISM 189

255. 'To speak with reverence of God.' *(A mock sermon)* 184
256. Reverence for holy things. *(Pretended sick call)* . 184
257. Reverence for God's House. *(Lifting his cap)* . . 185
258. 'To keep our lawful oaths.' *(Injured arm)* . . 186
259. Giving evidence on oath. *(Driver's mate)* . . 186
260. Respect for one's oath. *(A Roman General)* . . 187
261. 'Unlawful oaths.' *(Inscription at Devizes)* . . 187
262. Take advice before making a vow. *(St. Francis of Sales)* 188

BALTIMORE 236-240
ENGLISH CATECHISM 193

263. 'To keep the Sunday holy.' *(Seven peaches)* . . 188
264. 'By hearing Mass.' *(They had a motor-car)* . . 189
265. Social worship is due to our Creator. *'(Solomon's Temple)* 189
266. 'Resting from servile works.' *(The Paris jeweller)* . 190
267. Working on Sundays. *(Re gardening)* . . . 190
268. Necessary work is allowed on Sunday. *(Re needlework)* 191
269. 'The Sabbath is made for man.' *(Gospel incidents)* . 191

BALTIMORE 241-243, 250
ENGLISH CATECHISM 197

270. 'Honour thy Father.' *(Vienna convict)* . . . 192
271. 'Honour thy Mother.' *(Condemned murderer)* . . 192
272. Scripture stories about obedience. *(Two sons, etc.)* . 193
273. 'In all that is not sin.' *(An unscrupulous mother)* . 193
274. Remorse for disobedience. *(Doctor Johnson)* . . 194
275. Loyalty to our parents. *(King Lear)* 194
276. Our debt to our parents. *(A contrary account)* . 195

CONTENTS

BALTIMORE 244
ENGLISH CATECHISM 201
277. Parental instruction lasts best. *(St. Zita)*
278. What one good mother can do. *(St. Margaret as mother)*
279. Wise love puts spiritual welfare first. *(St. John Calybite)*
280. True charity begins at home. *(Sir Launfal)*

BALTIMORE 246-249
ENGLISH CATECHISM 198
281. The wider Family. *('Behold My mother and My brethren')*
282. 'Our Bishops and Pastors.' *(A by-election)*
283. The Lord's anointed. *(David and Saul)*
284. All lawful authority is from God. *(Christians and Caesar)*
285. We must obey the 'Civil Authorities.' *(Bicycle-lamp)*
286. Limits of Civil Authority. *(B. Sebastian Newdigate)*
287. Bad laws not to be obeyed. *(St. Thomas More)*
288. The Totalitarian State. *(In the Fiery Furnace)*
289. When is a law not a law? *(Kissing in public)*

BALTIMORE 251-253
ENGLISH CATECHISM 206
290. 'Thou shalt not kill.' *(Macbeth)*
291. Murderous motorists. *(Narrow escape)*
292. Lawfulness of just war. *(Four young men)*
293. There need be no war. *(Christ of the Andes)*
294. Cruelty is always in men's hearts. *(St. Telemachus)*
295. We must not take our own life. *(An African hero)*
296. When can we risk our own life? *(Captain Oates)*

BALTIMORE 253
ENGLISH CATECHISM 207
297. Hatred and Revenge. *(Portrait of Judas)*
298. 'Fighting, quarrelling, and injurious words.' *(Miraculous water)*
299. The sin of Scandal. *(Officers' Mess)*
300. Reparation for Scandal. *(Heir to a brewery)*
301. 'That's why I don't go to church!' *(Little girl's prayer)*
302. The force of a good example. *(Tin-whistle at St. Quentin)*

BALTIMORE 254
ENGLISH CATECHISM 210
303. 'Thou shalt not commit adultery.' *(King David)*

CONTENTS

		PAGE
304.	The havoc of passions uncontrolled. *(Herod the Tetrarch)*	212
305.	Marriage is a free promise. *(St. Bathilde)*	213
306.	Loving each other in God. *(St. Elizabeth of Hungary)*	214
307.	What real love means. *(Colliery disaster)*	217
308.	Loyalty. *(St. Louis of France)*	217

BALTIMORE 255-256
ENGLISH CATECHISM 211

309.	'Whatever is contrary to holy purity.' *(Tekakwitha)*	218
310.	Our Lady, safeguard of holy purity. *(St. Edmund)*	220
311.	Modesty. *(St. Bega)*	220
312.	Vanity. *(St. Rose of Lima)*	221
313.	How not to be vain. *(Royalty in Lambeth)*	222
314.	'Occasions of sin.' *(An Archbishop on dancing)*	222

BALTIMORE 259-261
ENGLISH CATECHISM 215-216

315.	'Thou shalt not steal.' *(St. Martin and brigand)*	223
316.	Habits of dishonesty. *(A policeman's note-book)*	224
317.	'Keeping what belongs to another.' *(The night's takings)*	224
318.	Finding is not keeping. *(The honest tramp)*	224
319.	Honesty. *(Abraham Lincoln)*	225
320.	Be worthy of trust. *(St. Eligius)*	226
321.	Carrying out a bargain. *(Bringing the penny back)*	226
322.	Bishops ought to defend God's poor. *(St. Hugh)*	226
323.	The best policy too. *(The Cardinal's mistake)*	228
324.	'Their master's time and property.' *(St. Zita, housekeeper)*	229
325.	One way of wronging our neighbour. *(Five boys)*	230
326.	Duty to employers. *(Young engineer)*	230
327.	Conscientious work. *(Sweeping under the mats)*	231

BALTIMORE 262-263
ENGLISH CATECHISM 217

328.	Restoring ill-gotten goods. *(A last burglary)*	232
329.	Rulers should protect the poor against the rich. *(St. Edward)*	232

BALTIMORE 265-267, 270
ENGLISH CATECHISM 220

330.	Telling lies. *(St. Andrew Avellino)*	233
331.	Lies of excuse. *(Two English Martyrs)*	233
332.	'Publicity.' *(Truth in business)*	234
333.	Lies in the Newspapers. *(Italy mobilizing)*	234
334.	Religious hypocrisy. *(Ananias and Saphira)*	235

CONTENTS

335. Secrets should be kept. *(A case of deception)*
336. 'Rash judgement.' *(Woman taken in adultery)*

BALTIMORE 268-271
ENGLISH CATECHISM 221-222

337. The sin of Detraction. *(St. Philip and the feathers)*
338. Gossip. *(Three ladies)*
339. 'Tale-bearing.' *(The Caliph's beard)*

BALTIMORE 273-276
ENGLISH CATECHISM 224

340. 'Blessed are the clean of heart.' *(Inferno and Purgatorio)*
341. 'Like the gentiles that know not God.' *(Episode in Uganda)*
342. No sin without wilful consent. *(St. Catherine of Siena)*
343. Remedy for sensual thoughts. *(Ignatius convalescent)*

BALTIMORE 257-258
ENGLISH CATECHISM 225

344. 'Gluttony, drunkenness, and intemperance.' *(St. Wulstan)*
345. Idleness. *(The desert hermit)*
346. Bad Company. *(Two Catholic soldiers)*

BALTIMORE 277-278
ENGLISH CATECHISM 227

347. 'Thou shalt not covet.' *(Naboth's vineyard)*
348. Money talks. *(The half-crown)*
349. Economics and Politics. *(The mirror)*
350. 'Nec speravit in pecunia et thesauris.' *(Irish navvy)*
351. The servant of Mammon. *(Miser in strong-room)*
352. Greed stops at nothing. *(Three gangsters)*
353. Envy will not share. *(Equal portions)*
354. The gambling fever. *(Oxford won)*
355. The gambling temperament. *(St. Camillus)*
356. One good side of gambling. *(Xavier and Vellio)*
357. What money is for. *(King Phythius)*
358. Our industrial system. *(In the canal)*
359. No need for Class War. *(Strike in Toulouse)*
360. 'Nobody starves, anyhow.' *(St. Columba)*

BALTIMORE 279-287
ENGLISH CATECHISM 229

361. Spirit of obedience to the Church. *(Choosing coin)*
362. Natural law and Positive law. *(A football player)*
363. Hearing Mass on Sundays. *(Dream about St. Peter)*

CONTENTS

PAGE

364. 'Do this in commemoration of Me.' *(Burning twigs)* 255
365. 'Therefore let us feast.' *(Paschal Lamb)* . . . 256
366. Easter Duties. *(The old grandmother)* . . . 256
367. The Offertory. *(Two shipwrecked sailors)* . . . 257
368. The Church's law of abstinence. *(Meat for the dog)* 257

BALTIMORE 288
ENGLISH CATECHISM 237

369. Days of abstinence. *(B. Conrad of Piacenza)* . . 258
370. 'All Fridays.' *(Martyrs of Gorcum)* 258

BALTIMORE: NONE
ENGLISH CATECHISM 244-242

371. 'As soon as they are Able.' *(Pius X)* 259

BALTIMORE 297
ENGLISH CATECHISM 246

372. 'To contribute to the support of our pastors.' *(Negro preacher)* 260
373. 'According to our means.' *(Widow's mite)* . . . 260
374. 'The Kingdom of his Church extended.' *(Collection for heathen)* 261
375. The pennies of the poor. *(St. Hugh and the Swineherd)* 261
376. When every Catholic does his bit. *(Bishop Wakelin)* 262

Part IV: The Seven Sacraments

BALTIMORE 305
ENGLISH CATECHISM 255

377. The Seven Rivers of Life. *(A Parable)* . . . 267

BALTIMORE 304
ENGLISH CATECHISM 249

378. 'An Outward Sign.' *(Traffic lights)* 268
379. The power of a few spoken words. *(Swiss avalanche)* 268
380. 'Ordained by Jesus Christ.' *(Baptism of John, etc.)* 269
381. 'By which grace is given to our souls.' *(Pliny's letter)* 269

BALTIMORE 109-115
ENGLISH CATECHISM 139

382. God dwells in our soul by Grace. *(St. Catherine's vision)* 270
383. Life, natural and supernatural. *(Oak, squirrel, etc.)* 271
384. 'A gift freely bestowed upon us.' *(St. Joan at her trial)* 272
385. Grace is the very life of our soul. *(The diver)* . . 272

CONTENTS

xxiii

PAGE

386. 'For our sanctification.' *(SS. Rufina and Secunda)* . 273
387. Grace and Glory. *(Solomon explains to Dante)* . . 274
388. 'A supernatural gift . . . for our salvation.' *(Out of a pit)* 274
389. Prompt correspondence with graces. *(The fortieth martyr)* 275
390. Meriting further grace. *(Napoleon and the private)* 276

BALTIMORE 306-309
ENGLISH CATECHISM 250-251

391. 'The Sacraments always give grace.' *(The white terrier)* 277
392. It is Our Lord who works in the Sacraments. *(Good Samaritan)* 277

BALTIMORE 315-317
ENGLISH CATECHISM 256

393. Baptism instituted by Our Lord. *(Gospels and Acts)* 278
394. Baptism begins a new life. *('O God of Clotilda')* . 278
395. Necessity of Baptism. *(St. Peter Claver)* . . . 281
396. Baptism 'makes us Christians.' *(St. Catherine of Alexandria)* 281
397. Baptism makes us 'children of God.' *(St. Francis of Sales)* 284
398. 'And members of the Church.' *(Two little stories)* . 284
399. The duty of godparents. *(Emergency godmother)* . 285

BALTIMORE 316
ENGLISH CATECHISM 257

400. 'In proper dispositions.' *(St. Francis Xavier)* . . 285

BALTIMORE 318
ENGLISH CATECHISM 258

401. 'When a priest cannot be had.' *(Baby sister dying)* . 286

BALTIMORE 319
ENGLISH CATECHISM 259

402. The Manner of baptizing. *(Desert story,* etc.) . . 287

BALTIMORE 330
ENGLISH CATECHISM 262

403. 'A Sacrament by which we receive the Holy Ghost.' *(St. Marinus)* 288
403A.'Strong and perfect Christians. *(B. John Ogilvie)* . 289
404. 'Soldiers of Jesus Christ.' *(The boy Roland)* . . 290

CONTENTS

PAGE

BALTIMORE 331-336
ENGLISH CATECHISM 264-265

405. The outward sign of Confirmation. *(Acts viii)* . . 292
406. 'I sign thee with the Sign of the Cross.' *(The First Crusade preached)* 292
407. 'I confirm thee with the chrism of salvation.' *(Chinese altar-boy)* 294

BALTIMORE 343
ENGLISH CATECHISM 266

408. 'My delight is to be with the children of men. *(Little prince)* 295
409. The Real Presence. *(Holy Child seen in Host)* . . 296
410. 'Ave verum Corpus.' *(A mediaeval crowd-vision)* . 297
411. 'True Body and Blood of Jesus Christ.' *(Wolves in the forest)* 298
412. 'Together with His Soul and Divinity.' *(About genuflecting)* 299
413. Divine power is in the Blessed Sacrament. *(St. Clare)* 300
414. 'Latens Deitas.' *(Canopy of singing birds)* . . . 301
415. 'Mysterium fidei.' *(St. Louis)* 301
416. 'Pledge of glory to come.' *(The Holy Grail)* . . 301
417. Devotion to the Real Presence. *(King Wenceslas)* . 302
418. Visits to the Blessed Sacrament. *(Various saints)* . 303
419. Going to Benediction. *(Film-star)* 303

BALTIMORE 344-350, 252-355
ENGLISH CATECHISM 267-268

420. 'The bread and wine are changed ...' *(Thoughts at harvest-time)* 304
421. 'By the power of God.' *(Two boys talking)* . . 305
422. The Consecration at Mass. *(St. Pascal Baylon)* . 305

BALTIMORE 356, 375
ENGLISH CATECHISM 269

423. 'I have compassion on the multitude.' *(Manna, etc.)* 307
424. 'Christ has given Himself to us.' *(Napoleon's happiest day)* 309
425. 'The same also shall live by Me.' *(Some mystical phenomena)* 309
426. 'Food of our souls.' *(Slum-clearance)* . . . 310
427. 'Yet a great way to go.' *(Elias)* 311
428. The Bread of the Strong. *(French soldier)* . . 311
429. 'He that eateth this bread . . .' *(Tongking Martyrs)* 311
430. All equal at God's Table. *(Archduke and servant)* . 312
431. 'Frequent Communion. *(Luke xiv, 15)* . . . 313

CONTENTS

432. 'With desire I have desired . . .' *(Communions by miracle)* 313
433. Desire for Communion. *(St. Juliana's Viaticum)* . 314
434. Our Guest. *(Holman Hunt's picture)* . . . 314
435. Spiritual Communions. *(Sister Paula, etc.)* . . 315

BALTIMORE 351
ENGLISH CATECHISM 270

436. 'Whole and entire under either kind.' *(A bit of Church history)* 315
437. Christ's Body and Blood inseparable. *('Tarry a little')* 316
438. 'Under either kind alone.' *(St. Peter of Cavanelas)* . 317

BALTIMORE 367-372
ENGLISH CATECHISM 271-272

439. 'That we be in a state of grace.' *(Parable of wedding garment)* 318
440. 'Free from mortal sin and pleasing to God. *(Miner's cottage)* 318
441. Confession before Communion. *(Case of needless scruple)* 318
442. Bad Communions. *(Gangster's advice)* . . . 319
443. Fasting from midnight. *(Various cases)* . . 319
444. Thanksgiving after Communion. *(St. Philip Neri)* . 320

BALTIMORE 357
ENGLISH CATECHISM 277

445. The Sacrifice of the New Law. *(The Mass ceremonies)* 320
446. Our High Priest. *(Restoring communications on battlefield)* 321
447. 'Under the appearances of bread and wine.' *(Melchisedech)* 321
448. The priceless privilege. *(Best gold coins)* . . 322
449. The Sunday Mass. *(Answer to Our Lord's command)* 323
450. Valuing the Holy Mass. *(Lieutenant de Lisle)* . . 324
451. Morning Mass. *(St. Isidore of Madrid)* . . 324

BALTIMORE 358-359
ENGLISH CATECHISM 275

452. What sacrifice is. *(Abraham and Isaac)* . . 325
453. 'To God alone.' *(Altar-stone in pavement)* . . 326

BALTIMORE 360, 362
ENGLISH CATECHISM 278

454. 'The same sacrifice with that of the Cross.' *(St. Colette)* 327
455. Calvary over again. *(Lay-brother's missal)* . . 327

CONTENTS

PAGE

456. 'Through the ministry of His priests.' *(Mass-vestments)* 328
457. Mass-servers and Martyrs. *(At Nagasaki)* . . . 328

BALTIMORE 361
ENGLISH CATECHISM 279

458. 'To give supreme honour and glory to God.' *(St. Henry)* 329
459. The supreme Act of Adoration. *(Empty church!)* . 330
460. The Angels at Mass. *(St. Bridget of Sweden)* . . 330
461. 'To thank Him for all His benefits.' *(The Eucharist)* 331
462. 'To satisfy God for our sins.' *(Soldier intercedes for his brother)* 331
463. Strength from daily Mass. *(Marshal Foch)* . . 331

BALTIMORE 379
ENGLISH CATECHISM 281

464. 'This man receiveth sinners.' *(Christ's Parables)* . 332
465. The Quality of Mercy. *(Abraham Lincoln)* . . 332
466. 'Sins committed after Baptism.' *('Is that what white people do?')* 334

BALTIMORE 380
ENGLISH CATECHISM 283

467. Christ institutes the Sacrament of Penance. *(From Gospels)* 334

BALTIMORE 381
ENGLISH CATECHISM 284

468. 'The priest forgives sins.' *(A priest in disguise)* . 336
469. The seal of Confession. *(St. John Nepomucene)* . 336

BALTIMORE 389, 409, 420
ENGLISH CATECHISM 286

470. God makes His own conditions. *(Naaman, also Ten Lepers)* 337
471. 'Three conditions for forgiveness.' *(Dante in Purgatorio)* 338

BALTIMORE 388-397
ENGLISH CATECHISM 287

472. 'A Hearty sorrow.' *(Pharaoh, also Antiochus)* . . 339
473. Constitution must be supernatural. *(Various instances)* 339
474. Sorrow because we have offended God. *(David, St. Peter, St. Paul, Parables)* 340
475. 'So good a God.' *(A small boy's idea)* . . . 341
476. Intention of Restitution. *(A dress for his wife)* . 341

CONTENTS

xxvii

	PAGE
477. 'Firm purpose of amendment.' *(St. Margaret of Cortona)*	341
478. Keeping our good resolutions. *(Ven. John Hambly)*	343

BALTIMORE 398-404
ENGLISH CATECHISM 293-294

479. Attrition, or imperfect contrition. *(More afraid of fire)*	344
480. 'Perfect contrition.' *(Magdalen, also the Good Thief)*	344
481. Saved through one poor tear. *(Buonconte)*	345
482. Forgiven even before confession. *(The duellist)*	345

BALTIMORE 408-418
ENGLISH CATECHISM 295-296

483. 'To accuse ourselves.' *(Only one guilty)*	346
484. 'To a priest approved by the Bishop.' *(At the seaside)*	346
485. Don't put off confession. *(Old woman)*	347
486. We accuse ourselves of sins. *(Two cases)*	348
487. Concealing a mortal sin. *(An Easter Confession)*	348
488. Bad confessions. *(Various cases)*	349
489. Such stuff as dreams. *(Two cases in point)*	350
490. When in doubt ask a Confessor. *(Advice in newspapers)*	350

BALTIMORE 426
ENGLISH CATECHISM 297

491. 'In order to prepare for confession.' *(Hilda in a hurry)*	350
492. 'Time and care to make a good act of contrition.' *(St. Francis of Sales)*	351
493. Contrition must cover every mortal sin. *(Man in fetters)*	351
494. 'A new life for the future.' *(Dangerous apples)*	352

BALTIMORE 420-425
ENGLISH CATECHISM 298-299

495. 'The penance given us by the priest.' *(Penances unperformed)*	352
496. 'Does not always make full satisfaction.' *(St. Anthony)*	353
497. The best penances are those God sends us. *(St. Margaret)*	354

BALTIMORE 435-442
ENGLISH CATECHISM 300

498. Penance can be remitted to the deserving. *(St. Vincent Ferrer)*	354
499. 'A remission granted by the Church. *(Martyr's intercession)*	355

CONTENTS

BALTIMORE 443
ENGLISH CATECHISM 301

500. 'The anointing of the sick.' *(Christ and Apostles)*	356
501. Through the gates of death. *(Fr. Capella)*	357

BALTIMORE 444-446
ENGLISH CATECHISM 303

502. 'To comfort and strengthen the soul.' *(The Oratory telephone)*	358
503. 'To remit sin.' *(Fractured skull)*	359
504. Why we should pray for the dying. *(Graces at last moment)*	360
505. 'To restore health.' *(Not dying yet!)*	361
506. Fortified by the rites of the Church. *(Bishop in the Highlands)*	361

BALTIMORE 451-455
ENGLISH CATECHISM 305

507. The priesthood of the New Testament. *(Scripture references)*	363
508. Dignity of the priesthood. *(St. Francis)*	363
509. Sharing Christ's priesthood. *(Martyrs in Spain)*	363
510. 'Thou art a priest for ever.' *(B. John Southworth)*	364
511. A true Father to his flock. *(St. Aelphege)*	366
512. Priestly zeal for souls. *(French revolutionist)*	366
513. 'His life for His sheep.' *(Invasion of China)*	367
514. 'Their sacred duties.' *(St. Oswald of York)*	367
515. Vocation to the priesthood. *(Working in the gold-mines)*	367
516. Fostering vocations. *(St. Brigid and Nennidh)*	369

BALTIMORE 457
ENGLISH CATECHISM 306

517. The plain gold ring. *(Pius the Tenth's mother)*	369
518. The Sacrament sanctifies the natural contract. *(Marriage with a Saracen)*	370
519. 'The contract of a Christian marriage.' *(St. Brigid and the horses)*	371
520. God must come first. *(SS. Marcian and Nicander)*	372
521. Married out of the Church. *(In Registry Office)*	372
522. Married as a Catholic. *(A Commissar resigns)*	374

BALTIMORE 458, 466
ENGLISH CATECHISM 307

523. Marriage is a true vocation. *(St. Margaret of Scotland)*	374
524. 'The difficulties of their state.' *(A shop-assistant)*	377
525. 'For better or for worse.' *(St. Bridgid's prayers)*	377

CONTENTS

526. Mixed marriages and their difficulties. *(Iron bar)*	378
527. 'To love and be faithful.' *(The Rose of England)*	378

BALTIMORE 459
ENGLISH CATECHISM 312

528. 'No human power can dissolve marriage.' *(Matthew xix, 3)*	380
529. Marriage is broken only by death. *(Episode from West Africa)*	381
530. 'Till death do us part.' *(St. Columba)*	382

Part V: Virtues and Vices

BALTIMORE, APPENDIX II, VII
'ONE LORD, ONE FAITH, ETC.'

531. 'One God above all, and through all, and in us all.' *(St. Guthlac)*	385
532. 'One Faith.' *(A perplexed Chief)*	385

BALTIMORE, APPENDIX X
OLD AND NEW TESTAMENTS

533. Two Testaments. *(President Kruger)*	386

BALTIMORE 189
TWO GREAT PRECEPTS OF CHARITY

534. We should return God's love. *(Converted by a placard)*	386
535. Love of God inseparable from the love of man. *(Mark xii, 28-34)*	387
536. What loving our neighbour means. *(Good Samaritan)*	387
537. 'Who is my neighbour?' *(St. Vincent de Paul's first earnings)*	388

BALTIMORE 121-124, 200-203
THREE THEOLOGICAL VIRTUES

538. Faith, Hope and Charity. *(Some Scriptural examples)*	388

BALTIMORE 196-197
THREE EVANGELICAL COUNSELS

539. Religious Vocation. *(Fr. Azevedo and companions)*	388
540. Commandments and Counsels. *(The rich young man)*	389
541. Faithfulness to the Vows. *(The monk Malchus)*	389
542. Following vocation under difficulties. *(In the Belgium Congo)*	390
543. The joy of being poor. *(Bernard de Quintavalle)*	391

544. The Vow of chastity. *(St. Bridgid of Kildare)*
545. The power in Obedience. *(Placid and Maurus)*
546. Obedience is fruitful. *(Watering a dry stick)*

BALTIMORE 425
THREE EMINENT GOOD WORKS

547. The treasurers that cannot be taken away. *(Raphael to Tobias)*
548. Rejoicing in the Living God. *(St. Francis and B. Bernard)*
549. The quality of prayer. *(Two friends)*
550. Daily actions can be made into prayer. *(The monastery cook)*
551. Self-denial as a form of prayer. *(Cup of coffee)*
552. Fasting as Penance. *(Jonas in Ninive)*
553. The pleasures of renunciation. *(Grapes in the desert)*
554. Suffering can help prayer. *(The Little Flower)*
555. The minor trials of life. *(No chair for twelve months)*
556. Christian care for the poor. *(St. Laurence)*
557. The open hand. *(King Oswald)*
558. Alms-giving at the expense of others. *(White mouse)*

BALTIMORE, APPENDIX VIII
THE FOUR GOSPELS

559. Reading the Gospels. *(St. Margaret's book)*

BALTIMORE 132-134
THE FOUR CARDINAL VIRTUES

560. Prudence. *(Ten Virgins and other parables)*
561. Justice for all. *(St. Margaret in Scotland)*
562. Fortitude means courage. *(A daring midshipman)*
563. The courage of endurance. *(A siege in Viscaya)*
564. Accepting trials gladly. *(St. Ignatius in prison)*
565. Thanking God for hardships. *(B. John Rigby)*
566. There is a cross for each one. *(The strange merchant)*
567. Taking God's part. *(Scriptural examples)*
568. Control of appetite. *(B. Henry Suso)*
569. Right use of money. *(How money talks)*

BALTIMORE 180-186
THE FOUR LAST THINGS TO BE EVER REMEMBERED

570. The eternal facts. *(Explorers in forest)*
571. We must all die some day. *('This is on me')*
572. Calm preparation for death. *(St. Phocas)*
573. Ready for the last crossing. *(Electric chair chaplain)*

CONTENTS

xxxi

PAGE

574. A good conscience need not fear death. *(Spanish priest and the Reds)* 410
575. Death is the gateway to Heaven. *(St. Catherine at the scaffold)* 410
576. The certainty of death and judgement. *(Not worrying about that')* 411
577. No appeal from God's Judgement. *(Wallisch of Vienna)* 412
578. We may lose our soul . *(Our Lord's parables)* . . 413
579. It is possible to lose our soul for ever. *(White people in hell!)* 413
580. 'Because they deserve Thy dreadful punishments.' *(Brigand on rack)* 414
581. No repentance in the next life. *(Johnny and the mission Father)* 414
582. Our choice at death is final. *(St. Martin and the devil)* 414
583. What is hell like? *(A Galway man's opinion)* . . 415
584. Desire of heaven. *(Frederick Myers)* . . . 415
585. Our true home-country. *(Martyrs of Caesarea)* . . 415

BALTIMORE 125-127
THE SEVEN GIFTS OF THE HOLY GHOST

586. 'The Spirit of the Lord.' *(The Seven Gifts seen in Christ's life)* 416
587. Remembering our final end. *(Solomon's sentence)* . 417
588. 'The foolishness of God is wiser than men.' *(Oberammergau players* 417
589. 'Lord, that I may see.' *(Pius XI and blind boy)* . 417
590. 'O guide our minds with Thy blest Light.' *(Some parables)* 418
591. Crosses need to be grasped firmly. *(A nun's dream)* . 418
592. The conquest of fear. *(Fr. Isaac Jogues, S. J.)* . . 419
593. The science of life. *(St. Dominic)* . . . 420
594. The essence of prayer. *(St. Teresa of Lisieux)* . . 421
595. God our Judge. *(St. Chad and the storms)* . . 422

BALTIMORE 191
THE SEVEN CORPORAL WORKS OF MERCY

596. Our Judgement will be decided on what? *(Matt. xxv, 31-36)* 422
597. 'You did it unto Me.' *(St. John of God)* . . . 423
597. Christ comes disguised. *(Returning home with a fortune)* 424
598. The duty of social justice. *(Old age pensions)* . 424
599. True love for the poor. *(St. Elizabeth of Hungary)* . 425
600. Giving drink to the thirsty. *(St .Giles)* . . . 427

CONTENTS

BALTIMORE: NONE
THE SEVEN CAPITAL SINS

601. Passions must be under control. *(Lion cubs grow up)* . 428
602. The seven weaknesses of human nature. *(School clock)* 428
603. Spiritual pride. *(Pharisee and publican, etc.)* . . 429
604. Arrogance. *(Scriptural examples)* 429
605. The achievements of Man. *(Tower of Babel)* . . 430
606. Vainglory. *('Only a mistake')* 430
607. 'Quia mitis sum et humilis Corde.' *(Our Lord's example)* 431
608. 'Learn of Me.' *('I'm the Corporal')* . . . 431
609. The charm of humility. *(Some saints, also Père Lagrange)* 431
610. Humility is not pushful. *(St. Anthony of Padua)* . 433
611. 'Be merciful to me a sinner!' *(Basket of sand)* . 435
612. Avarice. *(Judas Iscariot)* 435
613. The passion for security. *('Thou fool!')* . . 435
614. Greed takes us to hell. *('My onion!')* . . . 436
615. Greed does not pay. *(Two boys fishing)* . . 436
616. Travel light to heaven. *(Spanish and Aztecs)* . 437
617. Money is a danger to salvation. *(Torpedoed warship)* 438
618. You can't take it with you. *(Rockefeller)* . . 439
619. Surrender to unchastity is failure. *(Sir Lancelot and the Grail)* 439
620. Lust ends in cruelty. *(St. Agatha)* . . . 440
621. Dangerous companions. *(St. Teresa)* . . . 441
622. Indecent conversation. *(A doubtful collar)* . . 442
623. 'The spirit against the flesh.' *(St. Jerome)* . . 443
624. 'Mater castissima.' *(St. Anthony's Prayer)* . . 443
625. Quarrelling. *(Two hermits)* 444
626. Nursing a grievance. *(Two sisters)* . . . 444
627. Impatience can be checked. *(B. Peter Faber at the door)* 444
628. Gluttony ruins health and fitness. *(Millionaire kidnapped)* 445
629. We should know when to stop. *('That kid's never satisfied')* 445
630. Enough is as good as a feast. *(Bread and water)* . 446
631. The temperate are the trustworthy. *(Soldiers of Gedeon)* 446
632. The Drink habit. *(Village toper)* 446
633. What drink can do. *(Terrorising his mother)* . 446
634. The envious mind. *(Scriptural examples)* . . 447
635. The envious tongue. *(In painting and poetry)* . 448
636. Too much class-consciousness. *(A gloomy Communist)* 448
637. The generous mind. *(St. Thomas and St. Bonaventure)* 448
638. The poison of jealousy. *(Othello)* . . . 449
639. The sin of Acedia. *(In the parables)* . . . 449

CONTENTS

	PAGE
640. Facing up to difficulties. *(The blocked road)*	450
641. 'Be you also ready.' *(St. Charles playing cards)*	450
642. No hurry! *(The devil's council of war)*	451
643. Lost opportunities. *(The Emperor Titus)*	451

BALTIMORE: NONE
THE EIGHT BEAUTITUDES

644. The poor in spirit. *(A Franciscan queen)*	452
645. The Meek bear no grudges. *(James, son of Zebedee)*	452
646. Christian revenge. *(Cholera patient)*	453
647. Christian martyrdom. *(The old Japanese nobleman)*	453
648. 'Beati qui lugent.' *(Our Lord's tears)*	454
649. Hunger and thirst after justice. *(Lord Shaftesbury)*	455
650. 'Beati misericordes.' *(St. Brigid's motto)*	457
651. Mercy to one's enemy. *(General Dumas)*	458
652. Mercy to animals. *(St. Columba and the Crane)*	458
653. 'Beati mundo corde.' *(St. Anthony and the Holy Child)*	460
654. 'Beati pacifici.' *(During the Commune)*	461
655. Persecution is a privilege. *(B. Thomas Sherwood)*	461

APPENDIX

(Some stories which should have been included in the earlier parts.)

INTRODUCTORY   PAGE
   656. The Catechism is to be lived. *(Football in China)* . 463

BALTIMORE 6-7
ENGLISH CATECHISM 14
   657. The Creed is an act of Faith. *(Perishing in the Arctic)* 463

BALTIMORE 77-79
ENGLISH CATECHISM 32
   658. 'Who is Jesus Christ?' *(The strange altar-boy)* . . 464

BALTIMORE 90-94
ENGLISH CATECHISM 55
   659. 'His life for His friends.' *(Private of the Royal Irish)* 465
   660. The spirit of sacrifice. *(Smothering the grenade)* . 465
   661. Dying for his mates. *(Three workmen in Manchester)* 466

BALTIMORE 158
ENGLISH CATECHISM 97
   662. The Church of all ages and all nations. *(High Mass in Phoenix Park)* 466

CONTENTS

BALTIMORE 170-174
ENGLISH CATECHISM 102
    663. 'You are my friends.' *(St. Louis and Brother Giles)*   468

BALTIMORE 475, 477-485
ENGLISH CATECHISM 141
    664. By prayer we call on God's grace. *(The horn of Roland)*   468

BALTIMORE 476
ENGLISH CATECHISM 142
    665 Always something to thank God for. *(Rice pudding)*   470

BALTIMORE 493
ENGLISH CATECHISM 151
    666. Spreading the Faith. *(Blind Martha)*   471

BALTIMORE 496
ENGLISH CATECHISM 154
    667. Answers to prayer. *(Captives in Soudan)*   471

BALTIMORE 85
ENGLISH CATECHISM 167
    668. Mary is 'our Mother also.' *(Our Lady of Guadalupe)*   472

BALTIMORE 171, 172, 215-218
ENGLISH CATECHISM 158
    669. 'Their prayers have great power with God. *(St. Colette)*   474

BALTIMORE 207-209
ENGLISH CATECHISM 179
    670. The sin of Presumption. *(Answered according to his folly)*   474

BALTIMORE 246-249
ENGLISH CATECHISM 198
    671. Christ and Caesar. *(Napoleon's excommunication)*   474

BALTIMORE 265-267, 270
ENGLISH CATECHISM 220
    672. Atrocity stories. *(The priests of Antwerp)*   475

BALTIMORE 343
ENGLISH CATECHISM 266
    673. Reverence in genuflecting. *(St. Anthony and the horse)*   476
    674. 'I am the Living Bread.' *(Jewish girl at Benediction)*   476

CONTENTS

BALTIMORE 444-446
ENGLISH CATECHISM 305
 675. Once a priest, always a priest. *(War stories)* . . 477

BALTIMORE 35-37
ENGLISH CATECHISM 19
 676. God creates through Love. *(Juliana of Norwich)* . 478

BALTIMORE 158
ENGLISH CATECHISM 97
 677. No Race-distinctions in the Church. *(Twelve new bishops)* 479
 678. The one Ark of Salvation. *(Life-boat)* . . . 479

CREED

THE CREED

* WHO MADE YOU?
God made me.

We did not make ourselves

KIRCHNER, famous astronomer, had a scientist friend who professed disbelief in God. Visiting Kirchner one day, this friend was admiring a working-model of the solar-system that stood upon a table; by turning a handle the planets could be made to revolve in their respective orbits round the sun.

'Very ingenious indeed,' he remarked. 'Who is the maker?'

'Oh, nobody particular.'

'But tell me, I want to know—who made it?'

'Nobody made it. It just made itself.'

The friend began to see the point, and was annoyed.

'I see, you are trying to be funny.'

'Isn't it rather you that is funny? You can't believe that this little model made itself, and yet you can believe that the real sun and moon and stars, the whole vast universe in fact, came into existence somehow without any Maker!'

His friend went away rather thoughtful, and later changed his opinion.

You, too, did not make yourself. God made you—your body, allowing your parents to help Him; your Soul, direct from His own hands like a new coin from the Mint. [See also nos. 656, 676, and 178.]

*BALTIMORE 1, 2, 48-50
ENGLISH CATECHISM 1

'Blessed be Thou for creating me!'

Each human soul is a separate creation of God's love, planned from all eternity.

St. Clare of Assisi never left her native town, yet her life was filled with high adventures of the soul. After fifty-eight years she lay dying in her tiny cell at San Damiano. She was heard murmuring quietly, and one of the sisters asked her to whom she was speaking.

'I am speaking to my happy soul,' she answered. And these were the words they caught:

'Go forth, my soul, go forth without fear; for thou hast a good guide for thy journey. Go forth, for He who created thee hath sanctified thee, and protects thee always, and loveth thee with a love tender as that of a mother for her son. Blessed be Thou, Lord, for creating me!'

Since God made us, we belong to Him

A beach sand-building competition. One boy and girl finished a magnificent castle, and then wandered round looking at the other children's efforts. When they came back they found a boy had occupied their castle and was making alterations and adding what he thought were improvements.

'What are you doing—that's our castle!'

'No, it's mine now. You left it.'

'But it's *our castle!*'

'What do you mean, yours? You didn't pay for the sand, did you?'

'But it's *our castle*—we MADE it, and we can do what we like with it, or destroy it or anything, because we *made* it.'

And, of course, everybody said they were right, the intruder was turned out, and they won the prize.

God *made* me, out of nothing, and so I belong to Him. I am His to do what He likes with.

The soul is an immortal spirit, in God's likeness

Lacordaire relates that a Polish prince had just completed for publication a book denying the immortality of the soul. Walking in his domain he met a poor woman who told him tearfully that her husband had just died,

CATECHISM STORIES 3

and asked for an alms to have Mass said for his soul. For this superstition (as he considered it to be) the Prince, out of mere kindness, gave her a gold coin, and thought no more of the matter.

Late one night, soon afterwards, he was sitting up putting the finishing touches to his manuscript, when he seemed to be aware of a man in peasant dress standing before the desk. Greatly astonished, he was about to ask the man how he had entered the room, when the visitor spoke.

' Prince, I came to thank you. I am the man who died last week, to whose wife you gave money to have Mass said for my soul. Your kind act was pleasing to God, and He has allowed me to come and thank you. Prince, you must make a good use of this favour that is granted you.'

Suddenly, the peasant was no longer there. Deeply moved by the experience, the prince destroyed his book and lived the rest of his life as a good Catholic.

God upholds us in existence

We say ' God made me,' but it would be truer to say ' God makes me ' ; if His creative action ceased I should fall back into nothingness.

There is a quaint story of St. Kevin, sixth-century founder of the great Monastery of Glendalough. He used to keep Lent by retiring for solitude in the mountains to a tiny hermitage, so small that when he stretched out his arms in prayer (as his custom was) he had to put one hand through the window. Thus, one morning a blackbird alighted on his hand and laid her eggs in his palm ; whereupon Kevin neither drew in his hand nor closed it, but out of his tenderness for God's creatures held it there in the same way until the young brood was hatched. And, therefore (says Giraldus Cambrensis, Topography, *c*. 28) all his images represent him with a blackbird in his hand.

God's own tenderness for His creatures is no less, when He supports us in existence with His Almighty hand from one moment to another.

N.B.—A similar story is told of St. Malo, an Irish monk who made his home in Brittany. Digging one day, he left his cloak on the ground, and a skylark laid her eggs.

in one of its folds. Rather than disturb her, he endured the cold without a cloak until the brood was hatched. [See also no. 17, p. 11.]

> * WHY DID GOD MAKE YOU?
> *God made me to know Him, love Him and serve Him in this world, and to be happy with Him for ever in the next.*

God wants to share His happiness

(THIS might be introduced as a magazine or cinema story.) A New York millionaire's only son, twelve years old, found an old file of newspaper-cuttings; evidently some former secretary had collected paragraphs in which the millionaire was mentioned. Amongst them the boy found one headed: 'Millionaire adopts a foundling'; it stated that the unknown baby boy found abandoned some days previously in a church porch had now been taken into the home of Mr. H—— (the boy's father). He looked at the date of the newspaper-cutting. It was twelve years ago. That baby would be a boy now, as old as himself—strange he had never heard of him.

Just then his father came into the study, and the boy showed him the cutting.

'Look, Dad—tell me, what became of this baby they found?'

The father looked thoughtful for a minute, then put his arm round the boy's shoulder and told him the truth.

'That story is about *you*. You see how it was, son—I had everything that money could buy, but I could never feel quite happy because there was nobody to share it with. This is grand, I always used to think, but why can't somebody else enjoy it, too? So when I heard you were waiting in the orphanage unclaimed, I just took the opportunity.'

It took the boy a minute or two to take in the idea. Then he said:

'Well, here I am anyhow. Are you still glad you did it?'

'You bet I'm glad, son. We're friends, aren't we, and

you've always tried to be a good son to me : that's all I want.'

We all want to share our happy times with others, and God is the same. He wanted someone to be happy with Him in His home in heaven ; that is why He made us, and all He asks from us in return is our love and obedience.

God made me to love Him

St. John Vianney, Curé of Ars, was walking through the fields one spring day with a friend. The trees were full of birds and the air was full of their singing. The curé stopped to listen. ' Ah, little birds ! ' he said. ' You were created to sing, and you are singing. Man was created to love God, and he does not love Him.'

' Thou hast made us for Thyself '

St. Augustine of Hippo (d. A.D. 430), after his conversion at the age of thirty-three, became bishop, saint, thinker and writer : one of the very greatest figures in the Church's history. But his pre-conversion years are a striking instance of how men may know God without loving and serving Him.

His father was an elderly self-indulgent pagan, and Augustine was not baptised, though his young mother, Monica, managed to teach him the Christian religion. He went to pagan schools, and at the age of sixteen threw aside Christian ideas and lived as a pagan, especially giving himself up to sins against the sixth commandment, while making a name for himself as a teacher of literature.

The greatest happiness (he thought) was to be found in love—' to love and be loved ' was his aim in life. In vain he tried to satisfy this desire in worldly ways, but it was not until his thirtieth year that the all-importance of loving God began to dawn on him. He listened to the sermons of the great bishop St. Ambrose, and found himself believing in the Christian God, and even loving Him in a way, but still unwilling to serve Him by living a chaste life. ' Give me chastity, O Lord, but not yet,' was his prayer.

His final conversion (for which his mother Monica was always praying) came through reading about St. Anthony of Egypt and the thousands of monks who gave up all the world's pleasures for the love of God. Could he not do the same? In agony of mind he lay in his garden; from the next house came by chance the sound of a boy's voice repeating the words 'Tolle, lege'—'take up and read.'

Augustine took them as a sign from God, for there was a book lying near him. He opened it (like St. Anthony with the gospels) at random and saw the words: 'Put ye on the Lord Jesus Christ, and make not provision for the flesh.' From that moment he made his choice to put the love of God before everything else, and soon he and his friends were baptised.

In his 'Confessions' he sums it all up: 'Thou hast made us for Thyself, O God, and there is no rest for our hearts until they come to rest in Thee.'

Where are we bound for?

Two orphan sisters (or brothers, as the case may be), had been emigrated to Australia, where they were in service near each other. They were overjoyed when a letter came from an uncle in Sussex, inviting them to come and make their home with him. He had won £1000 in a sweepstake, and sent a cheque to each of them to cover their passage home.

At the shipping agency, where they went to make enquiries, the walls were decorated with advertisements of pleasure-cruises.

"Look, Brenda!" Alice pointed to a picture representing a gaily-dressed crowd of young people playing deck-games or lying in long chairs, with a bright blue sea in the background. 'Do let's go on a cruise—I've always wanted to!'

'But we couldn't—we've only got enough money for the passage home.'

'Oh, but just think of the grand time you could have. What an opportunity!'

'We've got our opportunity of getting home—that's what matters most.'

There was a warm argument. Finally Alice spent her money on a lot of holiday clothes and a fortnight's cruise. It was a luxurious boat and good weather, and Alice had a gay time; but at the end of the cruise the passengers disembarked where they had started. She got another situation and spent the rest of her life regretting her foolishness. Brenda went to England in an ordinary boat, second class, a long and dull voyage, and she was very seasick in the Bay of Biscay. But she found a warm welcome from her uncle and a very happy home; until she got married not long after, when her uncle bought her a house near his own.

God has destined us for heaven, given each of us sufficient help to get us to our Destination. Some keep the Destination in view—others don't. [See also nos. 197, 244, 464, 534.]

> * OF WHICH MUST YOU TAKE MOST CARE—OF YOUR BODY OR YOUR SOUL?
>
> *I must take most care of my soul, for Christ has said: What doth it profit a man if he gain the whole world and suffer the loss of his own soul?*

The Soul is the highest part of man

WHEN St. Anselm taught the boys at Bec, a monk from a neighbouring monastery came to watch his school at work and play. He was astonished to see them so happy and industrious.

'My own boys are hopeless indeed,' he complained. 'We do our best, we beat them from morning till night, but there is never any improvement.'

'And what are they like when they grow up?' asked Anselm.

'As dull and stupid as beasts.'

'A wonderful system, if it changes men into beasts!' said Anselm. Then he explained his own way, which was to treat the boys with patience and understanding, and win their hearts, and trust them with some freedom and responsibility. The other monk went away resolved to try it.

*BALTIMORE 4, 50
ENGLISH CATECHISM 7

The difference between man and animals is that man has a soul, with reason and free-will. It is wrong to treat men like animals, or to behave as if we were only animals ourselves. The soul should be master over the body. Soul and body are partners, but the soul should be the senior partner, with the final say in everything.

Bodily instincts are a useful part of our nature, but God meant them to be under control of reason. [See no. 344.]

'What doth it profit a man?'

On His last journey up to Jerusalem, Our Lord was trying to convince the Apostles that when they got there He would be handed over to the Romans and mocked and scourged and put to death. St. Peter was shocked at such talk and remonstrated with Him. Our Lord replied: 'Go behind me, Satan: you understand not the things of God, but the things of man.' Then He turned to all the disciples and said: 'If any man will come after me, let him deny himself and take up his cross and follow me' (i.e. like a man going to be crucified, like one who has finished with this world). 'For he that will save his life shall lose it; and he that shall lose his life for my sake shall find it. For what doth it profit a man, if he gain the whole world and suffer the loss of his own soul?' (Matt. xvi, 23–26).

Taking proper care of our soul often means denying the body what it would like, and sometimes suffering even to death like Our Lord and the martyrs.

This night they require thy soul

Our Lord has a story of a man who took most care of his body, and preferred not to remember that the soul can take nothing with it into next life.

Story in Our Lord's own words: Luke xii, 16–22 and verse 31.

Taking most care of his guinea-pig!

A priest visiting a careless family found a boy feeding his pet guinea-pig. 'How often do you feed him?' 'One good feed a day; he likes me to give it him. Then I get him some milk at night.' 'Certainly he looks well-cared for,' said the priest, and asked further questions. The boy explained how he collected potato-peelings for his pet, and cleaned out the hut every other day. 'That's the hardest part—takes half an hour nearly.'

'I reckon you must spend three hours a week taking care of your guinea-pig.'

'Yes, I expect I do.'

'Tell me now, were you at Mass last Sunday?'

'Not last Sunday, Father—but I go pretty often.'

'And what about prayers?'

'Well, I say them most nights.'

'How long?'

'Couple of minutes, I suppose.'

'On the average then, you spend about half an hour a week on your religious duties?'

'That's about it, I suppose.'

'Seems to me it's better to be your guinea-pig than your soul: he's better taken care of.'

'You're right, Father, I'll be at Confession on Saturday.'

The one thing necessary

A young friend of St. Philip Neri came to see him, and knelt by the old priest's chair as his custom was. In reply to enquiries, he said he was studying for an exam. and hoped to do well in it. The saint listened attentively to his plans for the future, nodding encouragement, while his hand played with the lad's hair.

'And after the exam.; what then?'

'Then I shall try for a degree in law.'

'And then?'

'I want to be a barrister: everyone tells me I'm cut out for it.'

'And then?'

'Well, if I make a name as a barrister, I could marry and settle down and be a rich man.'

'And then?'

'Oh, well, I might hope to end up as a judge, and obtain some high office in the court of Rome.'

'And then?'

'Some day I should retire with a big pension and be able to enjoy an honourable old age.'

'And then?'

'Then? Well, Father, some day I suppose I should have to die.'

The saint drew the boy's head closer and whispered in his ear:

'*And then?*'

This talk made a lasting impression on the youth, whose name was Francesco Zazzara, and later he threw up his worldly ambitions as a danger to his soul, and joined St. Philip's Congregation of the Oratory. [See no. 434.]

We make our own eternity

A young builder had just set up in business on his own. An old friend of his family, now a wealthy brewer, came to him and said: 'Jim, I want you to build me a house. Here are some rough plans. Use the best materials, I leave you a free hand. Bring me the bills whenever you like. Make a thoroughly good job of it.'

Jim took the job on, and at first meant to carry it out conscientiously. But gradually a greedy desire for more profits made him skimp the work, using cheap materials while charging for best quality, employing second-rate workmen, and so on.

When the house was finished, Jim took the keys to his friend, also the bills which came to over £2000. The brewer wrote out a cheque. 'Here you are, Jim,' he said, 'you can keep the keys and here are the deeds of the property. The house is your own, Jim, my present to you. I hope you will be happy there for the rest of your days.'

The builder settled down in his new house. Winter came. The damp crept up the walls, the wind whistled through the cracks, rain came through the roof, the windows jammed.

'And I've got to live in it the rest of my life,' thought Jim. 'What a fool I was not to make a good job of it.'

We are each of us building our own character and soul, and God has given us a free hand, with His grace to help.

CATECHISM STORIES

What we make of our soul in this life, we shall be for all eternity.

This life nothing compared with Eternity

Many years ago a British ship was wrecked in a storm off the coast of Brazil. It carried a large amount of Spanish dollars ; some barrels of these were brought up on deck, but the ship was sinking so rapidly that they were abandoned and everybody took to the boats. As the last boat left, a hammering noise was heard on board, and one of the officers went back to see if anybody was left behind.

To his surprise he found a man sitting on the deck surrounded with heaps of silver coins, and engaged in breaking open a second barrel with a hatchet. The officer tried to pull him away.

'The ship's going to pieces !' he shouted.

'Let it go,' the man replied. 'I've lived in poverty all my life, but now I'm going to die a rich man.'

When the officer persisted he was threatened with the hatchet, so he abandoned the madman to his fate and just reached the boat again as the ship broke up.

A madman, certainly. But hardly more mad than we are when we ruin our souls for the sake of a few short years of self-indulgence, which are only a few seconds compared with Eternity. [See also nos. 560, 570–576.]

> * WHAT MUST YOU DO TO SAVE YOUR SOUL ?
> *To save my soul I must worship God by faith, hope and charity : that is, I must believe in Him, I must hope in Him and I must love Him with my whole heart.*

The Three Theological Virtues

A LITTLE boy stood in the sun, on the edge of an open trap-door of a cellar. From above, nothing was visible down in the cellar, only a blackness. Up from the cellar there came the voice of the boy's father : 'Jump down, son ! I'll catch you !' 'But I can't see you, father.' 'Never mind, I can see *you*. Jump !' Summoning his courage, the boy

*BALTIMORE 120-124, 200-208
ENGLISH CATECHISM 8

jumped, and in a moment felt himself held safely with his father's arms round him.

A picture of the three virtues by which God's children turn to their Father. The boy *believed* that it was his father speaking, he *trusted* that his father would do what he promised, and he *loved* his father and showed it by obeying him. [See also no. 538.]

Our need of Revelation

A young Eastern king wished to be wise and good, and rule his people according to the will of Allah. He called together the wisest men of his realm and ordered them to gather all wisdom into books so that he could read and learn for himself how to rule well.

The wise men began on their tremendous task, and after thirty years it was finished. A long string of camels, bearing five thousand volumes, came to the palace. 'Here, O King, is all wisdom.' The king, already middle-aged, was occupied with many duties and plans. He looked at the loaded camels. 'I'm too busy to read so many books. Take them away and condense them for me.'

The work of condensing took fifteen years, and then the wise men proudly produced five hundred volumes.

'Still far too many,' said the king, 'fifty ought to be enough.'

Most of the wise men were dead, but their successors carried on and in ten years they brought the fifty books to the king. But by this time the king was old and tired. 'You must make a summary of it all into one book,' he said.

It took them five years, and when they brought the precious volume to present to the king, it was too late, he lay on his deathbed. (From Anatole France, in *La Vie Littéraire*.)

Very few people have the time, the intellect, the learning to work out for themselves the truth about God and why He has made us. We need to be told and God sent His Son to tell us.

We need correct information

People say : 'I don't think it matters what you believe, so long as you're sincere.'

Two boys in a Midland city had just left school and were

due for an interview with a large firm just outside the town. A number of jobs with good prospects were waiting for the applicants who would be selected. The candidates had to be there for 10 o'clock, and the boys arranged to catch a local train at 9.23. They arrived close on time at the station, where a train was waiting. 'Just caught it, what luck!' 'Are you sure it's the right one?' 'Must be, it's 9.23 and the right platform. Get in, it's going!' The train started off, and seemed to be getting up speed. The ticket-collector came along the corridor, and the boys asked him what time they would get to S——. 'You won't get there this morning, I'm afraid: you ought to have got on the 9.23 train, behind this one.' 'We believed this was the local!' 'No, this is the 9.20 express. First stop Manchester, 12.20.'

They missed the interview and the vacancies went to other boys. They honestly believed it was the 9.23, but their belief was mistaken and it didn't alter the facts and the consequences.

The gift of Faith

Edwin, young pagan King of Northumbria, married the Christian princess Ethelburga of Kent. With her as chaplain came St. Paulinus, an old Roman monk sent by Pope Gregory to help St. Augustine. Edwin himself was soon nearly convinced by Paulinus' instructions, and when a daughter was born he allowed her to be baptised. At last, after several signs from God, he promised to become a Christian, but wishing to bring others with him, he called his chieftains together at Godmundingham, near York, and asked them their opinions of the new doctrine.

One of the counsellors spoke thus: 'O King, the life of man is full of mystery before and after. You sit at supper with your chieftains in the winter-time, the fire is blazing and the room is warm, while the rain and snow whirl outside. Suddenly a sparrow flies through the hall, coming in at one door and escaping quickly by another. It comes from the darkness. For a moment it is in the bright light, and then it glides back into the dark storm again. So it seems with man's life, but of what shall follow it or what went before, we know nothing. Therefore, if this new teaching can tell us more certainly about it, let us hear what it says.'

The pagan chief priest, Coifi, proposed that Paulinus should be heard, so he preached the gospel to them all. Then Coifi said : ' I have long known, O King, that there was nothing in what we have worshipped. The more I sought for truth in it, the less I found. But now I openly declare that here in this new preaching there is the truth. Let us immediately desecrate and burn the temples and altars which we consecrated in vain.'

Edwin gave Paulinus leave to preach, and announced his own conversion. When the temple was destroyed, Coifi himself took the lead. ' Much rejoicing in confessing the true God,' he asked for a spear and a war-horse—both things forbidden to a pagan priest—charged up to the temple and cast his spear through the doorway, and gave the word for the burning. [Faith, see nos. 231–239, 657, 666, 674.]

Hope in God's promises

A boy going home from school always stopped to look in the window of a large old-fashioned house ; on a table near the window was a large red stamp-album, usually open at some page, with loose stamps lying on the table. One day an old gentleman, coming out, stopped and spoke. ' I see you are admiring my stamp-collection ? ' ' Yes, sir.' ' Would you like to have it ? ' The boy could only gasp with astonishment. ' Well, come along one day this week and you shall take them home.' The gentleman walked on.

The more the boy thought about it the more impossible it seemed. The gentleman couldn't possibly have meant what he said—must have been joking. So he never went to claim the stamps.

Some weeks later he went to tea at a school-friend's house. The first thing his friend showed him was the wonderful stamp-collection in its red album. ' Look, an old gentleman living in the square gave it to me.' So the old gentleman had meant it after all !

God makes us wonderful promises, but some people

CATECHISM STORIES

think they are too good to be true. He wants us to have trust in Him and take Him at His word.

Trust in God only

In the reign of Ezechias the Assyrian emperor Sennacherib invaded Judea with great armies, took all the fortified towns, and came up against Jerusalem. Some of the people had wanted to seek the help of Egypt, but Isaias always declared against alliances and exhorted the City of God to trust in God only and promised that it should not be taken. (Read aloud one of his prophecies, Isa. xxxi.) King Ezechias made energetic preparations for defence (read 2 Para. xxxii, 1-6) and encouraged his army with a grand fighting speech (2 Para. xxxii, 7-8). The Assyrians invested the city, and Sennacherib sent one of his generals to utter threats and blasphemies against God, as if He were like the gods of the gentiles (Isa. xxxvi, 13-15, 18-19; 2 Para. xxxii, 15). He also wrote a blasphemous letter to Ezechias (Isa. xxxvii, 10-11). Ezechias took it up to the temple and spread it before the Lord and prayed with supreme hope (Isa. xxxvii, 16-20).

Isaias answered the blasphemies of Sennacherib in a prophecy of glorious defiance (Isa. xxxvii, 21-23, 33-35).

And the Lord sent an angel who cut off all the warriors and captains of the besieging Assyrians (this is generally thought to have been a sudden pestilence) and Sennacherib had to hasten back with the survivors to his own country God had saved the Holy City that trusted in Him.

How God keeps His word

Another great example of Hope is holy Simeon, who lived in evil times when most Jews had ceased to expect the Messias or expected a worldly one. Simeon was one of the few who held to the pure faith of the prophets, and looked for a Saviour who should be a Light to all the world. God had given him an inward assurance that he should live to see that day, but when he lived to extreme old age and there seemed no prospect of God's Kingdom, he must have been tempted to lose hope after all. Yet still he ' waited for the Consolation of Israel ' and went every day to the temple to make sure of being there when the Saviour should appear. God kept His promise, Simeon held the Holy Child in his arms, and died (it is thought) that very day, broken-hearted with joy. [On Hope: see nos. 182, 214-216, 240-241, 538.]

The virtue of Charity

Charity is the love between man and his Creator. We should love God back because He loves each one of us 'with an everlasting love.'

St. Teresa of Avila (who was very fond of children, and always liked to have a child somewhere about her, if possible) once was aware of the presence of a lovely little boy. He came near to her and spoke :

'What is your name?'

'I am called Teresa of Jesus. What is yours?'

He smiled up at her joyfully :

'I'm Jesus of Teresa!'

It was the same Teresa, in her old age, who on one of her trying journeys in God's service, leading her companions on foot through a flooded bit of road, lost her footing and was nearly drowned. 'Oh, Lord,' she cried ; 'why do You put such difficulties in our way?' She heard an inward reply : 'Do not complain, my daughter —this is the way I treat my friends.' 'Yes, Lord, and that is why You have so few.'

To be on such familiar terms with God our Father is the genuine virtue of Charity. [On Charity: see nos. 241, 534, 538, 594.]

* SAY THE APOSTLES' CREED

Devotion to the Creed

IN the thirteenth century in Northern Italy there still survived many Manichean heretics, who believed in two gods, a good one who created the spirit-world, and an evil one who created the earth. In one heretical family at Verona there was a boy named Peter (born 1205) who was sent for convenience to a Catholic school. When his uncle asked him what he learned there, he recited the words of the Creed : ' I believe in God the Father Almighty,

*BALTIMORE 6-7
ENGLISH CATECHISM 14

Creator of heaven _and earth._' They tried hard to make him change his mind, but in vain.

At fifteen he went to the University of Bologna, where he joined St. Dominic, and the rest of his life was spent in preaching to the heretics all over Northern Italy. Every day as he lifted the chalice at the Elevation he prayed : ' Grant, Lord, that I may die for Thee, who didst die for me.'

He was forty-seven when two Manicheans plotted to murder him and waylaid him on the road. A blow on the head with an axe struck him down. He rose to his knees, dipped his finger in his blood and wrote on the ground : ' Credo in Deum.' The murderers then stabbed him to the heart. [See no. 657.]

> * WHAT IS GOD ?
>
> *God is the supreme Spirit, who alone exists of Himself, and is infinite in all perfections.*

' Alone exists of Himself '

THE children of Israel oppressed in Egypt (Exod. i, 8–14). Baby boys to be thrown in the river (i, 22). Moses adopted by Pharaoh's daughter and educated in the learning of the Egyptians (ii, 1–10). Has to flee into the land of Midian (ii, 10–21). While tending sheep he sees the burning yet unconsumed bush on Horeb, like a beacon signal.

'*Come not nigh hither . . . I have seen the afflictions of my people . . . I will send thee to Pharaoh. . . .*'

' Who am I that I should go to Pharaoh ? . . .'

' *I will be with thee. . . .*'

' If they should say to me, what is His Name ; what shall I say to them ? '

' *I am who am. Thus shalt thou say to the children of Israel : He-Who-Is hath sent me to you* ' (iii, 13–14).

So Moses went and after many adventures delivered his brethren, but that is another story.

In Hebrew this sacred Name is Jehovah, which the Jews in reverence left unuttered, substituting Adonai.

God's Name is holy because it belongs to Him alone, for God alone exists of Himself ; all other beings exist because

*BALTIMORE 8-11

of God (e.g. our shadow), but nobody made God; He is 'the One who *is*.'

The sanctuary of a Catholic church is holy ground like Mount Horeb, and we take (not our shoes) but our caps off and genuflect.

Infinite in all perfections

St. Patrick came to Connaught and set up his tents by the fountain of Clebach, near the dwelling of the king at Rathcrogan. In the early morning, while the praises of God were being sung, the king's two daughters, Eithne and Fedelm, came to the fountain where it was their custom to bathe. Wondering at the strangers, they asked: 'Whence come ye? Are ye phantoms or fairies, or friendly mortals?'

'Better that you should adore the true God, of whom we come to tell you,' replied Patrick, 'than waste time with useless questions.'

'Who is God?' the maidens asked eagerly. 'Where is his dwelling? Is he rich in silver and gold? Is he everlasting? Is he young or old? Is he beautiful to see? Is he in the heavens, or on earth? Is he in the sea and rivers and mountains? Tell us all about him, and how he is to be found?'

St. Patrick was filled with the Holy Spirit and answered:

'God whom we announce to you is the Ruler of all things. The God of heaven and earth, of the sea and the rivers. The God of the sun and moon and all the stars. The God of the high mountains and of the valleys. His dwelling is in heaven and earth and sea and everywhere. He gives breath to all. He gives the light to the sun and the brightness to the moon, and appoints the stars to serve them.'

'Teach us,' the maidens said, 'how we may know this King of heaven, and how we may see Him face to face. We will do everything you say to us.'

St. Patrick instructed and baptised them and so great was their longing to see the face of Christ, that 'when they received the Eucharist of God, they slept in death, and they were placed on à couch arrayed in their baptismal robes.'

CATECHISM STORIES

Thus, these maidens who so loved the beautiful things of earth, were led on by St. Patrick to desire God, who is Beauty itself and infinite Source of created perfections.

In the prayer called 'St. Patrick's Breastplate' he speaks in the same strain :

> 'I bind to myself to-day
> The power of Heaven,
> The light of the Sun,
> The brightness of the Moon,
> The splendour of Fire,
> The flashing of Lightning,
> The swiftness of Wind,
> The depth of Sea,
> The firmness of Earth,
> The hardness of Rocks.
>
> I bind to myself to-day
> God's Power to guide me,
> God's Might to uphold me,
> God's Wisdom to teach me,
> God's Eye to watch over me,
> God's Ear to hear me,
> God's Word to give me speech
> God's Hand to guide me.'

St. Francis of Assisi's Canticle of the Sun (which he made when he lay ill and nearly blind in a little hut at San Damiano, on a visit to St. Clare) is another glorious instance of the same rejoicing recognition that all earthly perfections have their Source in God, who is therefore worthy of all love.

The Footprints of Allah

A French scientist was travelling in the desert and sat outside his tent in the cool of sunset, talking with his young Bedouin guide about religion. 'Nobody knows,' said the Frenchman, ' nobody can know for certain that there is a God.'

The lad pointed to a smooth stretch of sand across which went a track of footprints.

'When I see those footprints in the sand,' he said, 'I know for certain that some man has passed this way. Only a man could have made them.'

He pointed to the fading colours of a glorious sunset in the west, and then overhead to the dark blue sky in which the great stars were coming out one by one.

'And when I see the sun, and the moon, and the starry heavens in their beauty, I know for certain that the Creator has passed this way. They are the footprints of Allah.'

The Bedouin was right. From the works of God which are seen we can know, even without revelation, that God exists. ' The heavens tell forth the glory of God

Infinite Beauty

'Let me see this God of yours,' a Roman emperor said to the Rabbi Joshua. The Rabbi pointed upwards: 'Lift your eyes to the sky, God is there.' The emperor looked up, but the sun was shining so strongly that he covered his eyes and looked away. 'What?' said the Rabbi. 'You ask to see the Master, when you cannot look even His servant in the face?'

All the various glories and beauties found in creation are faint reflections of something in God : He is infinite in all perfections, and worthy of all our desire and love. [See also nos. 152, 167, 169, 548.]

* HAD GOD ANY BEGINNING ?

God had no beginning ; He always was, He is and He always will be. He has no body. He is a spirit and He is everywhere. He can do all things ; He knows and sees all things, even our most secret thoughts.

Our Knowledge of God

CAN we know God, or is it all guess-work? Are we like the little girl of six or thereabouts, who was busy with paper and pencil? 'What are you drawing?' 'I'm drawing God.' 'Oh, but you can't—nobody knows what God looks like.' 'They'll know now.'

We can know something about God by our reason, and more by revelation. But *all* our knowledge of God is by analogy, that is, indirect and symbolic ;, as we might know a landscape only through a map ; or as a person born deaf might know the music of Handel's ' Messiah ' by watching

*BALTIMORE 12-23
ENGLISH CATECHISM 20-23

CATECHISM STORIES

it performed, e.g. in this Catechism answer, much is negative : no beginning, no body, etc. In this life we can never know God in Himself.

We know God by our reason

There is an anecdote of a worldly young French lady whose drawing-room, on her days for receiving visitors, was filled with distinguished people. One day the conversation turned on religion, and a fashionable journalist argued hotly against the existence of God. No one seemed to agree with him, and at last he turned to his hostess as if looking for sympathy : ' I simply couldn't have believed that in such a group of intelligent people as this I should be the only one not to believe in God ! '

' Oh, you're not the only one ! ' said the young lady.

Naturally, he looked pleased, but not for long. ' Here are two others,' she went on, and pointed to her dog and her cat. ' They don't believe in God either, but they have more sense than to boast about it ! '

Animals cannot believe in God because they are without reason, but men who have reason can and should know God.

The Unbeginning

A priest had done his best to instruct an old negro, and was asking him a few questions to see how much he had taken in.

' Who made you ? '

' De Lord God.'

' And who made the Lord God ? '

The negro looked puzzled, and then dismayed, but after a moment, his assurance returned :

' Ah'm glad yo' mentioned that, Father. That's one thing Ah've wanted to know all mah laife, who made de Lord God. Tell me, who was it ? '

If anybody had made God, He would not be God. God is by definition the One who *must* exist.

As He said to Moses : Tell the children of Israel : *He-Who-Is* hath sent me to you.

From eternity to eternity Thou art God!

Because God exists of Himself, He is for ever. We have to try and picture His eternity to ourselves.

At a school camp by the sea (*render it somehow as your own experience*) a priest was giving a little talk after night prayers to the boys round the fire.

'Take a handful of sand,' he said. 'If you tried to count the grains, how long would it take you—there are many thousands.

'Suppose you put your handful of sand into a little box, and take out one grain every day—the box would still seem just as full when you grew into an old man. We should all be dead for centuries before the box began to look even half empty.

'Suppose the grain of sand was only taken away once a year; and suppose instead of a little box of sand there was all the sand on this two-mile beach to be taken away, one grain every year, no, one grain every thousand years.

'Or, instead of this beach, think of all the sea-shores in the world, and all the sand in the Sahara, too, and all other deserts; and instead of a thousand years, take away one grain of sand every ten million years.

'When the last grain of sand was gone, eternity would still be only just beginning, whether you look into the future of the future or backward into the eternity before the world began.'

Before the mountains were made, or the earth and the world were formed; from eternity and to eternity Thou art God.

God is Spirit, present everywhere, all-mighty

St. Paul in his journeyings came to Athens, for so many centuries a world-centre of human wisdom and art. He wandered through its magnificent public places, looking at shrines and statues of the gods, in marble and gold and silver, one work of genius after another. God of war, god of poetry, goddess of wisdom, goddess of love—these were but ordinary human qualities and passions made into idols —how could these educated Athenians be so blinded! Then he noticed a small incense-altar in its shrine, with the surprising inscription 'To the Unknown God.' Evidently

CATECHISM STORIES 23

some Athenians were unsatisfied with paganism and seeking for something higher.

Soon he made some friends, both Jews and Greeks, and tried to tell them about Christ. Some of them arranged a public meeting for him on the Areopagus, a great open-air forum on a hill. A big crowd gathered, for the Athenians were always ready to hear about anything that was news. He began by referring to the altar he had noticed to ' The Unknown God,' and said he would tell them about Him. God made all things and is the Lord of heaven and earth, he said. He dwells not in temples made with hands, nor does He need anything from men. He is the great Spirit who gives to all life and breath and everything. He made us His children to His own likeness; and we live and move and are in Him, spiritual beings also. These pagan gods of gold or marble are not as much like God as we are ourselves—why worship such things?

So far the Athenians listened attentively; St. Paul was only saying what the wisest of the Greeks had said; that there is one infinite Spirit over all, from whom all things come.

But then he went on to tell them how God had sent His Son, and raised Him from the dead to be our Judge. This was too much for the clever Athenians; some treated it as a joke, others, more polite, said: ' Some other time, perhaps.' Nevertheless, from this meeting St. Paul got a handful of converts (Acts xvii, 34), and the Mass began in Athens. [See also nos. 265, 531.

God knows and sees all things

Mother Margaret Hallahan (foundress of the English Dominican nuns of Stone) began life as a child of poor Irish emigrants, who left her an orphan at nine. For two years she was at an orphanage in Somers Town, London, where the children attended the Church of St. Aloysius, Clarendon Square, near what is now Euston Station. Over the high altar was painted an Eye, within a triangle, to remind the worshippers that we are always in the sight of God.

This Eye made a deep impression on the child. She

continued to attend St. Aloysius's when she went into service at the age of eleven. When she was unhappy, as she often was from ill-treatment, the thought of this Eye comforted the lonely child with the sense of God's continual Presence; a sense that gradually became the strongest influence in her spiritual life. It led her (after thirty years in domestic service) to try her vocation as a lay-sister in Bruges, and then to work amongst the factory girls of Coventry under the direction of Dr. Ullathorne, and so finally to found her Congregation.

> * WHY IS GOD CALLED CREATOR OF HEAVEN AND EARTH?
>
> *God is called 'Creator of heaven and earth' because He made heaven and earth, and all things, out of nothing, by His word.*

Creator of Heaven and Earth

AN old Spanish woman upbraided some Red militia-men who arrived at the village in a lorry and were burning the beautiful old church. They told her the Anarchists intended to tear down and destroy everything that could remind the people of God and religion.

'Well,' retorted the sturdy old woman, 'you had better tear the stars down from the sky, and put out the Sun and Moon, for so long as they are there we shall be reminded of the good God who made them.'

Creator of Life

The pupils of a certain school were listening to a lecture on plant-life. 'All living organisms,' said the learned professor, 'are developed from a substance called protoplasm, which is made up of oxygen, hydrogen, carbon, and nitrogen. This we know. But from where does that protoplasm derive its power of living and growing? Does anybody know that?'

'I know,' said a boy at the back.

'You know what makes protoplasm grow? Then you are wiser than all the biologists. You must tell us.'

'God does,' said the boy.

*BALTIMORE 35-37
ENGLISH CATECHISM 19

CATECHISM STORIES 25

The answer went beyond physical science, but it was right, for, as far as we can see, the gulf between dead matter and living matter can be bridged only by the intervention of God.

St. Francis of Assisi had such respect for all living things that he could never allow trees to be rooted up, but had them cut so that new green shoots could grow forth again from the roots.

Creator of all things, visible and invisible

One of the oldest religions (Zoroastrian) said there is not one God but two ; a good one and an evil one, and that the whole bodily world was created by the evil one. This idea survived in some heresies in Christendom (Manicheans, Albigenses, etc.).

When St. Anthony of Padua became a friar, his 'first job was to preach to some heretics of this kind (Cathari) in northern Italy. During one sermon, at Rimini by the river-bank, they scoffed and refused to give him a hearing. At last he turned from them to the river : ' O little fishes, I have a message for you from Christ.' Whereupon (says the *Fioretti*) the fish came to listen, and ' all held their heads out of the water in great peace and order, so that in front were the smallest fishes, after them the middle-sized, and behind in the deepest water the largest fishes.'

He said : ' The greatness and goodness of God is shown forth in you, my dear fishes. You were the first living creatures that God created for man. You were the food in which Our Saviour Christ took much pleasure, and when He desired to pay the tribute to Cæsar He found it in the mouth of a fish. God has given you the whole world of waters to dwell in, so clear and transparent, and has furnished it with caverns and grottoes more wonderful than the palaces of kings. You are led by a deep instinct to obey nature with delight and to propagate your kind. Winter and summer are the same to you, the rain cannot harm you, nor earthquakes. You were safe even in the Deluge which destroyed the other creatures. You ought to be grateful to God ; and since you cannot praise Him with words, at least bow your heads now, as a sign of gratitude.' Whereupon (says the *Fioretti* again) the fishes bowed their heads in unison, and swam away.

The fish-congregation is presumably legend, but we can well believe St. Anthony did preach the sermon, and that the heretics listened and saw the point of it—the one God, whose Creation, matter as well as spirit, is all good.

God's Providence guides all His Creation

A small boy (I remember hearing about) went to a children's party; one of the games was a Treasure-Hunt in the garden. Each child was given an envelope containing the first clue. Tommy's message said: '*Look in the tool-shed.*' Searching in the tool-shed he found another message under a flower-pot: '*Try red.*' The only red he could see in the garden was some geraniums, and amongst them he found a third message: '*Apples are best.*' He discovered an apple tree, and looking carefully found a tiny note tied to a branch: '*Three paces to the south.*' The three paces brought him to the garden wall, where he noticed a hole in the bricks, and in the hole he found the Treasure—a bright shilling.

When he got home he told them all about it, very pleased with his own cleverness. His mother said: 'I hope you thanked Mrs. Brown properly.' 'I thanked her for the party, but not for the shilling, because I found it myself.' 'Silly boy, Mrs. Brown asked you to the party, and put the shilling in the wall for you, and arranged all the clues for you as well.' 'Did she? Well, next time I see her I will thank her for *everything*.' [See also nos. 182, 199, 594, 676.]

* ARE THERE THREE PERSONS IN GOD?

   There are three Persons in God: God the Father, God the Son and God the Holy Ghost. These three Persons are not three Gods: the Father, the Son and the Holy Ghost are all one and the same God.

The Mystery of the One and the Three

ST. AUGUSTINE was walking on the sea-shore, pondering the mystery of the Blessed Trinity and how it could best be

*BALTIMORE 24-34
ENGLISH CATECHISM 25-26

described in words. Close by he saw a little boy, who had dug a hole in the sand, and kept filling a big shell with sea-water and pouring it into the hole.

'What are you trying to do?' said Augustine.

'I am going to put all the sea into that hole,' replied the boy.

Yes, thought Augustine to himself, that is like me, trying to put all the vast mystery of God into a few human words.

He went home and wrote his book about the Trinity, in which he says that God is Love, therefore there must be somehow more than One in God; that the Father and Son love each other and the Love which proceeds from them is the Holy Spirit. That is the nearest we can get to so lofty a mystery.

Three Persons in God

On Holy Saturday, 633, St. Patrick blessed the new fire on the hill of Slane, and the Druids watching it from Tara said that if not extinguished it would blaze in the land for ever.

King Leoghaire, overlord of all Ireland, had forbidden any fire to be lighted until the beacon at Tara the next day, which would signalize a great assembly of all the chieftains of Ireland. But St. Patrick had determined to use the occasion to begin his preaching in such dramatic fashion that all Ireland would hear of it.

While he was waiting he composed the prayer called 'St. Patrick's Breastplate.' It begins and ends with God, Three in One :

> 'I bind to myself this day
> The strong power of the Invocation of the Trinity.
> I believe the Three-ness in the One-ness,
> The Creator of the Universe.'

Next morning, Easter Sunday, he and his monks came to Tara in solemn procession singing the Litanies. There he encountered and conquered the magic of the Druids, and was given leave to speak of his God to the assembled rulers from all over Ireland.

He plucked a shamrock from the ground and lifted it

up. 'See this tiny plant—three leaves exactly equal—yet all one growth from one stem. The God I preach to you is likewise One and Three—Father, Son, and Holy Spirit, three Persons, one God.'

He remained all Easter week at Slane and Tara, and then had the happiness of baptising Conall, the brother of King Leoghaire himself. Thus the conversion of the Irish began, and they have ever since loved the shamrock as the emblem of Faith and Country.

God is above our finite minds

We must expect mystery in God, because all human words must fall short of Truth when it is Infinite.

St. Thomas Aquinas, the Emperor's young cousin, who at seventeen ran away from home to join the Dominicans, became one of the very greatest thinkers and writers the Church ever had. Every word he wrote was treasured up by his friends. At forty-seven he was half-way through writing his greatest work, the *Summa Theologica*, all about God and His dealings with man. One morning at Mass he fell into an ecstasy; not unusual, for he had immense devotion to the Blessed Sacrament (it was he who had written the *Pange Lingua*, and the mass for Corpus Christi), but this was a longer ecstasy than usual. After a day or two it was noticed that he was writing nothing, not even to finish the *Summa*. To the anxious questions all he could say was: 'Such things have been shown to me that all the words I have written seem to me now not worth a straw.' A few months later God called him from this life, to the clear vision of eternal Reality and Truth. [See also no. 169.]

> * Who is Jesus Christ?
> *Jesus Christ is God the Son, made man for us.*

The Son of the living God

THE greatest moment in the founding of the Church was when the apostles, led by St. Peter, made their first open act of faith in Our Lord as the Son of God. They had been with Him about three years, watching His holiness and His miracles, and the conviction had been silently forming

*BALTIMORE 77-79
ENGLISH CATECHISM 32

CATECHISM STORIES 29

in their minds. One day, near the pagan city of Cæsarea Philippi, with its shrine of the great god Pan, they are all resting by the wayside, and Our Lord suddenly asks : ' Whom do men say the Son of man is ? ' They tell him the rumours—some say You are John the Baptist ; some Jeremias, or one of the prophets come back. ' But whom do you say that I am ? ' A silence, then Simon, speaking for all, uttered the momentous words : ' Thou art the Christ, the Son of the living God.' The act of faith is welcomed joyfully by Our Lord. ' Blessed art thou, Simon Bar-Jona ; flesh and blood hath not revealed this to thee, but my Father who is in heaven,' etc. Now the Twelve have hold of the great fact of the Incarnation. Now He can begin to ' build My Church,' and appoint His Vicar, and go up to Jerusalem to finish on the Cross the work His Father had given Him to do.

God so loved the world

The men who, out of all mankind, ought to have recognised that Our Lord was God, were the religious rulers of God's people—the High Priest and the Sanhedrin or Council. Only two of them, as far as we know, believed. One was Nicodemus, who when Jesus was in Jerusalem at a festival time, came to Him secretly by night and said : ' Rabbi, we know thou art come a teacher from God, for no man can do those signs which thou dost, unless God be with him.' He wanted to know more. Our Lord told him that to see the kingdom of God meant being born again and starting a new life, following the voice of the Holy Spirit instead of earthly prudence. Nicodemus asked how these things could be done. ' Art thou a master in Israel, and knowest not these things ? ' Then Our Lord revealed to Nicodemus that to save man God had Himself become man ; ' God so loved the world as to give His only-begotten Son, that whosoever believeth in Him may not perish, but may have life everlasting.'

Nicodemus crept home in the dark, believing but still not brave enough to profess his faith. At a later festival-day, when the Council had tried vainly to have Our Lord arrested, Nicodemus had courage enough to speak up and say : 'Doth our Law judge any man until it first hear him?' The other members replied scornfully : 'Art thou also a Galilean' (John vii, 50).

After that he seems to have kept away from the Council. In Holy Week, after Our Lord had driven the money-changers from the Temple, Caiphas called a meeting (Matt. xxvi, 3) to plan Our Lord's death quickly, before the Pasch. On Thursday after Our Lord's arrest He was brought before a midnight meeting at the house of Caiphas ; the false witnesses failed to agree, and at last the High Priest stood up, put Jesus on oath and as God's representative asked Him solemnly : 'I adjure thee by the living God, that thou tell us if thou be the Christ, the Son of God.' It was the supreme moment in the history of the Jews. Our Lord answered with equal solemnity : 'Thou hast said it.' The high priest rent his garments as a sign of horror at the blasphemy, and with great clamour they all agreed to pass sentence of death.

After Our Lord was dead, and His disciples scattered, the two secret believers on the Council found some courage. Joseph of Arimathea, who for some reason seems to have been absent from all the Council meetings, went boldly to Pilate and begged the body, and Nicodemus brought spices and helped in the burial.

We do not hear of them afterwards (except in legend—Glastonbury, etc.). Doubtless Nicodemus, too, became a Christian, and we cannot be sure that we should have been any braver in his place. But what an opportunity he missed, by not confessing his faith in the God-Man, in the very Council of the Jews.

Made man for us

Would God have become man if there had been no Fall ? Very possibly, but as things are, He became man to save us when we were lost.

Two of Our Lord's stories, one for men and one for women, picture the love of God which brought Him down from heaven.

In His own words, the lost sheep and lost groat : Luke xv, 1–10.

CATECHISM STORIES

What manner of Man is this?

In the stilling of the storm Our Lord is seen clearly as both divine and human (read story from Mark iv, 36–40).

Truly man, when He lies exhausted and asleep. Truly God, when He gives orders to the forces of nature themselves. No wonder the apostles are filled with awe, looking at one another with questions they can hardly put into words. [See also nos. 392, 658.]

> * WHY IS JESUS CHRIST TRULY GOD?
> *Jesus Christ is truly God because He has one and the same nature with God the Father.*

True God of true God

As soon as Constantine had given peace to the Church he had to gather the Council of Nicæa (325) to settle the Christian mind troubled by the Arian heresy. Arius was a priest of Alexandria, elderly, grave, ascetic; to him and his followers God seemed so high and remote that He could not have become man; the Son who became man was not really God, not consubstantial with the Father, but only the highest of God's creatures.

The great Council opened, with 318 bishops, some bearing marks of torture or maiming from the persecution of Diocletian. Constantine himself listened from his throne. The Patriarch of Alexandria brought with him a young deacon named Athanasius, who spoke with great effect on behalf of the true Faith. The Council condemned the teaching of Arius and defined the truth in the 'Nicene' creed which we sing every Sunday: 'Deum de Deo . . . consubstantialem Patri.'

This was not the end of the heresy, which became mixed with politics and went on spreading. The young Athanasius soon became Patriarch of Alexandria himself, and for fifty years he was the heroic leader on the Catholic side, with his life often in danger, and driven five times into exile. But the victory had really been won at Nicæa, by the test-word 'consubstantial,' which meant that the Son is equally God with the Father, and therefore that Jesus Christ is truly God.

*BALTIMORE 80
ENGLISH CATECHISM 84

CATECHISM STORIES

Consubstantialem Patri

For two incidents from Our Lord's life, in which His own words indicate that He is God, see *Teaching the Catechism*, p. 16, or John viii, 51–59 ('Before Abraham was made, I am': thus taking to Himself the very Name of God, cf. Exod. iii, 14); and John xiv, 4–9 (at the Last Supper: 'He that seeth Me seeth the Father').

' Indeed the Son of God '

A remarkable act of faith in Christ's divinity was that made by the centurion who was in charge at the Crucifixion. He had seen Our Lord in His deepest suffering and failure, he had got the procession with difficulty through the seething streets, he had superintended the nailing of the condemned to their crosses, witnessed the cruel mockery of the priests and scribes, had seen the darkness, and felt the trembling of the earth. He had heard Our Lord's seven words, His calling upon His Father; he had seen Our Lord die, and made his report to Pilate, and driven a lance into the Sacred Heart with his own hand. In all this he was a soldier obeying orders, but gradually faith was forming in his mind; and at last he says: 'Indeed this man was the Son of God!'

' Before the day-star have I begotten Thee '

This story is in three chapters: the first happened in the time of the ancient Jews, the second in Our Lord's time, and the third has not happened yet.

(1) Centuries before Christ, the shepherd-boy David became a great fighting man, beat the Philistines and other dangerous enemies, and reigned peacefully as king over the people of God. King David (or perhaps some inspired prophet speaking in his name) was shown by God a vision of the great King whom God would send one day—the Messias. He would be Priest as well as King, like Melchisedech. The vision showed him conquering God's enemies, trampling them under foot, terrible in his anger, breaking kings and nations.

All this is in Psalm 109 (*read it*) and it begins with God speaking to David's Lord, the Anointed King: ' Sit thou at My right hand, until I make thy enemies thy footstool.'

(2) In the last few days of Christ's life, in the Temple, after the Pharisees and scribes had asked him many questions to ensnare Him, Our Lord put one question to them. (*Read it:* Matt. xxii, 41-46.) The right answer would have been that David calls the Messias 'Lord' because Messias, invited to sit at God's right hand, is equal to God, and is God Himself.

When Our Lord asked the question in the Temple, there fell a silence. But in two or three days Our Lord gave the answer Himself. No longer free in the Temple, but bound before the High Priest, He was asked : 'Tell us if thou be the Christ, the Son of God.' 'Thou hast said it ; and hereafter you shall see the Son of Man sitting on the right hand of the power of God and coming in the clouds of heaven.'

(3) The third chapter will be at the end of the world, when Our Lord will come, with all the power of God, to conquer by force those who have not been won by His love.

> * WHY IS JESUS CHRIST TRULY MAN?
> *Jesus Christ is truly man because He has the nature of man, having a body and soul like ours.*

Our Lord has the nature of man

IN Gethsemane we clearly see that Our Lord has a body and soul like ours. Have story read from Matt. xvi, 36-46, adding Luke xxii, 43-44.

His agony is of His human soul ('My soul is sorrowful even unto death') and His sweat of blood indicates His human body, of delicate sensitiveness. Both soul and body are mentioned in His words (which refer to Himself as well as the apostles) : 'The *spirit* is willing but the *flesh* is weak.'

'He emptied Himself'

St. Paulinus (fifth century) was one of the richest men in the Roman Empire, but distributed all his estates in charity and became a priest, and finally Bishop of Nola, famous for his wisdom and holiness. When the Vandals from Africa raided the district, Paulinus spent all he could raise in relieving his people's distress and ransoming them from slavery. Then a poor widow came to say that her only son had been carried off by the Vandal king's son-in-law.

'I have no money left,' said Paulinus, 'but I will give what I can. Let us go to Africa, and I will exchange myself for your son.' Despite her objections, he insisted on carrying out this plan. In Africa the exchange duly took place, and Paulinus was put to work as a gardener. After some time it came to the king's ears that amongst his son-in-law's slaves was the famous Bishop of Nola. He at once had him set free, and sent him home together with a number of other men from Nola who had been made slaves in the raid.

St. Paulinus was acting in the mind of Christ Jesus, who came down from heaven and assumed our human nature, taking (as St. Paul says) 'the form of a slave, being made in the likeness of men, and in habit found as a man.'

Christ is our Elder Brother

A lady met a little boy of seven carrying a heavy baby in his arms. He looked tired and his thin arms did not look strong enough to bear the weight of the younger child.

'Isn't he too heavy for you?' the lady asked him kindly.

'Oh no, he's my *brother*,' the little boy replied. He seemed surprised at the idea that the little brother whom he loved could be a burden.

And that is the way Our Lord feels about us.

In all things like as we are

One Sunday morning in June, 1885, Father Damien was saying Mass as usual for his lepers. He had lived with them for twelve years, nursing them, building houses for them, doing everything to mend their broken lives, making their coffins when they died. This Sunday after the gospel he came to the rails to preach, and his very first words made a breathless hush in the church: instead of his usual 'My dear brethren,' he said, very slowly: 'We lepers . . .'

CATECHISM STORIES

That was his way of telling them that he was at last one with them in their affliction. For another four years, until his death, he worked amongst them, fighting for their rights with the Government, kindling a fire of charity that has since spread over the world.

In the same way, when Our Lord took our nature He took on Himself every sorrow and affliction of humanity, sin only excepted.

'We have not a high priest who cannot have compassion on our infirmities, but one tempted in all things like as we are, without sin.'

> * WHAT DO YOU MEAN BY THE INCARNATION?
> *I mean by the Incarnation that God the Son took to Himself the nature of man:* 'The Word was made flesh.'

Descendit de cœlis

THERE is a story of a young king in olden days who really cared about his people, and was grieved to know how much they suffered from hunger and cold and pestilence. He did what he could by gifts of clothes and food, but his own resources were scanty, and the people were often too ignorant to do the best for themselves. When the king tried to teach them better ways of farming and building, the people made little response. 'It's no good telling the King our troubles,' they would say. 'He could never understand what it is to work or to be hungry and cold.'

The young king felt discouraged and went to a wise old minister and asked his advice.

'How can I win the confidence of my people?' he said. 'I want to show them how to put an end to some of their misfortunes, and help them to bear the others with courage. They do not know their king cares about them—tell me how I can make them understand.'

'There would be only one way, I think, Your Majesty.'

'Tell me, for God's sake.'

'If Your Majesty could go and live amongst them, not as king, but as one of themselves. . . .'

That night a poorly-clad man left the palace; no one

*BALTIMORE 82-86
ENGLISH CATECHISM 40

recognised the King and no one knew his secret but the old minister and two or three trusted servants. It was given out that the King had gone on a foreign journey. For months he lived in a poor hut, and lived and ate and worked as a peasant, tended the sick and helped the workers. His fellows soon got to love him and came to him for help and advice, and were very sorry when he said good-bye to them.

When he reappeared at the palace and once more went amongst the people in royal fashion, he was soon recognised by those who had known him as a labourer. The story spread, and thenceforward his people loved and trusted him because he had shown that he loved and cared for them.

To make us understand God's love for us was the purpose of the Incarnation.

Christ the Bridge

In the book of Genesis we read a mysterious story of Jacob's dream of a ladder joining earth to heaven. (Read Gen. xxviii, 10-19, and then Our Lord's words in John i, 51.) It is Our Lord, therefore, who points to Jacob's ladder as a figure of Himself, the God-man who joins heaven to earth again, and restores communication of ascending prayers and descending graces. The Incarnation is a bridge built (Pontifex=bridge-builder) between God and man. [See also nos. 408, 607, 609.]

The Spirit of Christmas

There is just one season in the year when men seem able to realise for a moment what the Incarnation means for us all ; and never was this so strikingly seen as in the Flanders trenches at Christmas, 1914.

Just before Christmas there had been some attacks and counter-attacks here and there, and many casualties, but as the holy season drew closer the firing seemed to die down by a general instinct. On Christmas Eve in some sectors the German parapet was decorated with candles and the singing of carols was heard. In the morning from trench to trench were shouted greetings, and all along the

CATECHISM STORIES

line the bolder spirits began walking into no-man's-land for a talk with equally adventurous enemies. Officers entered into the spirit of the proceedings, and as the day went on a good part of both armies had left their trenches and were fraternising in crowds between the lines, exchanging cigarettes and chocolate from their Christmas parcels.

An eye-witness, writing twenty years after (in *Reynolds' News*), says : ' Our brigade was composed of the Gordon Highlanders, the Scots Guards, and the Border Regiment. On Christmas Eve a seventy-two-hour truce was arranged to bury the dead. We sent German identification discs and pay-books to the German lines. They replied by sending similar grim relics to our lines. We fraternised, exchanged views and rations. . . . When the truce ended the Germans fired three volleys in the air to indicate that hostilities were resumed. Even so, about twenty Germans were still walking about unarmed on the top of their trenches, and our lads did not attempt to shoot them down. Indeed, although many of us were threatened with court-martial, our unofficial armistice lasted for fourteen days.'

Another (Seaforth Highlanders) : ' On Christmas Eve German soldiers began to shout across that they wanted Christmas without firing. At first it was regarded as a joke. As night advanced there seemed to be more sentiment in the German's shouting, and one of our fellows, a daredevil corporal named Davie Flint, cried : " If you're not afraid, come right over." Someone came. Davie threw off his equipment and jumped forward to meet him. Others followed, and for four days Germans and Seaforths exchanged smokes and rations. It was glorious. We enjoyed the utmost freedom and officers joined in our rejoicing. Then we went out for our four-days' rest. On returning the Colonel said that fraternisation must cease, we were at war. A German was coming towards us. The Colonel shouted to him to go back. He failed to do so, and orders were given to fire over his head. This was done. The Germans replied with five shells. That is the true story of the first Noël of the war, before Messines in 1914.' (Isaac Sefton, Airdrie.)

Another : ' I was serving with the 2nd Bedfords. The

Germans put lanterns on the front of their trenches and called out to us not to fire as it was Christmas. There was singing on both sides. Before long British and German soldiers were exchanging cigarettes and souvenirs in no-man's-land. We were later relieved by the Royal Scots Fusiliers, and our opposite number, the Saxons, by the Prussian Guards. Orders were at once given reminding us that we were at war. Shots were fired over the heads of the Germans. Hostilities resumed. I don't know what happened to the Saxon soldier who was a waiter in a London hotel. If he had the luck to come through it all, here's Christmas greetings to him from G. L. Joyce, Peterborough.'

The Christmas spirit could go on all the year round if our Faith in the first Christmas was strong enough.

> * WHERE IS JESUS CHRIST?
> *As God, Jesus Christ is everywhere. As God made man, He is in heaven and in the Blessed Sacrament of the Altar.*

'As God, Jesus Christ is everywhere'

WHEN St. Edmund was a boy at Oxford, one day he wandered away from his companions playing in the meadows. Suddenly he heard his name called, and turned to see a young boy of wonderful beauty. 'Don't you know me?' said the boy.

Very much astonished, Edmund said: 'I do not know you, and I do not think you know me.'

'I wonder you do not know Me, for I sit next to you in the schools. I am with you all day long. Everywhere you go, I am at your side.' Then He said:

'Look in my face, and read carefully what is written on my forehead.'

Edmund looked, and read the words: 'Jesus of Nazareth.'

'I am Jesus of Nazareth, and this is my Name; trace it carefully on your forehead every night, and it shall fortify you against sudden death, and anyone else who shall do the same.'

*BALTIMORE 84 and 103
ENGLISH CATECHISM 46

CATECHISM STORIES 39

And when He had said this (says the chronicler) the Boy on whom the angels desire to look disappeared ; but in the breast of that boy whom He had deigned to visit He left no small sweetness.

Every night afterwards St. Edmund traced, with his fingers, the letters INRI upon his forehead, and recommended the practice to his friends.

'As God made man, He is in heaven'

ST. STEPHEN was the first martyr of the Church, two or three years after Pentecost. He was chosen to be one of the seven deacons, was an eloquent speaker, and carried on an active apostolate in the synagogues of Jerusalem, frequented by Jews from Alexandria. We do not know if he had ever seen Our Lord, but he was martyred because he insisted openly on Our Lord's teaching that God's kingdom was now world-wide and no longer confined to the Jews and the Temple. Accused before the Sanhedrin, he made a long speech to that effect ; at the end he reminded them that they were the betrayers and murderers of the Just One. Then, while his judges raged against him, Stephen was filled with the Holy Spirit and looking up to heaven saw the glory of God, and Jesus standing on the right hand of God, and he said : ' Behold I see the heavens opened, and the Son of man standing on the right hand of God.' The horrified Council stopped their ears, rushed upon him, hurried him out of the city and stoned him to death.

' Lord, lay not this sin to their charge,' he said, and perhaps he was praying specially for the fierce young Pharisee whom he could see holding the garments of the stoners.

This was Saul, who soon, riding to Damascus to persecute the Christians, is thrown and blinded by a great light from heaven, while Christ speaks to him : ' Saul, Saul, why persecutest thou Me ? ' ' Who art thou, Lord ? ' ' I am Jesus, whom thou persecutest.'

Our Lord is still living His risen life in heaven, still watching over the life of His Church, still interested in every move of His friends, still winning His enemies over.

Alpha and Omega

'One day, all on a sudden, St. John heard in the silence a voice like a trumpet call, clear and heart-stirring. "And I turned," he says, " to see whose voice it was that was calling me." And being turned, he looked up into heaven as through a door opened in the sky, and there in the midst of celestial light he saw someone like to his old Friend and Master, Jesus of Nazareth. It was in reality He, the very same, but different in appearance.

'Not now clothed in the common work-day garb of earth, but clad in kingly garments falling down to His feet, and girt about with a golden girdle. His head, with heaven's light playing through His flowing hair, looked bright and white as snow glistening in the sunshine. His voice was as the sound of many waters, and it thrilled through the disciple's soul and the burning splendour of the vision melted all his mortal strength, and he fell prostrate on his face. And Jesus our God, with whom St. John had walked arm in arm on earth, came forward and laid His right hand upon him, saying · " Fear not. I am the First and the Last. Alive and was dead. Behold I am living for ever and ever, and have the keys of death and hell "' (Apoc. i, 10–18. From *Daybreak in the Soul*, by Fr. W. Roche).

'And in the Blessed Sacrament'

St. Paschal Baylon (Franciscan lay-brother of Aragon, d. 1592) used to tell of an odd adventure on a journey he made to Paris, carrying a message for his superiors. He was on the road alone when a Huguenot lancer came riding. 'Is God in heaven, monk?' he shouted. 'Why, of course God is in heaven,' replied the astonished Paschal. Whereupon the soldier spurred his horse and galloped off. Then Paschal suddenly realised that the soldier had expected him to say 'in heaven and in the Blessed Sacrament,' in which case he would have run him through with his lance.

'Alas,' he said, 'I was not worthy of the crown of martyrdom, and I missed it for the second time.'

The first time had been when some Huguenots stoned

CATECHISM STORIES

him (and broke his shoulder) when he spoke up for the Catholic Eucharistic doctrine. Another time he was nearly hanged at a Huguenot chateau. This journey was so full of perils that when he returned to Spain his black hair had turned white as snow. [See also nos. 408-422.]

> * WHAT DOES THE THIRD ARTICLE MEAN?
> *The third article means that God the Son took a Body and Soul like ours, in the womb of the Blessed Virgin Mary, by the power of the Holy Ghost.*

Ave gratia plena

ST. LUKE himself tells us the story of the Third Article of the Creed, and his own words are the best (Luke i, 26-38).

Mary's place in the Creed

A Protestant clergyman was visiting an orphanage, and the children were each reciting their prayers for him to hear. One little boy, who had previously been at a Catholic school, after finishing the Our Father began the Hail Mary. ' No, no ! ' said the clergyman. ' We don't want to hear about her—go on to the Creed.' The little boy did so, but stopped suddenly when he came to ' born of the . . .' and said : ' Here she comes again—what shall I do now, sir ? '

Indeed we cannot have Jesus without Mary.

Mother of Christ

Some of the saints tell us of their visions which helped them to understand the joys of Our Lady's motherhood.

'While praying in the church early in the morning,' says B. Angela of Foligno, ' I was rapt in spirit, and I saw Our Blessed Lady come into the church. My soul was filled with intense joy when I saw her, but for a time I was afraid to go near. But Our Lady, seeing me hesitate, held out to me the Holy Child and said : "You love my Divine Son so much, come and take Him from me." She then placed Him in my arms. He seemed asleep, for His eyes were shut. Then she sat down as if she were tired from a long journey. She looked so lovely as she sat beside me that I

*BALTIMORE 85-87
ENGLISH CATECHISM 48

could scarcely take my eyes from her to look at the Holy Child whom I was pressing to my breast. At this moment Jesus opened His eyes and looked lovingly upon me; His look filled my soul with so much joy that I should have died on the spot had He not sustained me by His divine power.' [See nos. 225, 668.]

> * HAD JESUS CHRIST ANY FATHER ON EARTH?
> *Jesus Christ had no father on earth; St. Joseph was only His Guardian or foster-father.*

Guardian of Jesus and Mary

OUR LADY had told no one of Gabriel's message, trusting that God would make known whatever was necessary. When St. Joseph knew that she would have a child, he did not know the child was the Son of God. She was promised to him in marriage, and he could not see what to do for the best. It seemed that he had been somehow deceived, but his chief thought was not for himself but for Mary, for whom his trust and affection could not be changed. If he had to put her away, could it be done privately, so that her good name should not be harmed? God let him suffer these perplexities for a time to bring him to higher holiness and to let him prove his loyal affection; then in his sleep came the angel of the Lord: 'Joseph, son of David, fear not to take unto thee Mary thy wife, for that which is conceived in her is of the Holy Ghost. And she shall bring forth a son, and thou shalt call His name Jesus: for He shall save His people from their sins.' All St. Joseph's doubts were ended, and he understood the wonderful place reserved for him in God's plan (Matt. i, 18, etc.).

St. Joseph's power with God

The modern devotion to St. Joseph received a strong impulse from St. Teresa of Avila. She tells us herself how, after becoming a nun, she was reduced to a wretched state by a serious illness, made worse for some years by unskilled doctors, and she only recovered through praying to St. Joseph. Always afterwards she had the greatest possible devotion to him. Out of seventeen new convents she

*BALTIMORE 88
ENGLISH CATECHISM 49

CATECHISM STORIES

founded, all except five were dedicated to St. Joseph. Every convent had a statue of him over one of its doors; and inside the entrance there was always a picture of St. Joseph leading the Holy Family into Egypt, with the inscription: 'We lead a life of poverty, but shall have many possessions if we fear God.'

'Knowing by experience,' St. Teresa tells us, 'the amazing influence St. Joseph has with God. I would persuade everybody to honour him with special devotion.'

Her theory was that Our Lord delighted so much at Nazareth in doing St. Joseph's bidding, that He still likes to do it in heaven.

'Every year on St. Joseph's feast I ask for some special favour, and I have always had my desires fulfilled.'

> * WHY DID OUR SAVIOUR SUFFER?
> *Our Saviour suffered to atone for our sins and to purchase for us eternal life.*

' Our Saviour suffered '

IT seems a natural idea to us that the Saviour of mankind came to suffer, but it was inconceivable to everybody before it happened, especially to those who believed in Our Lord.

No doubt Our Lady was the first to know, by revelation at the moment of holy Simeon's prophecy; but she kept it in her heart.

In the last few weeks of Our Lord's life, when He had made sure that the apostles knew Him for the Son of God (St. Peter's confession of faith), and had appointed a visible head for His Church, He 'steadfastly set His face to go to Jerusalem.' On the journey He repeatedly told the apostles what would happen in Jerusalem—that He would be rejected by the Jewish leaders, and suffer many things, be mocked and scourged and spit upon and put to death, and the third day rise again. They simply could not believe it, and when it actually began to happen it seemed the end of everything.

Afterwards, on Easter Sunday afternoon, the risen Christ walked unrecognised with two disconsolate disciples going

*BALTIMORE 90-94
ENGLISH CATECHISM 55

to Emmaus. Read their account of the Passion, and His reply (Luke xxiv, 18–27). He went through the Scriptures reminding them of passages such as Isaias liii, 4–7, and Psalm xxi, 1, 7, 8, 17, 18, 19 ; and made them see that the Passion was foretold and therefore part of God's plan.

During the forty days He continued this ' opening the Scriptures,' and afterwards it formed a main theme of the apostles' preaching : ' How that Christ died for our sins, according to the Scriptures.'

Saviour of Mankind

Golgotha (' place of the skull ') was a rocky mound outside Jerusalem. Jewish legend said that the skull of Adam was buried there. It had been handed down from Noe to Sem, and finally to Melchisedech, priest-king of Salem, who buried it there. So when the precious Blood flowed down from the Cross, it is pictured (in Christian art) as falling first upon our first parent whose sin made the Redeemer necessary. Hence a skull and bones are sometimes seen on a crucifix ; it is Adam, representing the human race, on Calvary as in Eden.

' He shall save His people from their sins '

One day when the little Child Jesus was playing alone in the garden, He saw two archangels standing and looking at Him. One held the Cross and the nails, the other a lance and a reed with sponge on it. The Child was frightened and rushed to His Mother's arms for protection, so quickly that one of His sandals came unfastened. He clasped her right hand in both of His, and she held Him with her left. He could still see the angel with the Cross, but His Mother seemed to think it was all right, so He did not feel frightened any more.

This is the story sometimes told about the ancient picture called ' Our Lady of Perpetual Succour.'

' He died for me '

For many years after the Civil War an Illinois farmer used to visit a soldier's grave at Nashville, Tennessee, tending it and planting flowers with much devotion once a year. If

CATECHISM STORIES

some stranger asked him : ' Is that your boy ? ' he would answer : ' No, he just lived in our town. You see, when the war came I had seven small children, and my wife was not strong. I was drafted for the army, there was nobody to carry on the farm, and they would have nearly starved without me. We were in terrible trouble about it, and the very day I was going to report at camp my neighbour's boy came and offered to go to the war for me. He said he had nobody depending on him, so he could go better than me. He went, and was wounded at Chickamanga, and died here in hospital. This is his grave.' Then he would point to a rough inscription which he had cut with his own hand on the tombstone : *He died for me.*

Each of us can say of Our Lord : ' He loved me and delivered Himself for me.'

' I, if I be lifted up '

Our Lord died for us when we were His enemies. The sight of Christ on the cross made God forgive us, and makes us forgive each other.

In Florence, eleventh century, John Gualbert and his brother Hugo were rich young nobles. Hugo fought a duel and was killed unfairly, and John swore a blood-feud against the slayer. Riding into Florence, with some armed followers (it was Good Friday), he met the man riding alone and unarmed. ' You at last ! Get down, I am going to kill you ! ' The other knelt down and stretched his arms out in the form of a cross : ' It is Good Friday—give me my life, for the sake of Christ's holy Passion ! '

A wave of grace swept John's soul, and he sheathed his sword : ' I give you your life, and my promise of friendship too. Pray that God will forgive my sin.' He went into the city and into the Benedictine Church of San Miniato, and knelt before a large crucifix, a changed man ; and he saw the Crucified bow His head as if in approval and pardon. Filled with joy and gratitude, he went straight to the Abbot and asked to be received as a monk. Later on he founded a new order of monks at Vallombrosa in the mountains, hermit-like, with perpetual silence and great hardships, and died a saint in 1073.

What Our Lord did on Good Friday goes on and on, winning souls back for God.

' Greater love than this '

In the War, two friends were out with a night patrol together. When the party returned under heavy fire to their trenches, one of the friends was found to be missing. By this time it was getting light, and almost certain death to be out on top, but the one friend insisted on crawling out to look for the other, and reluctantly the officer gave permission. He was watched slowly working his way into no-man's-land, from shell-hole to shell-hole, and at last could be seen no more. When it became dusk again he crawled back and dropped into the trench, himself mortally wounded. While the stretcher-bearers were attending to him, the officer said : ' Well, I hear you found your friend.' ' Yes, sir, but he only lived for a few minutes.' ' I'm afraid it was hardly worth it—I wish I hadn't let you go.' ' Oh, yes, sir, it was worth it. He said : " Good old Jack—I knew you would come ! " '

Our Lord's love for us is like that—He would give His life again for each one, if it were necessary.

Dux vitæ mortuus

In 1386 the men of Lucerne and three allied cantons were fighting for their freedom against the Austrians. At Sempach there was a decisive battle, 1500 Swiss against 6000 Austrians ; but the Swiss, armed with swords and halberds, tried in vain to break the Austrian line of long pikes. A knight of Unterwalden named Arnold von Winkelried said to his comrades : ' Look after my wife and my children—I commend them to your care.' Then shouting : ' I will make a way for you ! ' he rushed towards the enemy, gathered a number of the pikes with his two arms into his own breast, and fell pierced with many wounds. His comrades forced their way into the gap thus made, threw the Austrian line into confusion, and won a complete victory.

Our Lord gave His own life to make victory and freedom possible for us.

A Ransom for many

There was one occasion when Our Lord spoke before-

CATECHISM STORIES 47

hand of His death as an atonement for our sins, and the story also shows us that we are free to take a share in His sufferings.

Read it from Matt. xx, 20–28.

'You are bought with a price'

In a remote town of North Africa the slave-market was being held in the square. A French missionary-father was passing by, when a young black slave-girl darted through the guards and flung herself on her knees before him. ' Please buy me ! I will be a good slave to you always. Oh, please buy me ! ' The missionary was touched, but said he had no need for slaves or servants.

' You have a kind face—I will work very hard for you all my life, if you will buy me, please ! '

' But I have no money to buy you with, my child.'

' Oh, don't go—listen ! If I am not sold to-day the dealer will give me to his uncle who is a chief, and he will be so cruel to me. Please, please buy me ! '

He asked the price, and the dealer agreed to wait. The missionary went home and sold his books and cloak and pawned his watch and managed to raise the money. He took the slave-girl (who was in transports of joy, of course) to a convent, where she soon became a Christian. Sometimes the nuns found her troublesome, but she would obey the lightest wish of the missionary because she said she belonged to him since he had bought her, and she worshipped him like a god as long as he lived. She was a native nun herself for many years till her death quite lately.

Our Lord paid ' the price by which we were ransomed,' and we belong to Him, once already by creation, and over again by redemption.

The price by which we were ransomed

Two boys went to stay with their uncle, an auctioneer, and one day he let them come with him to a sale held at an old-fashioned country-house. All sorts of people crowded into a big room, farmers and shop-keepers and parsons' wives, and dealers from London in fur-collared overcoats, smoking cigars.

Various lots of furniture and odds and ends were bid

for, and went for a few pounds or shillings. One grand-looking picture was put up of a military gentleman in a fine gilt frame, and the boys were sure it would fetch a lot, and were disappointed when the local inn-keeper got it for seven and six.

Then a dirty-looking little picture in a shabby and broken frame was put on the table. It seemed to be a portrait of a child, but you could hardly see what, it was so old. ' Lot twenty-five,' said somebody.

'Fifty pounds' was the first bid, and the boys could hardly believe their ears. The London dealers sat up and began to bid against each other, and in five minutes the picture had reached thousands of pounds: at last it went for £6500.

Going back in the car, the boys asked their uncle why the dingy little picture fetched all that money.

'Because it happens to be by a great artist. Anything from his hand is of immense value.'

'Well, it wasn't much to look at!'

'Ah, it'll look very different when the restorers have taken centuries of dirt off it. Then you'll see its beauty. Very likely some day you'll see it hanging in the National Gallery.'

Every human soul is of infinite value, because it is the work of God.

It is an image and likeness of God Himself, and however tarnished it may be it only needs cleaning for its beauty to be seen.

Because of this, Our Lord valued us so greatly that He bought us with the infinite price of His Precious Blood. [See nos. 248, 388, 446, 462, 511, 646, 654, 659–661.]

> * WHY DO WE MAKE THE SIGN OF THE CROSS?
> *We make the Sign of the Cross first to put us in mind of the Blessed Trinity; and secondly to remind us that God the Son died for us on the Cross.*

How to make the Sign of the Cross

BERNADETTE's first vision (February 11, 1858). As she was taking off shoes and stockings to cross the brook, a

*BALTIMORE 487-689
ENGLISH CATECHISM 59

CATECHISM STORIES 49

sound of rushing wind made her look towards the meadow, but the trees were not moving at all. Then in front of her she saw the brambles in the grotto tossing about. ' Behind these branches, in the opening, I saw immediately afterwards a white girl, not bigger than I, who made me a little bow with her head. At the same time she put her hands out a little from beside her body—her arms were hanging down like the (pictures of) Our Lady. A rosary was hanging on her right arm. I was frightened. I stepped back. I wanted to call the two little ones, but I dared not. I rubbed my eyes again and again : I thought I must be mistaken. Looking up, I saw the girl smiling at me very sweetly (*avec beaucoup de grâce*). She seemed to be inviting me to approach, but I still was frightened. All the same, it was not a fear like what I have felt at other times, because I would always have stayed to look at that (*aquéro*), but when one is frightened one goes away quick. Then l thought of saying my prayers : I put my hand in my pocket and took out the rosary that I always carry in it ; I knelt down and meant to make the sign of the cross ; but I could not put my hand to my forehead—it fell back. Meanwhile, the girl put herself sideways and turned towards me ; this time she was holding the big rosary in her hand. She crossed herself, as though to pray. My hand was trembling ; I tried again to make the sign of the cross, and this time I could. After this I was no more frightened. I said my rosary. The girl made the beads of hers slip (through her fingers), but she did not move her lips.

' While saying my rosary I was looking as hard as I could (*here follows a description of the dress, etc., of the Vision*). . . . The girl was alive, very young and surrounded with light. When I had finished my rosary, she bowed to me, smiling, retired into the niche and disappeared all of a sudden.' (Fr. Martindale's translation.)

At first it did not occur to Bernadette that ' the little young lady ' she had seen was the Blessed Virgin. But at once her own manner began to show the influence of what she had seen. She had a new way of bowing, and especially a new way of making the sign of the cross—

large, slow, recollected—which startled everyone who saw her. She was imitating the way she had seen Our Lady doing it.

We might well do the same, too. Remember the sign of the cross is the compendium of our religion : the Trinity, the Incarnation, and our own loyalty to the Crucified Son of God as our Leader. [See also nos. 566, 591.]

Strength from the Crucifix

WHEN we sign ourselves with the Cross, it is a sign that we are willing to take our share of Christ's Passion.

The Capuchin St. Joseph of Leonissa (d. 1612) had an intense devotion to the Crucifix, and always held it in his hand when preaching, e.g. to the Christian galley-slaves in Turkey, teaching them to accept their sufferings in union with Christ's Passion. Near the end of his life he had to undergo a most painful operation to remove a growth, and the doctors wished him to be tied down with cords (no anæsthetics in those days). But he had the Crucifix placed where he could see it, and said : ' This is the strongest cord, this will keep me still,' and with his eyes on the cross bore the pain without uttering a sound.

Welcoming the Cross

Of Blessed Osanna of Mantua (Dominican tertiary, fifteenth century) it is related that when she was a child her guardian angel came in vision and led her into heaven to see the glory of the saints. Afterwards, full of joy, she was praying : ' Dearest Jesus, I want to give myself to you. Do whatever you please with me,' when He appeared to her in the form of a beautiful little Boy, but crowned with sharp thorns and carrying a cross that He could hardly hold up. He smiled and held out His hand towards her and said : ' Osanna dearest, I am Jesus the Son of Mary. If it is Me you wish to please, you will have much to suffer in this life ; but you must not be afraid, dearest, I shall never leave you alone.' So saying, He disappeared, leaving her full of joy.

CATECHISM STORIES

Always afterwards the Passion was her favourite meditation, and we are told that she received the stigmata.

The joy of suffering with Christ

Once when Christ wanted to teach His apostles a lesson of humility, He called a little boy into the circle and said to them : ' Unless you become as this little child you shall not enter the Kingdom of Heaven.'

This boy (if tradition is correct) grew up to be St. Ignatius, a Syrian who was baptised by St. John the Apostle and made Bishop of Antioch by St. Peter when he left that city for Rome.

When Ignatius was an old man, the Emperor Trajan visited Antioch. The bishop was denounced to him as a Christian.

' Who are you, poor devil, to disobey my commands ? ' said Trajan.

' Call him not " poor devil " who bears a God within him,' answered Ignatius, and explained to the Emperor's questions that he had Christ crucified living in his breast, meaning that he had eaten the Bread of Life.

Trajan sent him in chains, guarded by ten soldiers, to Rome to the lions ; to his great joy because he longed to suffer with Christ crucified.

' My Love is crucified,' he said to his Christian friends. And again : ' I am the wheat of God, to be ground by the teeth of wild beasts that I may be pure bread.'

Everywhere along the journey the Christians crowded to greet him. We have several letters that he wrote on the way. His great fear was that the Christians at Rome, by their prayers and their pleadings with the authorities, might prevent his martyrdom. So he sent ahead a letter to them : ' Be only silent for me, and I shall soon enjoy God. . . . Let flames reduce my body to ashes ; let me die a lingering death on a cross ; let lions and tigers grind my bones and tear me limb from limb ; I shall suffer everything with joy, trusting in the grace of my Redeemer Christ. . . . If you really love me, let me tread the footsteps of my suffering Jesus ; let not your prayers delay my entrance into life by delaying my death.'

In the amphitheatre the lions left nothing of the martyr but a few bones, which were reverently gathered and are now in the Church of San Clemente in Rome.

> * WHAT DO YOU MEAN BY THE WORDS, ' HE DESCENDED INTO HELL ? '
>
> *By the words ' He descended into hell' I mean that as soon as Christ was dead His blessed Soul went down into a place of rest, where the souls of the just who died before Christ were detained.*

' He descended into hell '

THE ' descent into hell ' is as important as the other articles of the Creed (because it joins Old Testament with New, and shows Our Lord as the Centre of all history), but it is outside all our experience and imagination. Tell the children we have to make a picture of it as best we can.

The moment when Our Lord expired on the Cross was the moment when the atonement was made, the world was saved, the Old Law was ended, the New begun, Our Lord's work of redemption complete. That is why He said : ' It is finished,' and why the Veil of the Temple (before the Holy of holies) was miraculously rent in two.

While Our Lord's body still hung lifeless on the Cross, His Soul had gone straight to the world of departed spirits (' Hell,' Limbo, etc.).

Picture a vast ' place ' in the spirit world, and the souls of the just who waited there (we must picture the spirits in bodily form)—Adam and Eve whose sin had closed the gates of heaven, Abraham and the patriarchs who had believed so long ago, the prophets and kings who had longed for the Messias ; David, Isaias, and myriads of others who had done God's will as they knew it, down to holy Simeon and Anna, the Holy Innocents, John the Baptist, St. Joseph himself : all waiting patiently, and knowing the time near. Suddenly, the Soul of Jesus, bright with glory, appears in the sight of all, and they welcome Him with joy and adoration. He passes through them, with

*BALTIMORE 95-97
ENGLISH CATECHISM 63-64

CATECHISM STORIES 53

greetings for this one and that one, making His way to our first parents, and the second Adam meets the first Adam, with God's message of full forgiveness.

Then to all the vast throng of spirits Jesus announces the Good News of Redemption. He fills their souls with the light of glory, spreading from the glory of His own Soul as many lamps lighted from one; and then (either now or at the Ascension) He heads them in grand procession into heaven.

> * WHAT DO YOU MEAN BY THE WORDS, 'THE THIRD DAY HE ROSE AGAIN FROM THE DEAD'?
> *By the words 'the third day He rose again from the dead' I mean that after Christ had been dead and buried part of three days, He raised His blessed Body to life again on the third day.*

'Resurrexit sicut dixit'

FOR Catechism purposes, the Resurrection is perhaps best told from the point of view of the Apostles.

Our Lord had told them beforehand of His resurrection, over and over again, along with His Passion and death; but they could not take in the possibility of His being put to death, much less of His rising from the dead.

When the blow fell in Gethsemane, they all fled and scattered; Peter and John ventured back, only for the worse desertion of Peter's denial.

On Easter morning Peter and John are told of the empty tomb, and run there, but Our Lord does not show Himself to them (perhaps because He has His own reasons to see Peter alone first).

During the day eight of the Apostles gradually reassemble at the Upper Room, the only headquarters they know in Jerusalem, with its owner friendly to them. They discuss the stories of the women about the angels' message, and Mary Magdalen's account, but do not take them seriously. Besides, they are full of shame for their cowardice during the Passion, and hardly expect their Lord to own them any more, even if He *is* risen.

Then Peter and John come; Peter has seen the Lord

but will not talk about it (then, or ever afterwards) and they still doubt and fear. It is evening by now, and all (except Thomas, still absent) sit down to a meal, perhaps their first that day. The two disciples from Emmaus rush in, and eager explanations are beginning, when suddenly Jesus is standing quietly in their midst. A ghost, surely!

'Peace be to you! It is I, fear not!' He shows them His hands, His side; they begin to believe and dare to rejoice 'Have you anything to eat?' He joins them at the table and takes some fish and some honey. All their doubts vanish—it is He, and His own body, alive again. 'The disciples were glad when they saw the Lord.'

Before He leaves them on that wonderful night, He lets them know they are forgiven—by giving *them* the power to forgive the sins of others. [See also no. 365.]

Witnesses of His Resurrection

After the Ascension the apostles, and other disciples, and Our Lady and the women, went to the Upper Room and waited persevering with one mind in prayer. St. Peter reminded them that the apostles were only eleven, and proposed that one of the other original disciples should be '*made a witness with us of His Resurrection*,' and Matthias was chosen by lot.

On the day of Pentecost, when St. Peter preached the first sermon, it was to announce the Resurrection: he reminded the people that they had crucified Jesus of Nazareth, and then told them the news that He was risen: 'This Jesus hath God raised again, whereof all we are witnesses.'

Again when he preached in the Temple after curing the lame man; 'The author of life you killed, whom God hath raised from the dead, of which we are witnesses.' See also Acts iv, 33.

That was the apostles' chief duty, to declare the Fact that Our Lord was risen from the dead; it is still the chief duty of the Church, because on that Fact all our faith is built.

'He raised His blessed Body to life again'

When Our Lord had cleared the money-changers, etc., from the Temple, the Jews came and asked: 'What sign

CATECHISM STORIES

of authority from God dost thou show us, seeing thou dost these things ? ' His answer was to tell them beforehand of His own Resurrection : ' Destroy this temple, and in three days I will raise it up.'

Every human body is God's temple, when the soul is in God's grace ; much more Our Lord's Body, which belongs to God the Son.

Stupid and malicious listeners mixed up this saying with His prophecies about the destruction of Jerusalem and the call of the Gentiles.

At His trial before the Council two witnesses alleged that He said : I am able to destroy the temple of God and after three days to rebuild it.

At the crucifixion the Jews taunted Him with it : ' Vah, thou that destroyest,' etc. (Matt. xxvii, 40).

Three days later the Sign was actually given, and when the apostles had time to think it all over they remembered His words in the Temple.

' In three days *I will raise it up* ' : this shows He raises *Himself* to life, as the Catechism says.

A Sign from God

During the French revolution, when nothing was esteemed unless it were new, a philosopher named Reveillere drew up plans for a new religion which he considered would be a real benefit to humanity. He went to Barras, then a member of the Government, and asked his advice as to the methods by which the new religion could best be spread. ' Well,' said Barras, ' my advice is to get yourself killed on Friday, and rise from the dead the following Sunday.'*

The philosopher's answer is not recorded.

' My Lord and my God ! '

St. Marina (third century) was daughter of a pagan priest, who disowned her when she became a Christian. The Governor of Antioch made advances to her, and when she rejected him he had her denounced to his own tribunal. There she told him she would be faithful to

* Barras was quoting or adapting a remark of Voltaire on a similar occasion.

Jesus Christ. The enraged Governor exclaimed: 'How stupid to worship a man as if he were a god—above all a man who came to such a disgraceful end as crucifixion!'

'Why do you always bring up His crucifixion and never speak of His resurrection?' answered Marina. 'His death shows that He was a man, yes; but His resurrection shows Him to be indeed a God.'

The Governor condemned her to the stake, and when the flames left her unharmed, she was beheaded.

The Sign of Jonas the prophet

The tiny book about the prophet Jonas was one of Our Lord's favourite Scriptures, because it teaches (by what looks like a parable-story) that God grieves over sinners, and wills the salvation of all men, of Gentiles as much as of the Jews.

Jonas (in the story) is told by God to go and preach in Ninive, the great pagan capital of Assyria. Jonas is unwilling, because he cannot bring himself to preach to Gentiles especially the Assyrians who were a danger and terror to the Jews. So he takes ship for Spain (i, 1-3).

A great storm endangers the ship; Jonas tells the sailors it is on his account, since he is fleeing from God; and the storm will cease if they throw him overboard. They do so; and the Lord, determined to bring Jonas to Ninive, has prepared a great fish to swallow him up, and Jonas is in the belly of the fish three days and three nights (i, 12-15; ii, 1-2).

The book then gives a poem (ii, 3-10) which the prophet uses for a prayer in the fish. It is a cry to God in affliction, remembering the holy Temple. (Read it through with Our Lord's Passion and Resurrection in mind, especially ii, 7.)

The fish vomits Jonas on to land; once more the Lord tells him to go to Ninive, and this time he obeys (ii, 11; iii, 1-4).

He enters the city preaching: 'Yet forty days, and Ninive shall be destroyed.' The Ninivitans believe and repent. Even the king rises up from his throne, puts on sackcloth and proclaims a great fast to implore the Lord's mercy (iii, 4-10).

The prophet, knowing how merciful God is, fears they

CATECHISM STORIES 57

will be forgiven, and is angry. He still thinks they ought to be destroyed, especially as he has prophesied it; and he bivouacs outside the city to see what will happen. A palm or ivy grows up to give him shade, but next morning it withers away, and he suffers from the heat (iv, 1-8).

God draws the moral for him : You did nothing to make that tree grow, yet you loved it and are grieved for its destruction. And shall I not spare Ninive, that great city, in which are so many souls whom I created, of little children alone a hundred and twenty thousand, and many beasts ? (iv, 9-11).

The story ends at that point suddenly. We are left to understand that Ninive is spared, and the prophet is convinced that God is right in willing all men to be saved.

In Our Lord's own Mind, He was in several ways like Jonas in the story; or rather Jonas was like Our Lord : he willingly sacrificed his life to save others; he came forth from the fish after being buried for three days in it; and thus he brought God's salvation for all men, not only the Jews.

It was the fish that brought the prophet to save the Gentiles, and it was by descending to the grave that Our Lord saved the world. Read His words now in Matt. xii, 38-41.

> * WHAT DO YOU MEAN BY THE WORDS, 'HE ASCENDED INTO HEAVEN'?
>
> *By the words 'He ascended into heaven' I mean that Our Saviour went up Body and Soul into heaven on Ascension Day, forty days after His resurrection.*

The Ascension

MOST of the Forty Days is spent in Galilee, where the apostles feel at home; rest and instruction combined. Then the return to Jerusalem, because the Church must start there. There He made His final visit to them, once more at a meal, and told them to wait for the promised Holy Spirit (Acts i, 4-8). Then He led them out to Mount Olivet, and there we may picture Him saying His final words ('Teach all nations,' etc. Matt. xxviii, 18-20; perhaps they had already been said once to the five hundred at the mountain in Galilee). He raised His

*BALTIMORE 101-102

hands to bless them, and they saw Him lifted slowly from the earth until a mist quickly gathered round Him and, still rising, He went from their sight. Two angels speak to them and they return to Jerusalem 'with great joy,' thinking of Our Lord glorified in heaven and of His promise to be with them all days (Luke xxiv, 50–52, and Acts i, 9–12).

Christ the King

Reigning at the right hand of God, Our Lord still keeps His five wounds, still showing them to His Father to intercede for us.

St. Martin told his biographer that he was praying in his cell one day, when there was a blinding light and a figure stood near him, serene and joyous of aspect, wearing a jewelled crown and a royal robe, and golden sandals. St. Martin gazed in bewilderment and for a time the two were silent. Then the apparition spoke: 'Martin, behold me, I am the Christ, come down to earth, and I desired to reveal myself to thee before all others.' Martin remained silent, and the speaker continued: 'Well, Martin, can you not believe your own eyes? I am the Christ!' Then the holy bishop, enlightened by the Holy Ghost, knew that it was the devil and not the Lord. He answered: 'The Lord Jesus did not say He would come robed in purple with a glittering diadem. As for me, I will not believe in the coming of Christ unless He look the same as in the day of His Passion and show me the wounds of His Cross.'

At these words the apparition vanished like smoke and the cell was left full of a vile stench. [See no. 462.]

> * WHAT DO YOU MEAN BY THE WORDS, 'SITTETH AT THE RIGHT HAND OF GOD THE FATHER ALMIGHTY'?
>
> *By the words 'Sitteth at the right hand of God the Father Almighty' I mean that Christ, as God, is equal to the Father, and, as man, is in the highest place in heaven.*

'Viva Cristo Rey!'

A CERTAIN English priest happened to be in Mexico during the religious troubles of 1926. One day he saw four young

*BALTIMORE 103
ENGLISH CATECHISM 70

CATECHISM STORIES

men being taken to prison, surrounded by a strong guard of soldiers. They were Catholic rebels or suspects, who had been seized and roughly treated, for their clothes were torn and their heads and faces were bleeding. Nevertheless they seemed proud and joyful as they walked, each carrying his rosary, and calling out all together at every fourth pace : *Viva Cristo Rey :* ' Long live Christ the King.' The English priest never heard what became of them, but the episode was so inspiring that when he returned home he asked leave to give his new church the dedication of ' Christ the King.'

> * WHEN WILL CHRIST COME AGAIN ?
> *Christ will come again from heaven at the last day, to judge all mankind.*

The Day of Reckoning

OUR Lord asserted many times most solemnly that He would come in judgement at the end of the world, and related several parables to help us to realise it.

One thing He wanted us to know was that good and evil will go on side by side in the world (and in the Church, too) until that final reckoning. This is the main point in the parable of the Wheat and the Cockle (read Matt. xiii, 24-30) which Our Lord explains Himself (Matt. xiii, 36-43).

Fair warning

Another great parable is concerned more with what Our Lord will reward or condemn at the Judgement. Our fate will be decided (He says) on whether we have come to the help of our brother-men in their bodily needs, because this is a test (He says) whether we love and serve our Father, God. Read the parable in Our Lord's words (Matt. xxv, 31-46).

' To judge the living and the dead '

St. Methodius (ninth-century co-apostle of the Slavs, with his brother St. Cyril) came to the court of the pagan king of Bulgaria, who heard of this monk from Constan-

*BALTIMORE 104, 180, 182
ENGLISH CATECHISM 72

tinople who could paint pictures, and asked him to decorate the walls of a room in the palace. He was very fond of hunting and thought a hunting-scene would be suitable. Methodius set to work, and when the king came to watch he begged him to wait until it was finished. At last it was ready for inspection, and the king stood before it stupefied. It was a large-scale picture of the Last Judgement. On one side were the happy just who had served God in this life, being welcomed into heaven by smiling angels; and on the other side were the wicked, rushing about in terror, being hunted by hideous devils, loaded with chains when caught, and dragged down into a pit terrible with flames and smoke. The king was deeply impressed with the beauties and terrors of the scene, and wanted it all explained; so St. Methodius preached the gospel to him, beginning from this article of the Creed, and the king at once asked to be baptised.

The circumstances of the Last Judgement are beyond our imagination. Meanwhile it would be foolish to despise such mediæval representations, for the spiritual reality of losing our soul would certainly be more fearful than anything thus depicted. [See no. 595.]

> * WILL EVERYONE BE JUDGED AT DEATH, AS WELL AS AT THE LAST DAY?
>
> *Everyone will be judged at death, as well as at the last day.*

Everyone will be judged at death

'HALF an hour after the body of Mr. Percy Macbeth, the Salford Stipendiary Magistrate, was taken into Salford Cathedral on Sunday night, there was brought in the body of Mr. Thomas (Tommy) O'Rourke—a man who had appeared more than once before Mr. Macbeth in his judicial capacity.

'The coffins containing the remains of the judge and the man he had often judged remained side by side throughout the night until the Requiem Masses the following morning.

'Tommy O'Rourke was a street flower-seller.'

(From *The Universe*, Jan. 21, 1938)

*BALTIMORE 181
ENGLISH CATECHISM 76

CATECHISM STORIES

'The first five minutes after death'

A famous Scottish explorer, in his old age, was holding some young people enthralled by telling some of the most exciting moments in his life. How he shot a tiger springing at him, how he was saved from shipwreck after two days in a boat, how he saw the marvellous sunrise from a peak in the Himalayas, and so on.

'But I'm expecting to have another thrill soon, bigger than any of these.'

His hearers wondered, for they supposed his exploring days were over.

'Are you planning another journey, then, sir?'

'No,' he replied, 'I was thinking of the first five minutes after death.' [See also nos. 576–578.]

* WHAT ARE THE THINGS CHRIST WILL JUDGE?
Christ will judge our thoughts, words, deeds and omissions.

Our conscience will supply the evidence

AT the moment of death we go before God's judgement seat, to render account of our whole life. Instantaneously (theologians tell us) our eternal destiny will be decided.

Some help in picturing the judgement may be gained from incidents such as the following, which happened to the late Fr. John Gerard, S.J., and which he recorded years afterwards in his diary. (*The Month*, Feb., 1913, p. 126.)

He went skating with two fellow-students on Gore's Pond, near Stonyhurst, known to be very deep. 'Edwards went through the ice in the middle, and I, trying to help him, lay down flat and gave him my hand. He pulled me into the hole and I even went under the ice beyond. I well remember the dark grey roof above me with a bright patch a little way off, to which I somehow managed to struggle. I was not then a swimmer. At the moment of leaving the ice for the water there flashed across me, along with the realisation that death was, apparently, immediately inevitable, a perfect picture of my past life in every minutest detail. It was not a chronicle of successive events but a picture, or rather a map, which thought instead of

*BALTIMORE 181
ENGLISH CATECHISM 73

sight perceived—everything was seen simultaneously and everything with equal clearness. . . . Everything seemed to be included, however trivial—the walks I had taken and the stones I had thrown—but it was only my own part I saw, nobody else appeared. . . . I was in full possession of all my faculties and used them immediately afterwards to get out, so that the experience proves nothing as to drowning. . . . Any seemingly inevitable danger suddenly apprehended would doubtless operate in the same way.'

De Quincey (*Confessions of an English Opium-eater*) mentions some cases precisely similar to this, and remarks that probably 'the dread book of account, which the Scriptures speak of, is in fact the mind of each individual.'

'Be not to me a Judge but a Saviour'

Two men in a train-compartment up to London; one grey-haired and thoughtful, the other young, restless, worried, seemingly afraid of ticket-collectors, etc. At last the elderly man spoke: 'I feel you are in trouble. Can I help in any way.'

'No, sir—no one can help me . . . but you are a stranger, I shall never see you again, and I feel I can trust you. . . . It will be a relief to tell you my story!'

It was a sad story, told frankly. Small embezzlements at business, to help his widowed mother; then he had got into the power of two older men, fellow-employees, who turned out to be hardened villains. The three attempted a serious robbery, a night-watchman surprised them and gave the alarm, and was shot by one of the older men, who were both captured by the police. They blamed the murder on to the youth, who had managed to get away; and now there was a warrant out for his arrest. He was going to London to hide.

The old gentleman looked grave, but spoke kindly. 'I strongly advise you to give yourself up, and tell your whole story in court, just as you have told it to me.'

'Ah, but you are so understanding—it was easy to tell you. I would be afraid in court.' But at last he promised.

CATECHISM STORIES 63

The court was crowded for the trial, and the youth, pale and trembling, was led into the dock and stood with downcast eyes. The charge was read out and he was asked to make his statement. Hardly able to speak from fear, he raised his eyes to the judge—and started with amazement and relief. The judge was none other than his friend of the train !

It was easy to tell his story now, to one who knew it already. He was acquitted of murder and placed on probation for the attempted robbery, and needless to say kept out of trouble ever afterwards.

Our Judge will be Christ. We shall feel a like confidence when we stand before Him, if we have let Him be our friend in this life. [See also nos. 464, 465, 504.]

> * Is THE HOLY GHOST EQUAL TO THE FATHER AND TO THE SON ?
>
> *The Holy Ghost is equal to the Father and to the Son, for He is the same Lord and God as they are.*

The Holy Ghost equal to Father and to Son

ST. EDMUND, as a young man, at Oxford, was a highly successful lecturer in Logic and Mathematics, and had a great fondness especially for Geometry. Once even in his sleep he was trying to find the solution of some problem, drawing the diagrams on the ground.

But his mother Mabel, dead not long before, came to him in his dream and asked what these diagrams were. He explained them to her. But she took his right hand and drew on it three circles equal and interlocking, and wrote a name on each—Father, Son, Holy Ghost.

' Dearest son,' she said, ' these are the figures you should study in future. Leave those others alone, for they have not helped you towards gaining the heavenly treasures for which you were born. You know I have always told you the truth—believe me, these are the really interesting things and the most useful ones, too.'

From that time he gave himself to the study of theology and holy Scripture. [See no. 676.]

*BALTIMORE 105-107
ENGLISH CATECHISM 80

* WHY DID THE HOLY GHOST COME DOWN ON THE APOSTLES?

    The Holy Ghost came down on the Apostles to confirm their faith, to sanctify them and to enable them to found the Church.

'To enable them to found the Church'

OUR Lord had received the Holy Spirit Himself at His baptism in the Jordan; in some way we cannot understand, this gave Him light, and strength to enable Him to begin His public life. (Read Luke iii, 21–22; iv, 1; iv, 14–21.)

The same was to be true of His Church, and at the Last Supper, when the Church began to exist in the Upper Room, Our Lord promised to send the Holy Spirit. He called Him the 'Paraclete' (i.e. the One who would be at their side to back them up. Read John xiv, 16–17; xiv, 26; xv, 26–27; xvi, 7; xvi, 13).

On Easter evening He gave them, with His own life and breath, the first touch (as it were) of the Holy Spirit—the power of forgiving sins. During the forty days He was promising the Spirit to them. (Read Luke xxiv, 49; Acts i, 4–8.)

Obeying His instructions, they collected in the Upper Room (120 souls altogether) and waited ten days in prayer till on the Jewish festival of Pentecost Christ's promise was fulfilled (Acts ii, 1–4). Immediate result was they began to praise God in tongues, sign of universality of the Church; this phenomenon soon attracted crowds, and the apostles found themselves with sudden light and courage to begin their witness to Christ. The Church is begun; that night, still within the Jewish religion, there are 3000 baptised Catholics.

** WHAT IS THE CATHOLIC CHURCH?

    The Catholic Church is the union of all the faithful under one Head, and the Head of the Catholic Church is Jesus Christ Our Lord.

Union of all the faithful

THE Church began its work at Pentecost. But when did the Church begin to exist as a Society? You might say,

*BALTIMORE 108-140-143
ENGLISH CATECHISM 82

**BALTIMORE 136, 139
ENGLISH CATECHISM 84-85

CATECHISM STORIES 65

when the twelve were appointed to be apostles; or when Our Lord said: 'Thou art Peter,' etc.

But the real beginning was the Last Supper. Our Lord made the most careful preparations for it, and arranged with some friend (now unknown to us) for the use of his large Upper Room, to be not only the place of the Last Supper, but the future headquarters of the infant Church. (Read Luke xxii, 7-15.)

Then, at the Supper He gave them Holy Communion and so made them all into one with Him and with each other, one Bread and one Body. Afterwards He told them how they must always remain united, in faith and in love; all living with the same life, like branches of the same tree. I am the tree, and you are the branches, He said. (Read John xv, 1-7, and make sure the children know what a vine is and what it looks like.)

The apostles listened wondering, they understood only partly perhaps at the time, but after Pentecost Our Lord's words came back to them and they began to see all He had meant when He said: 'I will build my Church.'

Everything He said is just as true to-day. Each one of the faithful is a tiny branch of the great Tree of Life; and so long as you make your Easter Communion and keep in a state of grace you are a live branch, bearing fruit, and Our Lord is living His life in you.

'If I forget thee, O Jerusalem!'

An old missionary in Korea tells (in the A.P.F. *Annals*) this story of his younger days about thirty years ago.

He was making his twice-yearly visit to a village called Kong-so, hearing confessions daily. Hearing a commotion outside the little chapel, he found some people from another village who had brought a very old woman. 'She says she is a Christian, and hasn't seen a priest for years.' When she saw the priest she knelt down sobbing and clutching his cassock. With many a question he extracted her story.

Kim Agatha was her name. In her young days she and her husband, both converts, had lived in the next mission. There came the great persecution of 1866. Their pagan relatives made them go away to the south for greater safety, but soon they were denounced as Christians. On refusing to apostatise, the husband was executed, and the wife received eighty lashes, still unyielding. She went back to her own district, but both her husband's family and her own were afraid to help her. A young pagan, out of pity took her into his house, made her his lawful wife, and took her for safety to live in one of the southern islands. She heard that all the bishops and priests had been put to death. ' For forty-three years I said my prayers, and my Rosary every day until I broke it and had to count on my fingers. I counted the days with pebbles so that I could say extra prayers on Sundays, and try not to do unnecessary work. I did not eat meat at all and I fasted when I thought it was Lent.' Her pebble-reckoning had got badly out and she was keeping Sundays on Wednesdays.

In her old age she returned with her son to her former village, but never dared to ask about priests or religion. She seldom went out, but one day after a special journey to buy something, she rested in a stranger's house, and saw a crucifix. ' Are you Christians ? ' she asked in a cautious whisper, and was amazed to hear that persecution was long over, and priests were working again. ' One comes every autumn,' they said, ' in fact, we are all going to see him at Kong-so to-morrow. You can come with us.' So she came.

Everyone prayed with great fervour when they heard about the old woman who had suffered for the Faith so long ago, and they all wanted to have in their homes the wife of a martyr. ' I promise you there were tears in my eyes,' says the missionary. ' I no longer get discouraged. How do I know that the faith of my new Christians would not stand the test equally well ? I believe it would.'

That Korean woman understood well that the Church is ' the union of all the faithful.'

The story also helps us to understand how even non-Catholics, if they are in good faith, can be in union with the ' invisible Church,' or rather, in union with the visible Church in an invisible way : ' baptism by desire,' etc.

Christ the Head of the Church

In the beautiful seaport city of Corinth, a little crowd of people—perhaps three hundred or so—were gathered in a large room late at night. It was about twenty-four years after Our Lord's Ascension. They were all kinds of people —a few richly dressed, many poor, and some slaves. Mass was just over, and they had all received Communion; on the table in the middle there still remained some of the Bread of Life. Meanwhile an old man is reading something, and all listen with close attention. It is a letter from St. Paul, by whom most of them had been made Christians three years ago. In one part of the letter he tells them there is some work each of them can do for God.

' The body is one and hath many members; and although there are many members, yet they are all one body. So also is Christ; for in one Spirit were we all baptised into one body. . . . You are the Body of Christ, and members of member.'

They looked round at each other, and at the Body of Christ, under the appearance of bread, on the table. They suddenly understood they all belonged to each other, all one Body, and Our Lord the Head of it. ' One Bread, one Body ' : they remembered St. Paul saying that.

The same thing was being felt in Ephesus, and Antioch and Rome, and everywhere where a Catholic congregation was started, and the same thing happens now. Our Lord's love for us is contagious; we begin to love each other. ' I came to cast fire upon the earth, and what do I desire but that it be enkindled.' [See also nos. 393, 396, 398.]

> * WHO GAVE THE CATHOLIC CHURCH DIVINE AUTHORITY TO TEACH ?
>
> *Jesus Christ gave the Catholic Church divine authority to teach when He said : ' Go ye and teach all nations.'*

' Teach all nations '

AT the Resurrection the angels gave Our Lord's message to His disciples (there were many in Jerusalem besides the eleven) that He would see them in Galilee. In Galilee

*BALTIMORE 137, 144-145, 162, 165
ENGLISH CATECHISM 12

word was passed round from Him for a rendezvous in a certain mountain (Matt. xxviii, 16), and more than five hundred came together (1 Cor. xv, 6). It was then (following St. Matthew) that Our Lord gave His great commission and promise to the Church (read it, Matt. xxviii, 18-20). No doubt He repeated it just before the Ascension.

With these words in mind, Catholics can never have any doubts as to where the authority of the Church comes from. [See also nos. 233, 666.]

> * HOW DO YOU KNOW THAT THE CHURCH CANNOT ERR IN WHAT SHE TEACHES?
>
> *I know that the Church cannot err in what she teaches because Christ promised that the gates of hell shall never prevail against His Church; that the Holy Ghost shall teach her all things; and that He Himself will be with her all days, even to the consummation of the world.*

Christ's Promises to the Church

IN this Catechism answer we have three pictures.

First, Our Lord sitting amongst the twelve by the roadside; Peter has just said: 'Thou art Christ, etc.' Then Our Lord's words in Matt. xvi, 17-19.

Second, sitting round the table after the Last Supper; Our Lord is speaking of the Holy Spirit: read John xiv, 25-26, and xvi, 12-13.

Third, the moment before His Ascension: read Matt. xxviii, 18-20.

Add also other words of Christ: 'As the Father hath sent me I also send you' (John, xx, 21). And to the seventy-two: 'He that heareth you, heareth me,' etc. (Luke x, 16).

All these sayings came back to the apostles' minds after Pentecost, and made them sure that Our Lord would keep the Church from teaching wrong.

After St. Paul had made many Gentile converts, the question arose: must Christians keep the Law of Moses? The apostles held a Council at Jerusalem, and it was decided in the negative. The Council sent a letter to the

*BALTIMORE 162-165
ENGLISH CATECHISM 101

CATECHISM STORIES 69

Christians at Antioch giving their decision, and the letter said : ' *It hath seemed good to the Holy Ghost and to us* . . .' which shows they knew the Holy Ghost was guiding them.

The Church cannot err in matters of Faith

But sometimes other things are mixed up with the Faith and it may be hard to distinguish. From the beginning of the world until four hundred years ago, all men thought the earth was the motionless centre of the Universe, with the sun and stars moving round it. About 1520 Copernicus (Catholic, German, cleric, mathematician) put forward the idea that the earth and the other planets moved round the sun. It was a staggering notion, because it seemed to push mankind into a corner of the cosmic stage, and also to contradict the language used by the Bible, and the age-long notion of a heaven above the solid sky. Copernicus spread it discreetly, breaking the news gently so to speak ; the Protestant Reformers bitterly opposed it, some Catholic prelates encouraged it and most people thought it a mere crazy speculation.

A century later, a famous Italian scientist named Galileo made the first telescope. What he saw through it convinced him that the Copernican theory was true, and he began to preach it so ardently that many Catholics took alarm. After all, they said, Galileo had not proved his case yet, and it did seem contrary to Christian belief and to the words of Scripture. So in 1616 the opinion was condemned as ' heretical ' by the Roman Inquisition and all books advocating it were forbidden. Calling the Copernican theory ' heretical ' was equivalent to saying it is an article of faith that the sun moves round the earth.

This was the biggest blunder the Church's authorities have ever made (though it was not a ' definition of faith ' and the infallibility of the Church was not really involved) and a kind of warfare grew up between scientists and theologians. In some ways the blunder lasted for a long time, since it was another hundred years or more before the Copernican books were removed from the forbidden list. Cardinal Newman thought the blunder was allowed by God in order to teach the theologians and authorities of the Church how careful they must be in saying what is or is not of faith.

As for Galileo, he retracted his opinion, but still went on preaching it and ridiculing his opponents, so he was in trouble again in 1633 and was imprisoned (only nominally, though, in the house of his friends) until his death in 1642. It was Galileo's fame as a scientist that has made his case so notorious. [See also no. 532.]

> * Has the Church a visible Head on earth?
> *The Church has a visible Head on earth—the Bishop of Rome, who is the Vicar of Christ.*

Any Society needs a head

Some boy school-friends decided to start a new club. Several of them came to the father of one, and asked for the use of an empty shed in the garden. He asked what the club was for.

' Oh, just to have as much fun as we can. It'll be called the P.Y.L.—Please Yourself League.'

' Any committee, or rules ? '

' No, we can't be bothered with those things.'

' Which of you is the secretary, then ? '

' Nobody wants to be secretary. Besides, we don't need one, nor a president. That's the whole point of the club. We don't want any fuss about organisation, just the club, that's all.'

' Well, you can have the shed, but it doesn't strike me as a very practical proposition.'

So the society was started, and a board ' P.Y.L., H.Q.' was placed over the door.

Next week the lender of the shed asked his son how the club was getting on.

' Oh, it's pretty awful. Everybody wants to have his own friends in, and keep other people's friends out. Nothing but arguments.'

' You want a committee, I should think.'

Next week : ' Well, have you got the committee yet ? '

' Yes, I'm one—we volunteered for it. But they won't listen, they all talk at once. Besides it isn't fair, some of

*BALTIMORE 136, 147, 156
ENGLISH CATECHISM 86

CATECHISM STORIES 71

them had a meeting last night when the rest of us didn't know about it.'

'Didn't the chairman call the meeting, then?'

'There isn't a chairman.'

'Well, why don't you elect a good chairman? Every society needs a head of some sort.'

'Yes, it does look like it.'

So the P.Y.L. provided itself with a chairman and a secretary, and things began to go properly. When little matters cropped up to be settled the chairman decided them, and if it was something big he called a meeting of the committee. One of the first things they did was to change the name of the club to the P.T.L., the 'Pull Together League.'

If a club for a few boys cannot get on without a 'visible head,' how much more Our Lord's Church, which He wants every person to join?

Head of the Church on earth

Blessed Cuthbert Mayne was a young Oxford convert in Elizabeth's reign, who went to the new college at Douai and was the first 'seminary priest' to be martyred (at Launceston, 1577), after six months in prison. The day before his execution, after a whole day's 'disputation' with two Protestant ministers, some magistrates came with an offer from London that his life would be spared if he affirmed on oath that 'the Queen is supreme head of the Church in England.' He seemed to hesitate, then asked for a Bible, much to the satisfaction of the magistrates, since his apostasy would have been a greater triumph than his death. He kissed the Bible devoutly, held it up in his chained hands, and said: 'I swear that the Queen never was, nor is, nor ever will be, head of the Church of England.'

> * WHY IS THE BISHOP OF ROME THE HEAD OF THE CHURCH?
>
> *The Bishop of Rome is the Head of the Church because he is the successor of St. Peter, whom Christ appointed to be the Head of the Church.*

The First Pope

THE story of St. Peter. Brought to Christ by his brother

Andrew (John i, 40). He leaves his boat to follow Christ (Luke v, 1–11) 'Thou art Christ' and 'Thou art Peter' (Matt. xvi, 15–19). He objects to Our Lord foretelling the Passion (Mark viii, 31–34). Christ prays specially for him, that he may confirm his brethren (Luke xxii, 32). At Last Supper, denial foretold (Matt. xxvi, 33–35). Draws sword in Gethsemane (Matt. xxvi, 51). Denies Our Lord in courtyard of Caiphas (Matt. xxvi, 69–75). Our Lord appears to him on Easter Day (Luke xxiv, 34). 'Feed my lambs' (John xxi, 15–19).

After the Ascension, Peter takes the lead in choosing Matthias (Acts i, 15), on day of Pentecost (Acts ii, 14), and before the Sanhedrin (Acts iv, 19). Receives first Gentiles (Acts x). Declares the Church's teaching at Council of Jerusalem (Acts xv, 7). Later he moved to Antioch (as we see from the incident in Gal. ii, 11–21) and finally to Rome, where he ruled the Church peacefully until the persecution of Nero. During this (according to a story related by St. Ambrose) St. Peter was persuaded to flee from Rome, but met Christ; 'Lord, whither goest thou?' 'I come to be crucified again.' St. Peter returned to the city. Soon afterwards he was arrested and crucified (head downwards at his own request, because he felt unworthy of the same death as his Lord).

St. Linus then became Bishop of Rome. Altogether the Popes down to Pius XII number 262.

Successor of St. Peter

One of the strangest episodes in the Church's history is how St. Catherine of Siena brought the Pope back to Rome.

Under the protection of the French king, the Popes for a whole lifetime had held their court at Avignon. This caused disunion in Christendom. Italy especially was torn with dissensions and wars, Rome was decaying, cattle were actually herded sometimes in St. Peter's and St. John Lateran.

St. Catherine wrote often to Gregory XI (sixth Pope at Avignon, and a Frenchman) with great freedom, calling him *Babbo mio*, 'my dear Daddy,' urging him to come back to Rome and take charge. 'Return, return: resist no

CATECHISM STORIES 73

longer the Will of God which calls you. Your starving sheep are waiting for you to come and sit on the throne of your predecessor and chief St. Peter. . . . Courage and fear not, for God is with you.'

In 1376 the Pope was having a dispute with the republic of Florence, and laid the city under interdict.

To St. Catherine (then twenty-nine, and already a public figure in the life of the Church) Christ appeared, putting His cross on her shoulder, and an olive branch into her hand. Scandals must come, He told her, but the Church would rise glorious from humiliation. She was to go out into the world and say to the nations : Behold I bring good tidings of great joy.

At once she offered herself to Florence as mediator with the Pope. She set out for Avignon and arrived in June. Her objects were peace with Florence, the Pope's return to Rome, and a crusade against the infidels to unite Christendom.

Gregory XI was deeply impressed by the firm way in which she told him of God's Will. He gave her a free hand to settle the dispute with Florence. But as for returning to Rome, most of the Cardinals were strongly against it, as well as the King of France. The Pope knew his duty but was timid and hesitating. Once he sent for Catherine : ' I am not asking you for advice, but to declare to me the Will of God,' he said.

' Who knows the Will of God better than Your Holiness, who has bound himself by a vow to return to Rome ? '

He had told nobody of his vow, and her knowledge of it astounded him.

Suddenly he announced his departure from Avignon, and left on September 13. At Genoa he heard a report that Rome was in rebellion. He was just about to yield to the Cardinals and turn back to Avignon, when he remembered that Catherine, too, was in Genoa.

She was staying at a friend's house, besieged by visitors. After receiving the Cardinals' advice at a Consistory, he went disguised to see Catherine. She recognised him and knelt, but he bade her rise, for he was the suppliant this time.

He laid the situation before her, regained his courage

as he listened to her burning words, and went away resolved. He sailed on October 29, and in the following January he entered Rome.

The successor of St. Peter was back in the Apostolic See, and though sad times were still in front of the Church, at least the 'Babylonian captivity' of Avignon was over. But Gregory XI never saw St. Catherine again, for he died in a few months.

> * WHAT IS THE BISHOP OF ROME CALLED?
> *The Bishop of Rome is called the Pope, which word signifies Father. The Pope is the spiritual Father of all Christians.*

Father of all Christians

ANY Catholic boy can become Pope. This is the story of how a lonely English boy became the 'Father of all Christians.'

Nicholas Breakspeare was born at Langley, Herts., about 1100. While still a youngster he felt drawn to becoming a monk, and applied for admission to the famous abbey of St. Albans. For some reason or other the abbot refused to accept him, and young Nicholas turned away, disappointed.

Packing his few belongings into a bundle he stepped off along the road to the coast. Here he managed somehow to get a passage; and before long he was swinging along the roads of France. His hike finished up at Arles—for the monks of St. Rufus admitted him to their number.

Though handicapped by being a stranger and a simple country lad, he had actually been chosen abbot of these French monks before he was thirty-seven. Once in power he asserted his authority by a thorough revision of the abbey's discipline. A section of the monks resented this, and applied to Rome for his removal. But Nicholas Breakspeare, knowing he was in the right, decided to go straight to the Holy Father. He promptly took to the road, and in due course arrived in Rome; there, his sound arguments and energetic personality won over the Pope to his side.

After various other jobs he was sent on an important mission to Norway and Sweden, where the Church was not

CATECHISM STORIES 75

yet fully organised, and where troubles with heathen tribes and quarrels between princes needed a firm control. Nicholas succeeded not only in his political and ecclesiastical undertakings, but also in winning the friendship of these fierce Northerners—whom, as an Englishman, he must have understood better than a French or Italian legate would have done. Such a good father did he show himself, whether to monks of the south or fierce warriors of the north, that in 1154 he was chosen to be the 'Spiritual Father of all Christians,' and ruled the Church for some six years as Adrian IV.

> * WHAT DO YOU MEAN WHEN YOU SAY THAT THE POPE IS INFALLIBLE?
> *When I say that the Pope is infallible, I mean that the Pope cannot err when, as Shepherd and Teacher of all Christians, he defines a doctrine concerning faith or morals, to be held by the whole Church.*

Shepherd and Teacher of all Christians

CATHOLICS had always regarded the Pope as infallible in practice, but it was defined as an article of faith in the reign of Pius IX, providentially increasing the Pope's spiritual authority at the very moment when his temporal power was destroyed.

'Pio Nono' was a late vocation, being twenty-two when he began studying for the priesthood. When he became Pope in 1846 there were still several kingdoms in the Italian peninsula, the 'Papal States' being one. The new Pope was in difficulties from the beginning, with the movement for a united Italy, represented by the King of Piedmont, and the revolutionary Garibaldi with his red-shirts. When the Papal States were invaded Catholic volunteers from all countries came to fight in the 'Pontifical Zouaves,' but they were hopelessly outnumbered by their enemies. The Papal States were annexed to Piedmont in 1860, all, except a small territory around Rome. A few years later the red-shirts were threatening Rome itself, but the French Government sent a few regiments of soldiers to protect what was left of the Pope's Dominion.

*BALTIMORE 164
ENGLISH CATECHISM 93

Meanwhile, on account of the spread of irreligion in the modern world, the Church had decided to hold a General Council; seven hundred bishops met at the Vatican in December, 1869. Amongst other things, many Catholics wanted to have Papal Infallibility defined beyond any possibility of dispute; they felt that modern times being so critical for religion and General Councils so difficult to assemble, the Church needs a permanent dictatorship to deal with the permanent state of emergency. There were some (like Dr. Newman in England) who thought there was no real need of this, and said the definition would be 'inopportune.' Also there was a loud-voiced party who spoke as though every statement by a Pope, on any subject and in any circumstances, was inspired by God.

There were long discussions, and at last under God's guidance the Council declared that the Pope possesses the infallibility of the Church within certain limits; that is, when he speaks *ex cathedra* (i.e. as Shepherd and Teacher of all Christians), defining a point of faith or morals to be held by the whole Church.

The definition was promulgated on July 18, 1870, and the next day war broke out between France and Germany. Hundreds of bishops returned to their own countries. The French soldiers in Rome were recalled to France, and the Piedmontese Government at once seized the opportunity to march into what was left of the Papal States. When their troops reached Rome, their guns opened fire on the Porta Pia, and once it was clear that he was yielding to force, the Pope ordered his own little army to cease fire. Rome thus became the capital of the new Italy on September 20.

From 1870 to 1928 Pio Nono and his four successors, rather than recognise this robbery, remained of their own will in the Vatican, and all that time the Pope's spiritual authority, as Shepherd and Teacher, was more and more recognised and obeyed.

In 1928 Pius XI agreed to let bygones be bygones, and accepted a tiny independent territory in Rome called the 'Vatican City.' Catholics everywhere were glad, because it made the Pope independent of any earthly power, without his becoming a real earthly power himself.

CATECHISM STORIES

* HAS THE CHURCH OF CHRIST ANY MARKS BY WHICH WE MAY KNOW HER?

The Church of Christ has four marks by which we may know her: she is One—she is Holy—she is Catholic—she is Apostolic.

** WHAT DOES THE WORD CATHOLIC MEAN?
The word Catholic means Universal.

' Four marks by which we may know her '

ISABEL went to see her grandmother and found her quite distressed because she had just lost an umbrella—the last birthday present her husband gave her before he died. Isabel remembered the umbrella.

' A white ivory handle, wasn't it? And a brown cover? '

' Yes, very faded, and there was a little hole burnt in it, too, from your grandfather's cigarette once. Really, it wasn't worth anything now, but I wouldn't have lost it for worlds.'

Isabel said nothing at the time, but later went to the Police Lost Property Office in town. The policeman showed her two long racks crammed with ladies' umbrellas.

' What's it like, Miss? '

' It's a brown cover, and a white handle.'

' New one? '

' No, rather faded.'

' Any name on? '

' No, but there's a cigarette-hole in the cover.'

' Well, that's four marks to look for—look here, what about this one? '

Sure enough, there it was, cigarette-hole and all.

' Sign for it, please, Miss, and there's a charge of eighteen pence.'

Isabel had to go home first to get the money from her money-box, but she was fully repaid by the old lady's joy at seeing the umbrella again.

There are hundreds of Christian sects nowadays, but only one true Church given to us by Our Lord, and we tell it by the four marks which He placed upon it Himself.

*BALTIMORE 152-160
ENGLISH CATECHISM 94
**BALTIMORE 158
ENGLISH CATECHISM 97

What Our Lord said about His Church

When Our Lord was starting the Church, so to speak, at the Last Supper, He took care to give to it the Four Marks He wished it to have. In His discourse afterwards in the Upper Room, He told the apostles He was offering eternal life to *all* flesh (read John xvii, 1–3); that the *apostles themselves* were His appointed witnesses and workers (John xv, 16; xv, 27); and He prayed that His disciples should be *all one* (John xvii, 11; xvii, 20–21); and that they should be made *holy* in the truth (John xvii, 17–19), getting their holy life from His as the branches from the Vine (John xv, 4–5).

If there is a true Church of Christ still on earth, we must expect it to show those four marks still.

One Lord, one faith, one baptism

On April 26, 1642, an immense crowd was gathered round the triangular gallows at Tyburn, and an elderly Welshman, who had come to be hanged, stood up in the cart to make his speech. He was Edward Morgan, a Flintshire man who had been to school at Douai and made priest at Salamanca. He had been imprisoned in the Fleet for fourteen years, and suffered great hardships, before being brought to trial under the Parliament. He waited till the crowd was quiet, and everybody was astonished at his cool and smiling demeanour. He began with the sign of the cross, and gave out a text ' The Good Shepherd giveth His life for His sheep.' He explained that he was going to be hanged simply because he was a Roman Catholic priest, and was very glad to die for the Good Shepherd who died for His flock. ' I offer up my blood for the good of my country, and for a better understanding between the King and Parliament.'

Then he went on to preach a full sermon on the Unity of the Church, and persisted in finishing it in spite of several interruptions from the Protestant ministers. There is one God, one faith, one baptism, he said; so there must be one Church. He gave proof that the Catholic Church was the one true Church going back to the apostles, and showed that the recent sects are all too new to have any claim to be

CATECHISM STORIES

the Church of Christ. At the end he asked God to forgive all who had injured him, and also (he said) 'my own innumerable sins.'

Then, 'with a merry countenance,' he told the hangman to do his duty and said : 'I pray thee, teach me what to do, for I never was at this sport before.'

Whereupon the minister said : 'Mr. Morgan, this is not a time to sport, nor is it a jesting matter.'

'Sir,' he replied, 'I know it is no joking matter for me, but good sober earnest. But God loveth a cheerful giver, and I hope it is no offence to anyone that I go cheerfully and merrily to heaven.'

He was allowed to hang until he was dead, before the rest of the sentence was carried out. [See also no. 532.]

The Church makes people holy

Two girls came to the surgery for another bottle of medicine for their mothers.

'It did your mother good, then?' said the doctor to the first 'Here's another bottle, then. Make sure she has it *after* meals.'

The other girl said her mother wasn't any better.

'Too bad,' said the doctor. 'I wonder if I ought to change the medicine.'

'She said it didn't make her cough any better, though she rubbed it on her chest night and morning.'

'Rubbed it on ! No wonder she isn't better. Can't she read the label—" One tablespoonful in water to be taken three times a day "? No medicine is going to cure people if they don't use it.'

The same is true of prayer and the sacraments. The Church offers to us all the means of holiness, but if we don't use them, or if we misuse them, they will not help us.

Chesterton said : 'Christianity has not failed, it has never been tried.' The people who really have tried it are the saints : they are the people who make full use of the helps Our Lord has given us. [See also no. 656.]

The Church produces the saints

When St. Francis had gathered round him eleven others

who shared his desire to live up to Our Lord's teaching literally and persuade others to do the same, he set off to Rome to get the approval of Pope Innocent III for the new society. Innocent III was a very able but rather worldly-minded Pope, and not much inclined to favour such ideas. Some of the Cardinals were very much against Francis; after all, God had blessed the Church with riches, so what was the good of preaching poverty? But one night the Pope had a dream in which the Church of St. John Lateran (the mother-church of all Christendom) seemed to be falling over and a little man in a brown habit was holding it up. Next day St. Francis came for his audience, and the Pope recognised the man in his dream. So he gave his approval to the new Order and told them to go and preach.

The Church is human as well as divine. Even the rulers of the Church may sometimes set a bad example, but the holiness of the Church remains and God raises up his saints to carry on the torch and save the situation.

Unworthy Christians

Our Lord's Church is holy, but not all Catholics are. There will always be good ones and bad ones (Our Lord said), and we can't always tell which is which until the Last Judgement.

Read the story of the cockle (Matt. xiii, 24–30) and Our Lord's explanation in Matt. xiii, 36–43. Also the net full of fish (Matt. xiii, 47–50).

Catholic in place and time

Blessed Peter Wright, born at Slipton in Northamptonshire, became a Jesuit at St. Omer in 1629, and was martyred at Tyburn in 1651. Twenty thousand people came to see, and he was offered his life if he would apostatise. His speech was a brief one: 'Gentlemen, this is a short passage to eternity, and I have not much to speak. I willingly confess that I am a priest, a Catholic, and (as you call it) a Jesuit. For this alone was I condemned; and for propagating the Catholic Faith, which is spread through the whole world, taught through all ages from

CATECHISM STORIES

Christ's time, and will be taught for all ages to come. For this cause I would die a thousand times if it were necessary, and I look on it as my greatest happiness that my most good God has chosen me, so unworthy a sinner, for such a grace. . . . God bless you all, I forgive all men. From my heart I bid you all farewell, till we meet in a happy eternity.'

[See nos. 189, 190, 662, 677, 678.]

The Church of all nations

Our Lord often spoke of the future when the Gospel of the Kingdom would be preached to all the Gentiles, but He Himself preached only to the children of Israel. During Holy Week in the Temple at Jerusalem some Gentile foreigners came to one of the Twelve and said : ' Sir, we would see Jesus.' When Our Lord heard about it, He thought of how His Church would spread through the world after His death, and He said : ' Amen, amen, I say to you, unless the grain of wheat fall into the ground and die, it remains one grain alone. But if it die it bringeth forth much fruit. . . . He that loveth his life shall lose it. . . . And I if I be lifted up from the earth, will draw all things to myself.'

Then before His Ascension He told the apostles to preach to all nations. They knew the Gentiles must come into the Church, but at first they preached only to the Jews and waited for God to show them what to do.

The sign came when St. Peter was on a round of visits to the brethren in Lydda and Jaffa. A message came from the pagan city of Cæsarea, the Roman military headquarters in Palestine. It was from a centurion there named Cornelius, who had been long interested in the Jewish religion and had now been told in a vision to ask the help of St. Peter.

Meanwhile, St. Peter, too, had had a vision (read it from Acts x, 9–16), so he went with the messenger and found that Cornelius had assembled all his relatives and friends to meet him. The centurion related his vision, and St. Peter stood up and addressed the assembly :

' In very deed I perceive that God is not a respecter of persons ; but in every nation he that feareth Him and worketh justice is acceptable to Him.'

He went on to instruct them about Our Lord and His Resurrection, etc. Even while he spoke the Holy Spirit came down on them all, and Peter decided they should be baptised (Acts x, 44-48).

After this precedent, others of the brethren preached to the Gentiles in Antioch, the capital of Syria; Barnabas was sent from Jerusalem to take charge, and he went to Tarsus and brought back the converted Saul to help him; and thus the Church began really to spread to all nations (details in Acts xi, 19-26).

Catholic means Universal

During the War two friends, both in the Post Office Telephone service, joined the R.E.s together. In France they found themselves at an artillery headquarters in a little village a few miles behind the lines. One of them was a Catholic, and used to get up early on Sunday mornings and go to the village church to hear Mass with the French people. 'What's the good of doing that?' his friend asked. 'You can't understand a word of the sermon.'

'That doesn't matter. Catholics go to Mass to offer sacrifice to God, not to hear sermons. Here the Mass is just the same as in Birmingham.'

'Well, this doesn't seem fair—why isn't there a church for me to go to as well?'

'Well, you are Church of England, and that's only *in* England; and I belong to the Catholic Church, and Catholic means Universal—it's the Church for everywhere.'

When March, 1918, came, and the Germans broke through, the gunner staff hurriedly packed up and departed, leaving the two friends behind with orders to telephone the situation to Army Headquarters till the last moment. They stayed all night, the firing died down, and the first thing they saw in the early morning was some Germans coming across the château garden. They just had time to telephone the news, tried to escape from the back door, but ran into more Germans and had to surrender.

In the German prison camp one of the prisoners was a French soldier-priest, and he said Mass for the Catholics on Sundays. The Protestant went with his Catholic friend.

CATECHISM STORIES 83

There were French and English and Irish and Australian prisoners there, also Portuguese and some Poles from the Russian Army and a Catholic doctor from Chicago and two French-Canadians. Some of the German Territorial camp-guards came to the Mass, too, and several German men and women from farms near the camp.

Afterwards the Protestant said to his friend : ' Well, I see what you mean about the Church being universal. If I ever get home I'll be a Catholic myself. Seeing all that crowd going to Communion together gave me a new idea about Christianity—the people who do that wouldn't really want to fight each other, would they ? I mean, if all the nations went to Mass more there wouldn't be any wars.'

' I expect that was Our Lord's idea,' said the Catholic.

The true Church must be ' Apostolic '

When it was evident that the Jewish leaders would reject Our Lord, He willed to make beginning with His own Church, and the first thing was to create a body of leaders for it. How many should He have ? The answer was Twelve. The chosen people of God were the ' children of Israel ' descended from the Twelve Patriarchs, sons of Israel (otherwise Jacob) ; anyone belonging to one of the Twelve Tribes had a share in the Covenant, the Promises of God to Abraham, Isaac and Jacob. Now Our Lord was going to make twelve new Patriarchs to be the beginning of His new Covenant. (We can tell this from His words later at the Last Supper, Luke xxii, 30).

One evening He left His crowd of disciples, went up into a mountain and spent all night in prayer. Then next morning He came down, held a kind of parade, and solemnly called to Him the twelve He wanted : one by one—Simon, Andrew, James, John and the rest. He said they were to be ' apostles ' (' men sent on a mission ' ; it was the official term for delegates from the Sanhedrin), and to be with Him always and teach in His name. To them, obviously meaning their successors also, He promised later : ' I am with you always, even to the end of the world.'

After the Ascension the first thing they did in the Upper Room was to bring the number up to Twelve again, by choosing Matthias in the place of Judas. On the Day of Pentecost it was 'Peter with the eleven' who made the first sermon and brought the Church into existence.

Evidently Our Lord meant that the connection between His Church and the Twelve apostles should exist for all time, by a spiritual descent from one generation to another.

> * WHAT DO YOU MEAN BY THE COMMUNION OF SAINTS?
>
> *By the Communion of Saints I mean that all the members of the Church, in heaven, on earth, and in purgatory, are in communion with each other, as being one body in Jesus Christ.*

'In communion with each other'

IN a certain Spanish monastery there was an old Irish lay-brother, who always showed extraordinary devotion at the Elevation, and was present at every possible Elevation he could. Sometimes children asked him why, and he would answer to this effect:

'Some years ago, one morning I came in at the back of this church when it was full of people hearing Mass. It was All Saints' Day. The bell was ringing for the Elevation. As I came in God gave me a vision. Over the altar I saw all the Church triumphant in bright robes and glorious light, kneeling to adore the Sacred Host. There seemed thousands of them, right up into the roof of the church. I could see Our Lady and the Apostles, and St. Lawrence and St. Agnes and many more I recognised; and amongst them I could see some boys and girls I knew in Dublin when I was a lad, though I'd never heard anything of them since. Then I looked lower down, because all the people in church were bowing low, and I could see over their heads, and behind the altar there seemed to be a sort of great cavern opened, and the souls in purgatory had gathered in hundreds round each side of the altar, in dark-coloured clothes and all lifting up their arms to the elevated Host. Right in the front I saw two monks of the community who had died a year or two before, and who had often said Mass at that very altar.

*BALTIMORE 170-174
ENGLISH CATECHISM 102

CATECHISM STORIES 85

'God showed me all this in a moment or two, and left me shedding tears of great joy, to think how close we are, in the Church militant, to the Church triumphant in heaven and the Church suffering in purgatory. And always ever since I have a great desire to adore Our Lord at the Elevation together with that company.'

Our prayers can bring grace to others

When St. Thérèse of Lisieux was about fourteen, everybody was talking about a criminal named Pranzini, who had been condemned in Paris for murdering three women and a girl. He refused to make his peace with God. Thérèse was filled with compassion to hear of it, and began to pray hard, offering many self-denials for his conversion. She asked God for some sign that her prayer was granted, 'because he is my first sinner,' she said.

The weeks went by. Every day she looked in the newspaper, only to read that the condemned man continued unrepentant. She persevered in her prayers. 'My God,' she prayed in effect, 'I am sure you will pardon him, even if he makes no outward sign of contrition. I shall always believe You have pardoned him, so please do!'

After two months the day of execution came, with Pranzini still refusing the Sacraments. He was dragged struggling to the guillotine, but at the very last moment, before the knife fell, he asked for the priest's crucifix and kissed it three times.

When Thérèse read this in the newspaper she was so overcome that she had to run out of the room, and thanked God with tears of joy that He had given her the sign.

How the saints help us

The nuns at Kuala Lampur (Malaya) had just opened a new little school at Kajang, fifteen miles away, where the inhabitants had once been Catholics, but for lack of a priest were being lost to the Church. The chief difficulty was how to get the Sisters there and back every day, for the two hours' railway journey in the heat was unendurable. To hire a car would cost seven dollars a day—quite impossible.

So the nuns began a novena to St. Teresa of Lisieux for a motor car, and to make her understand how urgent it was, somebody made a miniature car and hung it round the little Saint's neck.

The novena ended and no car arrived. 'Make another novena,' said Reverend Mother. 'Bring in St. Joseph, too. I must have that car for Monday.'

On Thursday a Chinese man from Singapore came to see one of the Chinese nuns who was his daughter-in-law. He had heard she was ill, and was glad to see it was a mistake.

She showed him round the convent, and in the chapel he walked over to the statue of St. Teresa. 'What's that thing round her neck?' he asked.

'It's a motor car,' said the Sister. 'We want one to take the Sisters to Kajang.'

'Well, you can tell Reverend Mother she shall have one. Only do take that thing off the statue's neck.'

Three days later St. Teresa's motor drove up, all new and shining. It was blessed there and then. With the chauffeur leading, there was a procession and fireworks, and everybody rejoiced. Every day now St. Teresa can watch the Sisters start off to Kajang to look for souls. (*Holy Childhood Annals*, January, 1937.)

Praying to St. Anthony

The following is told (in *Catholic Times*, January 3, 1936) by Dom Ambrose Agius, O.S.B.

'I remember my father telling me the following story: One evening, on his way to America, he was smoking an after-dinner cigar before turning in when he heard the engines stop and the ship came round in a circle. "Man overboard!" Boats were lowered to search the seas. My father prayed to St. Anthony. The boats returned. The captain called: "Have you found him?" "No," came the answer. "Come on board, we cannot wait any longer," ordered the captain. Then, as an afterthought, "Oh well! Have one more try. If you don't find him, come back at once." "Ay, ay, sir." They rowed away, straight to the missing man.' [See also nos. 226, 227, 663, 669.]

CATECHISM STORIES

We can help the souls of the dead

St. Malachy of Armagh (twelfth century) had a sister whom he loved but whose life was so worldly that he felt obliged to have nothing to do with her. One day he heard she was dead, having first repented of her sins. For many days he offered Mass for her, and then more and more seldom.

One night he dreamed someone came into his room and said : ' Your sister stands at the door, and complains that for thirty days you have given her no food.'

He remembered that it was thirty days since he had offered Mass for her, and began to do so again.

After a few days he dreamed that he saw her at the church door, trying in vain to enter. She was clothed in dark-coloured garments.

He continued his Masses, and after a few days, in another dream, he saw her in light-grey garments ; this time she was able to enter the church, but could not approach near the altar.

Again he continued the holy sacrifice for her, and a third dream showed her in a robe of shining white, with a company of others attired in the same way ; they stood close to God's altar, and their faces were full of joy. So St. Malachy knew that at length his prayers for her were fully granted. [See also nos. 4, 675.]

> * WHAT IS PURGATORY ?
>
> *Purgatory is a place where souls suffer for a time after death on account of their sins.*

The necessity of Purgatory

JUDAS MACHABEUS (160 B.C.) had raised his countrymen against the oppression of King Antiochus of Syria. ' It is better to die in battle,' he said, ' than to see the evils of our nation and of the holy places.' He had won toleration for the Jewish Law and restored the Temple.

But the peace did not last long. The local governors treated the Jews badly, and at Joppe two hundred, including women and children, were put on boats and drowned. In vengeance Judas made a night raid on the harbour,

*BALTIMORE 173-184
ENGLISH CATECHISM 106

and set the shipping on fire. Hearing of another massacre planned at the port of Jamnia, he made another night attack there and burnt the city and ships, ' so that the light of the fire was seen at Jerusalem two hundred and forty furlongs off.' In the darkness and confusion some of the raiders looted the pagan temples, which was strictly against orders, since anything used in the service of idols was forbidden to the Jews by the Law.

After this exploit they made savage reprisals on other towns (remember it was before Our Lord had come to teach a higher morality) and returned to Jerusalem in time for Pentecost.

After the festival they marched again, this time east against Gorgias, the Governor of Idumea. There was an exciting battle, and Gorgias was defeated and nearly captured (details in 2 Mach. xii, 32–37). Judas led the final charge, singing psalms in Hebrew in a loud voice; perhaps Psalm 67. When they came to collect their dead for burial, they found some of the dead Jews wore round their necks for luck little golden trinkets, votive-offerings looted from the idols in the Jamnia temple.

Judas made a speech about this and said their death in battle was evidently a punishment for their sin. Yet also, they had surely died a good death, fighting for God's Law !

So everybody prayed to God to forget the sin, and Judas made a collection which realised 12,000 silver drachmas, and sent it to the priests at Jerusalem to have sacrifices offered for the dead. The chronicler, inspired by God, adds the comment that ' it is a holy and wholesome thought to pray for the dead, that they may be loosed from sins.'

It is only common sense to recognise that most of us, like those rough warriors, when we die may not be wicked enough for hell, but are certainly not fit to go straight into heaven. [See also no. 391.]

' A place where souls suffer for a time '

Dante's great epic imagines Purgatory as a long and toilsome mountain-climb up to heaven.

CATECHISM STORIES 89

The poet tells how he and his guide, Virgil, emerged from the pit of hell. It was just before dawn, and with immense relief he felt the fresh air and saw the stars again. They found themselves on the shore of the island of Purgatory, and on the sea they saw a little ship sailing in swiftly, steered by a shining angel whose high upright wings were the sails; it was full of new-departed souls.

Dante and Virgil turned to the mountain that rose from the middle of the island. Its rocks seemed so sheer that they could not see any way to begin the ascent, until some souls higher up pointed them to the beginning of a narrow little track that went up between walls of rock. Up this they scrambled, reached the open hill-side, and climbed upwards all day. They met many souls on these lower slopes, all sitting about wearily; they were the souls who in life had put off repentance, many of them till the moment of death: and now when they greatly desired to begin their purgation they were not allowed to do so, but had to endure an unwilling delay for as long as they had wilfully remained in their sins during life.

At last, after speaking with many of these souls, some of whom Dante had known on earth, the two poets found themselves next day at the great gate where Purgatory really began. The angel-sentinel let them through, and after climbing up a long zig-zag path they came out on to a wide ledge or terrace which encircled the whole mountain.

This was the first of seven such terraces, for the purging of the seven capital sins; they might be called seven training schools for the re-education of the soul.

This first terrace was to cure the effects of Pride. On the mountain wall were lifelike marble carvings, beginning with Our Lady saying: 'Behold the handmaid of the Lord': all meant to make the beholder love Humility. Further on were other pictures in stone, giving examples of the fall of Pride (such as Sennacherib being killed by his sons): but these pictures were in the pavement. Dante saw the reason when groups of souls came creeping by, all bent double under the weight of heavy stones fastened on their necks. They were all reciting together the Our Father, the prayer which prevents pride by putting us in our right relation to God. One of the souls recognised Dante and spoke to him; he was a famous book illuminator named Ortin, who on earth had been very boastful, but here he willingly told Dante that better paintings than his were now being done by his pupil, Franco.

After exploring this first terrace they found an opening in the rock with a steep stairway which led to the second terrace, where Envy was purged. Here the souls sat begging for prayers like blind beggars, and their eyelids sewn together with a wire (as the custom was with troublesome hawks) to prevent the envious glance. Voices in the air floated past, recalling examples of Charity (e.g. ' They have no wine '), or of the punishments of Envy (e.g. Cain's ' Whosoever findeth me shall slay me ').

They mount to the third terrace, which dealt with Anger. Here the penitents experienced inward visions showing the beauty of Mildness, and the sad effects of Wrathfulness, but the whole terrace was clouded with a thick fog, just as anger clouds the intelligence.

On the fourth terrace they found the Slothful, who were now ever hastening round the mountain at a run, urging each other on by calling out examples of Diligence (which means love, leading to interest and work).

On the fifth terrace were found the Avaricious, lying face downward on the earth, because in life they had given all their mind to earthly things. They wept bitter tears and their voices uttered the praises of Poverty.

While Dante and Virgil were here, the mountain suddenly trembled under them, and all the souls were heard singing ' Gloria in excelsis Deo.' This was because one soul had just finished its penance and felt free to mount to Paradise; in fact, this very soul (the ancient poet Statius) now overtook the two explorers and kept them company.

On the sixth terrace the Gluttonous were found; they seemed lean and starving. There was one tree by a spring of clear water, bearing fragrant fruit, and from its leaves came a voice relating stories of Temperance. A second tree was surrounded with souls still in an early stage of purgation, striving to get its fruit which was just out of reach.

Ascending to the seventh terrace, the poets found it

ablaze with flames issuing from the mountain-side, so that they had to walk warily along the outer edge. The souls, however, were careful to stay in the flames, which purified them from Lust, and as they suffered they sang.

Dante has to pass through the terrible fire himself, and then going up the last ascent they came at last to the top of the mountain, and find it a region of pleasant woods, streams and flowers. This is the Earthly Paradise, or Garden of Eden ; there Virgil leaves him, and there he meets Beatrice, his ideal woman, whom he had loved from a distance, and who had died young. With Beatrice as guide he goes on to explore Heaven itself.

' On account of their sins '

A Protestant went on a long country walk with the Catholic friend with whom he was staying, and in a friendly way they argued about religion. 'And then you believe in Purgatory ! ' he said. ' If I'm saved, I'm saved—why shouldn't I go straight to heaven ? '

When they got back home the servant told them that dinner was just being served.

' Splendid,' said the Protestant. ' I've never felt so hungry in my life ! '

' All right, come straight into the dining-room.'

' What, just as I am ? With these muddy boots and dirty hands and collar like a wet rag ? I wouldn't insult your wife that way. Let us go and tidy up first.'

Later at table the Catholic said to his wife : ' You ought to be very flattered. Our friend here pays more attention to what you think of him than to what his Creator thinks.'

' Whatever do you mean ? ' she asked.

' He would not come into dinner without washing and changing, but he hopes to go straight into heaven with all the dust and stains of this life still on his soul.'

' I never looked at it that way,' said the Protestant. ' Yes, after all, perhaps the souls of the departed would choose not to enter heaven till they are fit, however painful the waiting might be.'

It is the contrast between God's holiness and our own unholiness that we feel so much in Purgatory.

CATECHISM STORIES

* WHAT DO YOU MEAN BY ' THE FORGIVENESS OF SINS ' ?

By ' the forgiveness of sins ' I mean that Christ has left the power of forgiving sins to the Pastors of His Church. Sins are forgiven principally by the Sacraments of Baptism and Penance.

Christ's power over sins left to His Church

THE story of how Our Lord claimed power for Himself to remit sins, how He forgave the apostles their great sin, and at the same time gave them power to forgive others, how He sent them forth with authority to remit sins and how they began doing it by the sacrament of baptism, and later (when some of the baptised fell into sin) by the sacrament of penance, can be put together from Mark ii, 1–12; xiv, 27–31; xiv, 50; John xx, 20–23; Luke xxiv, 46–47; Acts ii, 36–38; 1 Cor. v, 1–13; 2 Cor. ii, 4–8.

' Whose sins you shall retain '

In the time of the Emperor Theodosius, a great champion of the Church against both Arians and pagans, there were serious riots at Thessalonica in the year 390, and some imperial officials there were murdered. The Emperor, acting on bad advice from those around him, gave orders for vengeance on the city in a way that horrified the world.

Public games were proclaimed at Thessalonica, the whole population crowded into the amphitheatre, whereupon soldiers surrounded them and set to work to kill the unarmed people to the number of seven thousand or more.

At this time Theodosius held his court at Milan, where the Bishop was St. Ambrose, who was very friendly with the Emperor; but rather than give communion to him after such a crime, Ambrose went into the country and wrote a letter to Theodosius telling him he must do public penance before entering the church. (Some say he actually met the Emperor at the church door and refused him admittance.) Theodosius argued he had only acted in the same way as King David had done to rebels: to which

CATECHISM STORIES

St. Ambrose said : ' If you have sinned with King David, repent with him, too.'

The Emperor was humble enough to obey. He did public penance in church, putting off all signs of royalty, prostrating himself on the ground and bewailing his sin, while the people prayed for him with tears.

Only after this was he readmitted to communion. [See also nos. 464-467.]

* WHAT IS ORIGINAL SIN ?

> *Original sin is that guilt and stain of sin which we inherit from Adam, who was the origin and head of all mankind.*

Our share in the sin of Adam

A CERTAIN young king in feudal times wished to honour a friend of his boyhood days and gave him large estates and the title of prince. By the royal decree not only himself, but all his children and descendants, too, were to be princes and princesses and take rank equal to the royal family.

Almost at once, however, the new prince and his wife revolted against the authority of their sovereign and tried foolishly to set up a kingdom of their own. They failed. The king was merciful and spared their lives ; but they lost their estates and their princely rank, and became once more mere subjects.

When their children grew up and realised that they would all have been princes and princesses if their parents had been more loyal, they were sorry, of course, but saw that it was the necessary result of their parents' fall, and they never dreamed of blaming the king.

This is a parable of original sin. God created Adam and Eve in a state of grace, that is, children of His own family with a right to heaven ; but they lost this supernatural gift for themselves and for us. So now we are all born merely men, without the grace God meant us to have.

Only, to make the parable complete, the King's own Son should come to live with the ex-princely family, and plead with his Father to restore them for his sake.

*BALTIMORE 51-61
ENGLISH CATECHISM 115

> * HAVE ALL MANKIND CONTRACTED THE GUILT AND STAIN OF ORIGINAL SIN?
>
> *All mankind have contracted the guilt and stain of original sin, except the Blessed Virgin, who, through the merits of her Divine Son, was conceived without the least guilt or stain of original sin. This privilege of the Blessed Virgin is called the Immaculate Conception.*

'I am the Immaculate Conception'

WHEN Bernadette had seen Our Lady several times she was told by her to give a message to the priests, telling them to build a chapel at the grotto. She did so, in fear and trembling, and the Curé (who did not then believe in the apparitions) said the lady at the grotto could have a chapel if she would tell her name.

Bernadette had asked her name already, but she had only smiled. On the feast of the Annunciation, when she saw the Lady again, she said during her ecstasy: 'Madame, will you have the kindness to tell me who you are.' At first the Lady still only smiled, but after Bernadette had asked three times, the Lady let her arms fall to her side (in the attitude of the Miraculous Medal) and joined them again on her breast. Then she raised her eyes and said: 'I am the Immaculate Conception.'

When her ecstasy was over, Bernadette went home with her friend Ursule, and could not help telling her about the name, because it made her so happy. She did not know what the words 'Immaculate Conception' meant, and she kept repeating them all the way home so as not to forget them.

Perhaps we may guess from this how much Our Lady thinks of this privilege of hers, since she chose that phrase to let us know that it was she herself at Lourdes.

> ** WHAT IS SIN?
>
> *Sin is an offence against God by any thought, word, deed, or omission against the law of God.*

Offending God: the only real evil

ST. JOHN CHRYSOSTOM at Constantinople was much loved

*BALTIMORE 62
 ENGLISH CATECHISM 117-118
**BALTIMORE 64
 ENGLISH CATECHISM 118

CATECHISM STORIES 95

by the ordinary people and the poor whose cause he championed, but many of the rich courtiers hated him because he preached against their evil ways. The Empress Eudoxia (it is related) discussed with some of them the best way of taking revenge on him. One said : ' Send him into exile, to some far country.' Another : ' Confiscate all his possessions.' A third : ' Put him in chains, in some dark dungeon.' A fourth : ' Persuade the Emperor to put him to death—that will silence him ! ' But a fifth, a cunning old man, said : ' You do not understand the man, any of you. Exile would not trouble him, one place is the same as another to him. If you take all his possessions, you are not punishing him, but the poor. If imprisoned, he would rejoice at the chance of suffering for God. As for death, you would only be sending him to heaven. If you really want to be revenged on him, there is only one way—you must get him to commit sin. I know him well, and I tell you sin is the only thing he fears.'

But there was no chance of success that way, and in the end St. John was exiled to the Caucasus. The guards were ordered to make his journey as rapid and full of hardship as possible, and he died on the way, saying : ' Glory be to God for all things.'

Sin is an offence against *God*, and that is why it is the only real evil. [See also nos. 439, 440.]

' Against the law of God '

We have the Ten Commandments, and the laws and teachings of the Church to help us. Even so, sometimes it may be hard to discern what God wills us to do, and then the great thing is to be true to our conscience as far as it is clear. Our conscience is God's law written in our heart.

General Robert E. Lee, of Virginia, was against slavery and against secession, but when the Southern states actually left the Union he felt he could not in conscience make war on them to force them back into it. He was invited to be Commander-in-Chief of the invading Union armies, but instead resigned his commission and joined the Southern armies to resist the invasion. Meanwhile his son was a lieutenant in the Union army. Lee, through his wife, sent him a message that he ought to be guided not by his father's wishes or example ('If I have made a mistake, he may be able to correct it'), but by his own judgement and conscience.

How we know the law of God

The 'law of God' is written in our hearts—what we call our 'conscience'; it is specially made known to us also in the Ten Commandments and the teachings of the Church. If we follow these signposts they will bring us to heaven. Turning aside from them is sin.

You ask the best way to some mountain summit. 'Go straight through the cross-road and when you come to a gate take the path to the right and then follow the stakes.' The cross-road is easy; you notice several gates, and wonder if you are right to disregard them; but at last your lane ends in a gate with two paths beyond. You take the right; there are no stakes in view, but in due course the first one appears; and though you can only see them one by one they lead you to the top.

The point is, you have to bear the instructions in mind; you can't picture the points, but when you reach them you can recognise them from the description.

So with the Church's teachings about life. You must take them on faith, and when the situation arises you will know what to do.

E.g. indissolubility of marriage, when a couple begin to have difficulties; they know they have to make a success of it; instead of drifting towards divorce.

> * WHAT IS MORTAL SIN?
>
> *Mortal sin is a grievous offence against God. It kills the soul by depriving it of sanctifying grace, which is the supernatural life of the soul. They who die in mortal sin will go to hell for all eternity.*

Mortal sin, greatest of all evils

WHEN St. Louis of France was a boy, his mother, Blanche of Castile, once said: 'You are as dear to me as any son could be to any mother, yet I would rather see you lying

*BALTIMORE 66-69
ENGLISH CATECHISM 121-125

CATECHISM STORIES 97

dead at my feet than that you should ever commit a mortal sin.'

He became king at eleven; and was a very good king because he always desired to avoid sin and do what was the Will of God. For instance, years afterwards he was talking with his friend and secretary, de Joinville, and asked him which he would choose, to catch the leprosy or to commit a mortal sin. De Joinville said he would commit a mortal sin. The king said: 'Oh, you are wrong. Nothing is more to be dreaded than to displease God.'

In 1244 the Christian capital of Jerusalem was taken by the Moslems, and St. Louis answered the Pope's call for a crusade. He led an army to Egypt and took Damietta, but his men were much reduced by pestilence. When they marched on towards Cairo, his brother Robert imprudently led the vanguard into a town called Mansurah, where it was caught by the enemy and cut up. The king himself was cut off from the base and captured.

During a captivity of many months, the Saracens tried hard to make him betray the Christian cause, especially to promise to hand over the Christian castles in Syria to the infidels. He was threatened with torture. Swords were held at his throat. 'You are masters over my body,' he said, 'do with it what you please.' Even when a massacre of all the Christian prisoners was threatened, he refused to do what he was sure would be a grave sin.

At last he was ransomed for a million gold bezants, took the remnant of his army on to Palestine and strengthened the Christian fortresses there, and returned to France in 1254, when news came of the death of his mother, who had been acting as regent.

During the next sixteen years he showed what a Christian king should be. Besides avoiding sin himself he did his best to remove the causes of sin by others. For instance, he worked hard for peace by removing the causes of war with other countries. He took care that justice should be done in France between man and man, and prevented oppression by the rich. Also he gave a wonderful example of charity to the poor, caring for the sick with his own hands, and feeding a hundred people every day.

In 1270 he took the cross again, and died of the plague in Tunis.

If heads of nations ruled with such a clear conscience as St. Louis, the world would be a happier place.

Three conditions to make a Mortal Sin

Four boys at work were talking about saying prayers. One, a Catholic, said: 'I generally say them, but I didn't say any all day yesterday. In the morning I was in too much of a hurry, and at night I was too tired.'

Another Catholic said: 'I haven't said any since we left school, three months ago. Can't be bothered with it, nor with Church either.'

A third boy: 'I always say prayers now, but once I didn't say any for over six months. I was smashed up on a bicycle, and lay unconscious for weeks. Even when I came round they used to give me drugs and things. Sometimes I used to think I ought to say my prayers, but I always seemed too drowsy somehow.'

The fourth boy said: 'Well, I can beat all of you—I've never said a prayer in my life. My father's a Communist and he wouldn't let anybody teach me religion, but I shall please myself now.'

Discuss whether any of the above boys have committed a mortal sin.

First: Venial only, 'matter' not grave enough.

Second: Lifting up mind and heart to our Creator, at least sometimes, is a natural duty; it seems difficult to acquit the second boy of mortal sin. All three conditions seem present, unless the general irresponsibility of youth is a mitigating excuse.

Third: Grave matter, also knowledge; but not sufficient consent of the will for mortal sin.

Fourth: Grave matter, also consent of will; but insufficient knowledge for mortal sin.

Mortal sin kills the soul

A rather terrifying story is told about Leonardo da Vinci. For his famous picture of the 'Last Supper,' he took as model for Our Lord a young man who sang in the choir of Milan Cathedral. His name was Pietro Bandinelli. Years afterwards the painter was looking for a model from whom to paint the face of Judas. One day in the streets of Rome he saw a man whose hardened eyes and countenance lined with vice and greed struck him as very suitable for the purpose. When they got to the studio something familiar in the man's manner made Leonardo ask his name.

'You have painted me before—I am Pietro Bandinelli.'

Mortal sin can make sad changes in outward appearance, but that is nothing to the fearful change it makes in the soul.

They who die in mortal sin

Along the road to a certain church was a row of fine horse-chestnut trees, but one was nothing but bare branches. It had been struck by lightning some years before and never recovered. A missioner noticed it and made a sermon out of it for the children. 'Mortal sin kills the true *life* of the soul,' he said. 'The soul is still there, like the tree, but the life has gone out of it, and nothing beautiful or good will come from it. One day some gale will blow it down, and it will lie there until it is chopped up or burned. That is what Holy Scripture says of a soul that dies in mortal sin : as the tree falls so shall it lie. A soul that is in a state of mortal sin is already in hell in a way, except that it still has a chance to repent.'

A tree that is dead would need a miracle to grow leaves and conkers again ; a soul in mortal sin needs a miracle of grace to repent, and God is always willing to work *that* miracle, in this life.

'Hell for all eternity'

It is said that some saint, in a dream, heard Satan complaining to God : 'Why dost Thou pardon souls who have offended Thee many times, and yet there is no pardon for me who have offended Thee once !'

'Hast thou ever asked pardon of Me ?' was God's answer.

After our death, theologians tell us, our will does not change its direction. If we died enemies of God, we should want to go on hating Him; we should not *want* to be pardoned. [See also nos. 493, 578–582.]

Men make their own hell

Dante, in his imaginary visit to Hell, found the souls of the damned punished by having to continue for ever in their sin and its consequences. The unchaste, who in life had let themselves be carried away by storms of passion instead of following the light of reason, were in the second Circle, blown about by violent winds in pitch darkness. The gluttonous grovelled in the mud, under a cold sleet, while the monster Cerberus barked over them and tore them to pieces, like the nightmares that come from overeating. The cruel were themselves hunted by merciless centaurs. The usurers, crouching amid a sandy waste, with flakes of fire falling like snow, had their money-bags tied round their necks.

People say, can a good God create hell? But it is really men who create their own hell. Even in this life men can make hell around them, by misusing God's gifts.

The story goes that a Scotsman died and found himself in the next world. To the first passer-by he remarked: 'Heaven seems verra little improvement on Glesca!' 'Mon, this is no' Heaven!'

> * WHAT IS VENIAL SIN?
>
> *Venial sin is an offence which does not kill the soul, yet displeases God, and often leads to mortal sin.*

Venial sin displeases God

WE are told of St. Philip Neri that he was always contriving some occupation for the boys. He used to make them sweep his room and dust his furniture, or make his bed, even if he had already made it once. Some of them he set down to read, and others who liked using their fingers better than their brains he employed in stringing Rosary

*BALTIMORE 70-72
ENGLISH CATECHISM 126

CATECHISM STORIES 101

beads, or in weaving garlands to deck Our Lady's statue. He knew that some of the boys needed real hard work to keep them quiet, and these he employed in dragging large, heavy pieces of furniture from one place to another. But all were equally happy, for it was a delight to do anything that St. Philip asked them to do.

He was always taking them on long, jolly walks on the hills, and organising ball-games or quoits. He used to play these games with them, and he never allowed a boy to sulk and fall out of the game for any reason.

They seem to have spent a great deal of their spare time playing ball in the corridors of the Oratory, and against the doors, and thereby driving nearly mad the unfortunate Fathers—especially Father Baronius, working at his *Annals*. When indignant Fathers burst out of their rooms and said it was *intolerable*, and for once the boys fell into an awed silence, St. Philip used to come out and say : ' Let them grumble as much as they please. Do not mind them. Go on with your play, and be as merry as you like. All I want is that you should keep out of sin.' It was rough on the Fathers, but no doubt it taught the boys to share St. Philip's conviction—that sin, even venial sin, displeases God more than anything else.

The greatest evil after mortal sin

St. Frances of Rome, great ' mystic ' of the fifteenth century, was privileged to see her guardian angel always at her side, as a beautiful little boy of eight ; his eyes were fixed on heaven and his hands crossed on his breast. Such radiance shone around his head that St. Frances could read her office-book by it. If anyone spoke any unbecoming words in his presence (she said) the little angel covered his face with his hands. But whenever Frances herself fell into some venial sin, he faded from her sight altogether for the time being.

Avoiding venial sin

Margaret Sinclair, Edinburgh factory-girl (french-polisher) ; fond of dancing, games, swimming ; engaged to be married at one time, but finally became a Poor Clare, died of T.B. in 1926, aged twenty-five.

The Jesuit priest Fr. A, who knew her well and to whom she made a general confession of all her life during her last illness, declared that all through her life Margaret had committed not a single deliberate venial sin.

In truth she had always made a complete gift of her will to God. She summed it up in the last prayer she uttered on her death-bed : ' Jesus, Mary and Joseph, I give you my heart and my soul.'

' That last prayer made such an impression on me,' says the sister who was looking after her. ' It was said with such fervour and confidence that we felt she was already in the arms of Jesus, Mary and Joseph.'

' Often leads to mortal sin '

When Arthur was first made king (a legend says) he used to ride out himself in search of adventures. One day Merlin told him : ' To-morrow you will meet a dwarf who will challenge you to fight. You will overcome him, and then you must kill him.'

Next day in the forest, the dwarf stood in his path, brandishing a sword, challenging Arthur to fight. He dismounted and fought ; the dwarf proved to be a good swordsman, but Arthur easily disarmed him, and when he begged for mercy he let him go.

On his return, Arthur was met by Merlin who shook his head and said : ' If you do not kill the dwarf he will destroy you one day.'

Next day the dwarf appeared again ; he looked an inch or two taller. They fought again, and again the king spared his life. This happened for ten days running, by which time the dwarf had grown nearly to full height. But at last, on the eleventh day, it was a great giant who rushed out from the trees, killed Arthur's horse under him, and set upon the king himself with his great sword. Only after a long and terrible fight did Arthur manage to cleave the giant's skull, then sank himself, sorely wounded, to the ground.

When he came to himself, Merlin had found him and

CATECHISM STORIES

was tending his wounds. Back at the castle, Merlin explained to the king that the dwarf was sin, which must be overcome in the early stages, otherwise its power grows, and a habit of venial sin will end in mortal sin. [See also no. 601.]

* WHAT DO YOU MEAN BY 'THE RESURRECTION OF THE BODY'?

    By 'The Resurrection of the body' I mean that we shall rise again with the same bodies at the day of judgement.

'We shall rise again at the Day of Judgement'

MAN is soul and body, and God meant them to remain united. On account of the Fall, death comes to dis-unite them. But soul is incomplete without body, so God will re-unite them, by a kind of universal miracle at the Last Day.

The resurrection of the body was a subject of controversy amongst the Jews; the Pharisees believed in it, but not the Sadducees. It was one of the questions they brought to Our Lord in the Temple, during the last few days of His mortal life. The Sadducees invented a possible case which (they thought) made this idea of resurrection seem foolish. Our Lord told them they were wrong, and taught clearly that the dead shall rise again.

Read story from Luke xx, 27–38.

'We shall rise again with the same bodies'

A pupil of Faraday once, by accident, dropped a silver cup into a jar of *aqua fortis*, and the cup was dissolved. Faraday came to the rescue, and put some salt in the jar. This precipitated the grains of silver to the bottom; Faraday took them out and had the cup made again from them, more beautiful than it was originally.

It was the same cup, inasmuch as it was made of the same material, but it was better than before. So with the risen bodies of the just. God can use the same matter for them, since matter is indestructible. Still, it is really our *Soul* which makes the body the *same* body; because the risen body belongs to the same soul.

*BALTIMORE 176-179
ENGLISH CATECHISM 129

CATECHISM STORIES

*WHAT DOES ' LIFE EVERLASTING ' MEAN ?
' Life everlasting' means that the good shall live for ever in the glory and happiness of heaven.

' The good shall live for ever '

HERE is the story of how the great St. Cuthbert heard the call to give his life to God's service.

Out on the hill-side a little group of shepherds slept beneath the stars. All except Cuthbert, who watched his sheep, and also watched in prayer. On a sudden he beheld a light streaming down from heaven, breaking the darkness of the night. And in this were choirs of the heavenly host coming down to earth ; and they forthwith, after taking away a soul of exceeding brightness, returned to their heavenly country. Waking his fellow-shepherds, he told them of the wonderful vision he had seen—' the gate of heaven opened, and the spirit of some saint introduced thither by an angelic company ; who is now, while we lie in lowest darkness, for ever blessed in beholding the glory of the heavenly country, and Christ its King.'

The shepherds were filled with wonder ; and all the more when, a few days later, news arrived that the great St. Aidan ' had departed to the Lord at the very time Cuthbert had seen him carried up to heaven.' From that time Cuthbert made up his mind to join a monastery if he could, so as to make sure of reaching heaven and becoming one of the glorious company he had seen.

Eternal bliss

A story is told of a monk, named Felix, who used to wonder what the saints would do in heaven and how anybody could be there for ever without getting tired of it.

One summer morning, walking near the monastery, he heard wonderful bird-music in a tree overhead. A little snow-white bird was there, the sight and sound of which filled him with rapture. He followed it as it flew from tree to tree, further and further away, over hill and dale, until at last it flew out of sight and in the distance he heard the

*BALTIMORE 186
ENGLISH CATECHISM 131

monastery bell ringing for Vespers. Marvelling that it was so late he returned.

To his surprise, the lay-brother who let him in was a new one whom he had never seen. Stranger still, every face he met about the house was new to him, though all wore the familiar habit of the Order. At last he spoke to a monk :

'Where have you all come from ? And where are all our fathers ? '

The other looked at him puzzled, and took him to the old Prior.

'Tell me your name and where you come from,' said the Prior. ' Have you been a monk in this house ? I have been Prior forty years, but cannot remember your face.'

The monk told his name, and how he had listened to the snow-white bird and followed it over the country for hours.

The oldest father of the community, who sat there listening, leaned forward and said :

'Did you say for *hours ?* What is your name in holy religion ? '

'My name is Felix.'

'Wait a minute,' said the aged monk, and then he took down an ancient leather-bound book which recorded all the professions and deaths of the community.

Sure enough, there it was written in faded ink how, ninety years before, a monk named Felix had left the monastery, without a word to anyone, and had never afterwards been heard of.

The monk, Felix, fell on his knees praying aloud : ' My God, I thank Thee, for now I understand how a thousand years would pass like a single moment in the joy of Thy presence.' And with that he fell forward and gave up his spirit.

Only a story, but it helps us to understand that ecstasy (of any kind, even natural, as in admiration of nature, or artistic creation ; much more in contemplation of God) makes time of no account while it lasts. In heaven it will last unbroken for ever.

Look forward to Paradise

We ought to have a belief in heaven as strong and as

contagious as had St. Dorothy, the fourth-century virgin martyr of Cappadocia.

Brought before the Governor Apricius, she said she would not sacrifice to the gods because she believed in the one true God; and she would not marry because she had chosen Christ for bridegroom. The Governor remanded her in charge of two girls, Chrysta and Callista, who had already renounced the Christian religion through fear. They were supposed to persuade her to do the same, but the opposite happened. 'How can you think so much of their threats?' she said. 'What can any pains in this life matter compared with heaven and its everlasting joys?' Their courage came back at her burning words, and when she faced Apricius again they went with her to share her martyrdom.

The Governor, after rackings and scourgings, tried his own arguments. 'You are young and beautiful,' he said. 'Your life is before you, full of happiness, if only you will renounce this foolery. It would be madness to choose death, and go down under the earth amongst the shadowy spirits of the dead.'

'I shall not be in those dark abodes,' replied Dorothy. 'I shall be with my bridegroom Christ, in His lovely garden where it is always summer and the trees are laden with fairest fruit.'

She was condemned, with the other two, to be beheaded. As she was led off to execution, a young lawyer named Theophilus called out mockingly: 'Dorothy, remember to send me some fruit from that garden!' and she turned to him and said smilingly: 'I will remember.' A few minutes afterwards she had her glorious martyrdom completed by the executioner's sword.

While Theophilus was telling his friends about this the next day an angel in the form of a little boy presented himself, carrying a beautiful basket of three roses and three apples. 'Dorothy told me to bring you these,' he said, and disappeared before he could be questioned. It was winter-time, and the roses and apples, and the boy, too, evidently came from another world than this. Deeply moved, Theophilus went to the Governor, declared himself

CATECHISM STORIES 107

a believer in the God whom Dorothy had worshipped, and soon went to join her in the heavenly paradise through the same gate of martyrdom.

That is the story as usually told. In its earliest form the legend has an ending less miraculous but equally impressive. In this version, Dorothy, preparing herself for the headsman, gave her veil to a six-year-old boy who stood near, asking him to take it to Theophilus. When the latter received it, he found it fragrant with the scent of roses and fruits. The fact of receiving such a token, sent at such a moment, filled him with a faith in heaven and a courage equal to hers. [See also nos. 184, 387, 585.]

> * WHAT IS THE GLORY AND HAPPINESS OF HEAVEN ?
> *The glory and happiness of heaven is to see, love, and enjoy God for ever.*

' The Glory and Happiness of Heaven '

IN the *Paradiso*, Dante tells how he was led by Beatrice through the nine heavens, until at last they came to the Tenth Heaven or Empyrean, which is pure light and love and joy. A river of dazzling light flowed there, and at Beatrice's bidding he bathed his eyes in it and so was able to see the glorious vision of the whole vast circle of the Redeemed, like the innumerable petals of a snow-white Rose, around the central Glory of God. The angels, like thousands of golden-winged bees, hover over the Rose and dart down amongst its petals.

Dante finds St. Bernard at his side, and he helps the poet to recognise Our Lady, St. John the Baptist, and many others of the Blessed, as well as Beatrice who has gone to take her own place in the Rose. St. Bernard prays to Our Lady that the poet may be allowed one glimpse of the Supreme Joy, the vision of God Himself, and receive from it the grace of final perseverance.

With eyes still more strengthened, therefore, the poet gazes up into the Eternal Light at the heart of the Rose. What he saw there (he says) is beyond all words to describe.

Everything in the universe seemed to be there, ' like so

*BALTIMORE 186
ENGLISH CATECHISM 132

many single leaves all gathered into one volume with love for a binding.' Looking deep into an abyss of radiance he seemed to imagine some signs of the Blessed Trinity, three orbs of living light united into one. As he tried to penetrate the mystery further, his mind was suddenly filled with a lightning flash of supreme illumination, and fell back helpless.

The moment afterwards everything he had seen was forgotten, his mind could recall nothing of it, but the sweetness of it still remained with him and the momentum of it carried his will forward, moved by ' the Love which moves the sun and all the stars.'

His great poem ends there, for after that anything else would seem anti-climax.

' Eye hath not seen . . .'

Mother : ' Time to go to Sunday school, Tommy ? '
Little boy : ' I don't want to go to-day.'
Mother : ' Now you be a good boy and get off quick. The Vicar will tell you all about heaven.'
Little boy : ' I don't want him to tell me. I want it to come as a surprise.'

That is just what heaven will be, even to the greatest theologian or mystic : an infinitely joyful surprise which God has carefully prepared for those who love Him. ' Enter thou into the joy of thy Lord.'

Where the true joys are

The Ven. Roger Wrenno (or Warren), a weaver of Chorley, was executed at Lancaster in 1615 or 1616 for harbouring and assisting priests. As companions in martyrdom he had a secular priest named John Thules, and several criminals whom the latter had converted in prison.

As Warren was hanging after being turned off the ladder, the rope broke and he fell to the ground. In a short time he recovered his senses completely, knelt up and began to pray, with his eyes lifted to heaven. The ministers came up to him, extolled this mercy of God towards him, and repeated the offer that had been made at his trial—that his life would be given him if he would take the new oath of allegiance. At once he rose and said : ' I am the same man as before, and in the same mind ; use your pleasure with me.' And with that he ran to the ladder and went up it as fast as he could. ' How now,' says the sheriff, ' what does the man mean that he is in such haste ! ' ' Oh,' says the good man, ' if you had seen that which I have just now seen, you would be as much in haste to die as I now am.' And so the executioner, putting a stronger rope about his neck, turned the ladder and quickly sent him to see the good things of the Lord in the land of the living, of which before he had had a glimpse.

(From Challoner's *Memoirs of Missionary Priests*, II, 101.)

[See nos. 584, 585.]

FATHER'

THE 'OUR FATHER'

* WHAT IS PRAYER ?
Prayer is the raising up of the mind and heart to God.

Our duty of prayer, as creatures

A famous conductor was rehearsing a great symphony orchestra. Everything seemed to be going well, 150 skilled performers responding to the conductor's inspiration. Suddenly in the middle of a *fortissimo* passage the baton raps the music-stand, there is a sudden silence :

' Where is the piccolo ? ' demands the conductor.

The piccolo player had missed his entry, and the trained ear of the conductor, even in that glorious volume of sound filling the hall, had noted its absence.

Man is created to give glory to God, and there ought not to be one voice missing from the chorus of praise. [See also nos. 7, 138.]

' We will never leave off praying '

Here is the story of some glorious boy-martyrs who show us that prayer to God is the supreme duty of all men.

One of the highest negro races lives in Uganda ; they were evangelised by the White Fathers in 1878 and many became Christians, notably amongst the noble families. The Moslem Arabs stirred up trouble, and in 1886 the then King Mwanga started a persecution at his court, where many of his own pages had just been baptized.

The missionary Fr. Lourdel, who had to witness what

happened, tells how 'the people who pray' (as the Christians were called) were collected into the courtyard. Mwanga addressed bitter reproaches to them; then he said: 'Let all who pray stand apart.' Charles Luanga instantly stepped out, hand in hand with Kigito, a catechumen, a boy of 13, but whose courage and firmness were far beyond his years. All the Christians in the company followed their example.

'At a sign from the King they were seized, bound with ropes and roughly dragged out of the courtyard. The young men of eighteen to twenty-five years of age were bound together; the children formed a second troop. They were tied so tightly and so closely to one another that they could only walk with the greatest difficulty, taking tiny steps and continually knocking up against each other. I noticed that little Kigito laughed at this as merrily as if he were at play with his companions. He was the son of one of the greatest lords of the kingdom. . . .

'Three of the youngest pages excited the compassion of the head executioner, who in the course of a long life had never had to practise such cruelties on children of such tender years.

' " Only tell the King that you will not pray any more, he said to them, " and he will pardon you."

' " We will never leave off praying as long as we live ! " was the indignant reply of the boys.

'They were accordingly bound and led out with the others, to the number of twenty-four, on to a hill which rises opposite to the mission-house. A quantity of dried reeds had been taken there, and of these the executioners made huge faggots, in each of which one of the victims was bound up. They were then laid on the ground side by side, the feet all being turned the same way. . . .

'Then the reeds were set on fire at the end where the feet of the victims were, in order that their sufferings might be more protracted, and that some might perhaps, when the flames reached them, be prevailed on to deny their Faith. A vain hope ! The martyrs' voices were heard, it is true, but only when joining in the prayers, which we had taught them to recite ! ' (From *Stories in School*, p. 128.)

CATECHISM STORIES

We have need of prayer

In the first part of 1918, when the final German offensive seemed to be overwhelming the allies, Foch was appointed Generalissimo on the Western Front. Dawn of July 18 was the day chosen for the great counter-attack on which the issue of the war depended. At the allied G.H.Q. on the evening before, all preparations were completed at last, and Foch left his office, telling his staff-officers to leave him undisturbed for an hour if possible.

A motor-cyclist rushed in with a very urgent telegram on which the staff felt Foch himself should decide. Thinking he was snatching some sleep, they went to his billet, but he was not there. At last they found his personal orderly, who, knowing the General's habits, led them to the village church. There was Foch, kneeling motionless before the altar. He read the telegram, gave his answer, and as the staff-officers left the church they saw him already on his knees again, with his eyes on the tabernacle.

'Always when I leave His temple,' wrote Foch once, 'I feel stronger, and above all more certain. It is there that I have taken the greatest decisions on the war.'

'We kept up our prayers'

If we have a good habit of prayer it will come to strengthen us when we need it most.

Three Manchester girls went hiking on Greenfield Moors one Sunday in December, meaning to go to Laddar Rocks and back. Thick mist came down, they lost direction, and wandered about for two days wet through and covered with mud, and with no food except a few sandwiches and one orange shared between them. One fell into a bog up to the waist, and the others struggled for over an hour to get her out. They lost their shoes in the mud. Two more days and nights went by. 'Our feet were swollen and aching with the cold and we tried to keep them warm by massaging each other. We slept huddled together under a bank. On Tuesday we saw the aeroplane searching for us, but we had not the strength to wave long enough to be seen. It passed over our heads and we really thought that was the end. The only drink we had was muddy water from a stream to which we could only crawl. Every night we prayed to St. Anthony of Padua. He is known as the helper of lost people. We hardly spoke all day, but we kept up our prayers each night. Edna was now very weak, and to-day we tried to walk again, but it was hopeless. We just lay and prayed in the grass.'

Meanwhile the organised search-parties had abandoned the search, as it was considered the girls must have died of exposure. On the fifth day, however, four policemen and four others went out on a forlorn hope to where the girls had last been seen ; they found a walking stick and part of a shoe. A policeman blew his whistle, was answered by a faint cry, and the three girls were found suffering badly from frostbite, exposure and lack of food. The doctor who first saw them said it was astounding how they withstood the bleakness of the winter moors. In hospital they soon recovered. The one quoted above said afterwards : 'This world used to seem a very unromantic place, but now I think I am lucky to be in it.' (In the *Daily Express*, Dec. 15, 1935.)

'Prayer gives power to action'

In their first year of wandering, at Raphidim, where Moses struck the rock, the Israelites had their first fighting. Word came that the rear party of stragglers had been raided and all massacred—men, women and children— by a savage desert tribe, Amalek ; and they were expected to attack the camp itself next day. Amid general alarm Moses sent for the brave young Josue : '.Choose out men to fight against Amalek ; to-morrow I will stand on the top of the hill having the rod of God in my hand.'

Next morning the attacking tribe appeared, riding across the desert, and Josue's unpractised warriors went out to meet them. Moses ascended the hill with Aaron and Hur, and lifted up his hands in prayer as he watched the battle.

At first Israel was standing firm. But when Moses dropped his tired arms Amalek pressed Israel back. This happened several times, and every time he raised his hands again he could see Josue rallying his men, and heard them cheering with fresh courage. So Aaron and Hur

CATECHISM STORIES

brought a stone for Moses to sit on, and held up his hands till sunset, when Amalek took to flight (Deut. xxv, 17–19 ; Exod. xvii, 8–13 ; Judith iv, 12).

Josue had won the battle by his bravery, but he could not have won it without Moses' praying for victory.

So it is in everything and especially in getting to heaven ; we must always do our best ourselves, but we must also pray that God will help us. Without prayer we cannot do anything ; with prayer we can do everything.

There was Someone else who prayed with arms outstretched, on top of another hill, for all men. And He still does so in heaven. The priest, too, prays that way in the Mass.

Prayer helps our work

John Wesley, great Protestant evangelist, used to spend two hours every day praying. Usually this meant that he had to get up very early in the morning to get in the two hours, before beginning his strenuous work or journeying. On one occasion he said :

'To-day I have such a busy day before me that I cannot get through it with less than two hours' prayer.'

And yet this Protestant servant of God had not the Holy Mass to look forward to each morning. (It is said that he would not allow himself to read the Fourth Book of the *Imitation* lest its beauty should make him a Catholic against his judgement.)

The Mass is the highest act of prayer, yet we Catholics are often too lazy to give even the half an hour needed for it.

'The raising up of the mind and heart'

One saint (St. John-Mary Vianney, curé of Ars) tells us a story of another saint.

In the village of Ars lived a farm labourer who always made a visit to the church on his way to and from his work. He would leave his spade and bundle at the door, go inside, and remain kneeling before the tabernacle, often for hours at a time.

The holy curé watched him and noticed that his lips

never moved, though his eyes were always fixed on the tabernacle.

One day the curé spoke to him : ' Tell me what you say to the good God during those long visits to Him.'

The farm labourer's answer has become famous. ' I say nothing to Him : I look at Him. And He looks at me.'

We cannot pray by proxy

Prayer is one of the things nobody else can do in our place. It is our own mind and heart we have to raise.

Once upon a time there was a monastery where the Office was sung every day, though the monks were all getting old and their voices were thin and cracked. One fine day a handsome young man rang the bell and asked to join the community. He was admitted, and when it was found that he had a beautiful tenor voice the old monks were overjoyed. ' Now we shall have the Office sung well.' So when the new postulant had been well trained in the chant, the great day came (it was the first vespers of the Assumption) when he was to sing in choir for the first time. Everything went off beautifully, the church was full of lay-folk come to listen, and all the old monks sat in choir and never sang a word themselves for fear of spoiling the effect. They wept for joy as they heard the beautiful young voice singing the praises of the Mother of God.

That night, as the Prior was praying in his cell, Our Lady herself appeared to him in light. But she looked reproachful. ' Why was not the Office sung to-day ? ' she asked. The Prior stammered out that it *was* sung—sung better than it had ever been before.

' Well,' said Our Lady, ' I ought to tell you that nothing was heard in Heaven.'

Prayer must be interior

One morning at Chapter St. Bernard told his monks a little vision or parable in some such words as these.

' Last night, as we were all reciting matins, I seemed to see all at once an angel standing beside each monk's stall. They were our guardian angels, and they held books in which they were writing. I could see that some were

CATECHISM STORIES

writing letters of gold, and some of silver, and some were using ordinary ink. There were some who were writing only with water; and some angels stood sadly with their books closed, not writing at all.

'As I watched and pondered, I understood that the angels writing in gold and silver were the angels of those monks who were saying their prayers with great attention and great love, some more and some less. The writing in ink was for those whose prayer was directed to God but without any fervour; and the writing in water was for prayers made only with the lips, while the mind was busy with other things. As for the angels who wrote nothing at all, their monks had already lost the grace of God and their prayers were nothing but a mockery of Him.'

Praying like a parrot

A lonely old man bought a parrot, thinking to pass the time teaching the bird to talk. The first day the parrot seemed shy, but at night when the old man knelt down to rake out the fire, he was startled to hear a small voice behind him saying very reverently: 'In the name of the Father and of the Son and of the Holy Ghost, Amen.' It was the parrot, which continued with the Our Father and Hail Mary, and short night prayers all complete. Next day the old man made enquiries and found that the parrot had belonged to a good family whose members had always said night prayers together, and by hearing them so often the parrot had learned to join in. The old man himself, who had not said any prayers for years, took it as a hint from God and began to practise his religion again. Thus the parrot had taught the man to speak, rather than vice versa.

But a question: Was the parrot really praying? (No, because it had no mind or heart to raise *up*.) It is to be feared that some boys and girls pick up their prayers like parrots, by hearing others, and repeat them with about as much inward understanding of what they are doing.

St. Edmund says: 'It is better to say five words devoutly with the heart, than five thousand words which the soul does not taste with love and intelligence.' (*Speculum Ecclesiæ*.)

Distractions sure to come

St. Benedict was journeying on horseback one day, and a peasant walking along the same road said : ' You've got an easy job. Why didn't I become a man of prayer, then I should travel on horseback, too.' ' You think praying is easy, do you ? ' replied the saint. ' Listen, if you can say one Our Father without any distraction, you can have the horse for your own.' ' It's a bargain ! ' said the peasant, who closed his eyes and joined his hands and began straightway to repeat the Our Father aloud : ' Our Father, who art in Heaven, hallowed be Thy name, Thy Kingdom come '—then he stopped suddenly and looked up : ' Shall I get the saddle and bridle too ? '

Wilful distractions

One hot summer evening a holy nun was kneeling in a crowded church where the congregation was saying the Rosary. A voice spoke in her ear : ' Do you think all you people are really praying ? '

Rather surprised, the nun thought : This must be my guardian angel ! ' Show me, dear angel ! ' she answered.

' Listen now, then : we shall hear only those who really *are* praying.'

A sudden hush—one quavering old voice saying ' Holy Mary, Mother of God . . .' The nun recognised the voice —it was Brigid Finnegan, old-age-pension widow.

Only old Brigid really praying ? Then what were all the rest of the congregation doing ?

' You shall hear now what they are all thinking of,' said the angel ; and immediately arose a great tumult and clamour of words—everybody speaking of all sorts of things —things to eat and drink, cricket and tennis matches, new hats, how to get some money, criticisms of other worshippers, etc., etc.

In the midst of all the clamour the good nun awoke and found it was only the people saying the ' Hail, holy Queen.'

So she made an act of contrition for going to sleep, and saved up the dream to tell to her catechism class.

Raising our heart

'When therefore you come to your prayers, *want* something. Want what? Well, to begin with, want something more, a great deal more than just to recite the words correctly. . . .

'Joyce Kilmer, a fine man of letters and equally fine soldier who fell for us in the Great War, wrote from the battle-fields of France to a priest I know, asking for prayers. I guessed what he wanted and guessed wrong. That life might be spared him, that he might soon get back safely to his dearly loved ones at home—to his children and their mother—that was what I thought he wanted most. But no, not that. Here's what he wrote: " Pray for me, my dear Father, that I may love God more and that I may be unceasingly conscious of Him. That is the greatest wish I have."

'When, therefore, you pray, want God, want His life in you, want His love around you, want His happiness to be yours, want to show that you know about Him and His goodness, want to fall in with His plans for you, want to please Him more than to please yourself, want Himself.' (From Fr. W. Roche, S.J.)

Note that the word ' Amen ' is an expression of *desire*, of wanting something urgently, and it is meant to speed our prayer up like an arrow to God. [Other stories on Prayer: nos. 24, 251, 363, 385, 417, 418, 451, 548–550, 565, 657, 664.]

> * HOW DO WE RAISE UP OUR MIND AND HEART TO GOD?
> *We raise up our mind and heart to God by thinking of God; by adoring, praising and thanking Him; and by begging of Him all blessings for soul and body.*

' By thinking of God '

AT the beginning of prayer we should always put ourselves in the presence of God.

An experienced big-game hunter was walking with a friend near the camp when suddenly round a bend in the

*BALTIMORE 476
ENGLISH CATECHISM 142

path there crouched a lion only a few yards away. The hunter raised his gun, the growling lion seemed just about to spring. Seconds passed like years, then the rifle cracked and the lion rolled over dead.

' I thought you were *never* going to fire ! ' said the terrified friend.

' I didn't want to miss,' said the hunter. ' I was taking aim.'

So it is with the arrows of prayer we send up to God. We should spend a few moments in aiming them, remembering Who it is we are going to speak to. [See no. 35.]]

The Prayer of Adoration

The prophet Isaias was granted a vision of the angels adoring God. In the Temple one day, at the offering of incense, he seemed to see the Lord God ' sitting upon a throne high and lifted up,' and all the Temple was filled with the angels attending on him. Two seraphim stood there, one each side : they had six wings, with two they covered their faces in awe, and with two their feet. And they cried one to another, ' Holy, holy, holy, is the Lord God of hosts : all the earth is full of His glory.' At the sound of their voices the door-posts of the Temple were shaken, and the whole Temple was filled with the clouds of incense. (Then the prophet's lips were cleansed and he was sent to prophesy.)

When we say God is ' holy,' we mean that He is far above and apart from all else, the transcendent Creator separated by an abyss from His creatures, like an unapproachable mountain peak.

Adoration of God is the first business of the creature, even before service of Him. Hence the feet of the seraphim (feet signify service) were veiled while they adored.

We should remember the vision of Isaias when the words of the seraphim are sung at the Sanctus. [See nos. 458–460, 661.]

The Prayer òf Praise

' When you come to your prayers, *want* something.' (Fr. W. Roche, S.J.) But it need not be something for ourselves : better still to desire simply the glory of God.

CATECHISM STORIES

To praise God is to express our wonder and delight, appreciating Him for what He is, as worthy of all love.

In parts of Germany, instead of 'Good Morning!' people say 'Praised be Jesus Christ!' and the answer is: 'Praised for evermore!'

In a German hospital a working-man lay on the operating table to undergo a serious operation for a growth in his tongue. The surgeon said: 'If there is anything you would like to say, you had better say it now, for after the operation you will no longer be able to speak.'

The man thought for a moment, and then said: 'Praised be Jesus Christ!'

'Praised for evermore!' answered the surgeon, and signalled the anæsthetist to begin his task. (From a pastoral letter of Cardinal Bertram of Breslau.) [See also no. 27.]

The Prayer of Thanks

Two Angels flew to earth. Each carried a basket, and wherever anyone knelt at prayer the Angels stopped and went in. Schools, churches, cottages and castles were each visited. Very soon the basket carried by one of the Angels grew heavy with the weight of what he had collected, but that of the other remained almost empty. Into the first were put the prayers of petition. 'Please give me this. Please I want that.' Into the other were the 'Thank you's.'

'Your basket seems very light,' said one Angel to the other. 'Yes,' replied the one who carried the 'Thank you's.' 'People are usually ready enough to pray for what they want, but very few remember to thank the good God when He grants their requests.'

Brother Deo Gratias!

St. Felix of Cantalice was a cattle-herd who at the age of thirty became a Franciscan lay-brother. For many years he collected alms in Rome and was very friendly with St. Philip Neri. (They used to wish each other 'great sufferings for God,' as other people might wish each other 'best of luck.') His usual greeting for everybody was 'Deo gratias!' and he used to teach it to all the children, who called him Brother Deo Gratias.

Once he saw two men fighting a duel, and called out to

them : 'Deo gratias, my brothers ! Say, both of you, Deo gratias ! ' They lowered their swords, then sheathed them, and became good friends.

On his death-bed, Brother Felix asked those present to go on saying 'Deo gratias' for him when he would no longer be able to speak. [See nos. 444, 461, 665.]

'And by begging of Him all blessings'

This is the prayer of Petition ; when we ask for something for ourselves or for other creatures, whether some spiritual or temporal blessing.

If it is God's grace we are asking for, we can be quite sure that it is God's will, and go on asking till we get it.

On this, see Our Lord's story (a man borrowing loaves at midnight) in Luke xi, 5-13.

Our Father will give us what is good for us, He says (verses 11-13) ; the 'good Spirit' to them that ask Him. (As an instance of praying with *confidence*, see story 240, of St. Martin.)

The Prayer of Contrition

(Not specially mentioned in this Catechism answer ; presumably included under 'all blessings for soul and body '—prayer for forgiveness.)

The best examples are in the Gospels, e.g. the publican's 'Lord, be merciful to me a sinner !' (Luke xviii, 13 : perhaps rather a prayer *for* contrition ?)

And the prodigal son in Luke xv, 17 ; he begins from the punishments of sin (' I here perish with hunger ') and rises to love for God and his Father (' against heaven and before thee ') and desire to make amends (' make me one of thy hired servants.')

'Blessings for soul'

During the War a German staff-officer lay very dangerously wounded in a French hospital. The nun who nursed him was herself a German, and knowing he was a Catholic she wished to send for a priest, but he would not hear of it.

'Well, I will pray hard for you,' she said, ' that God may touch your heart.'

'You will soon get tired and give up,'

CATECHISM STORIES

'No, I do not give up. There is one man for whose conversion I have prayed for sixteen years.'

'Sixteen years! That must be someone dear to you—father, or brother perhaps?'

'No, it is someone I never saw. You see, my mother was maid to a countess in Germany. Sixteen years ago that countess asked my mother to ask me to pray for her son, who was leading a wild life. Ever since then I have prayed for him every day, and so have the other sisters. He is with the army now—we heard so in a letter from his mother, the countess, last month.'

The officer was listening eagerly.

'Was your mother's name Beata?' he asked.

'It was. Can it be possible that you are Count Charles?'

It was indeed, and he could not prevent his tears—it seemed such a clear design of God who had brought him to the care of this very sister. He received the sacraments, and soon afterwards died in very good dispositions, to the great consolation of his mother when she heard. (*Spirago*.) [See also nos. 123, 474, 480, 492, 504, 525.]

'**Blessings for body**'

Many people asked Our Lord for temporal favours, cures chiefly, and He seemed sometimes reluctant to grant them, but would do so to strong faith.

E.g. (Matt. xv, 21–28) the touching story of the pagan woman whose daughter suffered from fits (this is a likely meaning of verse 22).

On the other hand, when praying for temporal blessings there should always be the proviso understood : *if* it is God's will. This would rather rule out some prayers altogether : e.g.

Mother : What are you praying for, Johnny?

Johnny : I want Pekin to be the capital of Mexico, because I put it in my exam-paper. [See also nos. 22, 202, 203.]

* WHO MADE THE LORD'S PRAYER?
   Jesus Christ Himself made the Lord's Prayer.

'**The Lord's Prayer**'

THE twelve were good Jews and had been brought up to say the usual prayers at home and at the synagogue. But living in the company of Our Lord they soon came to feel that He was closer to God than they had imagined anyone could be. Especially they saw Him going up often at night into the hills to pray alone ; and saw the joy that shone in His face when He came down in the morning as if refreshed and strengthened. So on one such occasion they came to Him and one of them said : ' Lord, teach us to pray, as John also taught his disciples.' They meant : teach us to pray in your way. We can imagine how glad He was : that was just what He wanted to teach them, and us.

' Thus then, shall you pray : Our Father, who art in heaven,' etc. They remembered the words carefully, and said them often, especially when they began to say Mass after the Ascension. (It comes after the Consecration.) It is the ' best of all prayers,' but even the best of all prayers is no use if we say it like a gramophone.

When He said ' Thus shall you pray,' He meant not that we should use only these words, but that all our prayers should be *like* that.

' This is the right way to approach God, these are the thoughts and desires you should have towards Him. Think of Him as your Father, think first of His glory and His Will, then ask Him trustingly for all you need.'

It is a sketch-plan, so to speak, for all our prayers, hence we study every sentence of it carefully.

> * WHY IS GOD CALLED ' OUR FATHER ' ?
>
> *God is called ' Our Father ' because He is the Father of all Christians, whom He has made His children by Holy Baptism.*
>
> *God is also the Father of all mankind because He made them all, and loves and preserves them all.*

God is Father of men in two ways

GOD is the Father of all men by creation, and He desires to be the Father of all men in a closer way by grace.

The book of Genesis gives us pictures (details not necessarily to be taken literally) of the Lord God creating the first man.

*BALTIMORE 492
ENGLISH CATECHISM 148-149

CATECHISM STORIES

After the earth had been created, and the lights of heaven, and the waters had brought forth the fishes and birds, and earth its living creatures, on the sixth day God said : '*Let us make man to our own image and likeness.*'

'*Let us....*' We can imagine God the Father speaking to God the Son and God the Holy Spirit.

'*Image and likeness.*' We may think ' likeness ' means the likeness in *nature*, man being in his soul a spirit like God ; and ' image ' means the higher resemblance of *grace*.

So ' God created man to His own image ; to the image of God He created him.'

In Gen. ii, 5–7, a different poem gives us a more detailed picture. The earth after creation was dry, because there was no rain yet, and no man to till the earth, but a spring rose up and watered all the earth. Out of the wet slime the Lord God formed the shape of a man, but he lay still with no soul yet. Then the Lord God ' breathed into his face the breath of life, and man became a living soul.'

Whether it was slime or long ages of bodily evolution doesn't make any difference : man became suddenly ' a living soul.' Adam opens his eyes and stands up, and then the first thing he does is to kneel down and lift his hands in adoration of God who has given him life.

Every time a new baby is going to be born God breathes into its face the breath of life, just as he did to Adam ; God makes every soul different.

And then in baptism the child is born again, and by grace adopted into God's own family of the Blessed Trinity.

' Father of all mankind '

A famous French Archbishop was told by his secretary that a poor woman had come to ask assistance. The secretary wanted to know how much to give her.

' How old is she ? '

' About seventy, I think.'

' Is she in great need ? '

' She says so, your Grace.'

' We must believe her. Give her twenty-five francs ' (then about a pound).

The secretary was astonished.

'Surely that is too much, your Grace ! Besides, she is a Jewess.'

'A Jewess ! Oh, that makes a difference. Go and give her fifty francs, and thank her for honouring me with a visit.'

All mankind are children of one Father. To despise others on account of colour or race is not Christian ; rather should we show them a greater charity. [See also no. 668.]

Men are all One Family

The beginning of March, 1939. World-insanity of suspicion, greed and hatred, rising to a climax. British ministers announce £580,000,000 to be spent in one year on arms, and steel air-raid shelters have begun to be distributed to all houses. German ministers announce that their air force could and would crush any opponent country 'in one short blow.' Italian newspapers filled with threats to France. American President warning dictators. War Commissar Voroshilov announcing that the Red Army had doubled its numbers and strength since 1934. Vast war in China, little war in Palestine, civil war in Spain, with several other countries joining in, and the Spaniards in Madrid beginning another war amongst themselves. Irish gun-men scattering bombs in English towns. On all hands nations being drilled to glorify and extend their own country and their supposed 'race' and to hate other countries and other races. In British Dominions and U.S.A. strict laws against immigration of most foreigners. Europe full of wandering exiles and refugees, Jews, Catholics, Socialists, bourgeois : robbed and beaten and interned in their native land, and driven to suicide by thousands, or escaping with bare life into countries willing to admit them.

From Germany 250,000 Jews had gone by now. On the French side of the Pyrenees 200,000 Catalonian refugees, interned under fearful conditions, but determined not to return to Spain.

Fifteen hundred Jewish refugees expelled from Italy and refused admission to France, said to be stranded in the Alps between the frontier posts, homeless and helpless.

CATECHISM STORIES

Amidst all this the Papal Conclave was held, and on the very first day elected the Cardinal who more than any was looked on as the champion of sane Christian reason against exaggerated claims of State and race. According to the supposed ancient prophecy of St. Malachy the new Pope was the ' Papa Angelicus '—' the Pope with a Message.'

Far into that night of March 2 Pius XII sat up preparing his first message to the world, which he spoke in Latin over the radio the next day.

To all Catholics and non-Catholics the world over he gave his greetings and the promise of his prayers. Above all he called men to ' peace, the fairest of all God's gifts, the peace which arises from justice and charity ; the peace of every soul in friendship with God, the peace of every family happily united in the holy love of Christ, the peace of nations joined to help each other in brotherly love, with each race under God's providence doing its share towards the happiness of the WHOLE GREAT FAMILY OF MANKIND.'

The true equality of man

Round a coffee-stall one night in a London street several men watched the rich people going home from the theatre in their big cars, and fell to talking about equality.

One was an American. ' Every man has equal rights with every other man,' he said. ' All men are born free and equal.'

' That's only talk,' said an English working-man. ' People aren't born equal. Some of them are born millionaires and some are born in the workhouse.'

' That's right,' said the coffee-stall keeper. ' And some are born with good brains, or good health, and some aren't.'

' It will be all the same when they're dead.' (This was a Russian Communist speaking.) ' One man doesn't matter more than another, because none of them matter at all. The only thing that matters is the mass of mankind— the whole community. The individual life is of no account.'

The next speaker was an Arab wearing a fez. ' Men are free and equal only when they are true believers in the

Prophet. Slavery is the lot of the infidel—such is the Will of Allah.'

'And what do *you* think?' said the stall-keeper to an old man who carried a bundle of newspapers.

'I think all men are equal in the sight of God,' said the old man. Then he took a handful of coppers from his pocket and spread them on the counter.

'See these 'ere pennies—there's bright ones and dull ones and thin ones and thick ones—but they're all worth a penny. And they're all stamped with the image of the King.'

Every human soul, created by God to His own image, is precious to God, is destined for heaven, and has been redeemed by the blood of Christ.

Loves and preserves them all '

God cares for us as a Father, but we must not measure His Providence by our own minds.

A boy found a snail crossing a motor road at a busy time of the day. He gave it advice and hints, with the point of his stick, but all in vain; so finally he kicked it gently with his foot into safety in the ditch.

Doubtless the snail regarded this as a catastrophe of undeserved suffering. But the boy's knowledge and intelligence were far greater than the snail's.

And God's knowledge is at *least* that much wider and His wisdom deeper than the wisest man's. We must have confidence in His good will towards us.

We are God's children by adoption

Moscow, about 1934; an early morning in winter. A boy and girl, aged about twelve and eleven, dressed in miserable rags, climb out of a lorry in a railway-yard (their lodging for the night) and go out into the hard snowy streets—first making sure no police are in sight—before stealing their way through the day. They are brother and sister, Sashka and Tania, and they have lived this way for months.

An hour or two later they are in the well-to-do part of the

CATECHISM STORIES

city, searching one of the dustbins on the pavement for scraps of food, but they couldn't find any, and Tania was crying with the cold.

The outside gate of the house opened and a boy of their own age came out. He wore a fur cap and a gaily coloured scarf and looked warm and happy. He called something to them, and they started to run away, but he caught them up easily, so they stood and looked at him suspiciously. They could not understand a word of his questions, so he produced some biscuits from his pocket and watched them eat them.

Just then a motor drove up to the house and a tall man in a rich fur coat got out, evidently the father of this foreign boy, who ran up to him and explained things. The man came up and asked them, in bad Russian, if they would come inside for a meal. Sashka made him promise not to hand them over to the police, and then they went in.

The inside of the house, large and comfortable, filled them with astonishment. The man took them to the housekeeper and she gave them a hot meal with some tea, and they found out that their host was Mr. K——, an American engineer working in Russia, and his son was named Andrew.

Afterwards Sashka and Tania told their own story to Mr. K——, as much as they knew of it. They remembered the small farm where they had been born; their father had been shot during some peasant riots, and their mother had died afterwards during a famine. An old grandmother had brought them to Moscow, and since she had died they had been homeless, living how they could. They did not want to be taken to the Government orphanages, because they wanted to keep their freedom till the summer came, and because in the orphanage they would not be able to say the prayers they had learned at home.

'Look, Dad,' said Andrew, 'why not let them stay here? I don't want them to go. We've got plenty of room!'

'Well, son, I guess they can stay till to-morrow, and we'll think about it. But you know we're going back to New York next week.'

So the housekeeper came and took them to have a bath and found some clean clothes for them, and all the evening the three children taught each other Russian and American games, and all got on very well. Sashka and Tania slept in proper beds for the first time since they had left their village years before.

When they came down next morning Mr. K—— was having breakfast.

'When we go can we take these clothes with us? Because they are warmer than ours.'

Mr. K—— said yes, they could take them. Then he looked at them and said: 'Look here, you two—would you like to come with us to America? Come and live with us there, I mean.'

It seemed too good to be true! The children stared, then Tania clapped her hands.

'Oh, that would be grand! Would you let us be your servants? Sashka would clean the boots and dig in the garden, and I would help the cook!'

'Well, no, I didn't mean that exactly. You see, I've only got Andrew—his mother is dead—and I thought it would be a good idea to have two more children in the family. If you'd like to come.'

When they realised that he meant it they threw themselves into his arms, speechless with happiness.

Everything went well. They are all in America now. Sashka has left college and gone into engineering. Tania has finished high school and is at home, learning to cook and looking after her adopted father and brother.

Our Father's home is heaven

St. Cyril was a boy who became a Christian at Caesarea in Cappadocia, third century. His rich pagan father reviled him, beat him, and at last turned him out of the house; but nothing could quench the joy in his heart, and he won many other boys to a Christian life also.

Soon he was brought before the tribunal as a Christian. Threats failed to move him. Then the magistrate offered

CATECHISM STORIES 133

to release him if he would return to his home and inheritance.

'Leaving home did not trouble me,' he answered. 'There is a real home waiting for me, much grander and more beautiful, where my Father in heaven lives.'

They took him to the fire as if for execution, then back to the tribunal. 'Why don't you get on with it?' he asked. As nothing could shake his firmness, he was led forth again to die. Some Christians around were weeping, but Cyril said : 'You ought to be a joyful escort for me. Evidently you do not know the City where I am going to live!' He watched the fire being kindled, and died in it brave to the last, with his mind fixed on his heavenly home. [See also nos. 2, 53, 383, 397, 430, 594, 677, 668.]

* WHY DO WE SAY : 'OUR' FATHER, AND NOT 'MY' FATHER?

We say 'Our' Father, and not 'My' Father, because, being all brethren, we are to pray not for ourselves only, but also for all others.

'Our Father,' and not 'My Father'

THE last words of St. Oswald, King and Martyr, are a notable instance of the prayer which thinks of others before self.

He was the pupil of St. Columba in Iona, became King of Northumbria (which he evangelised with the help of St. Aidan and Irish missionaries, for whom he often acted as interpreter) and overlord of the Christian part of Britain. In 642, being at war with Penda, the pagan king of Mercia, his small army was overwhelmed by a larger pagan force at Maserfeld (Oswestry in Shropshire). Oswald was slain with most of his followers. As the brave young king fell, with a forest of enemy swords and battle-axes brandished over him, his thought was not for himself but for his men who were suffering the same fate, and he cried out in a loud voice : 'God have mercy on their souls.' The words passed into a proverb in the North : 'God have mercy on their souls, quoth Oswald when he fell to the ground.' [See also nos. 122, 201, 364.]

*BALTIMORE 491
ENGLISH CATECHISM 150

CATECHISM STORIES

* WHEN WE SAY, 'HALLOWED BE THY NAME,' WHAT DO WE PRAY FOR?

When we say, ' Hallowed be Thy name,' we pray that God may be known, loved, and served by all His creatures.

God tells His Name to Moses

FOR this see Exod. iii, 1–14 (or No. 26, under Catechism 17). This is the name of Jehovah, or Iahveh; the Jews out of reverence never pronounced it (except the High Priest, once a year, when he entered the Holy of holies), but substituted ' Adonai ' instead when it occurred in the Scripture read aloud. Hence the true vowel-sounds of ' Jehovah ' have been forgotten.

Christians are not afraid to pronounce the Name of their Father; but they should ' hallow ' it—keep it holy—as much as the Jews did: above all by doing His Will. See parable of the two sons (Matt. xxi, 28–31).

We are made to give glory to God

Yo-San was an old Chinaman, a Christian, who worked in the rice-fields and lived in poverty in a boat on the river. One day he went to the missionary: ' Father, wouldn't it be good if we could have a real church instead of the wooden hut? '

' Indeed it would, but I'm afraid it will be a long time before we have the money.'

' Father, I should like to pay for the building of a new church.'

' Well, I hope you will be able to do your own little share towards it when the time comes.'

' But, Father, I should like to pay for the whole church myself.'

The missionary explained kindly that this was impossible, as the cost would be £500. Yo-San said he knew that, and finally produced the actual amount in money; and in answer to the questions of the astounded Father, he told how, long ago, as a young man under instruction, he had heard a former missionary explaining the words ' Hallowed

*BALTIMORE 493
ENGLISH CATECHISM 151

be Thy Name '—that the purpose of our life is to give glory to God—and had conceived the desire of some day building a temple to God's name ; so for forty years, living with no family and no house, eating only a little rice, he had managed to lay aside most of his scanty wages till he had the £500.

The missionary raised difficulties about taking all the money as Yo-San was old and would soon be unable to support himself ; but the old man said God would look after him ; and implored the Father to grant this life-long desire.

In a few months the new church was finished, and opened with a sung Mass and great rejoicings of all Christians in the neighbourhood, and Yo-San was there shedding tears of happiness. After Mass he stayed praying a long time, and was found lifeless—his heart broken with joy. That night the missionary in a dream saw Christ welcoming the old Chinaman into heaven : ' Well done, thou good and faithful servant, enter into the joy of thy Lord.'

We are made to give glory to God. ' Hallowed be Thy Name ' is a prayer that all men may do so. We should always put the glory of God first, that is why it comes first in the Our Father.

'We pray that God may be known '

In 1896 a British force conquered Ashanti and took Coomassie, the capital. Human sacrifice was a great feature of religion there, as the terrifying decorations consisting of innumerable human skulls gave evidence. King Prempeh was exiled to the Seychelles Islands, and there in due course he became a Christian (Anglican). At his first communion he said to the Bishop : ' I will give you my son : let him be ordained some day and send him to convert his own people.' After twenty-eight years' exile, Prempeh was finally allowed to return to Coomassie in 1924 and appointed chief of his former capital. On Sundays he acted as churchwarden. Four years later his son John, now an ordained clergyman of the Anglican Church, rejoined his father to labour in Ashanti.

We pray that one day all Our Lord's followers will be re-united in the one true Church ; meanwhile we can rejoice over every advance of the Christian name amidst the pagan darkness.

There is a story, rather sad, of another African chief, who died a pagan because he could never make up his mind whether to become Catholic, or Anglican, or Wesleyan. Christian unity would be the greatest help to the coming of God's kingdom.

' By all His creatures '

Thoughtless people sometimes disparage the work of the foreign missions, but of all good causes it is the closest to Our Lord's Heart.

A white trader arrived at one of the South Sea islands and a native offered to help him carry his baggage from the boat. On the way they talked about missionaries, etc., and the trader asked rather sneeringly :

' What good has Christianity done to you ? '

' I can tell you some good it has done to *you*,' replied the native. ' See that big flat stone over there ? If you had come here when I was a pagan I should have cut your throat on that stone and then I and my friends would have eaten you. Now here I am carrying your suit-cases for you instead.' [See also nos. 374, 666, 678.]

Seed of the Church

Thousands of Christians were martyred in China during the Boxer Rising of June and July, 1900.

At Tai-yuan-fou the massacre began with the burning of many Christian buildings. The Christians knew there was no hope for them, and gathered round the church and the house of the Bishop, Mgr Grassi. After several days of suspense and threatening proclamations, soldiers arrived and took away in carts the Bishop, four Franciscans, and seven Franciscan nuns, five Chinese seminarists, six orphan children, a widow and nine servants. They were lodged in a disgusting compound near the Mandarin's residence ; forty Protestants also were imprisoned next door. Three

CATECHISM STORIES

days passed, during which the priests were able to celebrate Mass and prepare their flock for martyrdom.

On the afternoon of July 8th, the clash of arms, with cries and lamentations, was suddenly heard from the next compound. The Protestants were being massacred. The Catholics gathered round their Bishop.

'The hour is come,' he said, ' kneel down and I will give you absolution.'

The soldiers came rushing in with a great noise. Seeing their victims kneeling in silence, they paused a moment in surprise, then threw themselves upon them, struck them, and, after having tied their hands behind their backs, made them come out into the compound. A Christian named Francis Lin, hidden in a corner of a street, saw the victims, as, tied in pairs, they were led or rather driven along the street under the curses and blows of the Boxers to the Viceroy's tribunal, and stopped at the *yamen* or entrance hall.

They were surrounded by soldiers and Boxers who cried : ' Down with the European devils.'. The confusion at this time seems to have been very great. Some say that the Viceroy came out and said : ' Kill them all.' Others, with more probability, say that he sat on the tribunal and made all the victims kneel before him, and then said with anger to one of the priests, whom he knew : ' How many years have you been in China ? ' ' More than thirty,' was the reply. ' Why then have you brought harm to my people; and for what end do you propagate your religion ? ' asked the Viceroy. The Bishop replied : ' We have done harm to no one, but have done much good.' ' That is not true,' shouted the Viceroy, ' you have done much ill to my people and for that I will kill you all.' ' If you do,' said the Bishop, ' you will suffer for your crime.' At this the Viceroy became furious with rage and struck the Bishop twice on the breast, calling out : ' Kill them all.' Soldiers and Boxers at once threw themselves upon their victims, striking at random, wounding right and left, cutting heads and limbs. In a few seconds they had killed them all. Then they discharged their guns with much noise, in order, as they said, to scare the souls away.

> * WHEN WE SAY, 'THY KINGDOM COME,' WHAT DO WE PRAY FOR?
>
> *When we say, 'Thy kingdom come,' we pray that God may come and reign in the hearts of all by His grace in this world, and bring us all hereafter to His heavenly kingdom.*

'Thy Kingdom Come!'

THERE is a story about a holy old monk named Cassianus. Weary of men's wickedness, he knelt alone in church praying to be taken to a better world. He fell into ecstasy with his eyes fixed on the large crucifix over the altar, and saw the five wounds on the figure begin to shine white like diamonds; then from each wound fell drops, not of blood, but of a sparkling crystal water, falling faster and faster till it formed a stream down the altar and the altar-steps and down the middle of the church and out at the main door.

The shining water lighted up the dark church and was so beautiful that the sight of it filled the monk with joy. He heard a voice at his side say: 'The living waters of Grace, which I won for men by My death on the cross,' and turned and saw Our Lord Himself standing.

Our Lord then said: 'Come with Me,' and they went through a little door to the top of the church-tower, and the monk could see all the town, streets and houses and people, spread out below. He saw the stream of living water flowing through the streets, into houses, seeking out all the people. Some people knelt down to drink from it, and he could see their souls within them become radiant like the water; he shouted to tell the other people to drink too, but he saw that nobody heard him. He asked: 'Who are these happy ones, Lord?' 'These are the souls in whom God reigns by His grace, so that they do His Will.'

Then Our Lord said again: 'Come with Me,' and in a moment they stood outside the closed Gate of Heaven, looking down from a balcony upon the earth far below. There the monk saw all the cities and countries of mankind, and the rivers of living water flowing through them, and

*BALTIMORE 494
ENGLISH CATECHISM 152

CATECHISM STORIES 139

everywhere souls in a state of grace, here few and there many, shining like stars and lighting up the darkness of the earth ; and sometimes he was terrified to see some of the stars go out, and sometimes he rejoiced when a new group of stars suddenly shone forth. Our Lord said : ' It is the Kingdom of God come upon earth,' and the monk felt that he could go on looking at that sight for ever.

Then Our Lord said : ' Now, Cassianus, you shall choose for yourself. You may go into heaven straightway by this gate, or you may go back to earth for seven years more to work and pray for the Kingdom of God. Which will you choose ? ' He fell at Our Lord's feet : ' Dear Lord, let me go back to earth for seven years.' Thereupon he came out of his ecstasy in church, and worked and prayed constantly to get men to live for the glory of God. His favourite prayer was the ' Our Father,' and whenever he came to the words, ' Thy Kingdom come,' he would stop and say them slowly over again for hours at a time. He died after seven years, with the same words on his lips.

The Kingdom of God means that God lives and reigns in the hearts of men by His grace.

God's grace is precious beyond all else

' *The kingdom of heaven is like a treasure hidden in a field* ' (Matt. xiii, 44). A rich man heard that brigands were approaching the village, and hastily threw his gold and jewels and plate into an iron box and buried it ; the brigands came and killed him in his house and burnt it.

A hundred years passed and the rich man and his house were forgotten. A poor labourer named Ephraim working for a farmer was digging a hole to plant a new tree and discovered the treasure ; too heavy and risky to carry off, he covered it up and dug the hole for the tree elsewhere.

After his work he went home, put on his best clothes, and went to the farmer and asked him to sell the field, offering ten pounds—all his savings. The farmer said fifty.

Ephraim was determined to get the field before night if he could. He went to a dealer and offered to sell his cottage. The dealer came to look at the cottage, but would only give £30. Ephraim then got from the dealer a further

£5 for his donkey, then £3 for his furniture, £1 for his bed, 10s. for his overcoat, and finally 10s. for the best clothes he was wearing.

So he put on his working-clothes (now his only possession) and hurried off with £50 to buy the field, and next day was a rich man.

Our Lord means that we must let God have His kingdom in our hearts, nothing else matters. That is the greatest Treasure.

We have found the Greatest Treasure, if we are in a state of grace, and we must be ready to let everything else go rather than lose it by mortal sin.

Grace is like the £50 the man had : he had nothing else, but he was rich with that, because it would get him the Treasure : and grace gives us a right to heaven.

The State of Grace

Grace makes our soul marvellously beautiful to the eyes of God.

Medical inspection day at school in a poor district. A little girl returns to the headmistress. ' Well, what did they say to you ? '

' They said I was a miserable little specimen. They thought I didn't hear, Sister. . . . Sister, they didn't know I made my first Communion yesterday, did they ? ' [See also nos. 382–386, 434, 439, 440.]

The Militant Kingdom of God

Some centuries ago, when Europe was in danger of being overrun by the Turks, two lads named Johann and Maurice were living in a border-province of one of the Christian kingdoms near the Danube. (Add Elisa, a sister of Maurice, if the audience is a mixed one.) There were rumours of war, then over the mountains poured the cruel hordes of Islam, who seized the whole province and terrorized the inhabitants.

One day the lads ventured near the headquarters, where the Sultan was holding a review. Black and hideous, he sat on a high throne, with an equally hideous General on each side, and thousands of his black-armoured cavalry in a

CATECHISM STORIES 141

motionless square. His recruiting officers led forward groups of inhabitants in chains, whom they had seized for military service.

The Sultan addressed these ferociously : ' Miserable dogs, you belong now to my army. I promise you plenty to eat and drink and you can plunder the people of the countries we pass through. In return you are my slaves, body and soul. I am a master without pity. I shall put you in front of every battle, and my captains will drive you on with whips. If you fall you will be left to your fate, for I can get plenty more like you. If you are caught trying to desert, you shall die with horrible tortures. At the end of the war, if you are still alive, we shall leave you to starve, and throw you into dungeons if you complain. So there is nothing for you to hope for, except the pleasure of destroying the cities of King Michael.'

The two lads saw that a sergeant nearby had noticed them and was pointing them out to his officer. They agreed they would rather die than join that army, and made a dash into a wood and got clear away after hairbreadth escapes.

After several days' travelling they fell in with a party of men who told them that the King was gathering an army, and they were going to join it ; and they told how everybody loved the King for his goodness and bravery ; so the lads kept with this party. Soon they came to the camp which was the assembling point for King Michael's army. The young King, on horseback, in white armour, was addressing his troops, who also wore white with red cross on breast.

' My comrades,' he said, ' you have answered my call to arms ; to-morrow we march together to rescue our countrymen from the cruel invaders. I tell you beforehand that it is going to be a hard and perilous campaign. Every man must obey my orders, for the safety of the army depends on it. But I shall order you to do nothing that I will not do myself. When you are hungry and tired out you will see your King hungry and tired out too ; you will see him with you where the battle-smoke is thickest, and you will see him riding in the front of the charge. But though the war will be long and severe, the final victory is absolutely certain, and then we shall all share the glory and rejoicing, and there will be great rewards especially for you who have been with me from the beginning.'

The soldiers cheered wildly. Then the parade was dismissed, and the King walked from group to group talking and laughing with his men.

The lads spoke to an officer and he took them as volunteers to the King, who said: 'Can you go through everything with me, and not turn back?' They promised. So they went with the officer, and he asked if they could ride, and gave them horses and uniform. (Elisa said: 'Is there anything the girls can do?' and was appointed to help with the wounded.) Next day they marched away, and all had many adventures at the war, and when victory came Maurice and Johann were captains in the King's bodyguard.

King Michael stands for Jesus Christ. The Catholic Church is the Army of the Kingdom of God, fighting not with worldly armament but with the 'battle-equipment of God' as described in Eph. vi, 13.

When we say 'Thy Kingdom come' we pray for the victory of the Church.

> * WHEN WE SAY, 'THY WILL BE DONE ON EARTH AS IT IS IN HEAVEN,' WHAT DO WE PRAY FOR?
>
> *When we say, 'Thy will be done on earth as it is in heaven,' we pray that God may enable us, by His grace, to do His will in all things, as the Blessed do in heaven.*

'That God may enable us by His grace'

THE room was full, and the auctioneer was selling different articles. After a time he picked up an old battered violin, and holding it aloft said: 'Any bids?' A smile went round, it was such a shabby-looking thing, then one man said 'a shilling.' There was a general laugh, and shouts of 'Give it him,' 'Let him have it.'

The auctioneer paused, and then said: 'Perhaps someone would like to play it?' There was a short delay and an old man stepped on to the platform; raised the violin to his chin, tried the bow across a few times; then he drew

*BALTIMORE 495
ENGLISH CATECHISM 153

CATECHISM STORIES 143

from the old instrument such an exquisite melody that his listeners were moved almost to tears. And as the beautiful strains died down there was a burst of applause from all in the room.

The auctioneer picked up the violin anew. ' Any bids ? ' ' Five pounds.' ' Ten pounds,' here and so on until it was finally knocked down at a hundred pounds. What had happened ? It was the same violin as before, but now they had heard it under the touch of a master's hand.

We feel very useless and worn and helpless, but under the touch of Our Master's hand we are of value and can achieve great things.

' I can do all things ' (says St. Paul) ' in Him who strengtheneth me.'

His Will, not our own will

Two mothers, one rich and one poor, each had an only son. During an epidemic both sons were at the point of death and the mothers were inconsolable. The rich mother would not listen to the priest who suggested resigning herself to the Will of God, but kept saying passionately : ' He must not die ! he shall not die ! O God, you must not let him die ! ' The poor woman—a widow—prayed God for her son's recovery, but added ' Not my will but Thine be done.'

The rich son lived, the poor son died. The rich young man lived to bring shame on his mother by a life of reckless dissipation with bad companions, ending after a few years with complicity in a murder and death on the gallows.

The poor widow, in her sorrows and difficulties, lived her remaining years still adoring the Will of God. She died a serene and happy death, holding out her arms as if she saw her son : ' Oh, my dear boy, you have come to take your poor old mother to heaven ! '

On earth or in heaven, God's Will

St. Ignatius one day said to Fr. Lainez : ' Suppose God let you choose, either to go to heaven now, or to stay on earth with the chance of doing something for His glory ; which would you choose ? '

'I would make certain of heaven now,' replied Fr. Lainez.

'Well,' said the saint. 'For my part I would remain on earth, to do the Will of God. As for the saving of my soul, I am sure God would take care of it. I don't believe He would let anyone perish who, for love of Him, had delayed entering heaven.'

'As the Blessed do in heaven'

Towards the end of the thirteenth century, in Florence, a young girl of noble family, Piccarda Donati, entered a convent of Franciscan nuns against the will of her family. She made her vows, but one day her brother forced his way in and dragged her home, where she was compelled to marry a turbulent noble named Rossellino da Tosa. In a short time, still only a young girl, she fell ill and died.

She was a relative of Dante, who some years later was writing the *Paradiso*.

In the poem he tells us that in the first or lowest of the heavens, that of the moon, he saw one of the spirits, a young and beautiful girl, who seemed to wish to speak with him, and he asks her name.

'If you will look at me carefully, you will soon know. I am Piccarda.'

Then he recognises her, though she is so transfigured by celestial joy that he had not known her at first. She explains that she is in the lowest heaven because she had failed to keep her vow, though submitting only to force.

'I see you are happy,' said Dante. 'But tell me—do you not long for a higher place in heaven, where you would know more and love more?'

The idea amuses Piccarda. She smiles at the question, and so do the other spirits that cluster round listening.

'Our will is at rest, brother,' she says, 'we could not wish for the higher heavens for that would be out of harmony with the Will of God, who has placed us here. Love makes our will one with God's Will. In His Will is our peace.'

The last six words, *In sua voluntade è nostra pace*, are one of the world's famous lines of poetry.

CATECHISM STORIES 145

It is as true for us on earth as for the Blessed in heaven. 'Thy will be done,' is sometimes considered as a prayer of sorrowful resignation, but it should be rather a prayer of joy and gratitude.

Our troubles are permitted by God's Will

There was once a woman who was always grumbling. Her husband, she thought, made more work than other husbands, her children took less care of their clothes than other children did. Her home seemed colder in winter and hotter in summer than anyone else's—in fact she thought God had given her a heavier cross to bear than He had given to any of her neighbours.

One night she dreamed that her Guardian Angel stood by her bed. He told her to rise as he had something he wanted to show her. She got up and followed him down the street. Many of the doors were marked with large crosses. The Angel beckoned, and she peeped through the windows. In one room she saw a mother and father kneeling by the bedside of a dying child. In another she saw a poor blind woman sitting beside an empty grate. In another, the bread-winner lay dead. Every house seemed to have some trouble. At last they stopped before a house with a tiny cross on the door, and as she looked at it she realised it was *her own* house.

When afterwards she was inclined to grumble she thought of all those who were worse off than herself, and instead of grumbling she said gladly and thankfully: 'Thy will be done, whatever it is.' [See also nos. 385, 388, 550, 554, 566.]

> * [1] WHEN WE SAY, 'GIVE US THIS DAY OUR DAILY BREAD,' WHAT DO WE PRAY FOR?
>
> *When we say, 'Give us this day our daily bread,' we pray that God may give us daily all that is necessary for soul and body.*

'Give us this day our daily bread'

THERE was once a man eating his dinner out of doors, some

[1] This and the three following Catechism questions are not included in the *Abbreviated Catechism* because the answers are so obvious; they are printed here for the sake of introducing the stories to the second half of the *Paternoster*.

*BALTIMORE 496
ENGLISH CATECHISM 154

bread and fish, and his little boy came along hungry, asking him for a piece of bread. The father picked up a stone, and tossed it to the boy : ' Eat that.'

The boy began to cry. ' Can't I have some fish ? '

' Here's a fish for you ! ' and the father captured a little lizard in his hand and held it out to the boy by the tail, so that the boy ran away screaming.

An impossible story, you say : no father would ever act that way.

Exactly, says Our Lord. And our heavenly Father is not like that either. He is a *good* Father, who knows how to give good gifts to those that ask Him. He is the Giver of all gifts.

Read aloud Matt. vii, 7–11 ; vi, 25–32. See also stories 39, 167, 173.

' Give us,' not ' give me '

We are told to say ' Give *us* this day,' not ' Give *me* ' ; this reminds us to think of all the other children of God. For instance, if we have any possessions we should be ready to share the use of them with our brothers and sisters in God's family.

A story is told of Lady Jane Grey, before she became the young ten-days' Queen of England. She was brought up very piously, though not as a Catholic. One cold winter's day at her country estate she dressed herself in rags, hiding her face with a shawl, and went round with a basket begging at the houses of her farmers and tenants. Some sent her away angrily, others gave her stale rubbish ; only at a poor labourer's cottage was she taken in to the fire and given some fresh cake.

Next day all these people received an unexpected invitation to the manor-house. On the dining-table there awaited them an equally unexpected dinner—stale crusts for one, a rotten apple for another, raw carrots for a third, an empty plate for some, and so on. Only the old labourer and his wife were served with good helpings of roast beef and plum pudding.

Then Lady Jane came into the hall and said : ' Yesterday I went to you disguised as a beggar to try your charity.

CATECHISM STORIES

To-day you have the same food served to you that you gave to me. Consider, that in the next world you will be served in the same way.'

The Prayer of Faith

The prayer of faith can work miracles, and the friends of God are not afraid to ask for them.

When St. Brigid was a girl she often used to go with her mother, a bond-woman, up to a mountain dairy on the green slopes of Faughart, to collect the butter of twelve cows belonging to the Druid for whom they worked. Making the butter, Brigid used to set aside a generous portion for the poor, and one day, after the poor had received their share, or perhaps more, there was not enough for the Druid's household. Fearing her mother would be distressed, Brigid knelt and prayed that everything would be right; and when her mother visited the kitchen there was so much milk and butter that she praised the maids for their industry; but the maids knew the real reason.

Brigid put her prayer into Gaelic song, and this is the English of it:

> *O my prince, O my prince,*
> *You can do anything like this!*
> *Bless, O God—it is a lawful prayer—*
> *Bless my dairy with Your right hand!*
>
> *My kitchen, O my kitchen,*
> *The kitchen that God gave me,*
> *The kitchen that my King has blessed,*
> *My kitchen now has butter!*
>
> *Mary's Son, my Friend, He came,*
> *He came and blessed my dairy!*
> *The Prince of the world came hither!*
> *May we have welfare with Him.*

(Acknowledgements to ' Roddy the Rover,' in the *Irish Catholic*.)

Praying for rain

One instance, famous in Christian history, of prayer for temporal favour, is the story of the ' Thundering Legion.'

The Emperor Marcus Aurelius (second century A.D.) was campaigning in the mountains of Bohemia. The army was surrounded by vast numbers of the barbarian tribes, and was suffering terribly from lack of water. The only chance was to fight a way through. In one of the legions there were many Christians, and these knelt down and prayed to the true God for help. Immediately dark storm-clouds rolled up and covered the sky, thunder crashed, lightning flashed into the faces of the enemy, and torrents of rain filled the Roman helmets and refreshed the whole army. They took advantage of the storm to attack and the barbarians were completely routed.

The event made a great sensation all through the Empire. The Emperor reported it to the Senate (ascribing it, however, to the pagan god, Jupiter Pluvius), and it is still to be seen commemorated on the column of Marcus Aurelius in Rome. He gave to this legion the title of *Legio Fulminata*, Thundering Legion.

His gratitude did not lead him to stop the persecution of Christians, but he did protect Christians in the army by decreeing the death-penalty for those who informed falsely against them. (*Clergy Review*, Dec., 1938, p. 492.)

Answered in a different way

A certain naval officer was very keen to get transferred to a particular ship. He made a novena and got all the prayers he could for this intention. He was very disappointed when he got orders from the Admiralty to join another ship. He was tempted to think his prayers were wasted, till one day he opened a newspaper and saw that the ship he had been so eager to join had been sunk and all on board had been drowned.

In this case the unexpected answer came soon and was easy to see, but if like God we could see the whole sweep of events we should see that all prayers are answered *somehow*. [See also no. 667.]

Refusal is an answer too

A little girl was travelling with her father in an express train. She noticed the communication-cord, and he explained how passengers could use it to have the train stopped. Later she was standing by the open window, and her doll fell through. In great distress, she implored her father to pull the cord and stop the train. He tried to dry her tears, but would not stop the train. Without listening to his explanations she went on : ' You can easily make it stop, Daddy, why don't you ? ' etc., etc. But he still refused. Afterwards in a calmer mood she was able to understand that it would not be right to upset the time-table and put all the other travellers to inconvenience merely for the sake of a doll.

So it may often be when God answers our petitions for temporal favours by refusal. He likes us to ask for them, but He also likes us to leave the decision to Him : ' If it is according to Thy Will.' (Illustration from Rev. G. R. Balleine, *The Young Churchman*. [See nos. 123, 423, 426, 431, 667.]

> * WHEN WE SAY, ' FORGIVE US OUR TRESPASSES, AS WE FORGIVE THEM THAT TRESPASS AGAINST US,' WHAT DO WE PRAY FOR ?
>
> *When we say, ' Forgive us our trespasses, as we forgive them that trespass against us,' we pray that God may forgive us our sins, as we forgive others the injuries they do to us.*

' As we forgive them that trespass against us '

FATHER ODIN, one of the early North American missionaries, tells us how one day returning from a journey he saw some Indians hunting ; on seeing him they rode up and greeted him gladly, and asked him to come to their chief who was ill.

He found the old man lying in his wigwam, desperately ill from poison which had been administered to him by an enemy.

' " You are very ill, my brother."

' " Yes, Black Robe, I am suffering very much pain."

' " I am sure that after you leave this world you would desire to be admitted into the palace of the Great Spirit ? "

' " Oh, yes, my Father, above all things."

*BALTIMORE 497

'"But you know that you could not enter therein unless I washed you on the head" (it is by these words that the missionary explains to the savages the Sacrament of Baptism).

'"Oh, Black Robe!" answered the chief, "wash me on my head, for I love the Great Spirit with all my heart!"

'On receiving this beautiful answer I at once began to instruct him in our Holy Faith, and from time to time I asked him if he firmly believed what I said.

'"Oh, yes, Black Robe," he said; "most certair'y I believe every word you have spoken."

'These savages have such horror of a lie that they cannot imagine it to be possible that anyone whom they respect could tell a lie.'

Next morning the priest came back to finish the instructions, but hesitated to baptize him because he knew the fierce vengefulness of the Indian character, and wondered how he would ever get the old chief to forgive the enemy who had poisoned him.

'With this thought in my mind I took the crucifix into my hands, and showed him the sufferings which the Great Spirit had endured from the hands of His white children. I told him that before dying He forgave them, and after His death went to His Father in Heaven to pray to Him that He might also forgive them. Then I told him that what the Great Spirit required of His children in this world, of whatever colour they were, was that they would from their hearts forgive all those who had ever done them any harm, and that unless they did this, He would not receive them into His kingdom.

'"Well, then," said the chief, "since such is the Will of the Great Spirit, I forgive from my heart him who has done me this evil."

'And in order to prove the sincerity of his words, he assembled around him the principal men of his tribe, and forbade them, on any account whatsoever, to take any vengeance on his greatest enemy.

'I could not restrain my admiration at this heroic deed, and from my inmost heart gave thanks to God for these Christian sentiments in the heart of one who, in his savage

CATECHISM STORIES

life, had never till now known God, yet who loved Him so truly.

'How could I for a moment longer defer his baptism? As soon as he saw me putting on the sacred vestments, he rose from his humble couch and sat upon it. Then taking into his hands the holy crucifix, he continued to gaze upon it, or raise his eyes heavenwards, while I performed over him the sacred rite.

'Four days afterwards he departed this life, to receive, let us hope, the crown of the elect in Paradise, from the just Judge who is not " a respecter of persons," and who, in a special manner, is the Father of those who are humble in heart.'

The necessity of forgiving

A priest of Antioch named Sulpicius had steadfastly refused to sacrifice to the gods, even under torture, and was being led away to be beheaded.

On the way, a Christian named Nicephorus ran up to him. He had quarrelled bitterly with Sulpicius and now sought reconciliation.

'Martyr of Christ!' he said, on his knees. 'Forgive me, for I have wronged thee.'

But Sulpicius refused to speak to him, even at the place of execution.

But when the moment came to kneel under the executioner's sword, he turned pale.

'No, no!' he said, 'I will obey the Emperor. I will sacrifice to the gods.'

Again Nicephorus ran up to him, and implored him not to lose his martyr's crown at this last moment. In vain. Sulpicius went off to sacrifice.

'Then I will take his place,' said Nicephorus. 'Tell the Prefect I am a Christian.'

So Nicephorus won the martyr's crown and Sulpicius turned coward, and all the Christians said it was because he would not forgive. (See also story 71, on St. John Gualbert.)

Forgiving our enemies generously

James Connolly, the Dublin labour leader, was commander at the General Post Office in the Easter Week rising of 1916.

He had signed the proclamation which said: 'In the name of God and of the dead generations from which she receives her old tradition of nationhood, Ireland through us summons her children to her flag and strikes for her freedom.'

Wounded, captured, court-martialled, sentenced to death, he was carried in a chair to the execution-yard.

'Will you say a word of forgiveness for the men who have to shoot you?' said the priest.

'I forgive all brave men who do their duty.'

The order to fire was given and the rifles crashed out.
[See also nos. 71, 297, 394, 626, 651, 675.]

> * WHEN WE SAY, 'LEAD US NOT INTO TEMPTATION,' WHAT DO WE PRAY FOR?
>
> *When we say, 'Lead us not into temptation,' we pray that God may give us grace not to yield to temptation.*

Keep out of temptation!

By the following story, St. Anthony of Egypt taught his followers that we are often the cause of our own temptations.

'One day there was a very loud knocking on the door of the monastery. When I opened it there stood a man of enormous size. Very frightened, I asked who he was.

'"I am Satan."

'"And what do you want here?"

'"I want to know why you monks and all Christians are always cursing me?"

'"They have good reason to curse you, wicked spirit; for you are always laying snares for them to lead them into sin."

'"Well, I am not so much to blame as you think. Men lead themselves into sin by seeking the occasions of sin, though they know they will probably fall. As for me, my

*BALTIMORE 498, 46-47
ENGLISH CATECHISM 156

CATECHISM STORIES

power is gone since God became man. Christians can easily overcome me, if they use the weapons they have. So why blame me when they lose their souls?"

'I said: "My Lord Jesus Christ, I thank Thee that Thou hast overcome the devil and given help to Thy servants."

'As soon as Satan heard that holy Name he vanished completely.'

Don't argue with temptation

Turn it down at once. To consider offending God as a possibility is more than half-way to sin.

A patrician came to the philosopher Epictetus and said: 'Nero commands me to play the buffoon in the arena. This is a grievous thing to me; what would you do in my place?'

Epictetus answered: 'In your place I would obey Nero.'

'What! you would play the buffoon in the arena?'

'No,' said Epictetus, 'I would not. But you may as well do so, since you are willing to discuss the matter.'

Making temptation remote

In Greek legend the Sirens, seeming like beautiful maidens, sat on the rocky shore of a dangerous, narrow strait through which ships had to pass. They sang so enchantingly that the mariners would forget their oars and helm, and the ships would drift on to the rocks and be destroyed.

When Odysseus sailed that way he wanted to hear the singing and yet to keep his ship safe. So he filled the ears of his sailors with wax; then had himself bound firmly to the mast with ropes, making the men promise to take no notice of his struggles or orders while the ship passed through the straits. By this exercise of foresight they passed through the temptation safe, though while listening to the Sirens Odysseus made frantic efforts to keep the ship in the enchantment.

We should not listen to temptation at all if possible;

but if there is a good reason for going into it, we should make the temptation 'remote.'

The best way of all (for those who are equal to it) is to overcome evil by good, e.g. meeting the seven capital sins by their opposite virtues, beating the temptation at its own game.

It is related that Orpheus with his lute once sailed through the straits of the Sirens; but he sang and played so divinely that the siren-song was drowned and the sailors were entirely absorbed in listening to Orpheus.

Temptations resisted bring strength

St. Thomas Aquinas, having become a Dominican novice, while studying at Naples at the age of nineteen, was kidnapped by his brothers and confined for two years in their castle at Rocca-Secca. To break down his vocation and vows, they paid a woman of bad life to hide herself in his room and tempt him. Failing by ordinary ways to convince her that she was not wanted, at last he snatched a burning piece of wood from the fire and forced her to retreat before it out through the door. Then he marked a cross on the wall and knelt down to pray: ecstasy came to him, and he seemed to see an angel who girded him with a cord in token of chastity. The girdle caused a pain so sharp that he cried out in his ecstasy, and his guards ran into the room. He told this vision years afterwards to his confessor, and said that he had never afterwards felt any difficulty in resisting temptations to impurity. [See also nos. 9, 11, 146, 243, 303, 319, 601, 602, 664.]

> * WHEN WE SAY, 'DELIVER US FROM EVIL,' WHAT DO WE PRAY FOR?
>
> *When we say, 'Deliver us from evil,' we pray that God may free us from all evil, both of soul and body.*

'Deliver us from evil'

THAT is, from all evil, whether of soul or body. Our Lord who taught us to pray for this, also Himself set many free from evil of both kinds. Besides His bodily cures, there

*BALTIMORE 499
ENGLISH CATECHISM 157

CATECHISM STORIES

were many whom he delivered from evil spirits. Two cases are related in detail : the man of the Gerasenes (Luke viii, 26-39) and the lunatic boy (Matt. xvii, 14-20).

Some evil spirits (He says) are cast out only by prayer and fasting. The prayer ' Deliver us from evil ' needs to be reinforced by self-denial.

' From all evil, past, present, and to come '

God's full answer to this prayer comes only when His friends are set free from all evils of this life and emerge into the glorious liberty of the sons of God. For some, like the martyrs, it is a sudden change from the worst that this world can do to the best reward that God's gratitude can devise.

'St. Joan of Arc, chained up in a dungeon, guarded always by soldiers, was questioned every day for three months ; and all that time her voices told her to " speak boldly, fear nothing ; God would help her, she would be delivered." But she thought it meant a miracle or a rescue. Then one morning they came and said she was to die that day. At first she could not believe it, passionate lamentations, then calmness, but (if we can believe the bystanders) she was filled with dismay and a kind of despair. Her voices, her mission from God, seemed all a deception ; her whole world fallen in pieces around her. Well, there was still God and the Blessed Sacrament ; they let her go to Confession and receive Holy Communion, for which she had so often asked in vain. Even then they worried her with questions about the voices. She said : " I believe in God alone, and not the voices ; they deceived me." And it was not until the very last moment, fastened to the stake and the fire lighted, that God made everything clear to her and the great crowd heard her crying out with a loud voice amid the smoke and flames : " My voices were of God ; they did not deceive me ! " ' (From *Two hundred sermon-notes*, p. 75.)

God can set us free

Acts xii, 1-17 (St. Peter's miraculous deliverance from prison, while the Church was praying for him) is a story that illustrates well the petition 'Libera nos a malo,' as regards bodily evils.

God's protection can work through natural means

Winter of 1812, Napoleon's Army retreating across Germany. In a lonely farm-house near the main road, the family awaited with dread the passing of the disorganised and desperate troops, who would certainly seize all food and animals, and even furniture, etc., for fuel, for the weather was very cold. Eastward the sky was red that night with the burning farms and villages; the family knew it would be their own turn next day. They knelt and prayed earnestly for God's protection. The old grandmother especially kept reciting the prayers for wartime, in which the words occur: 'Build Thou up a wall around us, that the enemy may not approach our habitation.' Hearing these words, the farmer said it seemed too much to ask of God to build a wall round them, but the grandmother shook her head; and they slept in their clothes, expecting to hear soldiers breaking in the door any moment. But the night passed without alarm; in the dawn they were astonished to see that there had been a deep fall of snow, and the wind had piled up a great snow-drift which completely hid the farm-house from the sight of anyone on the road. All that day and the next the French were passing, but behind its white wall the farm and its inhabitants remained unobserved and safe. [See also nos. 22, 241, 248.]

* WHAT IS THE CHIEF PRAYER TO THE BLESSED VIRGIN WHICH THE CHURCH USES?

The chief prayer to the Blessed Virgin which the Church uses is the Hail Mary.
We should frequently say the Hail Mary to put us in mind of the Incarnation of the Son of God; and to honour our Blessed Lady, the Mother of God.

The making of the 'Hail Mary'

STRANGE that any Christian should object to a prayer which is addressed to Our Lady in Holy Scripture itself.

*BALTIMORE 86-87
ENGLISH CATECHISM 160-164

CATECHISM STORIES

For the making of the first part of the Hail Mary see Luke i, 28, and i, 42.

Legend says that St. Ildephonsus, Bishop of Toledo (d. 667), was the first to combine these greetings in a prayer. Going into his cathedral at night he found Our Lady seated on his episcopal throne, with a choir of virgins round her singing her praises. He drew near to her, genuflecting three times, at each genuflection repeating the words of the Archangel and St. Elizabeth. Our Lady showed her pleasure and rewarded him with the gift of a beautiful chasuble. Later on was added the word 'Jesus' followed by 'Amen.'

The second part of the Hail Mary as we have it now probably came from Italy. A copy is said to exist in the handwriting of St. Antoninus of Florence (d. 1459). 'An *Ave Maria* identical with our own, except for the omission of the single word *nostrae*, stands printed at the head of a little work of Savonarola's issued in 1495, of which there is a copy in the British Museum.'

(For this, and further interesting information, see article 'Hail Mary,' by Fr. Thurston, S.J., in the *Catholic Encyclopedia*.)

The power of the 'Hail Mary'

A gangster convicted of several murders was awaiting the electric chair in the condemned cell, and the prison chaplain made endless efforts to get him to the sacraments, all in vain. 'Go away—leave me alone,' was the only response. Full of heartfelt compassion the priest sent up a lightning prayer to the Mother of God ; then he said to the criminal :

'I'll go, then, but will you do me one little favour first ? '

'All right, what is it ? '

'Let us say together one Hail Mary ! '

They began it together, but with the very first words the grace of repentance invaded the hardened heart ; tears flowed from his eyes, he asked for confession and absolution, and died calmly with Our Lady's rosary in his hand and her name on his lips.

'And at the hour of our death'

A true story. A priest was asked by a hospital sister to visit Number Seven in Ward 3, very ill. The priest found the patient (as he thought) not very ill, and in conversation found he had long ceased to practise his religion, but had always kept up a promise made to his mother, to say one Hail Mary every night before going to sleep.

Before the priest had left him the patient had made his confession, with much devotion.

Leaving the ward, the priest met the sister and found that he had been in Ward 4 instead of Ward 3, and had not yet seen the Number Seven of the sister's request. This was soon put right, but the priest felt thankful for the mistake which had led him to the lapsed Catholic's bedside.

He felt still more thankful next day when he heard that the man he absolved had had a sudden collapse and had passed away still unconscious.

The priest remembered that the man had always kept up his 'Hail Mary': 'Pray for us sinners now and at the hour of our death.'

Our Lady had not forgotten his prayer.

'To honour Our Blessed Lady'

'My special friends at Exeter (Cathedral) are the little street fiddler and the acrobat high up in the vaulting shaft corbel of one of the piers in the nave. The fiddler and the acrobat standing on his head are both on the north side of the nave, and immediately facing them, on the corresponding pillar, is the figure of Our Lady holding the Holy Child in her arms.

'The figures, of course, represent the old story of "Our Lady's Tumbler." He was a wandering player and dancer who wanted to serve God. But everyone despised him, for he was only a poor wretch and no scholar. The legend tells how one day he came upon a church, and crouched down by an altar. Above it stood the figure of Our Lady, the Holy Mary. He strips and dances. "Lady, I cannot chant, nor read to you; but, certes, I would pick for you a choice of all my finest feats. Now, may I be like the bull-calf that leaps and bounds before his mother. Lady, who are no whit bitter to such as serve you truly, whosoever I am, may it be for you."

'Then he began his leaps before her, low and small, great and high, first under and then over, saluting and vaulting. "Lady, you are the *mon-joie* that kindles all the world." At last he dies, and the people hear the angels singing for joy about him. The story ends thus: "In happy hour he tumbled; in happy hour he served; and thereby won high honour such that none may compare with." For many years he went alone each day to the crypt to do his tricks and dances for he would have no man know his doings save God alone and he believed that God understood his meaning. But some stone-carver remembered the story. For some six hundred years the little tumbler has stood on his head, and the fiddler has played away. For six hundred years their eyes have been fixed upon the pillar across the nave to the figures of "his most sweet, dear Mother and her Son, her Lord."'
(From the *Church Times*.)

Devotion to Our Lady

St. Crispin of Viterbo (Capuchin lay-brother, eighteenth century) had such devotion to Our Lady that he was called 'the apostle of Mary.' In the monastery garden he made a little shrine of boughs in which he placed her statue. He kept a lamp burning before it and strewed corn around so that the birds would come and join him in singing to his Queen. Some of the brothers said his shrine would be destroyed by the first wind or rain; but he said : ' What rain ? What wind ? The very mountains will be blown down before this little shelter of my Lady, who commands the winds and the storms and the whole heaven.' And so it happened, for great storms came and trees were blown down, but his little shrine stood unharmed through everything. In return for his devotion, Our Lady often cured the sick to whom were taken flowers from Brother Crispin's shrine or oil from Brother Crispin's lamp.

Our Lady answers a Novena

In the *Telegramme du Pas de Calais* of August 25, 1938, appeared an account of a Lourdes cure at Arras.

On the previous day Madame Debuisson had returned from Lourdes to Arras with her son Omer, who she declared was cured on the pilgrimage. Before his departure the doctor had certified that he was ' affected with paralysis of all the limbs, with cerebral trouble. His case must be considered absolutely incurable.'

Here is the mother's account as given to the newspaper reporter :

' My son has been ill for eighteen years and was affected with encephalitis. Twelve years ago, after a violent emotion, my poor child became completely paralysed. I consulted the best doctors ; one after another they gave me to understand that medical science was powerless to cure this kind of malady.

' Twice I went with him to Lourdes, begging the Holy Virgin to give him back his health, but she was deaf to my prayers.

' I went on looking after him. He could not move his limbs, nor speak, nor even masticate his food. All I could do was to pour some liquid into the back of his throat. I had to invent all sorts of little ideas to make things easier for him ; for he was incapable even of driving away a fly or of saying what he wanted, except by his look. I put all my trust in Our Lady of Lourdes, and decided to go for the third time with the National Pilgrimage. The journey was dreadful. At the Hospital de Lourdes the nurses had to send for me because they did not know how to give my son his food, so I went every day at meal-times. On Monday at midday I saw that his jaw had begun to work and I called the nurses' attention to this sudden change, then I hurried home for my own meal, and came back quickly to the Hospital, where my dear boy welcomed me by making the military salute. Soon afterwards I had the happiness of hearing his voice for the first time for twelve years.'

Full of joy she then made her son show the reporter how well he could walk, and make the sign of the cross.

CATECHISM STORIES

'This marvellous cure,' adds the newspaper, ' is truly a blessing on the parish of St. Nicholas-en-Cité, which together with its devoted clergy had made a special novena to Our Lady, every night at Benediction, for M. Omer Debuisson.'

Our Lady's power

As an instance of a recent miracle at Lourdes, a M. Auguste Brunet, of Boulogne, was cured of tuberculous kidney during the pilgrimage of the diocese of Arras, 1938.

The certificate of the Lourdes Bureau des Constations Medicales states :

' Auguste Brunet, aged 42, living at Boulogne : genitourinary tuberculosis : left kidney removed in 1936 by Dr. Houvel. . . . The patient suffering from cystitis, with great pain, had to travel as a stretcher-case.

'. . . At present the fistule lombaire is cured. The pains disappeared two days after bathing at the piscine. . . . Conclusion, under reserve of further examinations : Brunet appears to be cured of his cystitis and his tuberculosis of the kidneys.

' Lourdes, July 2, 1938.'

The people of Boulogne were very pleased because this cure happened on the eve of a Congress which was to be held there in honour of Our Lady of Boulogne.

'Ask Our Lady for everything '

Mr. John Traynor, of Liverpool, subject of a remarkable cure at Lourdes in 1923, says that his mother ' always taught us to ask Our Blessed Lady for everything and to thank her for everything, so all my life from a little child I have been devoted to Our Blessed Lady.'

He was a sailor in the mercantile marine, entered the Navy in 1914, took part in the defence of Antwerp, and was wounded by a shell-fragment in the head. Later, in Gallipoli, he took part in the landing of April, 1915, and the fighting ashore, finally in a bayonet-charge being wounded by machine-gun bullets, one of which did severe damage to his right arm, severing the large nerves, and causing paralysis and wasting of the muscles.

Several unsuccessful operations were performed during the next year or two, but he always refused to have the arm amputated. He began to have severe epileptic attacks, and the surgeons operated on his head-wound also. He was granted a war-pension for 100 per cent disability, and in 1922 at last left hospital and was put under special treatment at home. By this time he could not walk or stand, had no sensation in his limbs or control over bowels, had not moved his arm for eight years, and suffered frequent epileptic fits.

He was offered a place in the Home for Incurables at Mossley Hill, but instead went with the Liverpool Pilgrimage to Lourdes, July, 1923.

On the second day, on the way from the Grotto to bathe at the Piscines, he had a severe fit and blood flowed from his mouth. However, he insisted afterwards on bathing, and from that time he had no more fits. Otherwise his condition continued unchanged until the ninth and last immersion, when his legs suddenly became violently agitated, and he felt he could get on his feet, but the attendants would not let him do so. Afterwards at the Procession, just after he had been blessed with the Monstrance, he felt the same kind of agitation in his arm, and burst the bandages and suddenly felt he could do anything; but back at the Asile he only walked seven paces, with difficulty, and went to bed in great pain. After a good night's rest, however, he heard the bell of the Basilica ringing the Ave, jumped out of bed, and knelt on the floor to finish his Rosary.

'Rising, I ran bare-footed out of the Asile. Dr. J. Marley, who was in attendance near the gate, opened it for me and fell back in amazement. I ran on to the Grotto, many pilgrims following, and there I prayed. Then I returned to the Asile, washed, shaved and dressed myself, and put on a pair of shoes for the first time in four and a half years. Since that time I have not suffered any illness whatever, and have enjoyed—thanks to Almighty God and Our Lady of Lourdes—splendid health.'

CATECHISM STORIES 163

The medical examinations and certificates before, during and after the cure fully confirm its marvellous and almost instantaneous nature. Some medical opinion still considers that the troubles completely cured were chiefly functional, rather than clearly organic (there still remained some abnormality of the muscles of the right hand), but such distinctions make no difference to the gratitude of the faithful. If God has indeed intervened in some case, it matters not (except as a minor point in apologetics) whether He lifted the case outside all laws of nature, or whether He worked through natural causes that are still unknown or obscure to us.

In subsequent pilgrimages to Lourdes, John Traynor has been a familiar figure as a hard-working brancardier, trying to express the gratitude he naturally feels to Our Lady. (Facts from *The Case of John Traynor*, by Dom Francis Izard, O.S.B. One penny, from C.T.S. Office, 30 Manchester St., Liverpool.)

> * HOW IS THE BLESSED VIRGIN MOTHER OF GOD?
>
> *The Blessed Virgin is Mother of God because Jesus Christ, her Son, who was born of her as man, is not only man, but is also truly God.*

All women are honoured in God's Mother

IN China, as in most heathen countries, the lot of most women is a sad one. As soon as a little Chinese girl can understand anything she is made to understand that girls are useless and unwanted. The best of everything is for the boys. In some parts of China the winters are very severe, and warm quilted clothing is provided for the boys of the family, but the poor little girls are left to shiver.

One day a small girl was leading her smaller brother by the hand past a Catholic mission school when Little Dragon, for that was the boy's name, lost his hat. A gust of wind

*BALTIMORE 85
ENGLISH CATECHISM 167

took it off his head and they saw it disappear over the convent wall.

'I want my hat,' wailed Little Dragon.

'Then why didn't you keep it on, silly?' asked his sister, crossly, because she was frightened. 'If we go in to fetch it the foreign devils will catch us and make us into soup.'

Torn between fear of this terrible fate and fear of their mother's anger if they returned without Little Dragon's hat, the girl hesitated.

Just then a nun appeared carrying the hat in her hand. 'Is this yours?' she asked kindly. Then as she went forward to put it on the little boy's head the children shrank away. At that moment a Chinese nun passed the little group and the first nun beckoned to her and told her to take the children and show them the Crib in the Chapel. They were not afraid of her as she was Chinese, and they were soon gazing with interest at the Crib which was being prepared for Christmas.

The Chinese nun told them the Christmas story, how the great Lord of Heaven came to live on earth. She pointed to the Statue of the Holy Infant and then at the Shepherds.

'Ah,' thought the poor little Chinese girl, 'even the Holy Child was a boy, and only men are allowed near Him!' Her eyes filled with tears. 'Even here girls were not wanted,' she thought sadly.

But just then the Statue of Our Lady was put into position quite close to the Holy Child. It was shifted about until the Holy Mother was looking down lovingly on her Divine Babe. 'Tell me about *her*,' pleaded the little girl, pulling the nun's sleeve with her hand while she pointed with the other to the figure of Our Lady.

'Long ago there was a holy and beautiful maiden named Mary, and the Lord of Heaven chose her . . .' The nun retold the Gospel story that is familiar to every Christian child, but to this listener quite fresh. It was indeed 'good news' for the despised little Chinese girl. (Adapted from *Holy Childhood Annals*.) [See also nos. 63, 668.]

CATECHISM STORIES

* SHOULD WE ASK THE ANGELS AND SAINTS TO PRAY FOR US?

We should ask the Angels and Saints to pray for us because they are our friends and brethren, and because their prayers have great power with God.

'We should ask the Angels and Saints to pray for us'

AT Syracuse in Sicily, in the reign of Diocletian, lived St. Lucy, daughter of rich and noble parents. She had promised her virginity to God and hoped to give all her goods to the poor.

Fifty years previously, the noble and beautiful maiden St. Agatha had been martyred at Catania, not far from Syracuse, and many Christians used to go to pray at her tomb. Lucy persuaded her mother Eutychia, who suffered from an issue of blood, to make the pilgrimage. 'Agatha stands ever in the sight of Him for whom she died: only touch her tomb with faith and you will be healed.'

All night they prayed at the shrine, till they fell asleep; then Lucy beheld Agatha in a dream, with angels round her: 'What are you asking for, my sister Lucy?' She promised that Eutychia should be cured, and that Lucy should have the same crown of martyrdom as Agatha herself.

Eutychia woke up cured, and in gratitude agreed with Lucy to distribute all their goods to the poor. This enraged the young man to whom Lucy, against her will, had been betrothed. He denounced her as a Christian.

Before the court she answered the magistrate with great boldness, as Agatha had done, and was subjected to the same attacks by lust and cruelty combined that Agatha had withstood. When they tried to burn her at the stake the flames would not harm her, and at last a soldier plunged his sword into her throat. (See also stories 66, 124, 125, 158.)

The Saints are 'our friends and brethren'

Ignatius Loyola, worldly and ambitious young nobleman, was directing the defence of Pampeluna against the French in 1521. A cannon ball passed between his legs, breaking the right below the knee. The garrison lost heart and surrendered, and the French treated the brave officer well and carried him to his own castle of Loyola, where his leg was broken again, to be re-set clumsily, necessitating further painful surgery and a very tedious convalescence.

Ignatius asked for some of his favourite romances to read; they brought him the only books in the castle, a life of Christ and a volume of the lives of the Saints.

For want of anything better, he read these, and they took him into a new world of heroes serving a King far more worth serving than any king on earth. In that glorious company, he felt, his ambition would have fair scope. Like St. Augustine, he said: 'If those men and women could do things like that, I can, too!'

Sometimes his mind reverted to the old day-dreams of worldly love, but now there seemed nothing in them compared with the new attraction. By the time his leg was better, his soul was cured also, and he was fully determined to join up with the Saints he had read about and enlist in the service of 'that sweet captain Jesus Christ.'

[See also nos. 66, 124, 125, 144, 158, 525, 669.]

COMMANDMENTS

THE COMMANDMENTS

* Who gave the Ten Commandments?

God gave the Ten Commandments to Moses in the Old Law, and Christ confirmed them in the New.

'God gave the Ten Commandments to Moses'

In the third month after leaving Egypt (we read in Exodus) the Israelites encamped below the steep and terrifying rocks of Mount Sinai. Moses went up the mountain and returned with an offer from God of a covenant, and the people promised to keep God's word (read Exod. xix, 3–8). On the second day he went up again, and brought a message to the people to prepare for what should happen the third day (Exod. xix, 9–14).

The third day was the fiftieth day after the original Pasch: the day afterwards known as Pentecost. It dawned with thunder and lightning, and a thick cloud of smoke with flames, covering the higher part of the mountain; the mountain shook and a trumpet sounded louder and louder. The people waited below in terror while Moses and Aaron went up into the cloud, and returned with the Ten Commandments of God (Exod. xix, 16–19; xx, 18–21; xx, 1–17).

It was as if God had said to the people: 'If you fear Me, keep My commandments.'

'Christ confirmed them in the New Law'

Many times Our Lord said He was come not to destroy the Law but to fulfil it; especially the chief part of the Law, the Ten Commandments.

*BALTIMORE 195
ENGLISH CATECHISM 174

CATECHISM STORIES

For instance, once a young man came with a question (read the story from Matt. xix, 16–22 : ' If thou wilt enter into life, keep the commandments ').

What Our Lord changed was the *spirit* in which the Commandments were to be kept. No longer the terrors of Sinai, but the love of children for their Father.

At the Last Supper, He gave us a New Covenant to replace the Covenant made at Sinai ; and gave us a New Commandment which included all the former Ten.

' A new commandment I give unto you ; that you love one another as I have loved you. . . . If you love Me, keep My commandments ' (John xiii, 34 ; xiv, 15).

Then on the Day of Pentecost (the day of the giving of the Ten Commandments) the New Law was given, with sound of mighty wind instead of thunder, and tongues of fire instead of lightning, while the house shook as Sinai had shaken. The Holy Spirit, Who is Love, came to merge all the Ten Commandments into one (Rom. xiii, 8–10) and make it easy for us to keep it.

(N.B. On the Ten Commandments and Conscience, see also stories 135 and 136.)

> * WHAT ARE WE COMMANDED TO DO BY THE FIRST COMMANDMENT ?
>
> *By the first Commandment we are commanded to worship the one, true, and living God, by Faith, Hope, Charity, and Religion.*

' To worship the one, true, and living God '

A CATHOLIC artist once painted a picture of the Last Supper. Someone to whom he showed his work admired the beauty of a lamp over the supper-table in the picture ; whereupon with one stroke the artist painted it out, saying : ' I want Our Lord to be the central Figure and all attention to be focussed on Him. Anything that distracts attention from Him must go ! '

So should we be ready to sacrifice anything that prevents our making God the true centre of our lives. [See also nos. 17, 250, 252, 452, 453, 538, 674.]

*BALTIMORE 200-203
ENGLISH CATECHISM 176

CATECHISM STORIES

* WHAT ARE THE SINS AGAINST FAITH?

The sins against Faith are all false religions, wilful doubt, disbelief, or denial of any article of Faith, and also culpable ignorance of the doctrines of the Church.

Professing our Faith openly

PROFESSOR IVAN PETROVITCH PAVLOV, who died in Moscow in 1937, aged eighty-six, was one of the greatest physiologists of the age, and knew more about the brain and its functions than any other scientist. Long before the Revolution he was famous; and afterwards, although he criticised the Soviet Government as 'an experiment without proper scientific controls,' both Lenin and Stalin had the sense to protect him and his research work. He was given a pension of £2000 a year, and a Physiological Institute was built for him regardless of cost.

He maintained full scientific independence, and as he was a believing Christian this included for him the practice of his religion. He insisted on a church being kept open in which he could worship God, and he gained his point.

Refusal to deny the Faith

In 1841 Chinese Christians had to suffer some persecution as a consequence of the wicked 'opium war' waged by the British Government. A Chinese Christian girl knelt in the courtyard before a mandarin to be tried, and firmly refused to give up her Faith. Trying to break down her obstinacy by stratagem, or perhaps to give her an opportunity to escape easily from punishment, he did not comment on her refusal but merely ordered a guard to trace a circle round her with his spear in the dust.

'If you get up and go outside that circle,' he told the girl, 'I shall consider it a sign that you have given up the foreign religion.'

Then he left the courtyard with his guard, and the girl remained alone.

*BALTIMORE 204-206
ENGLISH CATECHISM 177

In the evening she was still kneeling motionless, and the mandarin's secretary returned and watched her secretly for some time. At last he went to her and said :

'My child, you can get up now and go home.'

'No, I would rather die than move from this spot.'

'But the mandarin was not serious.'

'I heard his words. I cannot know his intentions. I will not move.'

At last, after many more persuasions in vain, the secretary himself smoothed away the circle, and only then would the girl rise and go home.

Indeed an example to many a careless Catholic !

Zeal for the Faith

Nicholas Garlick was a yeoman's son in Derbyshire, went to Worcester College, Oxford, and became a schoolmaster at Tideswell. He had loved from his boyhood the daughter of the lord of the manor there, but she was too far above him in station, and at last he renounced his hopes and turned instead to the service of God. He became priest at Rheims, and worked in his own county. In the Armada year, 1588, he was captured in a hiding-place at Padley Hall by Topcliffe (through information by a traitor) and executed with two other priests at Derby. As he stood on the ladder he suddenly cast among the crowd a number of loose papers, written in prison, in defence of the Catholic Faith. Everyone into whose hands those papers fell was subsequently received (it is said) into the Catholic Church. [See also no. 666, in the Appendix.]

Avoiding 'all false religions'

The Ven. Ralph Milner was a farm labourer near Winchester in the reign of Elizabeth. He had lived through all the changes of religion ; but in his old age he was reconciled to the Catholic Church and became very active in assisting the priests who went about secretly saying Mass. At last he succeeded in securing a priest to work permanently in his own district ; and when this priest was captured, Ralph Milner was tried along with him, and both were executed at Winchester on July 7th, 1591.

Being asked by the judge why he would not go to church, he said that he was born in the reign of King Henry VIII and that he would live and die in that faith wherein he was born and christened.

Milner had a large family. As he went up the ladder to the gallows the Sheriff shouted to him : ' Come down, fool, and look after your children ! ' Thinking he was to be reprieved he came down the ladder again, whereupon the Sheriff offered him a pardon if he would go to the Protestant church. ' No, no, I'll hang ! ' said Milner, and at once went back up the ladder. His children were at the front of the crowd and called for his blessing as he stood with the rope round his neck. He said : ' God bless you, and send you no worse end than your father's.' (*Acts of English Martyrs :* Pollen.)

Taking part in a false religion

Mabel, a rather careless Catholic, had a Protestant girl-friend. She came with Mabel to midnight Mass, and later on asked Mabel to go with her to her chapel, which in spite of some misgivings Mabel did. She did not care much for the service, but there were some pleasant young people there, and she went with her friend again. Soon she was going regularly. ' Of course, I'm a Catholic ; but it's all the same, isn't it ? ' Later she and her friend began courting and she no longer went to the chapel, nor to her own church either. She married in the Registry Office, and went to live in a district where there was no Catholic Church near ; so she took her babies to be christened at the nearest Protestant church and sent them to the Sunday School there to get rid of them on Sunday afternoons. When a Catholic Sister heard of her and came to see her, she said : ' Yes, I was a Catholic once but I don't want to be now.'

Discuss : Can the ' supernatural gift ' of Faith be weakened, or lost, by our own fault ? What should Mabel have said to the friend who asked her to go to the chapel (extempore dialogue between two girls perhaps) ?

CATECHISM STORIES

Reading bad books

In a factory a man was selling many copies of a penny paper consisting entirely of attacks on God and religion. One Catholic boy, Dan, refused it. 'Afraid to read the other side?' sneered the seller. 'I'd rather not swallow poison either into my stomach or my mind' was the answer.

Jim, another Catholic boy, said: 'Let's have a penn'orth!' Then during the dinner-hour, sitting around with some of his mates, he read bits out of the atheist paper with comments of his own, showing its arguments up and where its facts about the Church were all wrong.

'Well, what about this?' said one of the listeners, pointing to a bit about something some Pope had done hundreds of years ago. Jim read it.

'Well, that's a new one to me. But I bet you a packet of Woodbines I'll tell you all about it to-morrow.'

So in the evening he took the paper round to a Catholic friend who could always put him wise on such occasions.

Dan's attitude and Jim's were both good in their way, but Jim's is evidently the best for those who can rise to it.

Heresy to be hated, but not heretics

Though avoiding heresy and false religions, we should use charity with those who adhere to them, since they are probably in good faith, and in any case our business is to win them to the truth.

In the days of the Arian heresy St. Hilary of Poitiers was a great champion of the truth, courageously attending various councils, where he found himself almost in a minority of one. He was denounced to the Emperor, who banished him to Phrygia. But there, by his writings and attending at councils, he proved himself such a thorn in the side of the Arians and semi-Arians of the East that they persuaded the Emperor to send him back to Gaul.

In spite of his hatred of heresy, he was ready for conciliation with semi-Arians who he thought were divided from orthodoxy only by verbal misunderstandings. In his earlier days he would not salute Jews or heretics, or eat with them; but later on, for their sake, he gave up this severity.

CATECHISM STORIES

Patience with unbelievers

There is a Jewish legend that tells how an old man approached Abraham as he sat at the door of his tent and asked for food and shelter for the night.

'Are you a believer?' Abraham asked.

'I worship the Sun,' the old man replied.

Whereupon Abraham drove him away, pouring abuse on him and calling him a dirty unbelieving dog.

That night as Abraham lay down to rest God's Voice spoke to him.

'I have put up with that old infidel for eighty years. Could you, My servant, not have borne with him for one night?'

'Culpable ignorance'

One cause of this is the way many people avoid sermons if they can.

St. Aldhelm, Bishop of Sherborne (d. 709), was distressed by the ignorance of his Saxon flock, who disliked sermons. Being somewhat of a musician he took his violin and stood on a bridge where everybody had to pass. He played and sang (possibly disguised as a minstrel) and when a crowd had gathered he taught them the Faith of which they were ignorant. 'Whereas if the bishop had proceeded with severity and excommunication,' says the chronicler, 'he would have made no impression on the people.'

But for Catholic boys and girls it ought not to be necessary for their pastors to go to such lengths. We should value our faith enough to learn it properly. [See also nos. 20, 25, 27, 38 (Culpable ignorance), 655, 656, 666.]

> * WHAT ARE THE SINS AGAINST HOPE?
> *The sins against Hope are despair and presumption.*

The virtue of Hope

OUR Lord tells us we should pray to God with great confidence.

St. Martin of Tours, preaching to some pagan villagers, wanted to cut down a great pine tree which stood close

*BALTIMORE 207-209
ENGLISH CATECHISM 179

CATECHISM STORIES

to the pagan temple which they had allowed him to destroy. After many objections, they said they would cut the tree down themselves if Martin would stand beneath it where he would be crushed, for ' If thy God is ever with thee as thou declarest, thou wilt run no risk.'

Martin agreed at once, and a great crowd of pagans came to see the spectacle, hoping to see the Christian Bishop killed.

The pine leaned to one side, and Martin was bound and placed in a spot where it seemed certain to fall. The treecutters began their work, with the other pagans cheering them on, and Martin's monks standing by, silent and terrified.

Soon the tree shook and with a rending noise began to fall. ' Martin, strong in the Lord, waits fearless, and calmly raises his hand and makes towards the tree the sign of the cross. The tree seems to be caught backwards by some unseen power and falls in quite the opposite direction to which it had inclined, so that the peasants who were standing in what they thought was a safe place had a narrow escape. At once a great shout rises up to heaven.' (*Chronicles of Sulpicius Severus*, C. *13*.)

St. Martin's confidence in God shows the essential virtue of Hope, reminding us of Job's words : ' Though He slay me, yet I will trust in Him.' Or the words of the Three Young Men in Daniel iii, 17–18.

' The lovely virtue of Courage '

A notable example of Hope (and of Courage in very dark days, which is somewhat the same) is St. Genevieve (*d.* 512). She was a child at Nanterre near Paris, when St. Germanus, Bishop of Auxerre, passed through and preached there. He noticed her eager face amongst the listeners and called her to him afterwards. She told him she wished to serve God entirely. He picked up from the ground a copper medal or coin, marked it with a cross, and gave it to her to wear always round her neck (he said) instead of gold and jewels. She wore it faithfully and kept all her resolutions. When her parents died she went to live in Paris, and became famous as a saint though many scorned and despised her. When Attila and his Huns threatened Paris she kept the people from panic by her

CATECHISM STORIES

courage and prayers. Later, when Paris was besieged for years by the Franks, she put courage into the citizens and organised a food supply by the river. When the Franks took the city she persuaded them to treat the people with clemency. It was she who led Clovis to the Christian faith and so laid the foundation of France. [See also nos. 21-23, 173, 182, 216.]

Despair

The terrible example of despair is Judas, after the betrayal. See Matthew xxvii, 3-5.

Despair is a sin because it misjudges God. He will forgive *anything* if only we are sorry. (See also no. 483.)

Over-confidence

One of the desert monks felt a desire to return to the cities and court martyrdom. He went to the holy Abbot Pachomius to ask his prayers and blessing.

'Stay in your desert cell,' said the saint. 'You will only be tempting God and perhaps deny your faith.'

But the young monk was bent on going. On his way to the city he was captured by brigands. They raised their swords to kill him, unless he would renounce his Faith.

When he saw the swords about to fall he gave in and they let him go. He returned full of remorse to the Abbot.

'Will God ever forgive me?'

'Yes, He will, if you are sorry in all humility. But you must never again rush into needless danger, for that is the sin of presumption.' [See also nos. 664, 670.]

> * WHICH ARE THE TWO GREAT PRECEPTS OF CHARITY?
>
> *The two great precepts of Charity are:* (1) '*Thou shalt love the Lord thy God with thy whole heart, and with thy whole soul, and with thy whole mind, and with thy whole strength*' (2) '*Thou shalt love thy neighbour as thyself.*'

'Thou shalt love the Lord thy God'

IN St. Benedict's time a certain hermit named Martin

*BALTIMORE 189-190
ENGLISH CATECHISM 320

CATECHISM STORIES

lived in a cave and was so much afraid of returning to the world and losing his soul that he had himself chained to the entrance of his cave. St. Benedict heard of this and was grieved. He sent a message to Martin telling him to break his chain : ' If thou art truly a servant of God, bind thyself not by a chain of iron, but by the chain of Christ.' The hermit followed this advice, and later St. Benedict received a message of thanks from Martin, who said that love was the safest chain of all and kept him as close to his cave as before (St. Gregory, Dial. III, 16).

' Love is the fulfilling of the Law '

At the Last Supper Our Lord said : ' A new commandment I give unto you, that you love one another as I have loved you. . . . By this shall all men know that you are My disciples, that you have love one for another.'

St. John, who was leaning on His breast, took these words to heart, and wrote them in his gospel in his old age. When he wrote a letter to the Christians he said : ' He that loveth not his brother whom he seeth, how can he love God whom he seeth not ? '

In extreme old age at Ephesus (St. Jerome tells us) St. John, whenever he was asked to preach a sermon, always preached the same one : ' Little children, love one another. Little children, love one another.' People began to think that perhaps his mind was failing and that he was too old to preach. So one day he was asked : ' Why do you always say the same thing in your sermons ? '

' Because it is the Lord's command, and if you do it, it is enough.'

' Thou shalt love thy neighbour '

Our Lord Himself gives us a story to illuminate this command. He was asked : ' And who is my neighbour ? ' Answer in Luke x, 30–37.

Loving our neighbour as ourself

Scene—a Somme battlefield in the spring of 1918. Mud, shell-holes, continual shell-bursts and machine-gun fire.

CATECHISM STORIES

The Germans had been advancing, but the British were now holding them up. A number of wounded were still out in what had become no-man's-land, but the heavy barrage from both sides prevented any rescue attempts for three days.

Then a chaplain managed to crawl out to them. He had on him a quart water-bottle. He found twenty men still alive, who had crawled into shell-holes near to each other for company. The first thing he had to do was to give them water. Holding his bottle to the lips of the first, he told him to drink, but not too much as there were nineteen other men dying of thirst. To the next one he said: 'Just a drop, lad—remember there are eighteen more.' Seventeen, sixteen, ten, eight, three. He shook the bottle: yes, still a little left. He crawled on to the remaining men. It was the last one who had the longest drink. This is a true story.

Heroic charity

When the troopship *Birkenhead* was sinking, Lieut. Russell, aged seventeen, was put in command of a boatload of women and children. After the ship went down a drowning sailor clutched the side of the boat and one of the women cried: 'It's my husband—oh, save him!' But there was no room, even for one more. Lieut. Russell stood up, jumped clear of the boat into the water (which was full of sharks) and the sailor was pulled on board in his place. All the women cried 'God bless you, sir!' to young Russell while they could see him, but in a few moments he sank from view.

'Where Love is, God is'

The story of Tolstoy with the above title could be read aloud in its entirety. Here is a bald summary:

An old cobbler, Martin, lived alone and read the gospels and tried to please God. Reading about the poor welcome given to Christ in the house of the rich Pharisee, Martin wished the Lord would come to his cottage.

One night, asleep, he heard a voice: 'Martin, Martin, look out of the window to-morrow, for I shall come.'

Was it a dream ? Anyhow, next day he prepared for a guest and kept watch. No one came, but outside he saw a poor old man sweeping the snow ; he called him in and gave him some hot tea, while he still watched the window.

'Are you expecting someone ? ' said the old man, and Martin told him about the voice, and spoke of Our Lord till the old man wept.

Soon after he had gone Martin saw outside a shivering woman with a crying baby ; he brought them in and gave them some of the soup, and an old cloak to wrap the baby in. The woman cried with joy, and he told her, too, about the voice he had heard.

' Who knows ? ' she said. ' All things are possible. Farewell, and thank you.'

It was evening now, and still the Christ had not come. Still watching, Martin saw a poor apple-woman resting, who caught a boy stealing one of her apples. Martin went out and made peace, paid for the apple, persuaded the woman to forgive, and made the boy feel so ashamed that he went off with the old woman carrying the basket for her.

Night came, and Martin opened his Bible again. From the dark corner a Voice : ' Martin, Martin, don't you know Me ? '

' Who is it ? ' said Martin.

' It is I,' said the Voice, and for a moment the old snow-sweeper was there. ' It is I '—and there was the woman with the baby. ' It is I '—the apple-woman and the boy smiled a moment and vanished.

So Martin was glad to know that the Christ had visited him that day after all. [On Charity : see also nos. 7, 8, 24, 534-538, 596-600, 643, 650, 659-661, 675.]

* WHAT ARE THE CHIEF SINS AGAINST RELIGION ?
The chief sins against Religion are the worship of false gods or idols, and the giving to any creature whatsoever the honour which belongs to God alone.

' Thou shalt not have strange gods before Me '

THE wickedness of idolatry is taught in the great story of

*BALTIMORE 212-223
ENGLISH CATECHISM 180

CATECHISM STORIES

the contest of Elias with the priests of Baal on Mount Carmel. Read it from 3 Kings xviii, 1-2, 16-45.

In these days we are not likely to worship graven things, or images of animals, etc., but we are liable to put something —money or pleasure, etc.—on God's throne in our heart.

The First Commandment means God must come *first*. [See also nos. 26, 27, 567.]

The virtue of 'Religion'

This means acknowledging the rights of our Creator. For us who have the true Religion it means being 'a practising Catholic.'

Molly was very keen to learn the piano, but when she found she was expected to practise five-finger exercises she soon grew tired of it.

One day a musician visited a neighbouring town, and Molly was taken to hear the great man play. After the concert she and her mother went to a hotel to have some tea. It happened to be the hotel where the pianist was staying, and someone pointed out the room where he spent many hours a day practising. '*Practising*,' said Molly in astonishment, ' I didn't think great players like that would have to *practise* ! '

' He would not long be a great player if he gave up practising,' she was told.

After that Molly was never heard to grumble about her five-finger exercises.

The five-finger exercises that we Catholics should always stick to are : (1) morning prayers ; (2) night prayers ; (3) Sunday Mass ; (4) monthly confession and Communion ; (5) visits to the Blessed Sacrament. So when we hear someone speak of a practising Catholic we can think of those five things. If we are faithful to these we shall probably do more later, but we are not likely to do anything much for God unless we do these five things.

'The honour that belongs to God alone'

On September 22 the Church commemorates SS. Maurice and Companions, martyrs. These are the famous Theban Legion, who, having proved their valour in battle, laid down their lives unresistingly rather than commit the sin of idolatry.

They had been brought from Africa (probably not the whole legion, but a detachment of several hundred) to help in suppressing a revolted tribe in Gaul about the year 287. After the victory the Emperor Maximian concentrated the army at Agaunum (St. Maurice-en-Valais, Switzerland) to offer sacrifice to the gods in thanksgiving. The Theban Legion were all Christians, and they marched out of the camp under their commander, Maurice, so as not to take part in the idolatry.

The Emperor ordered them back, but in vain. Then he surrounded them with the rest of the troops, and threatened them with massacre if they still refused to sacrifice.

'Know, O Emperor,' was the reply of Maurice, 'we are your soldiers, but we are also servants of the one, true and living God. We cannot obey your command without sin, and we would rather die without shame than live through sin.'

The Emperor ordered them to be 'decimated'—every tenth soldier was executed. Then he repeated his command, but exhorted by the brave Maurice they still remained firm.

Decimation after decimation was carried out, until the whole legion had given their lives for the true God.

Superstition

Any belief which takes away from the sovereignty or providence of God is a sin against the virtue of Religion.

' Early in 1928 the first Hindu baby was born in the new Zenana hospital at Rawalpindi, Punjab. The relatives all anxiously enquired the exact hour of its birth and the father rushed off to the family astrologer ! A few hours later the mother was found in tears and the baby pushed to one side. What was the matter ? Its horoscope was so bad that the family had decided it was better to let it die. This was a problem until someone had an inspiration—the clock was fast ! So fond father had to race off again to the astrologer with the correct hour of birth. This time the child was assured of a happy future and peace reigned.' (*A.P.F. Annals.*)

CATECHISM STORIES

Even if it be admitted that ' there may be something in ' astrology, it could only be a matter of tendencies and influences operating within God's providence, and leaving us quite free in our will.

' Superstitious practices '

' Here's a case. A woman, as she wakes one morning, is startled by a sharp " ping " on the little table by her bed. She looks, and finds to her surprise that a circular band a quarter-inch wide has broken off the top of her water glass. She rings for another glass.

' Within five minutes she again hears a " ping " and again the rim of the glass has broken away. Still more startled, she rings again. Another glass is brought. Within ten minutes there's yet a third " ping " and again a circular band is lying loose on the glass.

This is altogether too much for her ! No breakage of the kind has ever occurred in her life before : and now it's happened three times running in the space of half an hour. She gives up her belief in natural causes on the spot. This must be some spirit or what not, some agency or power behind the veil, playing tricks.

' The great Jung tells that story. (It's in his latest book, *Modern Man in Search of a Soul*.) He calls it a " disagreeable story." He himself, so far as one can judge, has, like the lady, no idea of the explanation.

' Years ago I ran across a precisely similar case, and was in at the tracing of the cause.

' Those tumblers had been wiped, the night before, by someone wearing a diamond ring. That's all. They'd each had the same scratch in the same place right round the inside. The change of temperature due to filling with water produced the same crack within ten minutes of the filling. And there you are.

' I don't deny, mark you, that mysterious forces outside human perception or reckoning *may* be at work doing queer things to us now and again or all the time. They may. Nothing's impossible. But most mysterious things have a traceable natural cause if only you'll keep on at it till you've found it.' (Professor John Hilton.)

The Professor's remarks could apply to most of the phenomena produced by spiritualistic mediums.

> *WHAT ARE WE COMMANDED BY THE SECOND COMMANDMENT?
>
> *By the second Commandment we are commanded to speak with reverence of God and all holy persons and things, and to keep our lawful oaths and vows.*

'To speak with reverence of God'

When the Spanish civil war began the Reds entered a certain church and destroyed and desecrated all that came within their reach. Then, finding some Mass vestments in the sacristy, one of the militiamen put them on and mounted the pulpit.

He was engaged in preaching a mock sermon, full of all kinds of blasphemies, when another party of Reds arrived. One of the newcomers, more drunk than sober, seeing what seemed to be a priest in the pulpit, fired at him and killed him.

Thus the blasphemer was sent to meet the very Judge whose Name he was insulting.

Reverence for holy things

During the French Revolution, when Catholic priests were in hiding or in prison, some *sans-culottes* drinking in an inn were discussing how they could discover the priest of that town, who was not yet arrested. The woman of the inn suggested a plan: her husband could pretend to be ill, and the report could be spread in the town that he wished for a priest to give him the sacraments. The priest would surely hear of it and come, and could then be detained and handed over to the revolutionary tribunal.

Everything happened according to plan. The priest soon arrived at nightfall, and was taken up to the 'sick' man's room, where two guards were also concealed. He spoke to the man in the bed, but there was no reply; he felt his hand—it seemed very cold.

*BALTIMORE 224-233
ENGLISH CATECHISM 189

'Why didn't you send for me sooner? The poor man is dead.'

The woman burst out laughing, and the two guards emerged from behind curtains. But the man on the bed remained still—he had indeed passed away—struck down by the judgement of God. Such terror paralysed all present that the priest was able to go away without interference.

Reverence for God's House

A priest in Liverpool was getting off the tramcar for the next stop, at his church, when a man in the car said:

'Father, there's a man dying that works at the same place as me. Couldn't you go and see him?' He mentioned the street and the number.

'Yes, of course I will. Isn't he a good Catholic?'

'Well, I don't know whether he's a Catholic at all, Father—I'm not much of a one myself. All I know is, he always lifts his cap when the car passes your church.'

The priest found the house, and the door was opened by a woman who stared at him uncomprehendingly—evidently she was unaccustomed to priests. After a question or two he found the dying husband upstairs. Sure enough, he was a Catholic who had been away from the Church ever since he left school fifty years before. He knew he was dying, and was glad to make his peace with God, and had not forgotten how to make his confession and Communion. At the end the priest told him of the request of the man in the tramcar.

'Yes, that's right,' said the dying Catholic. 'It's forty years since I said any prayers, but there's one bit of religion I always clung to—I always raised my cap passing a church, even though I never went inside. The priest who taught us for our first Communion made us promise to do it always, and somehow I always kept it up.'

That little habit of reverence had brought him the great grace of a happy death. [See also 412, 444, 508, 673.]

CATECHISM STORIES

'To keep our lawful oaths'

It is for the public good, and therefore lawful, that we should take oaths in a court of law ; and perjury is a great crime against God.

An employee went to court because he was not satisfied with the compensation offered to him for an injury to his arm when working his employer's lift.

'Ever since the accident I haven't been able to raise my right arm more than so high,' the plaintiff assured the court, raising his hand to about the level of his shoulder and screwing up his face as if even that caused him great pain.

'And how high could you raise it *before* the accident ? ' he was asked.

'Oh, as high as this,' and before he had time to think the man held the injured arm straight up above his head without the slightest effort. There was a roar of laughter in court.

But the judge said : ' I can see nothing to laugh at in a man perjuring himself as you have heard the plaintiff do. You all heard him call God to witness that he would speak the truth, the whole truth, and nothing but the truth, and almost in the same breath he tells a deliberate lie. His case is dismissed.'

Giving evidence on oath

A lorry which was travelling too much on the wrong side of the road was involved in an accident with another lorry, resulting in some damage. To the policeman, the lorry-driver insisted that he was on his right side till compelled to swerve by a small car which had passed and disappeared. The driver's mate knew that this was untrue, but backed up the driver's story out of loyalty to his friend. The case came into court, and the driver's mate gave evidence on oath—'the truth, the whole truth,' etc. He was asked : ' Are you sure the lorry was on its right side ? ' and answered yes. In his own mind he justified himself : ' It's perjury, of course, but everybody does it. If I told the truth, the driver would lose his job.' Was he right?

Loyalty to our friends is well in its way, but our first loyalty is to God and His law.

Respect for one's oath

Regulus, a Roman General, was taken prisoner by the Carthaginians. When they wanted to sue for peace they sent Regulus as one of their messengers, but made him promise, with solemn oath, to return to Carthage if peace was not concluded. Arrived in Rome, Regulus conveyed to the Senate the Carthaginian request for peace, but advised the Senators not to grant it, as he thought it would be against the best interests of Rome.

Peace was therefore refused, and everybody dissuaded Regulus from returning to Carthage. His answer was:
' I know the fate that awaits me, but I fear even more the dishonour of breaking my oath. I will return to Carthage. The rest is in the hands of the gods.' He returned, and the Carthaginians put him to death with great torments, which he met with fortitude.

Indeed, an example to those whose oaths are taken to the one true God.

' Unlawful oaths '

On the market cross in the town of Devizes there is an inscription which reads as follows :

'On Thursday, the 25th of January 1753, Ruth Pierce of Pottern in this County agreed with three other women to buy a Sack of Wheat in the Market, each paying her due proportion towards the same. One of the Women in collecting the several quotas of money discovered a deficiency and demanded of Ruth Pierre the Sum which was wanting to make good the amount. Ruth Pierce protested that she had paid her share and said " She wished she might drop down dead if she had not." She rashly repeated this awful wish when to the consternation and Terror of the surrounding multitude she instantly fell down and expired, having the money concealed in her hand.'

CATECHISM STORIES

Take advice before making a vow

Someone heard that St. Francis of Sales had made a vow when young to say the Rosary every day. She wished to take the same vow, and asked the saint's advice. 'Don't do it,' he said. ' I was young and did it without sufficient thought. Say the Rosary every day by all means, but as a good practice, not as a vow, then there will be no sin if you omit it. I must say my vow has sometimes been a hindrance to me and I thought of seeking dispensation from it.'

Vows once taken must be kept, and therefore should not be taken hastily, or without advice. [See nos. 539–542.]

> * WHAT ARE WE COMMANDED BY THE THIRD COMMANDMENT?
>
> *By the third Commandment we are commanded to keep the Sunday holy by hearing Mass and resting from servile works.*

' To keep the Sunday holy '

TOM was spending his holidays on his uncle's farm. There were many things to delight and interest him. On Sunday he grumbled because he had a long way to go to Mass.

His uncle said nothing, but on market day he brought home a paper bag containing seven large juicy peaches which he gave to his nephew. Tom thanked him warmly, and when his uncle asked if he could spare him one peach out of the seven, he replied : ' Of course, Uncle, take as many as you like,' and handed the bag for him to help himself.

' Ah, I see you are more generous to me than you are to the good God,' the farmer remarked.

' What do you mean ? ' the boy asked.

' Why, you do not grudge me a share of the fruit I have given you, and yet when God has given you seven days in the week you grumble at sparing a part of one day in seven to worship and thank Him.'

*BALTIMORE 236-240
ENGLISH CATECHISM 193

CATECHISM STORIES

' By hearing Mass '

A little girl once went to Catechism with a friend. She could not answer even the easiest questions, and when the priest asked about the Holy Mass she seemed not to know what he was talking about.

' My child, don't you ever come to Mass ? ' he asked.

' Oh no, Father, you see, we have a motor car.'

The family to which this child belonged were breaking the first Commandment, for they put their car and their own pleasures before their duty of worshipping God. (See also stories 362 and 363.)

Social worship is due to our Creator

The building and consecration of Solomon's Temple is one of the great scriptural examples of our duty of worshipping the Majesty of God, especially of public worship in churches.

Story of the building can be read as follows : 2 Paralipomenon ii, 1–9 ; iii, 1–8 ; iv, 19–22.

After seven years the Temple was finished, and Solomon gathered all the ancients and princes together, and the whole people marched in procession taking the Ark of the Covenant into the Temple, while one hundred and twenty priests sounded the trumpets, and the Levites sang to harps and cymbals and other kinds of music : ' Give glory to the Lord for He is good : for His mercy endureth for ever.'

When the Ark was taken in and the priests came forth the cloud of God's glory filled the Temple. Solomon explained to the people that he had carried out the desire of his father David in building the house of God.

Then he knelt down before the altar in the presence of all the multitude of Israel and lifted his hands towards heaven.

' O Lord God of Israel ! there is no God like Thee in heaven nor in earth. If heaven and the heaven of heavens do not contain Thee, how much less this house which I have built ! But to this end only is it made, that Thou mayst regard the prayer which Thy servant poureth out before Thee. Whosoever shall pray in this place, hear

Thou from Thy dwelling-place, that is from heaven, and show mercy. Hear Thou from heaven, and forgive and render to everyone according to his ways, which Thou knowest him to have in his heart : for Thou only knowest the hearts of the children of men.' (The whole prayer could be read : 2 Para. vi, 14-42.)

Everything Solomon said in his great prayer is a thousand times more true of the humblest church where the Real Presence is on the altar. [See·also nos. 169, 362, 363, 449, 450.]

'Resting from servile works'

A wealthy German officer was stationed in Paris after the Franco-Prussian War. One Sunday morning he called on one of the foremost jewellers and asked to inspect his wares. The jeweller explained that on Sunday his shop was closed but that he would be delighted to serve him on the following day. This did not suit the German, who had made arrangements to leave Paris early on the Monday.

He tried in vain to persuade the jeweller to break his rule for once, pointing out that he wanted to spend a good deal of money.

The tradesman was anxious to do the business, but he was yet more anxious to keep the Sunday holy according to God's law, and so he remained firm.

The German officer turned away, a little annoyed perhaps. But on thinking the matter over he began to see that a man who was willing to sacrifice personal gains for religious principles would certainly be a man to be relied on in business. Finally, therefore, the officer postponed his departure and not only bought a large quantity of jewellery from the conscientious jeweller himself but recommended him to a number of his friends so that his prosperity increased rapidly. Thus even in this life did God reward a faithful servant.

Working on Sundays

A Catholic man, who worked at a desk all the week, was fond of gardening and liked to put in an hour or two

CATECHISM STORIES

at his garden or allotment on Sunday mornings, after having been to early Mass. One Sunday while he was digging a trench for some onions a Catholic friend came by and said : ' Well, *I* don't know ! if that isn't servile work what is ? '

' It's just fresh air and recreation for me,' said the gardener.

' I'll bet Father A. wouldn't agree to your doing it on Sunday.'

' I don't know about Father A., but I know Father B. thinks it's all right because he's often seen me at it and made no remark.'

' Perhaps he didn't like to. Have you asked him about it in confession ? '

' No—why should I ? That's the sort of thing I can settle for myself.'

For discussion :

Would such Sunday gardening be sinful ? (*No.*)

What when priests' opinions differ? (*Follow which you like.*)

Must Catholics ask a priest about everything ? (*No. If properly instructed you can use your judgement.*)

Necessary work is allowed on Sunday

Sunday afternoon, two girls, one busy sewing.

' Sewing on Sunday ! What is it ? '

' This dance frock wants altering. I've got to wear it at the dance to-morrow night, and this afternoon is the only chance I shall get to do it.'

' Well, to keep you company, I'll put in an hour's work on a tennis dress for next season.'

(The dance frock was ' necessary work,' the other was not ; however, an hour's work would not amount to a great sin.)

' The Sabbath is made for man '

The Jewish scribes did not make allowance for human needs and were over-strict in their rules for the Sabbath. The gospels give several instances of how Our Lord

CATECHISM STORIES

openly broke these rules and argued it out with the scribes:

The woman in the Synagogue (Luke xiii, 10–17).
The disciples pluck ears of corn (Mark ii, 23–28).
The withered hand (Mark iii, 1–6).
The infirm man at the 'pool (John v, 2–18).
The man blind from birth (John ix, 1–41).

All these make interesting stories, showing Our Lord as the champion of common sense and the common people against the legalists.

> * WHAT ARE WE COMMANDED BY THE FOURTH COMMANDMENT?
>
> *By the fourth Commandment we are commanded to love, reverence, and obey our parents in all that is not sin.*

'Honour thy father'

IN olden times in Vienna the convicts were used as scavengers in the streets. One day a minister of State was looking out of the window and saw a respectably-dressed young student go up to one of the convicts clearing the snow and kiss his hand. The minister at once sent for the student to question him, thinking perhaps it was a case of some dangerous political leader and a young follower. 'Explain your behaviour just now—it is highly improper for anyone to kiss the hand of a criminal.'

'But that was my father, sir.'

The minister was much impressed with the son's devotion, and told the Emperor (Joseph II), who ordered the convict's release. 'He cannot be a bad man if he brought up his son so well and inspired in him such affection.' (Told by *Spirago*.)

'Honour thy mother'

A convicted murderer (in U.S.A.) had an old mother aged seventy-one. He made his relatives promise to conceal the death sentence from her and tell her that he was sentenced to twenty years' imprisonment. Then he filled in the six weeks before he went to the chair by writing

*BALTIMORE 241-243, 250
ENGLISH CATECHISM 197

CATECHISM STORIES

letters which were to be posted to his mother every month for twenty years.

The deception is not to be commended, but the consideration for his mother is. What a pity though that he had not considered her before taking to bad ways!

Scripture stories about obedience

The great example of obedience to parents is given by Our Lord at Nazareth.

Our Lady's remonstrance: 'Son, *why* hast Thou done so to us?' lets us see how considerate and reliable He had always been before. His three days in Jerusalem was not disobedience, but a foreshadowing of His future. Then He 'went down with them to Nazareth and was subject to them' in all the everyday things of house and workshop, He who knew that His Father was God.

Some of Our Lord's parables are concerned with home obedience. The Prodigal Son, of course (Luke xv, 11–32), though its point is rather that there are other virtues besides obedience and other things for parents to consider besides upholding their authority.

More to the point of obedience is the little story of the Two Sons (Matt. xxi, 28–32); neither of the boys were shining examples, but Our Lord as usual prefers *action* to good intentions, still more to mere outward professions.

There is also a parable about the obedience of servants to their master (Luke xii, 43–48).

Stories from Old Testament on filial duty: Joseph and Jacob (Gen. xlvi, 28, etc.), and Ru˙ and Noemi (Ruth i, 7–19).

'In all that is not sin'

Mary, aged twelve, had one of those mothers who, unfortunately, do not give their children a good example. One Sunday morning, just as Mary was getting ready for Mass, her mother said: 'You're not going to church this morning, I want you here to mind the baby.' Mary thought perhaps she ought to run off to Mass all the same, but in the end she did what her mother said and hoped it would not be a sin.

8

In the evening her mother found there was no milk for tea and she said to Mary : 'There's a bottle of milk on the doorstep of that house opposite—they've been out all day—it's getting dark, nobody will see you if you go and take it—hurry up now.' Mary said : 'No, it's a sin to steal. I won't do it.' Her mother was very angry, but Mary stuck to her word.

Mary was right in the first case, because the 'natural' law to obey our parents comes before the 'positive law' about going to Mass. She was also right in the second case, because taking the milk would be a sin of stealing ; except in case of extreme necessity (e.g. starving), when things become common property.

Remorse for disobedience

The great Dr. Johnson, between leaving school at the age of sixteen and going to Oxford, spent a year or two at his home at Lichfield. He spent most of his time devouring books. His father was a bookseller, and sometimes opened a bookstall in the neighbouring towns on their market-days. On one such occasion, when he wished his son to accompany him to Uttoxeter and help with the stall, Samuel refused to go. Many years afterwards, when he was a famous writer, the memory of this disobedience so troubled his mind that he did penance for it by making a journey to Uttoxeter market-place, and standing for an hour, bareheaded and in very bad weather, on the spot where his father's stall used to be. 'In contrition I stood, and I hope the penance was expiatory.'

Loyalty to our parents

For girls especially, Shakespeare's *King Lear* provides examples for the Fourth Commandment ; Goneril and Regan of unfilial greed and ingratitude, and Cordelia of loyalty to parents even when they are foolish and unreasonable.

Dramatic readings might be arranged in class : relevant scenes are Act I, scene 1, scene 3, scene 4 (last half) ; Act II, scene 4 (from Lear's second entrance) ; Act IV,

CATECHISM STORIES

scene 4, scene 7; Act V, scene 3 (omitting most of the middle part).

Our debt to our parents

A boy was often asked by his mother to go errands or do various jobs for her, and sometimes she gave him a penny afterwards. Once when he had been kept rather busy, he made out a sort of bill and presented it, half in joke, to his mother.

Going seven errands	7d.
Minding the baby	3d.
Washing-up twice	2d.
Total	1s.

She looked at it and said: 'All right, we'll settle it to-morrow.' Next day she presented him with a contrary account:

	£	s.	d.
Board and lodging for 12 years	250	0	0
Clothing for same period	30	0	0
Laundry for same period	20	0	0
Nursing through Chicken-pox	1	0	0
Nursing through Mumps	1	0	0
Nursing through Scarlet-fever	5	0	0
	307	0	0

'As far as I can make out, you owe me £306 19s. 0d.'

'All right, Mum, I'll start working it off.—What can I do to-day?'

> * WHAT IS THE DUTY OF PARENTS TOWARDS THEIR CHILDREN?
>
> *The duty of parents towards their children is to provide for them, to instruct and correct them, and to give them a good Catholic education.*

Parental instruction lasts best

ST. ZITA began her life of serving God as a little maid in a nobleman's house, and ended it as the housekeeper of this same house, never having had the chance to do anything more heroic than housework. And yet she was declared one of God's saints, and hundreds of miracles were performed at her tomb. It was her mother who set her feet on the road to sanctity when she was only a very little girl by teaching her to make a rule of always asking herself, before she did anything, ' Will this please God ? ' or ' Might this be displeasing to God, and against His Divine Will ? ' Zita remembered this rule taught her by her mother all through her life, and found, as she grew up, that, sure enough, *everything in life* is either definitely pleasing to God or definitely displeasing.

How happy her mother in Heaven must have been when she saw that rule of hers slowly moulding her daughter into a saint.

[See also nos. 137, 234.]

What one good mother can do

St. Margaret was an English princess who went to marry the rough warrior Malcolm, King of Scotland, and spent her life reforming the uncouth and careless life at Court ; seeing that her poor subjects had justice ; getting the Catholic Faith properly taught and observed in Scotland, and, in short, doing all that a great Christian queen could possibly do.

She became the mother of eight children. Though she was so busy with many important matters, she counted her children as one of the most important of all. She took great care to find the ablest and wisest teachers for them. She was specially careful to see that they grew up good Christians, loving and understanding their Faith, and this part of their training she did not leave to teachers but undertook herself. She was rewarded, for four of her sons became good and brave kings of Scotland, one daughter a good queen of England, another a nun, and—best of all—David, the youngest boy, and the last to become king, has always been known as Saint David.

A historian has said : ' It is in great measure owing to

the virtuous education given by St. Margaret to her sons that Scotland was governed for the space of two hundred years by seven excellent kings—that is by her three sons, Edgar, Alexander, and David; by David's two grandsons, Malcolm IV and William; and William's son and grandson, Alexander II and III; during which space the nation enjoyed greater happiness than perhaps it ever did before or after.'

To show how much St. Margaret thought even of the simple duties of motherhood, one of her good works during Advent and Lent was daily to feed nine orphan babies, who were brought to her at daybreak. Taking them on her knee, she would feed them with her own silver spoon.

Wise love puts spiritual welfare first

Some parents love their children in a worldly way, not caring for their eternal interests.

St. John Calybite was born in Constantinople of noble parents. His mother gave him a book of the gospels when he was about twelve, and from reading it he longed to give his whole life to God, but his fond mother would never agree to his living a life of poverty and hardship. So, when some years older, he ran away from home with an abbot who passed that way on pilgrimage. After six years as a good monk he longed to see his home again, and the abbot allowed him to go. On the way he changed clothes with a beggar, and so disguised was unrecognized by his mother, who drove him from the door. After that he lived in a hovel near his home, practising prayer and good works. After three years he knew he was dying, sent for his mother, and revealed himself by showing her the book of the gospels which she had given him in childhood. He made her promise to bury him in his beggar's rags, and then died in her arms. After his death, thinking more of what people would think than of her promise, she arrayed his body in rich garments for burial. But she was struck with paralysis, which only left her when she dressed her son's body again in the garb of poverty.

(See also story 234, Ven. Ralph Milner.)

CATECHISM STORIES

True charity begins at home

In a family or household one person can often make all the difference in creating a happy home. That is, after all, for most people the greatest thing they can do for God.

Sir Launfal (the legend says) rode out in his splendid armour to seek the Holy Grail. A beggar sitting at his gate asked him for a cup of water. Sir Launfal threw him a coin and rode on. After a year he returned to his castle, humbled and disappointed in his quest. The beggar still sat at the gate, and once more asked for a cup of water. This time Sir Launfal got down from his horse, took the beggar's wooden cup and filled it at the stream. Suddenly the wooden cup, with the water in it, glowed with heavenly radiance, and the air around seemed full of music. At his own home he had found the Grail, it had been there all the time !

> * ARE WE COMMANDED TO OBEY OUR PARENTS ONLY ?
>
> *We are commanded to obey, not only our parents, but also our bishops and pastors, the civil authorities, and our lawful superiors.*

The wider Family

THE love of our own family is God-intended and beautiful, but it should not become a sort of group-selfishness, shutting others out. Rather it should tend to widen out, taking in our friends, our own countrymen, our fellow-Catholics, all mankind.

Our Lord taught this dramatically one day when He was speaking to the crowds. Somebody came and said : ' Behold thy mother and thy brethren stand without, seeking thee.' (The ' brethren ' were Our Lord's cousins, children of Our Lady's sister, Mary of Cleophas : see *Twelve and After*, p. 43.)

But He answered : ' Who is My mother, and who are My brethren ? '

He stretched forth His hand towards His disciples : ' Behold My mother and My brethren ! For whosoever shall

*BALTIMORE 246-249
ENGLISH CATECHISM 198

CATECHISM STORIES

do the will of My Father that is in heaven, he is My brother and sister and mother ! '

Anybody who will obey the Father of the Family is counted as a full member.

' Our Bishops and Pastors '

There was a by-election in a certain town, and one of the party candidates, Mr. So-and-so, was a Catholic. On the morning of the election the town was flooded with handbills : ' All Catholics must vote for So-and-so. The Bishop of Bigtown says we need a Catholic M.P. Father So-and-so says So-and-so's programme is the best. Obey your Bishop and your parish priest, and vote for So-and-so.'

Some Catholics said they certainly would, especially those that were going to vote for So-and-so anyhow. Others said the Bishop and parish priest ought to mind their own business, as the election had nothing to do with religion this time. Others said the handbill was only an election trick, and these turned out to be correct, for in the evening papers the Bishop and the parish priest both denied that they had said anything of the kind. When the result was declared at night, Mr. So-and-so was the defeated candidate.

We are bound to obey the authorities of the Church, but only in matters which concern the Church, either altogether or principally. [See also no. 107.]

The Lord's anointed

It is God who clothes the civil ruler with authority. This is illustrated in the story of the outlaw David refusing to kill his enemy King Saul, when at his mercy. Read the story from 1 Kings xxvi, 1-25. Add if you like 2 Kings i, 1-27.

All lawful authority is from God

We see this clearly in Our Lord's double trial, before the two highest authorities then on earth.

God's High Priest puts a solemn question to Him in God's name; and Our Lord, recognising his authority, gives an equally solemn answer (Matt. xxvi, 62-64).

Pilate, representing the Roman Emperor, reminds his Prisoner that he has power to crucify or release Him. Our Lord answers that whatever power the Governor has, it comes like all other authority from heaven (John xix, 9–11).

The same teaching was given by the first Pope. While St. Peter was still alive, thirty years after the Ascension, the pagans began to notice the Christians as a separate body from the Jews. The Christians had all along suffered from the enmity of the Jews, but now the pagans, too, were watching them suspiciously; all the more as so many Christians were slaves, and the new religion seemed to teach that all men were equal. In Rome itself, under Nero, there was a decree against the Christians, and many had been arrested and suffered torment and death; and the same seemed likely in other parts of the Empire. It was just then that St. Peter wrote his first epistle from Rome, and one point that he stressed was obedience to lawful authority as from God, recalling the example of Christ before Pilate.

Read the passage in 1 Peter ii, 11–23. (See also Rom. xiii, 1–2.)

We must obey the 'Civil Authorities'

A schoolboy, starting off to cycle home through the country lanes in the autumn dusk, found his cycle-lamp empty of oil. He could have bought some in the town, but it would have made him late for tea and other affairs, so he preferred to risk the ride with an unlighted lamp. As it happened he met no policeman and practically no traffic, and he decided there would be no great risk in doing the same every night. He therefore did so, partly to save trouble and expense and partly out of bravado, and got away with it safely until the days began to lengthen again after Christmas.

Are we bound to obey the laws of the land such as the one concerning lighting-up time? Certainly we are. On the first evening the boy had a good excuse of inconvenience, but afterwards his action was a sin against God (by whose

CATECHISM STORIES

authority, in the long run, all just laws are made) and an offence against the general welfare of the community.

Limits of Civil Authority

B. Sebastian Newdigate and his two companion martyrs hanged, drawn and quartered at Tyburn, were Carthusian monks. He had been favourite friend of Henry VIII before entering the Charterhouse monastery. Both in the Marshalsea (where they had to stand in chains, bound to posts, for thirteen days) and in the Tower Henry VIII visited him and tried to make him yield on the matter of the King's new title (Head of the Church). He answered: 'When in Court I served your Majesty, I did it loyally and faithfully, and so continue still your humble servant, although kept in this prison and bonds. But in matters that belong to the faith and glory of our Lord Jesus Christ, to the doctrine of the Catholic Church and the salvation of my poor soul, your Majesty must be pleased to excuse me.'

The King replied: 'Art thou wiser and holier than all the ecclesiastics and seculars of my kingdom?'

He answered: 'I may not judge of others, nor do I esteem myself either wise or holy, being far short in either; only this I assure myself that the faith and doctrine I profess is no new thing nor now invented, but always among the faithful held for Christian and Catholic. We must obey God rather than man.'

Bad laws not to be obeyed

The ideal Catholic layman, both in private and public life, was St. Thomas More. At home he was devoted to his four children and his eleven grandchildren. One of the greatest joys of his life was to go on expeditions into the country with his children and grandchildren on feast days.

Throughout life he put God first and thus preserved an admirable balance between the conflicting claims upon him. He loved his professional work as a lawyer and his life at court, yet he did not allow these to encroach on his family life, nor his family life on his studies, nor his studies on his prayers. All the important events of his life he prepared himself for by receiving Holy Communion. He showed that a man can live for the next world and yet be merry. Consequently, when the call came for a heroic choice he was ready.

On Monday, April 13, 1534, he was summoned to Lambeth Palace to take the oath of succession which as a Catholic he had to refuse. He was flung into the Tower where he endured many privations for a year.

On July 6, 1535, a little before 9 a.m., St. Thomas More, aged fifty-seven, wearing a coarse garment of frieze, and carrying a red cross, was led out from the Tower. As he proceeded on his way a woman, a second Veronica, offered him a cup of wine. Gently he declined it. ' My Master had vinegar and gall given Him to drink.' Arrived at the scaffold, he made a brief speech to the crowd, desiring them to bear witness that he should there suffer in and for the Catholic Faith. He concluded with these words : ' I die the King's good servant but God's first.' Kneeling, he recited the ' Miserere ' ; he then rose, kissed his executioner, covered his eyes himself with a cloth he had brought for the purpose, and lay face downwards, his head on the block. The axe whirled and with one stroke his head fell. Thus died one of England's noblest sons. (Acknowledgements to *Messenger of the Sacred Heart*.)

The Totalitarian State

In the stirring narrative of the Three Children of Israel in the Fiery Furnace (Dan. iii, 1-24) we are given, in the setting of an ancient empire (the political atmosphere, scholars tell us, is that of Syria under Antiochus, rather than of Babylon), a vivid picture of the ever-recurring struggle between the religious conscience and the Totalitarian State.

All the features we know so well are indicated in the story : The dictator and his megalomania, the terroristic decrees, the mass-gathering of Party representatives, the whole nation paraded for a propagandist festival, the heroism of the few lonely souls who stand up against the tyranny.

In the story God protects the Three Children by a miracle. He does not necessarily do so, but He does always have the last word. The real point of the story is in verse 18 : 'Our God can deliver us out of thy hands, O King ; but IF HE WILL NOT . . .'

When is a law not a law ?

A young man in Warwickshire got to know an American family on their holiday and fell in love with the daughter. Some months later he got his motor firm to send him to U.S.A. ; there he was able to spend a week in the small town where the young lady lived, and before the week was through they were engaged. On the Sunday evening he walked home with her from church, and kissed her good night outside the house.

'My goodness !' she said. 'You didn't ought to have done that !'

A police officer on the corner strolled over and said he must take their names and addresses. The young man asked what for.

'Say, don't you know it's against the law to kiss in the public street ?'

The young man thought he was joking, but the officer insisted :

'I tell you there's a law in this State which forbids kissing in public on Sundays—and in plenty other States too. Say, where was you reared ?'

The young man explained that he came from Coventry, England.

'Where Shakespeare was born' said the young lady.

'O.K. I guess I'll have to let you go this time, but remember that sort of conduct may have been all right for Shakespeare but you can't get away with it here.'

Interesting discussion might be : Is kissing wrong ? Unhygienic ? Immodest ? Between young people, engaged or otherwise ? Is it wrong in public ? Or in public on Sunday ? If the civil authority makes such a law, must it be obeyed ? [See also nos. 472, 671.]

CATECHISM STORIES

* WHAT DOES THE FIFTH COMMANDMENT FORBID ?
The fifth Commandment forbids all wilful murder, fighting, quarrelling, and injurious words; and also scandal and bad example.

'Thou shalt not kill'

CHIEF scriptural example : Cain and Abel (Gen. iv).

The classical treatment in English literature of wilful murder and its sinfulness is *Macbeth*. Dramatic reading could be arranged from Act I, scene 5, scene 7 ; Act II, scene 1, scene 2 ; Act III, scene 2 ; Act IV, scene 1 ; Act V, scene 1.

Murderous motorists

'A short time ago I was being driven by a friend in Birmingham. We were in an unfrequented street, on the footpath of which a little girl of about eight or nine was running briskly. Suddenly she recognised a friend on the opposite side of the street and took a running leap into the radiator without the least precaution.

'Yet there was no accident, for the car was instantly stopped and turned at the same time from the child. If that accident could be avoided there scarcely need be a motoring fatality. The escape was due entirely to a driver who is skilled, is an abstainer and—what is still more to the point—keeps his wits about him. A pint or two of beer, an "upset nerve" or any inattention would have meant yet another death—with an exoneration from all blame by any jury, especially by one functioning in Birmingham.' (A letter in the *Birmingham Mail*.)

Lawfulness of just war

A certain country called its trained men to the colours as a war seemed certain to break out. Four young men stood reading the mobilisation placards.

'I shall not go' said the first. 'All war is sinful. The Bible says : Thou shalt not kill ; and Our Lord says : Love your enemies.'

'I shall not go either,' said the second, who had read

*BALTIMORE 251-253
ENGLISH CATECHISM 206

CATECHISM STORIES

and thought a good deal. 'This war is wrong on both sides—just a fight between two sets of financiers for rich territory and new markets.'

'I don't agree with you,' said the third. 'Of course there's a good deal of that, but our country is only sticking up for our rights. We are fighting for freedom against force.'

The fourth said : 'Well, it's all beyond me, I can't see what it's all about. I shall do whatever our Government says, and if they're wrong they must take the blame.'

Discuss these various attitudes :

The first is mistaken. The Fifth Commandment does not forbid killing in self-defence, e.g. in a just war. And we can love our enemies even when we are defending ourselves from them.

The second is right to decide for himself if he is sure about the facts ; if he is sure the war is unjust he would be doing wrong to kill in it.

The third is right also in using his judgement, though either he or the previous speaker must be mistaken about the facts.

The fourth is right too ; if he doesn't feel competent to judge for himself he can leave it to the authorities.

In general : unless sure that a given war is not justified, a Catholic should obey his Government when called on to fight, though even then he should not join in methods of war which are unlawful, e.g. deliberate killing of civilians.

There need be no war

In our own times Chile and Argentina disputed over their frontier which ran along the mountains of the Andes. Both were preparing for war. On Easter Sunday the Archbishop of Buenos Ayres preached a sermon urging peaceful methods for Christ's sake : the Bishops in Chile acted in like manner. Their people listened, and the dispute was brought to the arbitration of the King of England (Edward VII), and there was no war. In thanksgiving, and to show that henceforth war is impossible between the two countries, they decided to melt some heavy guns from the fortresses and make them into a gigantic statue of the Sacred Heart, and set it up at the frontier on the summit of the mountains. The statue was so heavy that the mules could not get it to the top, but the men of both countries dragged it the rest of the way by ropes. There, between the two nations, high on the mountain-top, stands the 'Christ of the Andes' to remind them of their promise of perpetual peace.

Cruelty is always in men's hearts

In spite of Christianity the cruel and bloody spectacle of the amphitheatres, especially the gladiatorial shows, still continued in the early fifth century.

An old hermit named Telemachus lived in the mountains, and heard at prayer a voice telling him : ' Go to Rome—I have work for you there ! ' He was old and reluctant and tried to treat it as illusion, but the voice persisted and at last he took the toilsome road to Rome.

Arriving there one morning, he was drawn along to the Coliseum with the crowds which were converging there. He took his seat, an incongruous figure, unmindful of the mocking smiles of the city folk around him.

Two parties of gladiators marched round the arena and lined up to fight. Then the old hermit suddenly knew what he had to do, and strength came to him to do it. He ran down the gangways, got into the arena, and stood between the combatants and shouted : ' In the name of Jesus Christ who died for men ! Do not kill each other ! '

A moment of silence, then laughter from the gladiators and an angry roar from the crowd. Someone threw a stone, many others followed. In a minute or two St. Telemachus lay dead on the sand.

But the incident was talked of everywhere, and many said he was right. The Christian conscience awakened, and soon the Emperor issued a decree which ended these cruel and murderous public entertainments.

Cruelty, blood-lust, even murder lives under the surface in the hearts of ordinary men. Only Jesus Christ is strong enough to hold it in check.

We must not take our own life

The first native of the Bakossi tribe (Cameroons, West

Africa) to become a Catholic was Pius Epic, a servant to a European near Victoria. This was in 1908, and in 1914 he returned to his own tribe and spread the faith with such success that in 1919 the pagan ju-ju men called a big council at Mesaka to decide what should be done. The judgement was that Pius must stop teaching or suffer death. He chose the latter.

He was taken to the top of a little mound, where a rope was thrown over a tree-branch and he was ordered to place his own head in the noose. Pius refused. 'If you wish to hang me that is your palaver—I will not kill myself.'

The pagans were enraged, but were afraid of the Government's vengeance on murder and thought better of it at the last moment. They sent a medicine-man to practise spells on Pius in his own house, but that also failed. Then the brave native went to Ktoko, the chief of the Bakossi, and got permission to build a doctrine house for his catechumens. He built it close to the mound where he had stood waiting to be hanged. To-day there is a wooden cross on top of the mound, which is one of the favourite places for the Mesaka Catholics to come and pray.

When can we risk our own life?

Captain Scott's little party reached the South Pole on January 17, 1913, and endured terrible hardships and discouragement on the return march. Evans was very weak, and died on February 17. The going was so rough they could only drag the sledges at one mile an hour. Oil supplies were short, and night-temperatures 40 degrees below zero. Captain Oates' feet were frostbitten, and getting worse. The entry in Scott's diary for March 3 was:

'God help us, we can't keep up this pulling, that is certain. Amongst ourselves we are unendingly cheerful, but what each man feels in his heart I can only guess.' About the middle of March, one night Captain Oates, knowing he was becoming a drag on his comrades, walked out quietly from the tent, right away, and did not return.

His body was never found, but the relief party which

came long after found the tent, built a cairn of ice, and placed a wooden cross with the inscription : ' Near to this place died a very gallant gentleman.'

Suicide is always a sin, but was this suicide ? No, because Oates did not take his life. What he *did* was merely to walk away from the party ; this action had two results, the first being to give the party a better chance of surviving, the second certain death for himself in the frozen wastes. He *intended* the first result, and *permitted* the second.

But is it not a sin to risk our life and health, e.g., for a boy to ignore warnings and sit about in a cold wind at the end of a hot football game ? True, we must not risk life *unreasonably ;* but Oates had a very good reason.

> * DOES THE FIFTH COMMANDMENT FORBID ANGER ?
> *The fifth Commandment forbids anger, and still more, hatred and revenge.*

Hatred and Revenge

A GREAT painter was at work on a picture of the Last Supper. He had an enemy and he decided to take a great public revenge. When he painted Judas in the picture he made it a portrait of his enemy. All the world would see—his enemy would be humiliated !

At last the picture was nearly finished ; but every time the artist tried to paint the face of Christ, he couldn't get on with the work ; he had to stop, and do another part instead. At last the whole picture was finished— all except Our Lord. The artist was in despair.

One day a holy friar visited the studio. He told the artist that no one who has *unforgiveness* and *revenge* in his heart can have Christ's likeness (i.e. grace) in his soul ; this was why he could not paint the picture of Christ. The great painter understood. He forgave his enemy, painted out the Judas and put another face instead. *Then* he was able to paint a beautiful portrait of Christ that all the world has admired ever since. [Against Revenge : see nos. 71, 206 ; On Anger : 131, 394.]

*BALTIMORE 253
ENGLISH CATECHISM 207

'Fighting, quarrelling, and injurious words'

A good deal of this would be avoided if people would control their tongues.

A woman came to a priest complaining that her husband knocked her about; but the priest guessed that he was provoked to it by his wife's nagging tongue. He gave her a bottle.

'Here you are, this is miraculous water, you'll find it will put everything right.'

'What do I do? Sprinkle it on my husband?'

'No, all you have to do is to keep some in your mouth. As long as you do that he will never feel any desire to hit you.'

On reflection she saw the point, and it worked.

(*N.B. on same topic:*

'Poor woman, she won't be able to nag her husband any more.'

'What, lost him?'

'No, he's gone deaf.')

The sin of Scandal

A young man got a commission in his father's old regiment. He was quiet and serious and seemed to find it difficult to make friends with his fellow-officers. For one thing, he drank no wine or spirits, and night after night he refused the drinks that were offered him. This annoyed the other young men, and one guest-night, by badgering and taunts, they induced the newcomer to have a drink. Then one drink followed another until the young man was hopelessly drunk. Someone helped him to bed and next day his fellow-officers awaited him in the Mess ready with jokes about the one-time teetotaller. The young man, however, never appeared among them again. He was far away in a sordid London lodging, drinking himself to death.

Then it became known that the boy had taken to drinking soon after he left school but had made a manful effort to conquer his weakness. When he got his commission he had promised his father not to take alcohol at all. All would have gone well had it not been for the cruel thoughtlessness of the other young officers.

Reparation for Scandal

' He gave up £1,000,000. A strange story, that of Frederick Charrington, who lived in two small rooms with his parrot, with an old friend and servant, fighting poverty, drunkenness, and prostitution.

' He lived among the people he served in the East End of London. He was the friend of thousands and the benefactor of thousands. He was born rich, heir to the Charrington brewery million. Years ago, " taking a night out," he saw a drunken man strike his wife into the gutter. And he looked up and saw above him the slogan, " Drink Charrington's Beer ! "

' He gave up that fortune, you may think foolishly, for he might have done much good with it. He thought not. Certainly Charrington did infinite good without it.' (*Daily Express.*)

' That's why I don't go to church ! '

Poor human nature ! It is a sad fact that religious people are often very unamiable, even to each other : even in connection with church work !

A little girl prayed : ' Please, God, make all the bad people good and all the good people nice.'

And some poet sang :

> ' Living with the saints above,
> All is peace and glory.
> Living with the saints below,
> That's another story.'

Let's avoid *that* pitfall anyhow. Good Catholics ought to be a recommendation for their religion by their inward joy and outward kindness.

The force of a good example

Just as scandal injures or kills our neighbour's soul, so good example fills others with life and courage.

CATECHISM STORIES

During the retreat from Mons in 1914, when several hundred British stragglers were left behind lying about exhausted in the streets of St. Quentin, waiting for the Germans to arrive, determined to surrender rather than go on, a British General managed to get them on the march again by playing a tin whistle.

About thirty years later, when the General (Sir Tom Bridges) had at last ended his fifty years' connection with the army, a newspaper reporter got from him a first-hand account of the incident which had long been famous.

'The men in the square were so fatigued that it was pathetic to see them. If one only had a band, I thought. Why not? There was a toyshop handy, which provided my trumpeter and myself with a tin whistle and a drum, and we marched round and round the fountain where the men were lying like dead, playing the "British Grenadiers" and "Tipperary" and beating the drum like mad.

'They sat up and began to laugh, and even to cheer. They began to stand up and fall in, and eventually we moved slowly off into the night to the music of our improvised band, now reinforced by a couple of mouth organs.'

> * WHAT DOES THE SIXTH COMMANDMENT FORBID?
> *The sixth Commandment forbids all sins of impurity with another's wife or husband.*

'Thou shalt not commit adultery'

IN this Commandment stories of happy and virtuous marriage are perhaps more desirable than stories of sin; but if the latter are deemed useful, the chief Scriptural example of course is of David and Bethsabee, with David's repentance, told marvellously in 2 Kings xi, 1–27, xii, 1–14. Commentators point out that idleness contributed to David's unchastity: he stayed at home instead of going with his army, and he stayed in bed all hours. Also that he broke the fifth Commandment by scandal, leading another into sin, as well as by murder.

*BALTIMORE 254
ENGLISH CATECHISM 210

CATECHISM STORIES

Add that in his contrition David composed the 50th psalm, *Miserere*, which could profitably be read aloud as the ending to the story.

The havoc of passions uncontrolled

Adultery, like suicide, is a selfishness or cowardice which leaves a tangle of every kind of calamity for others. Often it leads to other sins.

Another Scriptural instance is the sin which was connected with the death of St. John the Baptist.

Herod Antipas, tetrarch of Galilee, was on a visit to Rome, and was fascinated by his niece Herodias, a handsome and passionate woman, who was married to his brother Philip and had a young daughter named Salome. Herodias, tired of living in retirement with Philip, and ambitious for power, went off with Herod to Palestine (taking Salome with her) making the condition that Herod should divorce his wife and marry herself. Herod did so, and this brought about a war with his first wife's father, King Aretas of Arabia, in which Herod's army was slaughtered.

Meanwhile St. John the Baptist had rebuked the tetrarch for his sin, and Herodias sought revenge; the rest of this episode is told in Mark vi, 17–29.

A year or two later, Herod was in Jerusalem for the Pasch when Our Lord was arrested; Pilate sent Our Lord to Herod, who thus had an opportunity to set Him free, but instead he mocked Our Lord as a fool, and sent Him back to Pilate; which shows how, in many cases, a habit of impurity hardens the heart and darkens spiritual sight.

In the end, Herodias and her ambitions brought Herod to ruin. Her brother Agrippa got himself appointed to rule Judea, with the title of king. Herodias was envious because her husband was only a tetrarch, and she persuaded him to go to Rome and ask for the title of king also. He did so, but Agrippa was beforehand with messages accusing him of conspiracy. He was deposed and banished to Lyons, where Herodias followed him, and they seem to have ended up in Spain. [See also nos. 601, 619, 620, 623.]

Marriage is a free promise

Marriage is a free contract for life, freely entered into, and that is why the partners should be loyal to it.

Amongst the slaves exposed for sale in the market of Paris (roughly about A.D. 640) was a golden-haired English girl of noble family, about fourteen, who had been carried off in a raid by Frankish pirates. Her name was Bathilde. A Frankish chieftain, Erchinoald, Mayor of the Palace, was struck with her beauty, bought her for his household, treated her well and had her waiting at his table. His wife died and he wanted to marry Bathilde, but not liking the idea, she ran away and only came back when he had married someone else.

The young King Clovis II, aged seventeen, often dined at the house of the Mayor of the Palace, and fell in love with the young slave who waited on him. He proposed to marry her.

'Sire,' she answered quietly, 'I am your slave, and whether or no I am bound to submit.'

'No,' said Clovis, 'a slave cannot be Queen. I set you free henceforth, and you are quite free to accept or reject my offer as you choose.'

Secretly she loved the young king as much as he loved her, but she did not at once accept.

'I thank you for the great favour you show me, but I could not accept without leave from my father.'

So messengers were sent to England, consent duly obtained, and Bathilde became Queen in 649. She remained sweet and humble, and good to the poor, and everyone loved her.

After seven years Clovis died, and she had to rule France through troubled years until her sons were old enough. With the help of holy bishops like St. Eloi, St. Ouen, and St. Leger, she did great things for the people, founded many churches and hospitals, and did away with the trade in Christian slaves. After ten more years she retired to the Abbey of Chelles, where she insisted on her rank being forgotten, taking place after the novices, and serving the poor and infirm with her own hands. She died a holy death A.D. 680.

Loving each other in God

One of the most pleasing love-stories in the lives of the saints (though so tragically cut short in this earthly life) is that of St. Elizabeth of Hungary.

She was a princess of that country (b. 1207), and at the age of four was promised in marriage to the son of the Landgrave of Thuringia, and according to custom sent (in a silver cradle or litter) to be brought up at his court in the famous hill-castle of the Wartburg, where she was welcomed with festivities and fireworks.

The Landgrave's eldest son died soon, and Elizabeth was solemnly betrothed instead to the second son, Louis, then eleven years old. He was very fond of her from the first, and always called her 'little sister,' and took her side when she was in trouble; and she naturally worshipped him, but he was often away from court learning how to be a knight or on hunting expeditions. When he came back from these absences, he always brought some present for his 'little sister.'

Seven little girls of noble family were provided to live with Elizabeth and play with her; she should have been very happy, but as she grew older the ladies of the castle, especially (some say) the Landgravine and her daughter Agnes, took a dislike to little Elizabeth because she was not so worldly as they were. 'More like a nun than a princess,' they said. She loved being in church, disliked wearing fine dresses and jewels, and gave all her pocket-money to the beggars at the gates. Even as a baby at home she used to cry at the sight of the misery of the poor.

When she was nine the old Landgrave died, and the castle ladies treated Elizabeth more scornfully than ever. Louis would never marry her, they said; she would be sent back to Hungary in disgrace, or put in a convent.

She wept many secret tears, but her distress turned to joy one day when the old Lord Varila (who had escorted her from Hungary when she was only four) came to her with a message from Louis. He had told Louis himself about the rumours that he would not marry Elizabeth after all, and Louis had been very angry. He stretched his hand towards Mount Inselberg, the highest peak in the country. 'If that mountain were all made of gold and precious stones, I would not take it in exchange for Elizabeth. She is dearer to me than all the world besides.'

Lord Varila asked if he could tell this to Elizabeth.

'Yes, tell her! And give her this locket from me, as a pledge that my love cannot change.'

It was a locket he wore himself of jewelled crystal, enclosing a tiny mirror and a picture of Our Lord. After that Elizabeth was happy, whatever the castle ladies might say or do.

Some time after this they were married. Louis was twenty, tall, fair, strong, fearless, and very good-humoured; Elizabeth was fourteen, of an ethereal kind of beauty, perfect complexion, large dark eyes.

Now they could be together all the time; if Louis had to go journeying Elizabeth would go with him, however rough the road, in rain or in snow, riding by his side.

For seven years they were marvellously happy. Their great love for each other took nothing away from their love of God. During the night Elizabeth still rose to say her long prayers; sometimes Louis would kneel by her side, or sometimes keep her hand clasped while he slept.

Once at Mass she found her eyes fixed on Louis instead of the altar: the elevation-bell suddenly recalled her attention, and instead of the Host she seemed to see the crucified figure of Our Lord. She remained in church a long time, shedding tears of contrition for her distraction, until Louis came (while dinner and guests waited), and she told him her trouble. He told her to have more confidence in God, and she was reassured.

Louis helped her with her charities for the poor and suffering, which now had full scope. These were the years when St. Francis was preaching and his friars were beginning to spread; Germany was the first country they came to. Louis and Elizabeth welcomed them and gave them a monastery. They were both full of the spirit of St. Francis; in fact St. Francis himself sent his cloak to Elizabeth, as from master to disciple. She used to put it on when she wanted to pray specially for something.

Two well-known stories (the roses, and the leper) will be found in Part V under the 'Corporal works of Mercy.' In both legends we can discern Louis's wondering acceptance of her unconventional style in charity.

Once when Louis was away for a time attending on the Emperor, there was much distress in Thuringia through famine. Left in charge of the Wartburg, Elizabeth defied the officials and gave away all the money in the treasury, and had all the stores of grain made into bread and given away to all comers. Finally she sold all her own jewellery and all the gold and silver plate of the banqueting hall. When Louis came back, the officials met him with their complaints. But he still stuck up for her as when they were children.

'Tell me, how is my wife—is she well ? That is all I care about. She can give away as much as she likes : it's your business to help her do it.'

They had four children : when her babies were born Elizabeth would dress herself in a poor woollen frock like any peasant, and herself carry her baby to church and offer it to God.

After seven years of happiness came tragedy. Louis, on a visit to the Emperor, had taken the vow to join the crusade the Emperor was organising, but he intended to keep the news from Elizabeth as long as possible. Sitting with him one day, she playfully opened the wallet he wore at his belt to take some money for her poor and out fell a small cross, which she recognised at once as the badge of the crusade. She fainted right off, and then implored him : ' Dear brother, if it be not against the will of God, stay with me ! ' But when she knew he had made a vow to God she gave him up generously.

When the time of departure came he showed her his signet ring and said she must believe any messenger who brought it to her as a sign. She couldn't bring herself to say good-bye ; she rode to the frontier with him, then another day's ride, then just one more ; till at last she had to stop and watch the long troop ride on out of her sight.

CATECHISM STORIES

A few months later a knight came back with the signet ring and the news that Louis had died of a fever at Otranto. She was frantic with grief. 'Now is the whole world dead to me!' she cried.

She was twenty when this blow fell, and she lived only four years longer—four years of incredible suffering and hardships and of swift ascent to high sanctity. But that is another story.

What real love means

Real wedded love means that each partner is thinking of the other and how to please the other, more than of self.

On September 13, 1935, there was a colliery explosion at North Gawber (Yorkshire). Fifteen men were caught in a sheet of flame, burned all over, and then soon killed by gas.

Following is from the *Daily Express* of September 21, 1935:

'A dying message to his wife, chalked on a block of stone by one of the victims, was found in the mine yesterday by an official. It said simply : " Farewell, Fanny, old pet." Three crosses, representing kisses, followed.

'The writing was identified as that of Albert Edward Ibberson, of Maplewell.

'With the greatest care, to avoid obliterating the wording, the stone was cut out and taken to his wife and child at home.'

Loyalty

'The story of St. Louis (of France) gathers round two objects—a ring and a cross. The ring was his wedding ring and the cross was that of a crusader. . . .

'The young king inherited his mother's personal beauty and strong faith. . . . When he was nineteen he married, in the great Cathedral of Sens, the lovely Margaret of Provence, the sister of Eleanor, Queen of Henry II. For his wedding day, May 27, A.D. 1234, St. Louis had a gold ring made, which from that day forward he always wore.

On the ring three words were cut: "God, France, Margaret." It is said that he liked to show the ring to his friends, and that he would tell them what it signified to him. "Outside this ring," he would say, "I have no love; my God, my country and my home."

'The marriage was abundantly blessed by God with a loyal, happy union of hearts. Margaret bore him eleven children, and she was the most beloved and beautiful of queens and a devoted wife and mother.' (J. A. Bouquet, *People's Book of Saints*.) [See also nos. 517, 519, 527.]

> * DOES THE SIXTH COMMANDMENT FORBID WHATEVER IS CONTRARY TO HOLY PURITY?
> *The sixth Commandment forbids whatever is contrary to holy purity in looks, words, or actions.*

'Whatever is contrary to holy purity'

THE scene is the camp of the Turtle Clan of the Mohawks, in the year 1667. The tribe has been at war with the French, but one day the Mohawk messengers arrive from Quebec, bringing news of a peace treaty. Three French Jesuit missionaries, who had helped in the treaty, are with the messengers; they stay three days in the camp, and in conversation with groups of squaws and children they speak of the Christian religion.

One intent listener is a girl of eleven, shy and pretty, though with face marked by smallpox. Tekakwitha's father had been a Mohawk warrior; in a raid on the Christian Algonquins he saved an Algonquin girl from death and married her; but both these parents had died of smallpox when Tekakwitha was four, and her father's brother, the chief, had adopted her and treated her more or less as a slave.

She listened to the Black-robes without doubting, and from that moment was a Christian at heart, though she dared say nothing. But she held herself apart from the vices and bloodthirsty customs and frenzied dances of the Indians, and would have nothing to do with the plans which the squaws were always making for her marriage.

The Mohawks moved further north to another hunting-

*BALTIMORE 255-256
ENGLISH CATETCHISM 211

ground. When Tekakwitha was eighteen Père de Lamberville came to evangelise that district, and she went to his chapel-hut for instructions, braving the scorn and threats of the tribe, who hated her for living her own life so different from their own cruelty and lust.

The priest saw that she was like a white lily growing amid evil-smelling weeds. One day as she came from the chapel, where she had been praying before Our Lady's statue for help to lead a chaste and modest life, the children pelted her with mud and stones, while their elders looked on approvingly; the Black-robe came out to protect her. 'It is becoming dangerous for you here, I will baptize you to-morrow.'

Next day she waited at the river till Père de Lamberville came in his canoe, then knelt joyfully at his feet as he poured the water of baptism on her head and gave her the name of Kateri. 'Now you are truly a child of God. St. Catherine will protect you, and you shall remain as pure as the angels of God.'

After baptism she practised her religion faithfully, but her life was more and more in danger from the tribe because she would not join in their wicked ways.

One day some Christian Indians, of the Oneida tribe in the north, came to the camp. The Mohawks hated them, but could not refuse hospitality. Tekakwitha helped to roast a deer and served at dinner.

One of the visitors was an old man named Bright Shell, a cousin of her dead mother. As Tekakwitha passed close to him at dinner, he whispered: 'Be ready to-night! We are to take you to the Mission on the St. Lawrence!'

Wildly excited within, she gave no outward sign; but next time she passed near Bright Shell she said secretly: 'Does the Black-Robe know?'

'He has given me a letter for the other Black-Robe in the North.'

At night, when all in Turtle Chief's cabin were sleeping on their rush mats, Tekakwitha rose silently and ran with noiseless steps through the woods to the river. The Christian Indians were waiting, and as she jumped in one of the canoes they paddled swiftly away.

Next morning her flight was discovered, and a Mohawk party in war-paint raged through the forests, but it was too late. Tekakwitha reached the St. Lawrence, and went to live with a Christian squaw named Tegonhatsihonga. She soon reached high states of prayer, and everyone looked on her as a saint of God. She was only twenty-four when she died, and is known as 'the Lily of the Mohawks.'

(From *Catholic Encyclopedia* and Sister Rosa, S.S.I., in *Holy Childhood Annals*.)

Our Lady, safeguard of holy purity

St. Edmund of Canterbury, when a boy of twelve at Oxford, with the consent of his confessor, resolved to make a vow of perpetual chastity. He went to the church and uttered this promise aloud before the statue of Our Lady, and then placed on its finger a ring which he had bought for the purpose. 'To thee, O Virgin of virgins, I offer m' promise. And with this ring I choose thee as My Lady and spouse, that I may serve thee with more devotion in the future.' Then he knelt and prayed with tears : 'O my Lady, most sweet spouse of my heart, pray to thy Son that I may follow in the footsteps of St. John.' Then, lest the ring on the statue should attract notice, he tried to take it from the finger, but found it impossible to do so, and there it long remained and was seen 'by the whole University.'

Quite apart from vows of chastity, praying to Our Lady is one of the surest helps for everybody against temptation. [See also nos. 342, 624.]

Modesty

St. Bee's Head in Cumberland is named after St. Bega, a beautiful Irish princess who had many royal suitors, but who wished rather to consecrate herself to God in the religious life. One day a mysterious stranger stood before her, who seemed to know all her thoughts ; he told her to hold fast to her vow, and gave her a bracelet engraved with a cross as a token-gift from God. But her father—stern and dominating—arranged with a prince from Norway to come and claim her in marriage.

CATECHISM STORIES

The Norwegians arrived, and that day there was riotous feasting and revelry, the end of which was that everybody lay in a drunken sleep. Horrified at the prospect before her, and following an inspiration from God, Bega crept through the drunken warriors, went down to the seashore, and embarked in a boat which was just sailing for Britain.

It took her to Copeland Forest, on the coast of Cumberland, and there for some years she lived alone hermit-fashion in a cave near Kirkby. It is said the sea-gulls and wolves brought her food.

But pirates came to that coast, and once more modesty counselled flight. Bega fled over the hills to St. Aidan, who was then helping St. Oswald to convert Northumbria. She became the first nun in the north and founded a convent at Hartlepool, afterwards handing it over to her friend St. Hilda to govern, herself retiring to Tadcaster to live as a hermit.

(The story of the thirteen-year-old St. Agnes is the traditional example on this topic : one version of it will be found in *Stories in School*, page 22.)

Vanity

Another fault that may sometimes lead to breaking the Sixth Commandment by oneself or others, is vanity.

St. Rose of Lima as a girl was remarkable for her beauty, and had a rather foolish mother, who tried to show her daughter off. In reaction against this, and in order to fulfil her desire of remaining single, Rose took desperate measures against vanity. When her beautiful hair was praised, she cut it short. When some young man had paid compliments to the smooth skin of her hand, she plunged it into quicklime. When forced to go to some party to be admired, she rubbed on her face an Indian pepper which caused blotches and pimples. When her mother made her wear roses in her hair, she wore a pin beneath them to prick her forehead.

At twenty she was at last allowed to go her own way. She became a Dominican tertiary, lived in a cell in her garden, and died aged thirty-one. Our Lord often appeared

CATECHISM STORIES

to her, and she would offer Him all her penances in reparation for men's sins.

Ordinarily girls should try to look their best, even if they intend not to marry. Don't imitate St. Rose in her singularities, but in her determination to avoid the sort of vanity which shows off and tries to make others jealous.

How not to be vain

'When Queen Mary drove through Lambeth with the Princess Royal she saw fair-haired Rosemary Jenkins and asked: "Where did you get that lovely hair?" and Rosemary replied: "I got it from God, Your Majesty." Rosemary is seven, the daughter of a railway porter, and was waiting outside the Old Vic with a bouquet.'—*Daily Express*, March 22, 1939.

'Occasions of sin.'

In the years after World War I there was an enormous craze for dancing, especially for the newer one-partner dances. Many people of stricter views disapproved strongly.

The learned and saintly Archbishop McIntyre (of Birmingham) was asked by a parish priest to give his approval to some Sunday-night dances which were being arranged for the young people, in the old schools belonging to the church.

'Certainly I approve,' said the Archbishop, although he knew that many people, both Protestants and Catholics, would profess to be shocked at what was then an innovation. 'In fact I will come there and give them all my blessing.'

So during the first evening the Archbishop, in cassock and feriola, came in with the parish priest, and spoke informally to the dancers as they stood round him.

'Dancing is a healthy exercise,' he said, 'and a good and natural form of social recreation. The Church likes to see you enjoy yourselves. It is sin that spoils everything, so keep out of sin and be as happy as you please.' Then the dancers all knelt down and the Archbishop gave them his blessing.

'Puritan' principles in their extremest form (Manichean)

are heretical. But there is a common puritanical outlook, or temperament, which exaggerates the danger in occasions of sin, or sees an occasion of sin where for most people is none.

In such matters people are different, and the only way is for each person to decide honestly what is a danger for himself or herself. But the Puritan is always trying to make all sorts of little rules to be kept by *everybody*. [See also nos. 340–346, 621, 622.]

> * WHAT DOES THE SEVENTH COMMANDMENT FORBID ?
>
> *The seventh Commandment forbids all unjust taking away, or keeping what belongs to another. All manner of cheating in buying and selling is forbidden by the seventh Commandment, and also every other way of wronging our neighbour.*

'Thou shalt not steal'

ST. MARTIN, after leaving the army and staying some time with St. Hilary (who made him an exorcist), thought he ought to visit his own province and parents still pagan. While crossing the Alps he fell amongst brigands ; one was about to split his head with an axe, but was restrained by another. Then Martin was bound and left with one brigand to guard and search him. He began by asking Martin who he was.

'I am a Christian.'

'Aren't you afraid ? '

' I never felt more confident in the Lord's mercy. *You* are the one to be pitied, not I, since you practise the trade of a a robber and so make yourself unfit for the mercy of Christ.'

The brigand was listening. Martin proceeded to expound God's word to him, and he believed. He showed Martin the way back to the road, and said farewell, asking his prayers. Henceforth the man led a blameless life, and later told the story to Sulpicius Severus, who tells it to us.

St. Martin in due course reached his home, converted his mother, but not his father, got into much trouble with the local Arians, and at last rejoined St. Hilary at Poitiers.

*BALTIMORE 259-261
ENGLISH CATECHISM 215-216

Habits of dishonesty

The habit of making free with other people's belongings is easy to acquire and not so easy to give up. An illustration in lighter vein :

'The Bishop of Leeds told an entertaining tale of a Manchester priest. This priest picked up in his car a man who emerged from Strangeways Gaol and asked for a lift. In conversation he said he had been inside for picking pockets. This rather disturbed the priest, and driving in a little agitation he disregarded the traffic lights and was brought to book by a policeman, who took down all particulars. When the time came for him to drop his passenger the man said : ' Thank you, Father. As one good turn deserves another, here is the policeman's notebook.'—D. W. in *The Tablet*.

'Keeping what belongs to another'

Some people are not above ' keeping what belongs to another ' when given too much change, etc. They should learn from such an example as the following :

'A homeless and nameless man approached a coffee stall in Waterloo Road yesterday and begged for some scraps. The kind-hearted woman in charge, Mrs. Varney, collected every spare bit of food she could find and gave them to him in a paper bag.

'Some hours after he had gone she discovered she had placed the scraps in the bag containing part of the night's takings. She was much distressed, the man she had helped could not be found, and she resigned herself to the loss.

'Suddenly her tattered beneficiary reappeared at the stall. He had £6 10s. in his hand. " I found this in the bag with the food you gave me," he said, and vanished.'

A newspaper cutting, date uncertain.

And this?

" I say, have you still got Jones's lawn mower ? "

" What's that to do with you ? "

" Well, lend it me and I'll lend you his roller."

Finding is not keeping

It is a comfort to know that there are people in the world who remain honest under the greatest possible temptation, and when they would never be found out. Let us hope that we should all have done the same as the man in this story :

'Police-Superintendent Arnold, of Burton, on Saturday handed £6 8s. 6d., publicly subscribed by post and through a local fund, to Alfred Pierce (36), a native of West Ham, who gained notoriety as the "honest tramp" when, in July last, he found £29 in Treasury Notes and 6s. 6d. in silver wrapped in a red handkerchief on the Derby Road and took the money direct to the police station. At the time he had only a halfpenny in his possession, and the police gave him sufficient for his night's lodging and food.

'Although the £29 was claimed in September by an Irishman, who established his ownership, nothing was heard of Pierce until he called at the police-station on Friday night. He was then told that there was some reward for him, although the owner of the money had only proffered a half-crown.'—*Birmingham Mail*, in March, 1938

Honesty

'Honest Abe' was Lincoln's nickname as a store-keeper in New Salem ; his fellow-citizens knew he could always be trusted, and they elected him postmaster.

Once a stranger left seventeen dollars for some reason with the postmaster, and disappeared without claiming it. Many years after, when Lincoln was a famous politician, this man turned up and asked for the money. Lincoln promptly opened a box and produced a little bag in which the seventeen dollars had been kept ready all that time.

As a lawyer in Springfield, he often let business take second place to honesty. To one client he said : 'I can win your case and get 600 dollars for you. But if I did, I should bring misfortune on an honest family, and I can't see my way to it. I would rather get along without your case and your fee. I will give you a piece of advice without charging you for it. Go home and try to think of some honester way of earning 600 dollars.'

CATECHISM STORIES

Be worthy of trust

Many places and churches in Northern France are named after St. Eloi (Eligius). He was at first a goldsmith, and it is related that he was commissioned by King Clotaire II to make a throne covered with beaten gold. When the time came for the completing of the work and the King came to see the result, the honest goldsmith showed him two magnificent thrones which he had been able to make out of the gold supplied to him for the work. Struck with such notable honesty, the King gave him a post of great trust at his court. Later St. Eligius became a priest and a great bishop.

Carrying out a bargain

A business man, anxious about the success of some plan, came out of a Liverpool church and met a very small girl just going in to make a visit after school. He stopped her and gave her a penny.

'Say a Hail Mary for my intention, please.'

He went on down the road, but had not gone far before the little girl came running after him. She offered him the penny back.

'Please, I can't say the Hail Mary all through!'

Bishops ought to defend God's poor

St. Hugh, a monk of the Grande Chartreuse, was sent to England to be Prior of a monastery recently founded by King Henry II, at Witham in Somerset. When he got there he found that its land had been provided by driving poor peasants off their holdings; these now lived in the woods, troublesome and discontented, and had already made life miserable for two former Priors. Hugh had been sent for because he had the name of being tough and shrewd, and likely to succeed where others had failed.

The first thing he did at Witham was to go to the King and tell him he had done an injustice to the peasants, and unless it was righted his monks could not keep the monastery. To everybody's amazement, the King listened and arranged for the dispossessed to be well compensated with other land elsewhere.

Not only so, but he took such a liking to this fearless Prior that when the See of Lincoln fell vacant he got the reluctant St. Hugh elected to fill it. The new Bishop came to his Cathedral for enthronement not riding but walking on his bare feet. Instead of the usual banquet to the nobles and clergy of the district, he insisted on inviting all the poor as well, and the keeper of Stowe Park was thunderstruck when he was told to kill three hundred deer for the feast in place of the usual thirty.

One of his first tasks at Lincoln was to rebuild the Cathedral which had fallen in an earthquake just before he came. He was not content with making the plans, but loved to roll his sleeves up and carry a few baskets of stone himself.

As Bishop he defended the poor more stoutly than ever; he denounced the cruel forest-laws and once he excommunicated the chief Royal forester for oppressing some poor labourer, nor did the King's intercession make any difference until the forester had made amends. To the King, St. Hugh said: ' The poor men who are tortured by your foresters will enter heaven while you and your foresters have to stay outside ' (*foris stare*—a play on words).

King Richard came to the throne and demanded a tax for a war with France. St. Hugh condemned the tax and went to Normandy to see the King, who refused to speak to him or give him the kiss of peace. But St. Hugh insisted on giving the kiss, and then, with perfect good-humour and sweetness, talked to the King about his conscience.

' Every day,' he said, ' I hear complaints of the oppression of poor men, the innocent wronged, and crushing taxes levied on the people. Not only that, but I hear also that you are unfaithful to your wife.'

The King was furious, and the saint, still smiling and calm, left him.

' Truly,' said the King later, ' if all prelates were like that one, not a King in Christendom would dare to raise his head in the presence of a Bishop ! '

Jordan de Turri, a rich man in the City of London, had defrauded two orphans. St. Hugh was appointed by the Pope as judge in the case. Jordan came arrogantly to the trial surrounded with his rich friends, who made a noisy demonstration to intimidate the Bishop.

'You are powerful,' said St. Hugh, 'and you can get your way. But I can write to the Pope and tell him there is one man in England that disputes his jurisdiction, and his name is Jordan de Turri.'

In the end the case was settled by Jordan making full restitution.

Another interesting fact is that St. Hugh defended the Jews against persecution. Twice he faced and quelled angry mobs intent on a pogrom, and he exposed the current atrocity-stories about Jews murdering Christian children.

St. Hugh died on November 16, 1200. During his illness they wanted him to make his will.

'All I have belongs to the Church,' he said. 'But to prevent disputes after my death I here solemnly bequeath all my goods to the poor of Christ.'

(For another story of St. Hugh, see No. 375.)

The best policy too

The saintly Cardinal François de la Rochefoucauld (Clermont, early seventeenth century) was once approached by a widow and her daughter, who said they were to be evicted from their cottage by the landlord to whom they owed five crowns in rent.

The Cardinal knew the landlord, a wealthy and profligate man, and seeing the good looks of the daughter he guessed that she had offended the landlord by declining his attentions.

He wrote a note for the mother to take to his almoner's office ; on receiving it the latter counted out fifty crowns.

'Oh, but the Cardinal has made a mistake,' said the woman, and insisted on the almoner going back with her.

'Yes, I *did* make a mistake. Madame's conduct proves it.'

He then wrote another note, this time for five hundred

crowns, and begged the mother to accept it as a marriage-portion for her daughter.

'Their master's time and property'

Those whose work means that they have control of other people's goods or other people's time can easily slip into dishonesty, merely by not being careful enough. For such St. Zita would make a good patron.

As housekeeper in the big house at Lucca we find her described as a perfect patron-saint of thrift—a virtue that some of the other saints seem to have found too dull. Now Zita was such a good manager that her master, we are told, found his goods seeming 'to multiply in her hands.' In other words, she checked waste and extravagance: this seemed the only honest thing to do, as they were not her own goods she was handling. Also she was most scrupulous about not wasting her time—since it was her master's time—and occupied it in his service just as fully as ever, though now she could arrange her work as she liked. All this appealed to her master, Fatinelli—anyone who could do miracles with the account books and reduce the household expenditure and make his goods multiply was indeed a person to be encouraged! It even made him feel quite generous, and knowing he could trust Zita not to go too far with it, he 'gave her ample leave to bestow liberal alms on the poor.' You can guess what some of our dear saints would have done under such circumstances—Fatinelli would soon have been bankrupt. Not so Zita; she was careful in her charity to the poor, and used her master's permission 'with discretion.' This, of course, was very much more sensible than rushing at it, and giving away so much that next time the poor needed help she would not have been allowed to give. By doing it carefully she got a very large amount of Fatinelli's superfluous wealth into the pockets where, in fairness, it belonged. As to her own possessions—probably such presents as a family gives to a beloved servant—we are told she gave away everything to the poor, only keeping her necessary clothes.

One way of wronging our neighbour

Five boys, at a loose end one day in the summer holidays, amused themselves by getting into the garden of a house whose occupants were away. They smashed a hole through a wooden fence, cut up a carefully kept tennis lawn by playing football on it, trampled down the rose trees and broke all the glass in the greenhouse by throwing stones at it.

One of them, named John, felt rather ashamed when they were going away and he noticed how much damage they had done. A week later, when the family came back, he heard one of them talking to his mother, telling her of the damage they had found on their return—it had cost over £2 to put it right, she said. This made John feel more ashamed than ever.

Just then came his birthday, and various money presents he received totalled 12s. 6d. He put it in the Post Office, where he already had 30s. saved.

Then he got an idea, and went to the other four boys and told them how much the damage in the garden had cost. He suggested that they should each put a share and repay the owner but they only laughed at him.

For discussion :
What should John do now ? (*He should offer to repay the whole amount himself, since he is able to. Mostly in such cases boys are not able to make restitution and are not expected to.*)

Duty to employers

A young engineer (true story) applied for a highly paid post offered by a mining company. He needed the salary badly in order to help his parents in their old age.

He knew that there would be keen competition for the position offered and he considered himself fortunate to be one of the six singled out for an interview. Doubtless he owed this to the excellent references he had from his late employers for whom he had worked conscientiously in the East for over three years. This firm owned important oil-fields and the young man had been in charge of some of the recent boring.

The momentous day of the interview arrived. At first all seemed to go well and the board seemed satisfied with his answers. Then suddenly his hopes fell with a flop for the chairman fixing him with an eagle eye said: 'Can you tell the board at what depth the company for whom you worked struck oil at such and such a boring?'

For one moment the young man hesitated and then he answered firmly but politely: 'I am sorry, sir, but I do not feel at liberty to disclose information that I came by when working for my previous employers.'

The board received his answer in silence, and the chairman intimated that the interview was at an end.

With a heavy heart the young man made his way out of the board-room. Perhaps he had been a fool, and by being over-scrupulous had lost the job. Then the early training his father had given him reasserted itself: 'Honesty is the best policy.' 'Never have one standard for business and another for your private life,' and so on.

When he told his parents what had happened they both assured him warmly that he had done the right thing. He went to bed somewhat comforted and came down next morning prepared to begin afresh his search for a job.

The first post brought him a long envelope, and when he had opened it he could hardly believe his own eyes, for the letter offered him the envied position.

It was many years afterwards that the young man learned that it was his refusal to give away a secret that had secured the job for him.

The question was asked by the chairman simply to test his loyalty and trustworthiness.

Conscientious work

A little maidservant once made a Retreat, and when she returned to her work somehow her fellow-servants got to hear of it and laughed at her for 'wasting her holiday,' as they put it.

'What difference does it make anyway?' one of them asked her.

'I sweep under the mats now,' the girl answered simply.

The resolution that she had made during the Retreat

was to do each part of her work with the thought that God had sent her to do that particular thing and that He looked on to see how she did it. This thought gave a new interest to even the humblest tasks and made the whole difference to life.

Another aspect of the servant question :
Mistress : ' If you can't get on better with your work, Jane, I shall have to get another maid.'
Jane : ' Thank you, mum, I could do with some 'elp.'

> * ARE WE BOUND TO RESTORE ILL-GOTTEN GOODS ?
>
> *We are bound to restore ill gotten goods if we are able, or else the sin will not be forgiven ; we must also pay our debts.*

Restoring ill-gotten goods

IN a cinema story a young gangster had a girl-friend, who implored him to give up his life of crime and settle down to married life and a quiet job. He said he would in a week or two. He did not tell her that first he had one final burglary to bring off at a jeweller's shop ; he had promised his fellow-gangsters to take part, and if successful he would be able to buy a nice house for his wife to live in. So the ' job ' duly happened ; the police turned up before it was finished, and there was a struggle in the dark, but the young gangster got away safely with £1000 worth of diamonds, which he managed to sell all right, and then bought the house and got married, and kept his promise to lead a law-abiding life for the future.

Query : Do you think he ' lived happy ever after ' ?

Rulers should protect the poor against the rich

When St. Edward the Confessor came to the throne a tax called the Danegeld, originally levied to buy off the Danish ships, was still being enforced though the reason for it had lapsed. The treasurer took the king down into the treasure vaults and showed him many chests of gold

*BALTIMORE 262-263
ENGLISH CATECHISM 217

brought in by this tax. Edward moved the lantern to and fro to see every corner of the vaults.

'On every chest I can see a black devil sitting and sticking his hooked claws into the money. They are the rulers down here, not I. Let the money be distributed to the poor, and stop collecting the tax, and so we shall rid the realm of these devils!'

So it was done. Later on the lords of the kingdom thought the king had spent all his own money on alms and church building and determined to give him a surprise. They sent out their soldiers and forced a large contribution from all their poor vassals; then on Christmas Day begged him to accept the large sum as a free present from his grateful subjects. But Edward knew what a burden it must have been upon the people, and while he thanked the lords for the gift, he also said that he could not bear such a pillaging of the poor, and commanded it to be returned, every farthing, to those who had given it. So the strange sight was seen of tax-collectors making their rounds, not to ask for money, but to give it back in the name of the king.

> * WHAT DOES THE EIGHTH COMMANDMENT FORBID?
>
> *The eighth Commandment forbids all false testimony, rash judgement, and lies.*

Telling lies

ST. ANDREW AVELLINO (*d.* 1608) began his career as a priest-lawyer in the ecclesiastical courts of Naples. One day, being very anxious to win some not very important case, he allowed himself to make a statement which he knew was untrue. Disturbed afterwards about what he had done, he came across the words of Scripture (Wisdom i, 11): 'The mouth that lieth killeth the soul,' and was filled with deepest remorse. He gave up altogether his work in the law-courts, and devoted himself to penance and the care of souls.

Lies of excuse

Robert Anderton and William Marsden, two Lancashire

*BALTIMORE 265-267, 270
ENGLISH CATECHISM 220

men ordained at Rheims, set out to work in England in 1586, but the ship was blown by a storm to the Isle of Wight. There they were suspected, arrested, and not denying their priesthood, were committed to prison. At the trial the judge, knowing they had not actually exercised their priesthood in England, tried out of compassion to suggest a plea by which they might escape the law.

'I suppose,' said he, 'gentlemen, you came out of France, not with the design of coming into England, but of going into Scotland, and that you were driven into England by a storm against your will ? Tell me, is not this the truth ? '

'God forbid,' said they, ' my lord, that we should tell a lie for the matter. Our lives would be a burthen to us if we should save them by an untruth. We were sent hither to preach truth, and we must not, at our first setting out, give in to a lie. The truth is we are both priests, and we set out from France with a design of coming for England, that we might here exercise our priestly functions, and reconcile the souls of our neighbours to God and His Church.'

They were accordingly executed in the Isle of Wight, and suffered with a constancy and cheerfulness which gave inspiration to the Catholics and astonished their adversaries.

'Publicity'

Too often in business, and especially in the advertising of goods for sale, truth is considered a long way after profits.

Head of the firm (*reprimanding office boy*) : ' Do you know what happens to lads who trifle with the truth ? '

Boy : ' Yes, sir. You send them out as travellers.'

Lies in the newspapers

' Last week (March 2) we in the City were frightened out of our wits by newspaper posters at lunch-time proclaiming that Italy had called 1,000,000 men to the colours. As a direct result War Loan shed an eighth and all other stocks reacted in concert. . . . Within a few hours we knew that the notices which had been posted in Italy were mere routine.

'By three o'clock the number had decreased to less than half, and at six o'clock we were told by another evening paper: "Reuter says . . . that the number affected is estimated to be between 60,000 and 200,000," and that B.U.P. says that the notices affect those conscripts of the 1915, 1916, 1917 and 1918 classes who were previously exempt for various reasons, and that the number involved is at most 30,000.' (From letters to *The Times*, March 8, 1939.) [See also no. 672.]

Religious hypocrisy

The story of Ananias and Saphira (Acts iv, 32 to v, 11) is used to illustrate the eighth Commandment, but it needs careful explanation otherwise it bristles with moral difficulties and seems more in the atmosphere of the Old Testament than the New.

Note first that Ananias and Saphira were doing no wrong in itself by keeping part of their goods for themselves; the sharing-up practised by the Jerusalem Christians was entirely voluntary.

It was their deception that was so mean; not simply lying, but lying to be thought good. They were exploiting the beautiful love of Christians for each other, Christ's 'new commandment,' and doing their best to turn it into a sham. It was the first instance of what would always be one of the standing scandals of the Church; hence possibly the striking and dramatic fate of these two, as a warning to other Christians, including us.

Even so it may seem rather excessive, and we can explain that it does not necessarily mean that Ananias and Saphira were damned. Perhaps their sin in itself was only venial, or perhaps they received grace for repentance at the very moment of death.

As for St. Peter, he did not bring about the deaths, though in the case of Saphira he saw it beforehand and foretold it.

CATECHISM STORIES

Secrets should be kept

Annie and Freda worked together as waitresses in a restaurant where married women were not employed. One day Freda said : ' Listen, here's a secret : I got married last week, but I'm not telling anybody. I want to go on working here as long as I can because my husband lost his job a week before we were married.'

For a few weeks nothing happened, but then some rumour got round to the manageress. She came to Annie and asked : ' Is it true Freda is married ? '

' Freda married ? Not that I know of. Whoever told you that story ? '

For the moment the manageress was satisfied, but a few days later she put the same question to Freda herself.

' Me married ? Certainly not. When I get married you'll all know about it, I can tell you ! '

However, the manageress had good information. this time, so at last Freda gave in and produced the wedding-ring from her pocket and put it on. She lost the job, but it did not matter so much since her husband had just found a good one.

For discussion :

(a) Was she justified in concealing her marriage ? (*Yes, for a good reason.*)

(b) And in denying it when questioned ? (*No, because that was direct lying.*)

(c) Was Annie justified in denying knowledge of the marriage ? (*Yes, because she was told as a secret—she hadn't the knowledge to use.*)

' Rash Judgement '

Only God can see the heart, and its guilt in His sight, and when we pass judgement on our neighbours it is always rash to some extent ; even if we are not mistaken we may still commit the sin of ' detraction.'

It is not for us (unless we are H.M. judges, etc.) to blame and punish sinners, that is God's affair, and He is more likely to be merciful.

Our Lord teaches all this most powerfully in the incident of the woman taken in adultery (John viii, 2–11). [See also no. 611.]

CATECHISM STORIES

> ARE CALUMNY AND DETRACTION FORBIDDEN BY THE EIGHTH COMMANDMENT?
>
> *Calumny and detraction are forbidden by the eighth Commandment, and also tale-bearing, and any words which injure our neighbour's character.*
>
> *If I have injured my neighbour by speaking ill of him, I am bound to make him satisfaction by restoring his good name as far as I can.*

The sin of Detraction

A LADY once went to confession to St. Philip Neri and accused herself of frequent sins of detraction. As a penance St. Philip told her to go out and buy an unplucked fowl in the market-place, and during her walk back she was to pull the feathers out one by one and scatter them along the way. Then she was to return to him and he would tell her what she was to do next.

It seemed a strange penance, but she went off to the market and did exactly what she was told, no doubt feeling a little foolish. On her return St. Philip praised her obedience.

'Now to complete your penance,' he said, 'you must go back and pick up all the feathers and bring them here to me.'

'But, Father,' the lady exclaimed, 'you *know* that is impossible. The wind blew them away, and I could never hope to recapture them now.'

'Quite true,' the saint replied. 'Neither can you recall the damaging words about your neighbours which by this time have passed from mouth to mouth far beyond your reach. Be careful in future to watch every word you utter.'

How it grows.

'I hear you won £5000 at Monte Carlo.'

'Well, to be precise, it wasn't Monte Carlo but Manchester, and it wasn't £5000, but ten bob, and I didn't win it—I lost it.'

Gossip

Some people live in a perpetual web of meanness, deception, intrigue and gossip.

*BALTIMORE 268-271
ENGLISH CATECHISM 221-222

CATECHISM STORIES

Mrs. Brown (very annoyed): 'Look here, Mrs. Green, Mrs. Gray told me that you told her the secret I told you not to tell her.'

Mrs. Green: 'Oh, the mean creature, and I told her not to tell you that I told her.'

Mrs. Brown: 'Well, look here. Don't you tell her that I told you she told me.'

'Tale-bearing'

Once upon a time in an Eastern city there was a riot. The people were hungry and blamed the Caliph. When he rode through the streets of the city some of the citizens mobbed him; and one man more desperate than the rest, caught him by the beard and but for the intervention of the guard would have dragged him from the saddle.

Order was restored, food distributed, and the discontent subsided; but a shopkeeper named Hassan sought to curry favour with the Caliph by telling him the name of the man who had pulled him by the beard. The man's name was Khasim.

The ruler sent for him. Khasim arrived at the palace trembling with fear. He threw himself at the Caliph's feet, begging for mercy.

'Get up, Khasim. I did not send for you to punish you, but to warn you that Hassan is a bad neighbour; for he it was that told me that you were my chief assailant in the riot. Go in peace, and never trust a tale-bearer,' said the Caliph.

> * WHAT DOES THE NINTH COMMANDMENT FORBID?
> *The ninth Commandment forbids all wilful consent to impure thoughts and desires.*

'Blessed are the clean of heart'

DANTE, in his journey down into the pit of Hell, comes to the second Circle. Pitch darkness reigned there, and a perpetual tornado of wind roaring and moaning. There, like flocks of starlings blown helplessly in a winter gale, souls were driven, sometimes singly and sometimes in couples, through the black air, whirled to and fro and dashed against the rocky cliffs. There was never a moment's rest for them.

*BALTIMORE 273-276
ENGLISH CATECHISM 224

Their wails and curses were heard through the noise of the gale. These were the souls who had given themselves up to impurity and not repented. They had allowed themselves in life to be blown to and fro by gusts of passion uncontrolled by reason and this was to be their eternal fate now.

On the Mountain of Purgatory, again, the poet found sinners against chastity, but here they were making amends for their sin and setting themselves free from it. They were in the last and highest terrace of the mountain, because (according to Dante) this is the last sin that men get rid of. Here from the mountain-side there shot forth flames of fire nearly all across the path, so that Dante had to walk on the very edge of the precipice. But the souls who were atoning for the sins walked willingly in the flames, singing a hymn to the god of purity (*Summæ Parens Clementiæ*). The flames caused intense suffering but no injury ; the opposite of the earthly fires of lust, which cause pleasure but also harm. At last they came to an Angel of God, the Cherubim with flaming sword of Gen. iii, 24, who seemed full of joy, and sang ' Blessed are the clean of heart.' He warned Virgil and Dante that they must pass through the flame themselves if they wished to climb the little path up to the Earthly Paradise at the summit.

Dante was paralysed with fear of the purifying flame, but Virgil reminded him that if he went through it he would find Beatrice, and this gave him courage to face the fire. Thus love, true and unselfish, drives out mere lust.

' Like the gentiles that know not God '

It is through Christ and His Mother that women are held in honour, and treated as free persons with souls. Where pagan customs reign, the same cruelties happen now as in the time of Nero and Diocletian.

' Arua (West Nile, Uganda, British East Africa) : The scene is thousands of miles up the Nile, fifty miles from the point where the great river takes its start from Lake Albert. The heroine is Martha, an eighteen-year-old girl of the

Alur tribe and a convert of but a little while ago. Martha has been brutally killed, but the story of her constancy has moved to the depths all the Christians of this new station in the mission-field.

'Two years ago Owi, chief of the Alur, died, poisoned by the women of his harem. His son Ali succeeded Owi. Ali followed the vicious traditions of his people, inherited his father's harem and increased its number to thirty. He sought further additions, and his eye fell upon Martha, to whom he made known his intentions. The Christian girl learned them with horror, and after a thrilling flight through the forest at night, arrived at the mission station at Angal. The priest noted the next morning with what fervour the girl received communion, and how she remained a long time in the chapel, but said nothing.

'Ali was furious when he discovered Martha's flight to the mission, and commissioned a lieutenant, Wakili, to use every wile to get the girl back to him.

'Wakili waited and finally Martha sought to slip back to her village. Wakili took her prisoner, used arguments first, then bound her to a tree and beat her with a whip. The poor victim fell in a faint, recovered, refused, was beaten again, and again replied with all her courage. 'No!' and murmured an aspiration to the God of martyrs.

'The patience of the savage was exhausted.' He threw the girl on the ground, kicking her in the chest, the face and throughout the body : when his fury had abated, Martha expired.

'Details of the murder were hushed up, lest British troops should punish the malefactors. Martha left the mission on August 9 to return to her village, and three days later the priest of Angal got the story of her death ; the precise date is not yet known.' — *A.P.F. Annals*, January, 1930.
(See also story 226, St. Lucy.)

No sin without wilful consent

Impure thoughts and desires may be very strong and

persistent, but they are not sinful unless we give consent to them. They do not kill God's grace in the soul, however little we may *feel* His presence.

St. Catherine of Siena tells us herself that at one time she was continually tempted by wicked thoughts, so long that the little room where she lived and prayed seemed to her full of devils, and at last she fled up the hill to the great church. Even there the temptations came as thick as ever. Then she prayed : ' I have chosen suffering for my pleasure, and I willingly accept this suffering, too, for as long as it shall please God's Majesty.'

At last the temptations ceased, and her mind was cool and calm again. In vision Our Lord appeared, carrying His cross, and He praised her for her constancy. She was consoled to see Him, but why had He not come before when she had needed Him more ?

' And *where* were You, my Lord, when my heart was filled with such foulness ? '

' My daughter, I was in the very centre of your heart all the time.'

Remedy for sensual thoughts

While St. Ignatius lay convalescing in the Castle of Loyola, a struggle went on in his soul. He felt drawn to imitate the example of Our Lord and His saints, of whom he had been reading ; but there were days, too, when he gave himself up to his old day-dreams of earthly romance and sensual satisfactions. But he found less pleasure in them than before. Then lying awake one night (he tells us about it himself) ' he saw clearly the image of Our Lady with the Holy Child Jesus, at whose sight for a notable time he felt a surpassing sweetness, which eventually left him with such a loathing for his past sins, and especially for those of the flesh, that every unclean imagination seemed blotted out from his soul, and never again was there the least consent to any carnal thought.' (See also story 310, St. Edmund.)

CATECHISM STORIES

* WHAT SINS COMMONLY LEAD TO THE BREAKING
OF THE SIXTH AND NINTH COMMANDMENTS?
The sins that commonly lead to the breaking of the sixth and ninth Commandments are gluttony, drunkenness, and intemperance, and also idleness, bad company, and the neglect of prayer.

'Gluttony, drunkenness, and intemperance'

IF we wish to keep the sixth and ninth Commandments we need to cultivate control over all bodily desires, especially eating and drinking.

St. Wulstan, the sturdy Saxon Bishop of Worcester in the time of the Conqueror, is an example against gluttony. To guard the district against Danish raiders, he had reluctantly agreed to have under his orders a party of men-at-arms. He used to dine with the soldiers in the great hall, and when they sat in Saxon fashion for hours drinking after dinner, he stayed with them to restrain them by his presence, pledging them when it came to his turn in a little cup which he pretended to drink, and in the midst of the din ' ruminating to himself on the psalms.'

During Lent he tasted nothing at all three days of the week, and only bread and vegetables on the other three, with some fish and wine on Sundays.

He was fond of roast goose, and once when he was saying Mass, the smell of a roasting goose floated into the chapel from the kitchen, and the Bishop could not help his mind wandering from what he was doing at the altar to the dinner which was awaiting him afterwards. This distraction so grieved him that he would not eat roast goose either then or ever afterwards.

As for the sixth Commandment, however, St. Wulstan had fought that battle and won it in the days of his youth. He was a handsome, athletic lad, the son of a Thane, with nothing much to do with his time, and a young woman had set herself to lead him into sin. One day on a crowded sports' field, where Wulstan had been the winner in races and feats of strength, she put forth her best efforts of flattery and allurement, and he felt himself yielding. But only for

*BALTIMORE 257-258
ENGLISH CATECHISM 225

CATECHISM STORIES

a moment. He left the field and threw himself down on a lonely heath, and shed tears of contrition. Then he fell into a deep sleep and woke up with his soul clear and fresh, and was never again tempted. [See also nos. 568, 628–633 ; and on control of instincts, 10.]

Idleness

A young hermit of the desert was troubled much with unchaste imaginations, and went to his superior and asked his advice about it. The superior knew that he was of indolent disposition, often letting himself off his prescribed tasks of digging or mat-weaving, and spending his time in day-dreaming. Accordingly the superior said nothing about unchaste thoughts, but imposed on the other a heavy programme of work, to be finished as soon as possible. A few days afterwards he met the young man again, and asked him about the temptations.

' Temptations ! ' exclaimed the hermit. ' I never get time to be tempted now ! I scarcely have time to draw an occasional breath, there's so much to do ! '

The remedy had succeeded, and will often succeed with ourselves.

Bad Company

A young Catholic soldier in training in England during the War, 1914–1918, became friends with a rather older Catholic in the same platoon. Unfortunately the latter was already associating with two other young men of loose conversation and conduct. The younger Catholic was drawn into the group, and was soon neglecting his prayers, learning to exchange unseemly stories, and coming back to camp at night more drunk than sober. The older Catholic encouraged him in all this, made fun of him when he hesitated, and finally after a few weeks persuaded him to come with the others to a certain place with the object of breaking the sixth Commandment, and lent him some money for the expedition.

Next day, when the younger man was full of shame and

remorse, sudden orders reached the camp and a draft for France was hurriedly assembled. It included the two Catholics. They would have liked to go to confession before leaving, but nobody could leave camp. After two days of continual trains, boats and lorries, they found themselves a mile or two behind a great battle, and joined a battalion going up that night to relieve another which was holding on to a line of shell-holes under continual bombardment. Amongst the very first casualties during the relief was the younger of the two Catholics, killed with several others when a shell fell right amongst them.

His friend, when he had time to think, was horror-stricken at the thought of the part he had played in trying to ruin a soul, perhaps for ever. As soon as the battalion came out of the line, he sought out a priest and made a sincere return to the sacraments. After coming unhurt through the rest of the War, he became a religious and is spending the rest of his life praying fervently for his friend's soul, and trying to do penance for his own sins, especially his great sin of scandal. [See also nos. 299, 302, 621.]

> * WHAT DOES THE TENTH COMMANDMENT FORBID ?
> *The tenth Commandment forbids all envious and covetous thoughts and unjust desires of our neighbour's goods and profits.*

' Thou shalt not covet '

THE story of the coveting of Naboth's vineyard by King Achab and Jezabel is told in 3 Kings xxi, 1-19. The sequel as regards the fate of the king is in 3 Kings xxii, 29-38 ; and of the queen, 4 Kings ix, 14-36.

Money talks

Some people let their religion go for the sake of some financial or worldly advantage, but they do not like to think that is the reason.

*BALTIMORE 277-278
ENGLISH CATECHISM 227

CATECHISM STORIES

With one such man, who said he had given up belief in God and in a life hereafter, a priest was reasoning and trying to get him to remember his duty.

'I'm afraid I don't see it,' the man kept saying.

The priest took a piece of paper and wrote on it one word : '*God.*'

'Do you see that?' he asked, and the man said yes. The priest covered the word with a half-crown he took from his pocket.

'Do you see it now?'

'No, but I know it is still there.'

'Exactly. And you are letting money come between you and God, but if you will think you will know God is still there.'

Economics and Politics

A rich man was grumbling loudly to a certain monk about proposals for increasing old-age pensions. The nation couldn't afford it, he said : the old people would have too much to spend on pleasure, etc., etc.

'Come over to the window,' said the monk. 'Tell me what you see through the glass.'

'Only people walking along the street.'

'Right—now come and look through this other glass.' This was a large mirror over the fireplace. 'Tell me what you see now.'

'Only myself, of course.'

'Only yourself. That is the difference it makes when the glass is covered with silver.'

The possession of wealth affects our point of view, and gives a selfish turn to all our thinking.

' Nec speravit in pecunia et thesauris '

'Michael Mannion, aged 61, an out-of-work navvy on tramp, penniless and hungry, was on his way to the casual ward in Amersham when he found two £1 notes. He handed them to the police, and was advised to call at Amersham police-station this morning. There he was told that the money belonged to a working-woman, the mother of eight children. She had left a reward of five shillings for him. He was told also that Mr. Jarvis, of Mantles Green Farm, who had heard of the incident, would provide him with a job that would last for two or three weeks.

' " I took the job," Mannion told me this morning, " but I would only take 1s. 6d. of the reward. Sure they're only poor people and I wouldn't be wanting any more than that." . . . Mannion became a tramp on the road as the result of illness which prevented him from following the heavy work of a navvy, which he had carried out for many years. He had a long illness in a Hampshire poor-law infirmary.' (*News Chronicle*, March 8, 1939.).

The servant of Mammon

Centuries ago in France lived a rich and avaricious nobleman, who to make his money quite safe had a secret strong-room made in the foundations of his château. A passage led from a deep unused cellar to the iron door, with a spring lock that shut of itself when closed. Here for many years the miser used to go and enjoy the contemplation of his gold, unknown to all.

One day, having received the quarterly rents from the oppressed peasants of his estate, he waited till night and carried the money-bags to his secret treasury, and spent his usual hour admiring and adoring its contents. At last, turning to go, he found to his horror that he had left the key on the outside and closed the door ; he was a prisoner. Shouts and hammerings were of no avail, the strong-room had been purposely made far from sight and sound. His household made every effort to solve the mystery of his disappearance, but at last could only conclude that he had been enticed away and murdered.

Months afterwards an old locksmith in a distant town heard of the Count's disappearance, and remembered the eccentric strong-room for which he himself had fitted a special lock thirty years before. He went to the château with his information, and led the relatives to the secret door where the key was still in the lock. Inside, the decomposing corpse of the miser was discovered, lying on heaps of gold which he had evidently embraced in his death-agony.

Greed stops at nothing

Three gangsters in the Middle West kidnapped a jewel-merchant in their motor-car, murdered him, and took his jewel-case to their headquarters, a cottage in the country, to divide the spoils. Two went into the cottage at once, and the youngest gangster was sent to drive to the next town for a bottle of whisky.

While he was gone, the two older ones said: 'Say, why should we give that kid a third of the jewels? When he comes back we'll give him the works and share fifty-fifty.'

Meanwhile the younger man was thinking: 'Those two will double-cross me over the share-out if they can. Why shouldn't I have the whole winnings and be a rich man? All that's needed is a little dope in the whisky I'm going to take back.'

So he bought some suitable poison at a drug-store and put it into the whisky.

As soon as he got inside the cottage and put the bottle on the table, one of the others shot him dead from behind; then they sat down and divided the jewels while they drank the poisoned whisky. In an hour, after terrible agony, they were both dead. The police found all three bodies, traced the shopkeepers who sold the whisky and the poison, and were able to reconstruct what had happened.

Envy will not share

A man once died leaving his possessions to be equally divided between his two sons. During the old man's lifetime the sons had worked happily together, but directly it came to dividing their father's things they each began to be afraid that the other would get more than his fair share, and they wrangled and bickered from morning till night. At last they sought the advice of an old friend of their father's. 'How would you advise us to set to work so as to be sure we each get an equal share?' they asked.

'You must pull down the house, and count out the bricks. You must saw the furniture in half, chop the cows and horses in half, break the plates in two, cut up the sheets and blankets, and so on. That is the way to make certain that neither of you gets an advantage over the other,' the old man replied.

As the old man spoke the brothers were ashamed. They saw that their covetousness was leading them into destroying the home, and they soon found a way to share fairly.

God has put us in a world where there is plenty for all, but our covetousness and self-seeking leads us into quarrelling and war, and we destroy the very things that God intended for our use and comfort.

[For stories of Greed in general, see nos. 201, 317-320, 543, 588, 598, 612-618, 649.]

The gambling fever

One Saturday, Jenkins asked his landlord what won the 2.30.

The landlord replied: 'I don't know. I'm not interested in racing.'

'Then you ought to be. Your rent was on the 2.30,' Jenkins replied.

Jenkins and his mates had a good laugh at the landlord's expense, but a few days later the following dialogue took place between Jenkins and his employer:

Employer: 'Who won the boat-race, Jenkins?'

Jenkins: 'I don't know, sir, I'm not interested.'

Employer: 'Wel! you ought to be. As a matter of fact Oxford won and unfortunately I had put your wages on Cambridge.'

Jenkins was speechless with indignation at such injustice, but all his employer said was : ' What's sauce for the goose is sauce for the gander.'

None of us have any right to gamble if we have any unpaid debts, nor if those who are dependent on us have to suffer if we lose.

The gambling temperament

St. Camillus of Lellis (d. 1614) at the age of seventeen ran away to share the life of his ne'er-do-well father who was a professional soldier serving any prince who would pay him. His father took him into a gambling partnership, making a living at cards when there was no fighting.

Then his father died (after a death-bed repentance) and Camillus was left destitute and with a wounded leg which had gone septic. For a while he reformed and worked in a hospital in Rome. Then the old gambling fever returned, he taught his companions to play cards, and was dismissed for demoralizing the hospital. Once more he went to the wars, and when the company was disbanded he gambled away his sword and gun and uniform, and was once more destitute. He found a disreputable gambling-partner, and became the lowest kind of vagabond, still only twenty-four years old.

At last, when he stood amongst the beggars outside a church one day, a wealthy charitable gentleman got into conversation with him, and finally gave him a note for a job on a monastery that he was building near the town.

Camillus went to say good-bye to his gambling-partner, but the latter laughed to scorn the idea of work. ' You'll never stick it ! You'll quarrel with everybody, just like in the army, and get the sack. And you'll have to do what you're told—you might as well be in prison. Come, let's get on the road again ! '

Camillus yielded, and they started off for the next town. But on the road grace came to him ; he realised that the job offered was a real opportunity that might never come again. Suddenly he made up his mind, left his companion and ran back and took the job.

It was the turning point of his life. He stuck to the regular work in spite of all temptations (including the ridicule of his gambling-partner who came back to torment him). Later on he tried to be a Franciscan, and finally, after working amongst the sick and poor in Rome, he founded an Order for nursing them. He got permission for his Order to wear a red cross on their mantles, and that is how the Red Cross comes to be the sign of mercy and care for the suffering.

The recklessness of the gambler still remained, but it was turned to the service of God. He gave recklessly without thought for to-morrow. When his disciples remonstrated he would say : ' O cowards ! Trust in God, and cast your bread into the river of life. Soon you will find it in the ocean of eternity.'

One good side of gambling

When St. Francis Xavier was at Sancian Island a rich merchant named Vellio became friendly and often helped with his charities, though his own life was given up to pleasure. Needing some money for an orphan, Xavier went seeking Vellio till he found him gambling at a friend's house. Vellio gave his key to Francis and told him to go to his chest and take all he wanted. In the chest was 45,000 ducats. Francis took only 300 scudi—a trifle— and when Vellio heard he was quite angry. ' I meant to go shares in it with you,' he said. Xavier was touched. ' God sees your generous good will. In His name I promise you that you shall never come to destitution. You will be very near it, but at the last moment your luck will change.' The prophecy was later fulfilled exactly. From that day, too, Vellio lived a better life.

What money is for

Phythius, King of Lydia, was very wealthy but very avaricious, and would spend as little as possible. His queen determined to cure him. One day when he came home hungry from the chase she told the slaves to place before him at dinner dishes filled with gold, fresh from the gold mines. He admired it for some time and then asked for some food.

'Food? Surely they have brought you what you love best in the world?'

'What do you mean? Gold cannot stay my hunger.'

'No? Is it not foolish then to have such love for something that cannot be useful so long as you keep it? Believe me, gold is truly of service only to people who exchange it for the good and useful things of life.'

Phythius realised the truth of this and afterwards opened the royal treasury more freely, to the great benefit of his subjects.

Saving money is a bad thing for everybody when it goes beyond what is necessary to provide for a rainy day or future needs and emergencies.

Our industrial system

The following story, unless its humour is deemed too grim, might illustrate either the social injustice of unemployment, or the desperate selfishness it may induce in some of its victims.

'Tha knows Joe Brown?'

'Aye.'

'Ah've joost seen 'im in t' canal. 'E's drahnin'.

'Aye.'

'Well, Ah've coom fer 'is job.'

'Tha's too late. T' chap pushed 'im in's gettin' it.'

No need for Class War

In Toulouse, 1919, a big strike broke out for higher wages following a sudden rise in the cost of living. Catholic trade unions took part in the strike and exercised a restraining influence against violent methods. One morning, when the trouble was at its height, the son of one of the chief employers was at Mass, and at the altar rails he found himself next to several of the trade union leaders. To speak to each other afterwards seemed a natural thing ; one word led to another, and the result was a round-table conference next day, which soon settled the strike on terms satisfactory to all.

'Nobody starves, anyhow'

In his old age St. Columba one day saw an old woman gathering herbs for food, and she was so poor that she gathered even nettles. This filled him with self-reproach because he fed so much better than she. He went home to his monastery and gave orders that his dinner was to be nothing but wild herbs and nettles. One of the monks, however, put some butter into the saucepan where the nettles were boiling and the old saint was very displeased when he noticed it.

If everybody shared St. Columba's feeling such things as the 'Household Means Test' would very soon be abolished.

> * WHAT ARE THE CHIEF COMMANDMENTS OF THE CHURCH ?
>
> *The chief Commandments of the Church are :*
>
> *1. To keep the Sundays and Holy Days of Obligation holy by hearing Mass and resting from servile works.*
>
> *2. To keep the days of fasting and abstinence appointed by the Church.*
>
> *3. To go to confession at least once a year.*
>
> *4. To receive the Blessed Sacrament at least once a year, and that at Easter or thereabouts.*
>
> *5. To contribute to the support of our pastors.*
>
> *6. Not to marry within certain degrees of kindred, nor to solemnise marriage at the forbidden times.*

Spirit of obedience to the Church

UNCLE ARTHUR came to tea and found out that his small nephew Peter was saving up to buy a dog.

*BALTIMORE 279-287
ENGLISH CATECHISM 229

'Splendid,' said the uncle, who was a bit of a practical joker. 'Look here now, here's two coins, you can choose which one you like to help your fund.'

He put on the table a bright new penny and a worn, dirty-looking half-crown.

Peter was too young to know the values of coins, but he knew some counted more than others. He much preferred the bright penny himself, but he did not want to make a mistake. He looked at them seriously; then he turned to his mother:

'You choose for me, Mummy!'

Uncle Arthur was so pleased with this solution that he added another half-crown, and there was enough in the money-box to buy the dog.

We don't always know what is best for us, but we can look to the experience and wisdom of our holy Mother the Church.

Natural law and Positive law

The Church does not want us to think that these precepts have the same force as the Ten Commandments.

One Wednesday afternoon (it happened to be in Lent) a lad was due to play in an away match for the football club he belonged to. He worked in a shop, and Wednesday was early closing day. At dinner-time his mother served up some roast beef, having forgotten about the abstinence. There was no time to do anything about it if he was to get to the match. He wondered if he should have some bread and cheese only, but decided that he would not play his best if he did, and it would not be fair to the team. He ate the meat with a good conscience.

Later on he discussed the incident with the priest. Had he committed a sin?

(*No, because he was honestly acting according to his conscience.*)

Was the judgement of his conscience a correct one?

(*Yes, because to go without meat in the circumstances would have been a serious inconvenience, and the law of abstinence would cease to apply.*)

On the last Saturday of the football season his team

was to play in a final for a cup and he was chosen to play centre-half. Unfortunately, his football boots were quite worn out and he could not afford new ones. During the morning it occurred to him that he could easily take a few shillings from the shop without much risk of being found out and pay it back later perhaps.

He remembered the previous occasion, when the law of abstinence ceased to apply. 'It would be a still more serious inconvenience if I couldn't play to-day. Surely the seventh Commandment would cease to apply under the circumstances!'

Somehow, however, this seemed unlikely, and he decided to stop thinking of that possibility. Instead, he managed to get his employer to let him have his week's money in advance, and after a hasty arrangement with his mother about future pocket-money he was able to buy the boots and score the winning goal. Would it have been sinful to steal the money?

(*Yes, because stealing is wrong in itself; not like eating meat on abstinence days, which is not wrong in itself, but only because of the law against it.*)

From the lawyer point of view the principle is as follows: What we call the 'Natural Law'—the eternal law of God, of our reason, of the Ten Commandments—tells us what is right or wrong in itself. It cannot be changed. In cases where it seems lawful to break one of the Ten Commandments (e.g. killing in self-defence, or a starving man stealing a loaf of bread) it is simply one natural law taking precedence over another.

When God, or the Church, or the State, commands something that is over and above the Natural Law (e.g. Sabbath rest, Friday abstinence, dog licence) it is called a 'Positive Law.' A 'positive law' must be obeyed, but it is not meant to apply in case of 'serious inconvenience.'

'Serious inconvenience' must be understood *relatively* to the importance of the law.

The Ten Commandments on the whole simply declare the Natural Law; the Commandments of the Church are on the whole 'positive law.'

Hearing Mass on Sundays

A careless Catholic dreamed that he arrived at the gate of heaven and gave his name, but St. Peter shook his head.

' You can't come in here. We don't know you.'

' Well, you know my wife anyhow. She's at St. Patrick's every Sunday at the eight o'clock.'

' We know your wife. But we don't know you.'

' The children go to the half-past nine—I always send the children.'

' Yes, we know your children. But we don't know you. You cannot come in.'

The dreamer was so upset that he woke up. It was Sunday morning, so he turned over a new leaf at once and took the children to Mass himself.

A variant: On Sundays husband used to say to wife: ' Oh, you can go for both of us.' He dreamt they came together to heaven's gate and St. Peter said : ' Mr. and Mrs. Smith ? Well, Mrs. Smith can come in for both of you ! '

' Do this in commemoration of Me '

A rich, careless Catholic had a gardener who insisted on time off on Sunday mornings to go to Mass.

' Can't understand you Catholics—surely you could say your prayers at home ? '

' Well, sir, it's like this. When I've been cutting the shrubs and hedges I have to tidy up, and all the twigs must be swept up and burnt. If I tried to set fire to each twig separately most of them would never burn at all. But when I gather them all into a big heap there's a fine big blaze and they all catch fire. And I reckon that's how it is with prayers, and that's why Our Lord wants us all gathered to Mass of a Sunday.'

' I see . . . well, wait for me a minute, I'll come along with you.'

[See also nos. 263, 264, 449-450. Also suggestions for stories or cases illustrating Mass obligation in *Teaching the Catechism*, Vol. I, p. 43.]

CATECHISM STORIES

'Therefore let us feast'

The eating of the first Paschal lamb is the Scriptural 'type' of our Easter Communion.

Read the passage Exodus xii, 1-42, and also xiv, 5-31; xv, 1-4, 11. But first try to stir the children's imagination to share the joy of the Jews set free from Egypt; then to look ahead at all the commemorative paschal suppers through fifteen centuries, as far as the distant Supper in the Upper Room, and Our Lord saying: 'With desire I have desired to eat this pasch with you before I suffer.'

Our Lord is the true Paschal Lamb, spotless, sacrificed, with bones unbroken in dying; His blood saving us from the vengeance of God.

Similarly the true eating of the pashal lamb is our Easter Communion. 'Christ our Pasch is sacrificed,' and gives Himself to be our Food, to be eaten with 'bitter herbs' of penance (confession) and the 'unleavened bread' of sincerity and truth (amendment of life). Thus with our Easter Communion we are delivered from the captivity of sin, passing through the Red Sea of Christ's Passion to the journey which will take us to the promised land of heaven.

Easter Duties

If we understand what Easter Communion means we shall want all Catholics to make their Easter duties.

A girl (I have heard of) named Joan heard a sermon one Lent about Easter duties. Next Saturday, as usual, she spent the day with her old grandmother, who had not been to church for many years and now had a good excuse on account of her infirmities.

'I say, Gran, shall I ask Father to bring you Holy Communion this Lent because you can't get to church?'

'No, don't ask him—I might be able to get there somehow.'

'Oh, Gran, I'm sure you can't. He'll be ever so glad to come.'

'Ah, it's so long since I went to confession.'

'Well, that's all the more reason for going this Easter!'

'I don't do anything wrong; I'm as good a Catholic as any of them, even if I can't come to church.'

'That isn't it,' said Joan, trying to remember the sermon she had heard, and sending up a prayer for a special grace for her grandmother. 'But if you miss your Easter Communion you'll be like a little branch that has no life in it when all the rest of the tree is coming out in green leaves. Our Easter Communion joins us all together to Our Lord and puts His life into us. We are one Bread and one Body, and I shouldn't like to feel you were being left out of it, Gran!'

The old lady was very fond of Joan and grateful for the help she gave her on Saturdays, and to please her she agreed at last. But after she had made her Easter duty, and had arranged for the priest to come once a month in future, she was more grateful to Joan than ever and said she felt happier than she had ever been before.

The Offertory

Two shipwrecked sailors clinging on a raft.
'Say, Bill, can you say a prayer?'
'No.'
'Well, can you sing a hymn?'
'No.'
'Neither can I. Well, we'd better do *something*. Let's have a collection.'

Everybody knows that giving is somehow an essential part of religion.

The Church's law of abstinence

A Catholic tourist in a hotel dining-room on a Friday asked for fish or eggs in vain, and contented himself with bread and cheese. Some other guests in loud voices made mocking remarks about such folly, as they called it. The tourist called out: 'Waiter, bring me a plate of beef,' and the others thought their mockery had taken effect. But when the beef arrived the tourist said: 'Put it under the table, it is for my dog. The lower animals eat meat every day of the week.' The mockers had no more to say.

CATECHISM STORIES

* WHAT ARE DAYS OF ABSTINENCE?
Days of abstinence are days on which we are forbidden to take flesh-meat and soups made from meat.

Days of abstinence

BL. Conrad of Piacenza was an Italian nobleman who gave up all and became a hermit. He lived for forty years in a cave.

It is related that one day some worldly men persuaded him to dine with them on a Friday and then served up pork prepared so as to look like fish. At the end of the meal his hosts turned on him in mockery for having broken the abstinence ; but Conrad showed them his plate of fish-bones, and they were forced to conclude that God had done this wonder to shame their contempt for the laws of the Church.

'All Fridays'

During the struggle between William of Orange and Philip II of Spain seventeen priests (including nine Franciscans) and two Franciscan lay brothers were cast into the dungeon of the citadel of Gorcum, July, 1572. Some were quite old, one was ninety. For two days and nights they were crowded together like sheep, with neither fresh air nor light, and the assurance of their captors that they would in the end be hanged unless they renounced belief in the Blessed Sacrament and the papal supremacy.

All day Friday they were unvisited even by the gaoler, and were faint with hunger and weariness. Some were for making a pretended submission to the heretics, though Nicholas Pieck, the Franciscan Guardian, strove nobly to keep the little band united.

At dusk footsteps sounded without ; the door was flung open, and a savoury smell filled the dungeon. A captain of William's army entered. Mockingly he bid them partake of the supper—'good Protestant meat'—which if they refused because it was Friday so much the worse for them.

*BALTIMORE 288
ENGLISH CATECHISM 287

Clearly their condition dispensed them from abstinence; but when Pieck suggested that they refuse the food rather than give the enemy occasion to blaspheme they all agreed—even the waverers. The captain withdrew, vowing that they should most certainly be hanged, and the supper was removed untouched. And hanged they were, after a great deal of suffering.

There was no spiritual exaltation about nineteen hungry men saying 'No thank you' to a good supper: just the ordinary Catholic instinct of faithful observance. And yet it was surely one of the really heroic moments in their passion.

> * HOW SOON ARE CHRISTIANS BOUND TO RECEIVE THE BLESSED SACRAMENT?
>
> *Christians are bound to receive the Blessed Sacrament as soon as they are capable of distinguishing the body of Christ from ordinary Bread, and are judged to be sufficiently instructed.*
>
> *Children are generally supposed to come to the use of reason about the age of seven years.*

'As soon as they are capable'

AN English lady one day took her little son to a private audience of Pope Pius X. The tiny boy leaned trustfully against the Holy Father's knee, such a serious, understanding look on his small face that the Pope asked how old he was.

'He is four years old,' answered his mother.

The Pope leant down to him and asked quietly: 'Tell me, little one, whom do we receive in Holy Communion?'

'Jesus,' said the tiny boy, without hesitation.

'And who is Jesus?' asked the Pope.

'Jesus is God,' said the little boy.

With a smile of happiness the Pope turned to his mother. 'Bring him to me to-morrow morning,' he said, 'I will give him his first Communion.'

*BALTIMORE (None)
ENGLISH CATECHISM 244-242

It is thanks to Pope Pius X that children now make their first Communion so much earlier than they used to. His message to children was :

'Come to Him as soon as you are old enough to understand and love Him.'

> * IS IT A DUTY TO CONTRIBUTE TO THE SUPPORT OF RELIGION ?
>
> *It is a duty to contribute to the support of religion according to our means, so that God may be duly honoured and worshipped and the kingdom of His Church extended.*

'To contribute to the support of our pastors'

GIVING our share to the ordinary collections for the Church is not a charity, but a duty.

A coloured parson preached on the text ' Salvation am free ! ' At the end a member of the congregation got up with a question :

' Pardon, parson ! Yo' jest been telling us Salvation am free and then yo' sends round de hat fer a collection. Dem statements don't kinder coincide.'

' Have patience, brother. Hold yo' talk while I explain. If you was parched and came to a rivuh you'd jest drop on yo' knees and lap up de good water, and it wouldn't cost you a dime, eh ? '

' Now, parson, dat's jest what I was beginning to say ! '

' Yes, brother, dat glorious water would be free, but now, a'supposing dat' water was pumped up t'roo pipes till it poured t'roo de taps in yo' house, you'd have to pay. Well, brother, it is de same with de gospel of de Lord. It's free, but it's having it piped up to you what costs de money. Pass de hat, deacon, pass de hat.' (Acknowledgements to Lord Castlerosse.)

'According to our means'

The story of Our Lord's comment on the widow's mite

*BALTIMORE 297
ENGLISH CATECHISM 246

(He 'called His disciples together' to tell them about it) is in Mark xii, 41–44.

The point is that God looks at the generosity of our heart, not at the amount of the gift.

It happened, of course, during Holy Week, and in the verses immediately before (Mark xii, 38–40) and immediately after (Mark xiii, 1–2) there are words of Our Lord bearing on the same subject. The upshot is that God cares for religion in the heart, and the buildings and outward prestige of religion are quite secondary.

'The Kingdom of His Church extended'

Our desire to spread the Faith is a proof of our own love of the Church. A lady once attended an A.P.F. lantern lecture, and when a collection was made she refused to contribute, saying that she didn't believe in foreign missions. Whereupon the man taking the collection said : 'In that case, Madam, as the collection is for the heathen, you are entitled to take something off the plate !'

The pennies of the poor

Over the great west door of Lincoln Cathedral are two stone figures. One represents a bishop in his mitre, the other a swineherd blowing his horn—St. Hugh of Lincoln and the swineherd of Stow. Here is the story told about them :

A poor swineherd, coming one day into Lincoln, was glad to see the walls of the new cathedral rising on their foundations—for the old cathedral had lately been destroyed by an earthquake. The great rebuilding was due to the zeal of the new bishop, Hugh, a Carthusian from France whom the worldly nobles had resisted at first, but who had won them over by his patient humility and courtesy. As to the poor, they loved him from the first, for he treated them as his brothers. Both nobles and poor were deeply impressed at the sight of their bishop working with his own hands on the cathedral site, carrying stones or mixing mortar.

The swineherd returned to the fields of Stow, a great

wish in his heart to have some share in the building of God's house.

Seven years passed by, and then, one day he presented himself at the Bishop's door. He was admitted, as poor men always were ; and St. Hugh, with the courteous smile he had for rich and poor alike, asked him his errand, expecting some request for help.

To his surprise the swineherd tipped up his horn and poured out a handful of silver coins. Full of awkward shyness, he held them out, the greater part of seven years' wages, asking the Bishop to use them for the building of the cathedral. He would have hurried away, but St. Hugh would not let him go. The astonishèd people of Lincoln saw their bishop and a swineherd walk up together to the great new altar and place a little pile of silver coins upon it.

The incident was remembered, and when his grateful people placed St. Hugh's image above the doorway, in memory of all that he had done, they showed how well they had understood his spirit when they chose the swineherd of Stow as representing the poor whom he had so loved, and who had helped him in his work for God.

When every Catholic does his bit

Bishop Wakelin was building the Cathedral at Winchester. He couldn't get enough wood for the roof, and was anxious to have oak from the royal forest of Hanepinges, on the road to Aresford. He asked William the Conqueror. William said he could have as much timber as he could cut down in four days and four nights.

Meanwhile the King had to go up to London. His business done, he was riding back to Winchester. Nearing the city, he seemed puzzled, turned to attendants and asked : ' What is that great building ? '

'The new cathedral of Winchester, sire.'

' But we haven't passed the forest of Hanepinges yet.'

' There is no forest of Hanepinges now—Bishop Wakelin has cut it down, all except the Gospel Oak, where St. Augustine preached.'

' But only four days and four nights . . . ! '

'Yes, but he had gathered all the axemen in this part of England.'

Nowadays the outdoor collection-card takes the place of the parishioner's axe, etc., but the zeal is the same and the church or school goes up like the cathedrals of old.

SEVEN SACRAMENTS

THE SEVEN SACRAMENTS

* HOW MANY SACRAMENTS ARE THERE?

    There are seven Sacraments: Baptism, Confirmation, Holy Eucharist, Penance, Extreme Unction, Holy Order and Matrimony.

The Seven Rivers of Life

A CERTAIN holy Cistercian, in a dream, was taken by his guardian angel and shown a vast plain peopled with many men and cities. On one side of the plain a copious spring of water gushed out from a hill-side, dividing into seven clear streams, which flowed down into the plain. At the other side of the plain another fountain rushed up from a dark cavern, also spreading out into seven streams.

He watched the streams that came from the cavern, and saw that many people drank from them eagerly, for their waters were sweet to the taste; but soon after drinking these people were seized with violent pains and vomiting, and many died.

'That is the cavern of Self-will,' said the angel. 'And its seven poisonous streams are the seven deadly sins. Now look across the plain to where the seven rivers of life take their rise from the hill of Calvary.'

The seven rivers of life were not so sweet to the taste, but they had wonderful properties, for the sick who drank them were being healed, the old were being made young again, the ugly becoming beautiful; and in some of the rivers the beholder could see the dead being brought to life again.

The vision filled him with grief for so many souls who were deceived by poisonous pleasures, and with a great

desire to bring them all to the saving waters of life. He understood that these seven rivers were the seven sacraments which are the channels of Christ's grace to mankind.
(See also story 191.)

> * WHAT IS A SACRAMENT ?
>
> *A Sacrament is an outward sign of inward grace, ordained by Jesus Christ, by which grace is given to our souls.*

'An Outward Sign'

AN old Irishwoman in London was puzzled by the electric traffic-signs at a cross-roads, and a humorous policeman undertook to explain.

'The red light is for the English, so you stay where you are ; the green is for the Irish, that's your turn to go.'

She watched the lights changing for a minute or two. 'Bedad,' she said, 'ye don't allow much time for the Orangemen to get across ! '

A traffic-light is an outward sign for stopping or going ; when the green light is on it is the cause of the traffic moving forward, somewhat as the outward sign of a sacrament is the cause of inward grace.

Of course, it is really the human will of the citizens which decides what the traffic-lights shall be, and also makes the cars move when the green light is on. And so, in the sacraments, it is God's Will which decides the outward sign and also ' releases ' the inward grace (according to His promise) when the outward sign is performed.

The power of a few spoken words

A young Englishman, staying at a Swiss mountain village in spring, went for a walk on a steep path up a mountain-side. The sun shone brilliantly on deep new-fallen snow. He rounded a bend in the path, and about twenty yards further along he saw a man standing and admiring the view. He recognised a fellow-guest from his hotel, a well-known mountaineer. By way of greeting he called at the top of his voice : ' Hello, there ! What a grand morning ! ' To his great surprise the other turned on

CATECHISM STORIES

him a gaze of horrified rebuke, then hurried down the path, seized the young Englishman round the shoulders and put a hand over his mouth. 'Keep quiet and listen!' he said in a low voice, looking with apprehension at the slope above their heads.

Even as he spoke a movement of the snow was visible in a great cleft on the other side of the valley. It gathered momentum, and in a few moments thousands of tons of snow were rushing down into the valley at two hundred miles an hour with a mighty roar. Then the two men had to crouch down clinging to each other for security as a tremendous blast of wind, lasting only for a few terrifying seconds, came up from below.

'Thank God it wasn't on our side of the valley!' said the mountaineer. 'It's just the weather for avalanches, and those few words you shouted were enough to start one, by the vibration they caused in the air.'

In each of the seven sacraments, as part of the 'outward sign,' there are the few essential words which cause a great avalanche of sanctifying grace, life-giving instead of destroying, falling into the soul to melt into fertilising streams of actual graces in daily life.

'Ordained by Jesus Christ'

This is essential for a true sacrament. Take, for instance, baptism. St. John the Baptist came out of the desert and preached his mission of penance to the Jews (read Mark i, 4–8, adding details from Luke iii, 10–16). He used the (already well known to the Jews as a ceremony of admitting gentile proselytes) outward sign of washing his penitents in the river to express the inward grace of repentance and change of life. Outward sign and inward grace were there, yet it was not the sacrament of baptism. (*Why?*)

Later, when Our Lord commanded the same sign to be used (Matt. xxviii, 19), it became a true sacrament.

'By which grace is given to our souls'

The word 'sacrament' was originally a Roman army word, meaning the sacred oath which a soldier took to obey the Emperor.

About eighty years after the Ascension a well-known Roman author named Pliny (the Younger) was Governor of Bithynia in Asia Minor. During his otherwise tranquil term of office one thing rather worried him : the remarkable spread of a new sect called Christians. They were getting so numerous that the pagan shrines were neglected, and the trade in animals for sacrifices had suffered badly. This led to many complaints and accusations against the Christians. Pliny regarded them as harmless, and certainly not guilty of any crimes. Even when he arrested two Christian slave-women, who were deaconesses in the church, and questioned them under torture, he could find nothing worse than ' low unreasonable superstition.'

Accordingly he wrote to the Emperor Trajan asking for instructions, and we still have his long letter. Here is his description of the Christians :

' They meet together on fixed days, before dawn, to sing antiphonally a hymn to Christ, as to a God, and to bind themselves by an oath (' *sacramentum* '), not for wickedness of any kind, but not to commit theft or brigandage, not to commit adultery, not to break a sworn promise and not to refuse the return of trust-money when claimed.'

The oath or ' sacrament ' was evidently the Holy Eucharist. Pliny had somehow got hold of the main point : in all the Sacraments, not only the Holy Eucharist, we do pledge ourselves to keep the Ten Commandments and lead a good life, because the sacraments supply us with the grace to do so.

(Trajan's answer to Pliny was that the Christians were not to be sought out ; but if denounced by informers they were to be punished, unless they would sacrifice to the gods.)

* WHAT IS GRACE ?

> *Grace is a supernatural gift of God, freely bestowed upon us for our sanctification and salvation.*

God dwells in our soul by Grace

ST. CATHERINE of Siena once saw, in some kind of vision, a soul in a state of grace. It was so entrancingly beautiful

*BALTIMORE 109-115
ENGLISH CATECHISM 139

CATECHISM STORIES

in its dazzling brightness that she could not bear to look steadily at it, and she cried out:

'If I did not know there is only one God, I should think this was another God!'

To her confessor, who asked her to describe it, she said:

'There is nothing in this world that can give you the smallest idea of what I have seen. If you could only see a soul in the state of grace you would sacrifice your life a hundred times for its salvation.'

'I asked the angel who was with me what made that soul so beautiful, and he answered that it was the image and likeness of God dwelling in it by Grace.'

(See stories 191, 192, 193, 342, 383-386, 439, 440.)

Life, natural and supernatural

'See how big I am. My peaks rise up to Heaven. I am so big no one can move me,' boasted the mountain to the oak.

'Oh, yes,' agreed the oak, 'you are big, but you can't *grow*.'

'I can grow,' boasted the oak to the squirrel. 'My roots go down into the earth and my branches stretch up towards the sky, and I get bigger and bigger each year. I give shelter to birds and to little people like you.'

'Yes, you can grow, but you can't *crack nuts*,' said the squirrel.

'I can crack nuts and I can spring from branch to branch,' boasted the squirrel to the old woman.

'But you can't *read* or do *sums*,' said the old woman.

'I can do sums. I have learned a great many things,' boasted the old woman to her little grandson.

'Yes, Grannie, but have you been *baptised?*' asked the child.

'No, I don't hold with such things,' replied his grandmother.

'Then, Grannie, I have something you haven't. I have two lives,' said the little boy.

'What do you mean?' his Grannie enquired.

'I have my own little life that I got on my birthday,

and I have a share of God's life in my soul that I got on the day of my baptism,' the child replied.

This parable shows us that all life comes from God, but God's own eternal Life of Joy is something no creature could ever reach, unless God 'freely bestowed' it as a gift.

(See also stories 191 and 192.)

' A gift freely bestowed upon us '

It is not possible for us to know with absolute certainty (except by special revelation from God) that we are in a state of Grace ; but we may confidently trust that we are, if we are conscious of no grave sin.

At the trial of St. Joan of Arc (for heresy, witchcraft, etc. etc.) her judges were Bishop Cauchon and an Inquisitor, assisted by a score or more professional theologians and canon lawyers, including some of the keenest minds in Europe. Some of these, all through the long trial, did their best to entrap her into heresy by cunning questions. Once she was asked :

' Are you sure you are in a state of grace ? '

To say Yes would have been heresy. To say No would have been taken as a confession of dealing with the devil. Her answer is famous :

' If I am in a state of grace, may God keep me therein ; if I am not, may God soon place me in it.'

A prayer which any Christian, even the greatest saint, may well have on his lips. Also perhaps for the scrupulous, always tempted to worry whether they have committed mortal sin.

Grace is the very life of our soul

A diver was going down into the sea to try and find a treasure in a sunken wreck. He was newly trained and this was his first big job. Just before his helmet was screwed on the captain gave him a final word of advice. ' Watch your two lines, keep them free and working, remember your life depends on them.'

The two lines were the tube that supplied the helmet with air, and the telephone wire that communicated with the boat.

The diver went overboard. Down by the wreck it was dark, and he could not see much of the two lines. Soon something seemed to be going wrong—he could hardly breathe—the air-tube must have got entangled in the wreckage!

He made the telephone signal, and heard a voice say: 'Hello, what's the matter?'

'Air-tube doesn't seem to be working.'

'Keep still, we'll get it right.' In a few seconds he found he could breathe well again, and was able to finish his work and locate the treasure.

Next Sunday the diver happened to be at Mass when the priest was preaching a sermon on Grace. The priest said our real home is heaven; here on earth we are strangers and pilgrims, and we need God's grace to keep our soul alive.

'That is like me,' thought the diver. 'The fishes are at home in the water, but I can't live there without a constant supply of air through the tube. The air-tube is like the sacraments, and the telephone wire is like prayer.'

(See also story 663.)

'For our sanctification'

There are instances in the lives of saints when the beauty of the grace-life in their soul has been allowed to shine forth in some outward radiance, somewhat after the fashion of Our Lord's transfiguration.

SS. Rufina and Secunda were two sisters in Rome, third century. Their father had promised them in marriage to two young Christian men, but when the persecution under Valerian broke out both the young men gave up their faith and tried to persuade the two girls to do the same. The latter refused, and in due course found themselves before the Governor's tribunal. He had Rufina scourged, whereupon Secunda was indignant at being left out of it.

'Why such honour for my sister, and such a slight upon me? Order us both to be scourged—we are confessing Christ together!'

The exasperated judge sent them to be shut up in a pitch-dark and filthy dungeon cell, thinking this would soon break their spirit. But as soon as they entered it their presence radiated a heavenly light around them, and sweet perfumes filled the dungeon. Finally after other trials the two maidens were taken outside the city along the Via Aurelia to the tenth milestone, and there beheaded. (*Breviary*, *July*, 10.)

Grace and Glory

Grace in this life turns into Glory in the next.

In the fourth heaven of Paradise, Dante and his guide Beatrice are greeted by twice twelve blessed spirits, who circle round them, resplendent as suns. St. Thomas Aquinas and St. Bonaventure are amongst them ; these name the other saints, and answer some of Dante's unspoken questions. One thing the poet wonders about is what will happen to the glorious brightness of the souls after they have been rejoined to their bodies in the resurrection ; will the brightness of the soul be hidden or diminished ?

This question is answered by King Solomon, lover of wisdom, and the most radiant spirit of the first circle.

' The light that shines in us will last as long as Heaven itself. It is the Light of Glory ; its brightness corresponds with our growth in Grace on earth. It is the Light by which we see the Vision of God : the greater the Light, the higher our vision, and the more burning our love. And when we regain our visible garment of flesh we shall seem even more resplendent than now ; and our bodies and eyes will be made strong to bear the brightness and enjoy all delight.'

And the other blessed spirits uttered a heartfelt prayer ' Amen,' signifying their desire to be reunited with their former bodies, not only for their own sake, but still more for the relatives and friends

> ' And those whom best they loved
> Ere they were made imperishable flame.'
>
> (*Paradiso*, Canto XIV.)

(See also story 149.)

' A supernatural gift . . . for our salvation '

A certain Chinese philosopher was first a follower of Confucius, then became a Buddhist, and finally a Christian.

Someone asked him to put into a word the difference between the three great religions.

'Yes,' he said. 'Suppose a man has fallen into a deep pit and cannot get out. Confucius would fold his arms and say: Serve you right for being such a fool as to fall in. Buddha would be full of sympathy and give the man advice about climbing out. Our blessed Lord would stoop down and lift the man right out of the pit.'

The Christian religion not only tells us what to do, but makes us able to do it: through God's life in us, which we call Grace.

(See also story 195.)

Prompt correspondence with graces

After Constantine had given peace to the Church, persecutions revived in the East under Licinius (316). In a Roman legion at Sebaste in Armenia forty soldiers openly confessed themselves Christians and persisted in spite of all punishments. At last the Emperor's legate decided to threaten them with a lingering death, in the hope of overcoming their will.

It was mid-winter, bitterly cold; close to the military headquarters was a frozen pool, and the forty soldiers were warned that they should be stripped of their clothing and exposed on the ice all night until they recanted.

They still refused, and that night they were duly placed naked on the frozen pool. Fires, hot baths and warm food were close at hand, near a little temple to Mars, the god of war, ready for any of the forty who should change his mind and sacrifice to the gods.

Gathering together on the ice, they prayed for strength to bear their trial, so that in the morning the bodies of forty soldiers of Christ might be found all faithful unto death.

Meanwhile in the priest's house, where the warm fire was, sat Sempronius, the centurion who had been charged with the duty of seeing the sentence carried out. Sleep overcame him, and he fell into a strange dream. He seemed to be close to the pool, watching the martyrs' courageous endurance. Then, from out of the darkness appeared an angel, carrying a shining crown—heaven's prize for the victorious. Again and again he came—thirty-nine crowns he brought in all. Wondering that there should not be forty, Sempronius awoke. One of the guards was entering the room, and he reported :

'One of the forty has sacrificed.'

There stood the unhappy man—shame and sorrow on his face. The soldiers had clothed him and were warming him with spiced wine.

His dream still vivid in his mind, Sempronius made his way down to the pool. Some of the martyrs lay unconscious. One was praying aloud :

'Forty athletes we have entered the arena, O Lord. Let forty victors receive the prize.'

'That passes the power of your God,' cried Sempronius, 'one of you has sacrificed.'

But the man continued to pray his strange prayer.

Then into the mind of Sempronius came light and a great wave of grace. 'One has lost his crown—I may attain to it!'

He hesitated not a moment. Straight to the legate he went and confessed his belief in the God of the Christians and his desire to die among them.

A few of the forty were still alive to welcome this new soldier of Christ as he took the place of the faithless man on the frozen pool.

The martyrs' prayer had been heard. Morning light revealed forty bodies lying on the ice. In heaven there was joy over the crowning of forty victors.

Meriting further grace

'Actual' graces (i.e. graces that come and go) are given to be acted on at once, if we want to get further graces.

At a big review in the Champs-Élysées Napoleon's horse bolted and a young private soldier ran out of the ranks, seized the bridle and stopped it.

'Thank you, *mon capitaine !* ' said the Emperor.

Like a shot the soldier answered : 'Of what regiment, sire ? '

Pleased with such readiness, Napoleon said : ' Of the Guard ! ' and rode away.

The young soldier at once laid down his musket and went and joined a group of officers. One of them spoke indignantly :

'What are you doing here ? Get back to the ranks !'

'I am a captain of the Guard : the Emperor made me one just now.'

'Ah—I did not know—please accept my apology, Captain, and my congratulations too.'

(See also stories 115, 671.)

> * Do the Sacraments always give grace ?
>
> *The Sacraments always give grace to those who receive them worthily. They have the power of giving grace from the merits of Christ's Precious Blood which they apply to our souls.*

'The Sacraments always give grace'

THAT is, sanctifying grace. And we need all they can give us.

A boy had a little white terrier and looked after him carefully. One winter morning, when the dog had just been bathed and brushed and combed, the boy and his sister agreed admiringly that Elfin looked really beautiful, perfectly white for once.

It had snowed all night, but now the sun was shining. They went across the fields to the village shop, and suddenly the boy said : 'Why, look at Elfin ! He's dirty again already !'

'So he is !' said his sister. Then, 'No, of course ! it's only seeing him against the fresh sparkling snow !'

Even when we are in a state of grace our souls appear soiled compared with the Holiness of God. Increase in sanctifying grace means increase in likeness to God : hence the oftener we go to the Sacraments the better.

It is Our Lord who works in the Sacraments

The story of the Good Samaritan (Luke x, 30–37) is often re-told as a parable of man's salvation. The man

*BALTIMORE 306-309
ENGLISH CATECHISM 250-251

lying wounded and helpless is Mankind after the Fall ; the Good Samaritan is Our Lord ; the oil and wine are the Sacraments ; the inn is the Church. This is only an ' accommodation ' perhaps, but it helps us to see the Sacraments as (what they are) a personal activity of Our Lord, and consequently always giving grace.

(See also stories 56, 671, 674.)

* WHAT IS BAPTISM ?

Baptism is a Sacrament which cleanses us from original sin, makes us Christians, children of God and members of the Church.

Baptism instituted by Our Lord

IN Our Lord's time the Jews already used baptismal washing sometimes as a ceremony of receiving proselytes. St. John the Baptist used it for everybody, as a sign of penance and remission of sins (read Mark i, 2–11).

Add that Our Lord Himself, through His disciples, practised baptism in the early days of His ministry (John iii, 22–26 ; iv, 1–2). Also His words to Nicodemus (John iii, 3–5). Finally, His formal command to the apostles (Matt. xxviii, 19).

The apostles evidently understood this quite literally, hence the Church began at Pentecost with a baptism on the grand scale of three thousand believers (Acts ii, 37–41).

Baptism begins a new life

A new life of happiness in heaven, for those who die just after baptism ; or else a changed life on earth, lived in faith, hope and charity instead of in sin.

Amid the wreckage of the Roman Empire a fierce young pagan chieftain of the Sicambri, named Clovis, managed to defeat all rivals and united the various tribes of the Franks into one kingdom. Then hearing of the beauty of Clotilda, Catholic Burgundian princess, he sent his friend Aurelian (it is said) disguised as a beggar to give her a message and a gold ring ; then he asked for her hand and they were married in the year 493.

Next year a baby son was born, and Clotilda wanted

CATECHISM STORIES

him baptised a Christian. Clovis agreed unwillingly, for he still preferred his warlike pagan gods. The baptism was performed with grand ceremonies, for Clotilda hoped to impress the king.

A week afterwards the baby died. Clovis blamed his wife: 'My gods are angry because the child was baptised, and your God could not save him!'

But Clotilda spoke up loyally for her Faith: 'I loved my boy, but I am not sad at his death; I know that because of his baptism he is happy now in the presence of God. I thank God that I am worthy to have a son in heaven!'

Clovis loved and looked up to his wife, and when their second son was born he again allowed her to have her way about the baptism. This child, too, became ill, and again Clovis blamed the Christian God, but Clotilda prayed and the child recovered.

Soon afterwards Clovis was in a great battle at Tolbiac with a German tribe, the Allemani. His soldiers were giving way and things seemed desperate. 'O God of Clotilda!' he prayed, 'give me the victory now and I will be baptised!' The tide of battle turned, the Franks rallied and swept all before them.

Clovis kept his promise, and Clotilda helped to instruct him. When he heard about Our Lord being nailed to the cross he cried out: 'Ha! if only *I* had been there with my Franks!'

He addressed his battle-comrades in full assembly and they all agreed to become Christians along with 'him.

The baptism of Clovis and three thousand of his warriors took place on Christmas Day, 496, at Rheims, with great splendour. Through garlanded streets, into the church, illuminated with thousands of candles and lamps, the holy bishop St. Remigius (St. Rémy) led the king by the hand, in procession with his warriors.

At the font Remigius addressed the king: 'Bow thy head, brave Sicambrian: adore that which thou hast burned, and burn that which thou hast adored.'

The chrism for his christening was missing, and a dove (legend says) came flying from heaven with a vase of chrism ; it was ever afterwards kept at Rheims and used at the coronation of the kings of France.

After baptism, Clovis was clothed in the white garment ; and immediately, with the people looking on, he set free all the captives taken after the battle of Tolbiac.

For the rest of his life (he died before Clotilda, at the age of forty-five) Clovis was a faithful Catholic, protecting the Church and helping forward its civilising work. His reign was the beginning of France.

Here are some verses about Clovis being instructed :

CLOVIS, OF CLOTILDE

' Is Peter, who put up his sword
before his lord avenged be,
is he forgiven of his lord ? '
So Clovis questioned.
    ' Even he.'

' Had I been there with valiant bands
the mob that mocked, the priests who schemed
and Pilate washing guilty hands
had all been slain ! '
    ' These are redeemed.'

' But those who plaited thorns, and they
who scourged Him, spat on Him, and cried
to crucify Him, dost thou say
such are redeemed ? '
    ' For such He died.'

' The thieves perchance. But not His foes
who drove the nails, who proffered gall,
who thrust the spear, who jeered, not those
can merit His salvation.'
    ' All.'

' For them who came with staves and knives
we still should make a bitter way,
for their sons' sons, their babes and wives,
through time and times and places . . .'
    ' Nay.'

' Must we not make their woes increase
by whose dark envy He has died ? '
' Until thou make this travail cease
His soul cannot be satisfied.'

'Yet was His innocence wounded sore !
Say then, how can forgiveness be
for them who did such things ? '
            ' Yea, more,
mayhap one day for even thee ! '

RUTH EVELYN HENDERSON,
in The Commonweal.

Necessity of Baptism

St. Peter Claver, S.J., worked for forty-four years at Cartagena, in Central America, as the heroic apostle of the poor negro slaves who were brought there from Africa to work in the gold-mines. A thousand every month used to arrive, after a frightful voyage, crowded in the holds of ships. Claver used to meet them with food and drink, and win their confidence by his kindness and his efforts to alleviate their oppression.

The first thing he usually did was to seek out the babies who had been born during the voyage. Many of them must have been dying already, and the others would mostly be dead soon owing to the terrible conditions in the slave-markets ; as for their poor parents, if still alive after the voyage, they were helpless to care for the future of their children. Claver had no scruples therefore in taking the black babies one by one into his arms and baptising them there and then, so giving them their 'spotless white garment' for the heavenly home which their living Father had waiting for them after the cruel hardships of their entry into the world.

In the same way, missionaries to-day baptise Chinese babies in thousands, not asking the parents' permission because the parents have abandoned them to die ; if they live they are brought up Catholics, if they die they are sure of heaven.

Baptism 'makes us Christians'

The medieval legend of St. Catherine was a parable teaching the necessity of baptism ; also illustrating the 'baptism of blood.'

She was a maiden of Alexandria, age eighteen, brilliant scholar, noble, beautiful, but when urged by her mother to choose a husband, she was positive that she would accept no spouse unless he should be her equal, not only in birth and riches, but also in beauty and intellect. Her mother (says the legend) became a Christian under the influence of a certain holy hermit. Catherine still defended the pagan gods; and her mother, being no equal to her in argument, went to the hermit and implored him to pray for her daughter's conversion.

Next night as mother and daughter were asleep, they both had the same vision. A great Lady, richly robed and crowned, came to them with a resplendent train of followers, all wearing diadems in royal state.

'See, my daughter!' said the Lady to Catherine. 'All these are kings, who reign under my Son the Emperor of Glory. Choose one of them now who shall be your spouse, for I know you are yet unbetrothed.'

As she was speaking her Son came, too, in very glorious array, with many shining followers. And when Catherine saw Him she had no eyes for any of the others.

'See, this is my Son, the Emperor of Glory—would you choose *Him* for your spouse?'

And with great fervour Catherine answered that she would choose no other at all, but Him alone.

Then her mother made the request of the Empress, and the Empress asked her Son, if He would agree to the betrothal. But He turned away.

'It would not be fitting, for I am the King of Christians, and this maiden serves the pagan gods. But if she were a baptised Christian, I promise that I would fulfil your request and give her a ring in token of betrothal.'

On awaking from sleep mother and daughter told each other the vision. Henceforth Catherine did nothing but sigh and weep with longing to see the Emperor of Glory, and she felt more and more drawn to the thought of becoming a Christian.

At last her mother took her to the old hermit, and when he had heard the vision he told them that the Emperor of Glory could be no other than Jesus Christ Himself, the Empress was his Mother Mary, and the kings who served Him were the saints of heaven. He

Baptism makes us 'children of God'

St. Francis of Sales even as a boy showed an apostolic zeal for souls, having great influence over his youthful playmates. Sometimes he would lead them into church and arrange them in a circle around the font. 'Look, this is the place we should love best of all! Here is where we were made children of God! Let us say one *Gloria Patri* to thank God for that.' They would all kneel down and say the prayer, and kiss the font itself, and then go back to their games. (See also story 178.)

'And members of the Church'

In a Cardiff hospital an old Arab seaman lay dying. He was a Mohammedan, and said he did not wish to see any Christian minister. A Catholic nurse thought perhaps she ought to baptise him before he died, and she did so while he was asleep. Did she do right? (*No, baptism is only to be given to those who are willing. The Church asks: Wilt thou be baptised? And the candidate replies: I will. Unconscious people may be baptised if they have previously showed some sign of willingness.*)

A schoolgirl named Annie used to take a baby out for one of the neighbours every day after school. She knew the baby had never been baptised, so one afternoon she took it to the priest and asked him to baptise it. When he heard that the parents were Protestants he said he couldn't as there was no likelihood of the child being brought up a Catholic. Annie thought this was rather hard on the baby, and as she was very fond of it she baptised it over the fountain in the park herself, in the way she had learned at school. Was the baptism valid? Did she do right? (*The baptism was valid, but Annie would be wrong in doing it against the will of the parents, even if the child had seemed dying. Baptism admits a person to be a member of the Catholic Church, and the Church will not admit them if she knows they will never live up to it.*

If babies can rightly be baptised it is our duty to baptise them, but those who die unbaptised are still in God's loving care and we can safely leave them to Him.)

CATECHISM STORIES

instructed her in the mysteries of the Faith, and she listened humbly, putting aside all her pride of learning, and at last, with great devotion, she was baptised.

Then at home, while she was praying alone, Our Lord came to her in vision with His angels and saints, and put on her finger a ring, promising great grace and glory to her if she would remain true to Him. When she came out of her ecstasy the ring, a real ring, was there on her finger.

From that time she gave her whole mind to the study of the Scriptures and to conversation with the servants of Christ.

When the emperor Maximin began a cruel persecution of the Christians, Catherine went to him and spoke boldly in defence of the Faith. Startled by the ability of this girl of eighteen, the emperor gathered a number of the pagan philosophers for a public debate with her. Her arguments and eloquence were so irresistible that several of the philosophers declared their belief in Christ and were ordered to immediate execution by the emperor. They were distressed at the thought of dying without baptism, but Catherine assured them : ' Have no fear, you will be baptised in your own blood.'

The enraged tyrant had Catherine scourged and put in prison. There she was visited out of curiosity by the emperor's wife, and a high officer named Porphyry ; these also after conversing with Catherine declared themselves believers and were put to death.

She was brought out to be martyred on a spiked wheel, but it was broken to pieces at her touch. Then she was beheaded, and angels carried her body to Mt. Sinai for burial.

Nearly all this story is legendary, but St. Catherine was one of the most popular saints all through the Middle Ages ; and she is still honoured as the patron of girl students and philosophers and wheelwrights.

Every human soul is made to be the bride of God, and sanctifying grace is the betrothal : God's promise of eternal happiness with Him, the soul's promise to be true to Him.

CATECHISM STORIES

The duty of godparents

The candidate for baptism is brought by one or two persons who are already 'members of the Church'—the godparents.

A young couple, a careless Catholic and his non-Catholic wife, took their first baby to be baptised, and asked the wife's brother and his fiancée to be godparents. These were both Protestants, and when they told the priest this he said: 'Well, you are very welcome to the baptism, but we must have a Catholic godparent somehow.' 'Why can't a Protestant stand?' 'Because the godparent has to say the Creed, and I don't suppose you know it, do you? Also the godparent is the one who undertakes to see that the child is brought up in the Catholic Church, and that is a thing that only a Catholic can do properly.'

Just then one of the big girls from the school (Linda was her name) came into church to make a visit, so the priest asked her to stand godmother. She made the answers and put her hand on the baby when it was held over the font.

Afterwards she used to go and see the baby boy sometimes and got quite friendly with the family, and when he was five she made sure he went to the Catholic school. Soon afterwards she got married and had him for her trainbearer. When he made his first communion she gave him a prayer-book. By that time his mother was a Catholic, too, and both parents went to Communion with him; and Linda felt that with God's help she had not done so badly as a godmother.

> * DOES BAPTISM ALSO FORGIVE ACTUAL SINS?
>
> *Baptism also forgives actual sins, with all punishment due to them, when it is received in proper dispositions by those who have been guilty of actual sin.*

'In proper dispositions'

ST. FRANCIS XAVIER was very ready to baptise simple savages and little children, even with but a short instruc-

*BALTIMORE 316
ENGLISH CATECHISM 257

tion, for his loving heart was eager to put heaven within their reach.

But with educated men whose knowledge made their sins more serious he was more strict.

For instance, St. Francis very much wanted leave to preach to the subjects of the king of Bungo (in Japan). But this king would have had nothing to say to a poor priest in an old black cassock, carrying his own pack, and begging his food along the way. Consequently it was necessary to impress him with what little pomp it was possible to arrange. So a procession was formed of thirty Portuguese from the ship, dressed in their best clothes, carrying whatever impressive things they could collect—a large book in a white satin bag, a magnificent parasol, a pair of fine black slippers worn only by great dignitaries, and so on, all to the music of a band. In the centre walked St. Francis in cassock and cotta and embroidered stole.

The king of Bungo, duly impressed, invited him to preach at Court. Large numbers of people were converted, and, in time, baptised. The king himself was so much taken with the Catholic Faith that he gave up the worst evils in his life and asked for baptism. But St. Francis saw that he was not yet willing to lead the Christian life; he refused to baptise him. It was some years before the king had got rid of all his evil habits and St. Francis felt able to allow him into the Church.

(For another story of adult baptism and its necessary dispositions see No. 206.)

* WHO IS THE ORDINARY MINISTER OF BAPTISM?

The ordinary minister of Baptism is a priest; but any one may baptise in case of necessity, when a priest cannot be had.

'When a priest cannot be had'

DAISY had to stay at home from school to look after her mother and the new baby, both very ill. One day the doctor said the baby would only live a few hours longer.

*BALTIMORE 318
ENGLISH CATECHISM 258

CATECHISM STORIES

Daisy's father, a Catholic, was at work. Daisy asked her mother (a Protestant) if she should ask the priest to come and baptise it, and her mother said: If you like. She ran to the presbytery, but the priest was out, so she thought she had better baptise the baby herself. She begged a bottle from the priest's housekeeper and went for some holy water from the church, but there was none left in the big jar. Then she ran home, put a towel under the baby's head, and took some water from the tap in a little jug, and said: ' I baptise you in the name of the Father and of the Son and of the Holy Ghost '—and when she said ' in the name of ' she poured some water on the baby's head.

Did she act rightly in all this? (*Yes, except that there was no need to use holy water, anyhow.*)

Is there anything else she should do? (*Tell the priest later on so that he can enter it in the Register; and if the baby lives bring it to church for the ' ceremonies ' and chrism.*)

* How is Baptism given?

> *Baptism is given by pouring water on the head of the child, saying at the same time these words:*
> *' I baptise thee in the name of the Father, and of the Son, and of the Holy Ghost.'*

The manner of baptising

An odd story is told (in Spirago) to illustrate the manner of valid baptism. A Christian catechumen was taking two poor old Christian beggars across the desert: one was armless, the other dumb. Their water supply ran out, and the catechumen was dying of heatstroke. He asked the others to baptise him. There was no water, so they decided to use sand (which is sometimes used in the desert for bathing purposes). The dumb man poured sand on the head of the catechumen, while the armless man uttered the words ' I baptise thee,' etc. Then the catechumen died. Was this baptism valid? (*No; water must be used, and the person who pours it must also say the words. But the catechumen received at death the ' baptism of desire.'*)

*BALTIMORE 319
ENGLISH CATECHISM 259

Is it enough if the water is *sprinkled?* Many Protestants do this and it may be valid, but the Catholic rule says the water is to be poured, e.g. made to flow on the head. If the sprinkling is generous enough it would be pouring. A Chinese war lord, the so-called ' Christian General,' is said to have baptised a whole battalion at once with the help of a fire-hose.

VICAR : How well your baby behaved during the christening !
PROUD MOTHER : Yes, I've been getting him used to it with the watering-can all the week.

* WHAT IS CONFIRMATION ?

> *Confirmation is a Sacrament by which we receive the Holy Ghost, in order to make us strong and perfect Christians and soldiers of Jesus Christ.*

' A Sacrament by which we receive the Holy Ghost '

WHEN the Holy Ghost came down on the apostles it filled them with courage ; Confirmation does the same for each Christian.

At the time of the Emperor Gallienus (A.D. 264) a Roman soldier named Marinus at Cæsarea, in Palestine, was about to be promoted to a high rank when some jealous fellow-soldiers denounced him as a Christian. The emperor called him and asked him if this were true, and he said it was. The emperor said his promotion would stand if he gave up the Christian faith, otherwise he must die. He gave Marinus three hours to decide. Marinus went to the bishop who had only recently baptised him. The bishop then and there laid his hands upon him in the sacrament of Confirmation, to strengthen him with the Holy Spirit. Then he put before him a sword and the book of the gospels, and said : ' Make your choice.' Without hesitation Marinus chose the gospels, and went back to meet his martyrdom and his reward.

(On Confirmation see also stories 99, 586.)

*BALTIMORE 330
ENGLISH CATECHISM 262

'Strong and perfect Christians'

B. John Ogilvie was one who lived and died as a valiant 'soldier of Jesus Christ.' Of a noble Scottish family, he was brought up Calvinist, but was converted at the age of seventeen, went abroad and joined St. Ignatius Loyola's 'Company of Jesus.' In 1613, aged thirty-three, he volunteered for the perils of the Scottish mission and worked in Glasgow and Edinburgh, reconciling many to the Church, until his arrest after nine months. 'During a long imprisonment' (says the *Catholic Encyclopedia*) 'no torture could force him to name any Catholics. Though his legs were cruelly crushed, and he was kept awake for nine nights by being pricked with needles, scarcely a sigh escaped him. Under searching examinations his patience, courage and gaiety won the admiration of his very judges —especially of the Protestant Archbishop Spottiswoode; but he was condemned and hanged as a traitor at Glasgow.'

On the scaffold he was offered life, wealth and other rewards if he would apostatise. '"Do you hear this?" said the father; "and will you confirm it when occasion arises?" "We hear," the people shouted, "and we will bear witness. Come down, Mr. Ogilvie, come down." The Catholics now began to tremble, the heretics to rejoice. "There is, then, no fear," said Fr. Ogilvie, "that I shall hereafter be held guilty of treason?" "None at all," shouted the mob in the market-place. "For religion's sake alone, then, am I brought here as a criminal?" "For that alone," came the answering shout. "It is well," said the father triumphantly; "it is, then, clear that for religion's sake alone I am condemned. For that I am prepared to give even a hundred lives, and to give them freely, gaily. Take, then, the one I have, I am quite ready. You shall never take my religion from me."'

A young Protestant Hungarian who was travelling in Scotland happened to be present, and wrote afterwards: 'I can find no words to describe his proud and noble bearing as he went to death.' He also tells how the rosary which Fr. Ogilvie threw into the crowd, as a souvenir for the Catholics, fell upon him, and how the incident set him thinking about religion, and remained as an unescapable thought in his mind, until after many years he became a Catholic.

'Soldiers of Jesus Christ'

Every Christian is adopted into God's family at baptism and taken into God's army by Confirmation.

Legend tells how Charlemagne forbade his sister Bertha to marry one of his own Frankish warriors, but the two married nevertheless and fled into exile in Italy. Soon after their son Roland was born, his father died; Roland and his mother made their home in great poverty in a hill-side cave near a town.

Roland grew up a brave little boy of noble bearing, and in spite of being so poor was a leader amongst the other boys, especially when they played at being soldiers with him as the captain. His great friend was Oliver, son of the town's governor.

One day Roland asked his mother why he had to wear rags when other boys wore velvet or silk. She explained how poor she was, and as he continued his questions it came out that she had once lived in a fine palace, and then that she was the daughter of a king.

'Then you are a princess, Mother! But how can you be a princess without servants and soldiers?'

'I need no soldiers, my son will wait on me and fight for me.'

'Yes! the cave is your palace and I will be your army!'

Not long afterwards Charlemagne came into Italy with his army and stayed some days in the town near by. He and his officers feasted at great tables spread under the trees in the meadows, and all the townsfolk were welcome to come and eat and drink. When the boy Roland saw this he walked boldly up to the tables, and instead of eating took up an armful of bread and meat and fruit and walked away with it to give his mother a good meal for once. The servants were going to stop him, but the emperor,

CATECHISM STORIES

who had noticed the boy and liked the look of him, signed to them to let him alone.

Next day again Roland came to the feast for an armful of food and this time Charlemagne called him and asked him to sit down and eat, but the boy replied he was taking the food home to his mother.

' Who is your mother ? '

' My mother is a princess.'

The people laughed, but Charlemagne liked the fearless look of the boy more than ever, and asked :

' Where is your mother's castle ? '

' Round there on the hill-side.'

' Has she many servants and soldiers ? '

' My hand will serve her, and fight for her, too.'

Charlemagne smiled and told the boy to run home ; then, rising from the table, followed him to the cave. There the emperor found his sister and was reconciled to her, to the boy's great wonder and joy.

' Roland, will you come and live with me as my son and learn to be a real soldier ? '

As soon as Roland understood that his mother was to come, too, he was only too pleased to be adopted by this marvellous emperor-uncle.

They all went to France, where Roland lived in the palace and learned to ride a horse of his own and to use lance and sword. As the years went by he was always begging to be allowed to go with the army.

At last the day came when he was a real knight and rode out with the others on a campaign. In the first battle he fought like a hero, and saved the emperor's life when it was in danger. Soon he was a great leader whom men would follow anywhere, and whose deeds were told far and wide in the world. His happiness was complete when his boyhood friend Oliver arrived from Italy to become his comrade-in-arms. They went campaigning together against the Saracens who had invaded France, and after seven years hard fighting they drove them into Spain and pursued them there. (For the end of Roland's story see Appendix, No. 664.)

* How does the Bishop administer the Sacrament of Confirmation?

The Bishop administers the Sacrament of Confirmation by praying that the Holy Ghost may come down upon those who are to be confirmed; and by laying his hand on them, and making the sign of the cross with chrism on their foreheads, at the same time pronouncing certain words:

'*I sign thee with the sign of the cross, and I confirm thee with the chrism of salvation; in the name of the Father, and of the Son, and of the Holy Ghost. Amen.*'

The outward sign of Confirmation

As soon as the Church began to spread beyond Jerusalem we read of the sacrament of Confirmation. In the persecution which followed the martyrdom of St. Stephen many Christians were dispersed to other districts. Philip went to the city of Samaria and made converts there, especially amongst the followers of Simon Magus (Acts viii, 1-12). Then Peter and John were sent from Jerusalem to hold a confirmation for the newly-baptised converts (read Acts viii, 14-17).

They were passing on the Gift of Pentecost by the outward sign of laying-on of hands. That is what our bishops do now.

'I sign thee with the Sign of the Cross'

It was at Clermont in France (1095) that Pope Urban II preached the great sermon that started the First Crusade.

It was an age when the warlike character was held in supreme honour; Christian princes and lords were constantly fighting amongst themselves, often bringing misery and famine on their poor subjects.

Meanwhile in 1077 the Turks had captured Jerusalem (from the Egyptians) and showed a cruel hatred for Christians. They desecrated the holy places, destroyed St. Helena's church of the Holy Sepulchre, oppressed and

CATECHISM STORIES

sometimes massacred or made slaves of Christians in Palestine, and often attacked and maltreated the bands of pilgrims who still went to the Holy Land. Also they were over-running the lands of the Christian Emperor of Constantinople, and he sent a letter to the Pope appealing for help.

So Urban II summoned a Council at Clermont (he was a Frenchman himself, and hoped for most help from Normans and French); over three hundred bishops and abbots came, and many great nobles camped with their followers in the plain near the town.

After dealing with Church matters the Council turned to public affairs and renewed the 'Truce of God' between Christians, which had been decreed in old days and was now neglected. 'Peace with justice,' said the decree; and to prevent the oppression of the people the Council took widows, orphans, merchants and labourers under the protection of religion. Finally it was decided to preach the Crusade.

The whole Council went in procession with the Pope to the great market-square, where thousands of people awaited them, including great leaders like Robert of Flanders, Godfrey of Boulogne, his brother Count Baldwin and Raymond of Toulouse.

At the Pope's side on the platform stood a strange figure, tall, gaunt, dressed in rough pilgrim-fashion amongst the purple and scarlet and gold. It was Peter the Hermit, who had seen the Turkish cruelties in the Holy Land and was trying to rouse Christians to go to the rescue. He spoke first, and told what he had seen.

Then Pope Urban spoke, with marvellous eloquence. He called on them to live up to the glorious traditions of the Franks, to give up their selfish quarrelling and go forth to rescue from captivity the Holy Sepulchre of Jesus Christ, promising them the Church's blessing and a plenary indulgence for the sins of the past. 'You have been fighting brother against brother—if you must fight, fight the infidel! You have oppressed the widow and the orphan, you have robbed the poor—go now to fight for the weak against their oppressors!

'You have seized the goods of the Church and violated sanctuaries—go forth instead to rescue from captivity the holy places, the very Sepulchre of Jesus Christ!'

His words filled the crowd with wild enthusiasm : 'Dieu le veult!' they shouted : 'God wills it!'

'Yes, God wills it!' cried the Pope. 'Those words shall be your battle-cry. When you have enrolled yourselves you shall wear a sign on your breast to show it : and the sign shall be the Cross of the Lord. You are soldiers of the Cross, and your leader is Jesus Christ who died on the cross that all might be saved.'

At the end of the sermon the whole crowd knelt and recited the Confiteor, and received the Pope's blessing. Then they pressed forward in thousands to volunteer : hundreds of knights enrolled at once, tearing up any red material that came to hand to improvise a cross. Differences of rank were forgotten : lords and vassals, knights and merchants, all who had taken the Cross felt themselves brothers and comrades together.

It would have been a great thrill to be at Clermont that day, and become a soldier of Christ ; but Our Lord needs us just as much to-day for the war that is always going on.

The wave of enthusiasm then started spreading everywhere ; soon all Europe seemed on the move eastwards.

The crusaders were not all saints nor the leaders all wise ; terrible things and sad things happened on the way to their goal. But at last, four years after Clermont, the main army reached Jerusalem, the Holy Sepulchre was set free, and a Christian kingdom was set up there under Godfrey of Boulogne ; he was unwilling to wear a crown of gold in the city where Christ had worn a crown of thorns, so he called himself not 'King' but 'Defender of the Holy Sepulchre.' Away in Rome Pope Urban died a week or two after the victory, before the news of it had reached him. (See also story 78.)

'I confirm thee with the chrism of salvation'

That is : 'I make you strong, dedicating you to God.'

A Chinese mission was being looted by a large party of bandits. The priest lay wounded and unconscious, and the bandits had got hold of a Chinese boy of twelve who usually served at Mass. For some time the bandit chieftain questioned and threatened the boy, trying in vain to make him say where the chalice and other sacred vessels were hidden. At last the chief lifted his hand with an angry oath, and with his open hand struck the boy a great blow across the face that sent him crashing against the wall.

'Come back here!' said the chief, and the boy slowly recovered himself and came back to stand before his brutal questioner.

'Do you want another like that?'

'Go on—I'm ready if you are. It is what I bargained for.'

The bandit grinned with puzzled admiration.

'How do you mean, bargained for?'

'We were confirmed last month. The Bishop struck me on the cheek. He said that is what a soldier of Christ must expect.'

'Look here, you're the sort of lad we want. Tell us where these things are hidden and I'll let you come with me and my troop!'

'No, I'd rather be a soldier of Christ.'

The chief took out his revolver, but just at that moment there were shouts and rifle-shots in the street, and the bandits all rushed out leaving the boy forgotten. Some regular soldiers had arrived, the bandits were soon cleaned up or driven from the village and the Christians were able to repair the damage and take care of the mission father, who wrote a proud account to the Bishop of the behaviour of his newly confirmed altar-server. (See also stories 241, 562–567, 592.)

> * WHAT IS THE SACRAMENT OF THE HOLY EUCHARIST?
>
> *The Sacrament of the Holy Eucharist is the true Body and Blood of Jesus Christ, together with His Soul and Divinity, under the appearances of bread and wine.*

'My delight is to be with the children of men'

THERE was once a little prince, the son of a king. He lived in a splendid palace, filled with playthings and games of

*BALTIMORE 343
ENGLISH CATECHISM 266

every kind. He looked out of the window one day and saw some poor children playing with each other in the streets. His tutor saw him looking out, and said : ' What would you like to do to-day, stay in the palace and play your own games or go out into the street and play with those poor children ? ' ' Oh, can I go out to them ? That is what I would love to do ! ' And he put on his oldest clothes, so that they would not be shy of him, and went out and played with them from morning till night and had a very happy day.

The above story, or comparison, was told by Our Lord to St. Gertrude (she says) while she was meditating on the Blessed Sacrament wondering how He could bring Himself so low as to live on the altar under the sacramental species. ' I am like the little prince,' He said. ' It is a pleasure to Me to be with you men and women. Anyone who keeps people away from Communion deprives Me of a great joy.' (See also story 55.)

The Real Presence

The ardent faith of the saints can sometimes by God's favour get past the outward appearances of bread and wine.

St. Veronica of Milan (1489) saw the Holy Child instead of the Host in the monstrance during a Corpus Christi procession.

Blessed Beatrice of Lier in Brabant, Cistercian nun (*d.* 1269), just before communion when the priest was saying ' Ecce Agnus Dei,' saw in the priest's hands instead of the Host the Child Jesus holding His arms out wide in welcome. She forgot everything else and pressed up to the altar rails out of her turn, and her communion that day filled her with ecstasy.

Blessed Peter of Toulouse, holding the Host over the chalice during Mass, saw in its place the Infant Jesus in such brightness that he had to close his eyes ; and the same thing happened to him nearly every day for four months.

Yet we know that such appearances are still only a kind of inner sacramental veil behind the bread-and-wine appearances, because Our Lord is present actually not as a Child but in the fulness of His Manhood as now in heaven.

'Ave verum Corpus'

Thomas of Cantimpre was a notable Dominican of the thirteenth century, contemporary of St. Thomas Aquinas; made long studies under the best masters of the time, was himself professor of philosophy and theology at Louvain, a renowned preacher, and author of a number of books. We have his own account of a remarkable occurrence at Douai on April 14, 1254. He was fifty-three at the time.

He heard a report of a marvel that had happened in the church of St. Amatus there. A priest giving communion had dropped a Host, and as he knelt down to take it up, it had risen of its own accord and returned to the corporal on the altar. He called out to the other priests, and when they looked they saw on the corporal a beautiful little Child smiling at them. The people in the church, and other townspeople who crowded in, all saw the same vision.

Thomas of Cantimpre, when he heard, hurried into Douai. When he reached the church the Host had been replaced in the tabernacle, but the church was still crowded with people. The dean of the church was a friend of his, and at his request opened the tabernacle.

Immediately from all over the church people cried: 'Look! There He is! I can see Him! Look, there is Our Lord!'

Thomas could see nothing but the Host, and began to wonder if he had committed some sin which prevented his seeing the vision; but his conscience did not reproach him.

'As these thoughts were passing through my mind I suddenly saw a most wonderful thing. Jesus Christ appeared to me, not indeed as a little Child—the form in which the others saw Him—but as a full-grown Man. On His head was a crown of thorns, and two great drops of blood trickled down from His forehead, one on each side of the nose. Instantly I fell on my knees, and with tears in my eyes I adored my Saviour, who had thus, in so special a manner, showed Himself to me. Then I rose up. To my astonishment there was now no longer on His head the crown of thorns, nor the two drops of blood on His forehead, but His face appeared to me to be that of a man of the most venerable appearance, more so than can possibly be expressed. It was turned a little to the right so that the right eye was scarcely visible to me.'

(He describes the appearance in detail, the high forehead, the ascetic cheeks, the long hair and beard, the eyes looking downward.)

' During the space of an hour the vision assumed various appearances, and Our Lord appeared in different ways to different people. To some He appeared as if attached to the cross ; to others He seemed to be the Judge of the living and the dead ; but to most He appeared as in the beginning, under the form of a little Child.'

What are we to say of such a marvel ? Clearly whatever happened was in the minds of the observers, not in the Host itself, since different observers saw different visions.

A psychologist would call it a collective imagination, but a Catholic would have no difficulty in believing that such a favour might come from God to increase people's faith. Certain it is that the people of Douai were grateful, and held an annual commemoration of the event ; and from this Douai pilgrimage, extra large in 1875, was born the idea of the present great Eucharistic Congresses.

The fact that different people saw Our Lord in different ways is a true picture of the character of the Real Presence. We can find Our Lord there in all the different mysteries of His life and the different moods of the Church's year.

' True Body and Blood of Jesus Christ '

We should value this gift above all things and be ready to guard it with our life itself.

In a village of Lithuania years ago a boy named Cyril lived near the church and served Mass every morning. One winter day the priest took Cyril with him on a sick call to an old man who had been for years away from the Sacraments. It was a long journey through the forest and the priest harnessed two ponies to his little sleigh, for there was danger from wolves.

Sure enough the distant menacing clamour of wolves was soon heard.

'Pray hard,' said the priest, 'that we may get through the forest safely and reach the old man in time.'

Nearer and nearer came the noise, and at last the hungry pack was close behind them. As the only chance of escape, the priest loosed the foremost of the ponies and left him to the wolves. For a time they got clear away, but soon the ominous baying drew near again. Cyril had made up his mind what to do. If the second pony was sacrificed the priest would never reach the dying man, and would himself be killed and devoured, and also (terrible thought) the Blessed Sacrament which he carried would become the food of wild animals.

Praying for strength, the boy waited until the wolves' eyes were gleaming in the dusk close behind the sleigh.

'Farewell, my father!' he called to the priest, 'Love and good-bye to my mother!'

Then he sprang into the midst of the pack, to be instantly torn to pieces. The priest could have done nothing to save the boy, even if he could have stopped the terrified pony. He got safely out of the forest and reached the sick man just in time to reconcile him to God.

Returning through the forest next morning, the priest found the boy's fur cap and scarf and took them home to the poor widow, who, though stricken with grief at the loss of so dear a son, was also proud to be the mother of a hero who gave his life for the Blessed Sacrament.

'Together with His Soul and Divinity'

A famous Protestant architect went to look at a new Catholic church. The priest was not at home, and an altar-server who happened to be at the presbytery was sent to show the visitor round. As they passed the altar the lad genuflected.

'Tell me why you do that,' said the Protestant.

'Because the Blessed Sacrament is kept on that altar.'

'What Blessed Sacrament?'

The lad explained what Catholics believe about the bread and wine being changed at Mass.

'So you believe that it is really and truly God present in that tabernacle?'

'Yes.'

'Why, if I thought that was true I would come all the way up the church on my knees!'

The altar-server felt a little ashamed, for his genuflection had been rather a careless one.

We are not asked to go all up the church on our knees (as pilgrims go up the Scala Santa in Rome, the steps said to be brought from Pilate's hall in Jerusalem), but the least we can do is to make our genuflection reverently, with a real inward act of faith. (See also story 670.)

Divine power is in the Blessed Sacrament

In 1234 an army of Emperor Frederick II was ravaging Umbria and prepared to attack Assisi. Some Saracen mercenaries came at night to the convent of San Damiano (outside the city walls) and tried to force an entrance. They were putting a ladder up to a balcony where there was a large entrance-window, and the terrified nuns went to St. Clare, who was lying ill.

A sudden inspiration from God came to her in this emergency. She promised the nuns protection in the name of Jesus Christ, and told them to bring up from the church the Blessed Sacrament in its pyx, and then she went out on the balcony herself, holding the pyx aloft, just in time to face the first soldiers coming up the ladder. Her action was a supreme prayer of trust in God, as if to say: 'Lord, you must save the Blessed Sacrament from the infidels, and us too!'

The Saracens seemed as if dazzled and blinded by sudden light; they fell down the ladder in fear and all rushed away.

When it was daylight the main army moved their camp near to the city to prepare an assault. Clare gathered her nuns in fervent prayer, and soon a tremendous storm broke, beating down the tents and blowing them away, and spreading panic amongst the army, which turned away and left Assisi alone.

The citizens gratefully attributed their deliverance to St. Clare. The ivory and silver pyx is still shown at San Damiano.

CATECHISM STORIES

Our Lord's Real Presence is a sure shield against temptation, and our faith in its power should be as strong as St. Clare's. (See also story 671.)

'Latens Deitas'

During a Corpus Christi procession at Valencia, when B. Nicholas Fattori was carrying the Blessed Sacrament, a flock of little birds suddenly appeared and formed a moving crown just above the canopy, singing most melodiously in a way that seemed to blend perfectly with the *Pange Lingua*. They accompanied the procession some distance. Afterwards, when Blessed Nicholas was asked about it, he said with a smile that no doubt they were angels who came from heaven to adore their hidden King.

This may have been so or not, but we do know that wherever the Blessed Sacrament is it is the centre of legions of adoring angels, happy to serve the God-man now as during His thirty-three years of mortal life.

'Mysterium fidei'

The Holy Eucharist is a 'mystery of Faith.' 'Blessed are they who have not seen and yet have believed.'

In the time of St. Louis, King of France, there was great excitement one morning at one of the churches in Paris; Mass was being celebrated at the high altar, and those present beheld Our Lord in the sacred Host in the form of a little child. Word got round immediately, and crowds of people came running to see the marvel. The King himself happened to be hearing Mass in his own chapel. Someone ran and told him what was happening, but he stayed where he was.

'Our Lord is present here as truly as there,' he said. 'Such miracles are for the benefit of unbelievers. Let those go and see it who do not believe. For me, Faith is enough. I prefer to believe in Our Lord's real presence simply because He has said it.'

'Pledge of glory to come'

The various legends of the Holy Grail are a reminder of how eagerly our hearts should seek after the Mystery of Faith.

St. Joseph of Arimathea is supposed to have been the owner of the house lent for the Last Supper. The legend says that he kept safe the chalice that had been used at the Supper, and used it also to gather Our Lord's blood when He was taken down from the Cross. Later he went to Gaul with St. Philip the apostle, who sent him with eleven other disciples to Britain. The twelve lived in community at Glastonbury, where they built a wattle-church. One version of the legend says the Grail is buried in the hillside there, where strange music is said to be heard and mysterious lights seen. For centuries Glastonbury was a famous place of pilgrimage.

Alternatively, legends relate how the Holy Grail was finally hidden in a secret city or castle, guarded by a king and an order of dedicated knights. Many of King Arthur's knights went out to find the Holy Grail, but Sir Percivale and Sir Galahad were the only successful ones in the quest, because of their chaste minds and holy lives.

(Details in Malory's *Morte d'Arthur*, Book XIII, c. 7 ; Book XVII, c. 18 to 23.)

The Holy Grail signifies the supernatural happiness of heaven ; our hearts must needs seek it ; Holy Communion is the pledge and promise of it.

Devotion to the Real Presence

The graces of a ' visit ' remain with us long after we leave the church.

' Good King Wenceslas ' of Bohemia had great devotion to the Blessed Sacrament. When the Emperor summoned him to Worms for the Diet, or conference of princes, he turned into a church on the way to visit Our Lord. This made him late for the opening ceremony of the Diet. The other princes were already seated, and when Wenceslas entered unattended, they made no sign of welcome, thinking he had come late on purpose to draw attention to his higher rank. But the Emperor received him with the highest honour, rose to greet him, and gave him a place next to himself ; and in explanation afterwards he said that he saw two angels entering with Wenceslas, acting with great reverence as his bodyguard.

The incident in the carol (of the servant keeping warm by treading in the King's footprints) was originally told about a journey made to visit the Blessed Sacrament.

Visits to the Blessed Sacrament

St. Mary Magdalene of Pazzi used to make thirty-three visits to the B. Sacrament every day, one in thanksgiving for each year of Our Lord's life on earth.

St. Elizabeth of Hungary, as a child, would often visit the Blessed Sacrament, and if she found the church closed would affectionately kiss the lock of the door and the outside walls, for love of Our Lord's presence.

St. Vincent de Paul used to take any unusually important matter or decision to the Blessed Sacrament and ask Our Lord's help and blessing on it; and also after it was concluded he would make a special visit of thanks.

B. Balthasar Alvarez was kneeling before the altar, when Jesus appeared to him as a little Boy, with a great double handful of precious stones : ' Oh, if I could only find someone to give these graces to ! '

A Countess of Feria who became a Poor Clare was called on account of her long and frequent visits the ' Spouse of the Blessed Sacrament.' Someone asked her what she did all the time before the altar. ' Oh, I could stay there for ever ! What do I do ? What does a beggar do when he is with a rich man ? What does a sick man do when he goes to see his doctor ? What does a thirsty man do at a cool spring ? What does a starving man do at a table loaded with good things ? '

(See also stories 157 and 161.)

Going to Benediction

A cinema actress whose face and name are familiar in five continents was on holiday in England, and spent one Sunday afternoon looking up an old school-friend. The friend was at home, and they sat over the tea-cups telling of old times.

' What would you be doing this afternoon,' said the

film-star, 'if I hadn't come and disturbed your arrangements?'

The friend had become a Catholic some years before.
'I suppose I should have gone to church,' she said.

'To church!' said the film-star, who had never had any special religion herself. 'Look here, I won't let you make me your excuse for staying away. Come on—I'll come with you!'

She came out of church rather impressed, but also mystified.

'Do tell me what they were doing in the last part of the service, after they lighted all those candles?'

The Catholic explained all about Benediction as well as she could. The film-star listened attentively.

'And you believe that God Himself was actually there in what you call the monstrance? The same God that created heaven and earth? You really believe that?'

'Yes, all Catholics do.'

'Well! If I believed that, nothing would ever keep me away from Benediction—I would be there every Sunday, and every week-day, too, if there was one, and everything else could wait.'

* HOW ARE THE BREAD AND WINE CHANGED INTO THE BODY AND BLOOD OF CHRIST?

The bread and wine are changed into the Body and Blood of Christ by the power of God when the words of consecration, ordained by Jesus Christ, are pronounced by the priest in Holy Mass.

'The bread and wine are changed . . .'

'IT is 1917. The harvesters are at the front. Two girls are cutting the wheat with sickles, working alongside one another. They look serious and also mild, like people who speak little and think a good deal. One of them stands and looks all along the stacked sheaves, in the sunshine . . . she looks at them as if she were holding a conversation with them.

*BALTIMORE 344-350, 352-355
ENGLISH CATECHISM 267-268

' " A penny for your thoughts, Madeleine ? " '
' " I was thinking that the Blessed Sacrament is there in the harvest." '

'This was in la Vendée, la Vendée the holy.'—RENÉ BAZIN.

'By the power of God'

Some factory-workers were talking about religion during the dinner hour (it was the day after the open-air Corpus Christi procession) and a Catholic boy had to explain about the real Presence of Our Lord under the outward appearance of bread.

'I don't see how anybody can believe it,' said a non-Catholic. 'Even God couldn't do a thing like that.'

'Oh, you do believe in God then ? And the Creed, do you believe in that ? '

'Yes, but there's nothing in it about God changing bread into His body.'

'Isn't there ? Will you just say the Creed for me then.'

'I believe in God the Father Almighty, Creator of heaven and earth——'

'Stop, that's enough ! If God created all things, out of nothing, mind you, surely after that it's a simple matter for Him to change one thing into another ? And even to leave the outward appearances unchanged at the same time ? You and I couldn't do that, but it ought to be easy for God, if He made all things out of nothing.'

'I suppose He *could* do it, but that doesn't mean He *has* done it.'

For discussion :

What should the Catholic answer to that ? (*We know that He* HAS *done it because Our Lord said,* This IS My Body. *We Catholics merely believe that He meant exactly what He said.*)

The Consecration at Mass

St. Paschal Baylon (Franciscan lay-brother in Spain, *d.* 1592) had a remarkable devotion to the moment of Consecration at Mass, partly derived no doubt from his holy parents.

When he was still a baby in arms his mother carried

him to High Mass for the first time. He remained motionless in her arms all through the Mass (she told long afterwards) with his blue eyes fixed on the celebrant. But when the sacred Host was lifted at the Elevation, a tremor passed through his body and his mother felt her own heart throb as if in sympathy.

When as a lad he became a shepherd, he went to Mass to see the Host whenever he could, but if it was impossible he would listen eagerly for the church bells (sanctus-bell, elevation-bell, etc.) and so follow the Mass from the hillsides amongst his sheep.

One day at sound of the elevation-bell he fell on his knees with a longing prayer : ' O my adorable Master, if only I could behold Thee ! ' Raising eyes, he saw in the sky a blazing point of splendour like a star ; it blazed, then faded, and the sky seemed to part asunder and revealed a vision of angels kneeling before a chalice surmounted by the Sacred Host.

Later on as a lay-brother he spent every moment he could spare kneeling before the tabernacle ; he had a special attitude for prayer, with hands raised to the level of his forehead, fingers interlaced, eyes fixed on the tabernacle ; ' one would have taken him for a seraph about to spread his wings and take flight towards heaven.' He loved serving Masses, and after serving eight or ten his devotion seemed even greater than at the first.

When dying on Whit Sunday he asked : ' Has the bell rung for High Mass yet ? '

Yes, they answered, Mass had begun. He rejoiced to hear it, for he knew that he would die on that day of Pentecost at the moment of Elevation. The elevation-bell rang out, his dying lips twice pronounced the name of Jesus, and he gave up his soul to God.

A final marvel is recorded as happening next day while his body lay on the bier in church, surrounded by crowds of people. Mass was being celebrated, and several witnesses relate that at the Elevation they saw the dead man open his eyes to gaze upon the Host, and again at the ' little elevation ' before the Pater Noster. The report is deemed worthy of mention by Pope Leo XIII in his

Apostolic Letter. Here is the testimony of a woman named Eleanora Jarda Mildes :

'I must confess, to my shame,' she deposes, 'that I was more attentive in watching what was going on round the holy man than in following the Holy Sacrifice. When I saw him open his eyes at the Elevation, I was so astounded that I gave a loud scream : "Mamma ! Mamma ! " I exclaimed to my mother, who was with me : " Look, Brother Paschal has opened his eyes ! " She looked and she, too, saw the eyes of the saint open and shut at the second Elevation. All who were witnesses of this miracle, like ourselves, had one and the same idea about it : namely, that Our Lord wished in this way to reward Paschal's extraordinary devotion to the Sacrament of the Altar, and that He gave him a new life, so that even on the other side of the tomb, he might still have the consolation of adoring Him in the Holy Eucharist.'

(See also story 661.)

> * WHY HAS CHRIST GIVEN HIMSELF TO US IN THE HOLY EUCHARIST ?
>
> *Christ has given Himself to us in the Holy Eucharist to be the life and the food of our souls. ' He that eateth Me, the same also shall live by Me ' ; 'He that eateth this bread shall live for ever.'*

'I have compassion on the multitude'

A EUCHARISTIC drama, so to speak, in four scenes.

First scene : In the dim, remote age of the Exodus. The ancient narrative shows us the Israelites, only a few weeks after leaving the plenty of Egypt, plunged now amongst the terrifying rocks of the Sinai Desert. Starvation seems inevitable, and panic seizes the people :

' Would to God we had died in Egypt, where we sat over the flesh-pots ! Why have you brought us into this desert, to destroy all the multitude with famine ? '

And the Lord said to Moses : ' Behold I will rain bread from heaven for you. Say to them : In the evening you shall eat flesh and in the morning you shall have your fill

*BALTIMORE 356, 375
ENGLISH CATECHISM 269

of bread. And you shall know that I am the Lord your God.'

In the evening therefore came flocks of quails ; and in the morning the ground was covered with small grains ' like coriander-seed white, and the taste thereof like to flour with honey.' The people said : ' Manhu ? ' (What is this ?) And Moses answered :

' This is the bread which the Lord hath given you to eat. Gather each morning enough for each tent, and no more ; but on the sixth day gather enough for the Sabbath also.'

And the children of Israel ate manna forty years, till they came to the land of Canaan (Exod. xvi).

Jewish legend added that the taste of the manna was different for each person according to his desire, having in itself all that is delicious (cf. the versicle sung after the Tantum Ergo).

N.B.—The manna, though presumably miraculous in quantity or frequency, may not have been in its nature a miraculous food, any more than the quails. Observers in the East have reported an occasional phenomenon answering to the description, and an actual fall of such manna in Natal was described in the *Morning Post* of March 29, 1932.

Second scene : Fifteen hundred years later, in another desert, east of the Lake of Galilee. Our Lord feeds the five thousand people with five loaves (John vi, 1–15), thinking meanwhile of how He will feed all mankind with the Blessed Sacrament.

The crowd seek Him out again at Capharnaum and ask Him to give them a sign : ' Our fathers did eat manna, bread from heaven, in the desert : give us another sign like that.'

Our Lord answers with the promise of the true Bread of Life (read His words from John vi, 32–35, 48–55). His disciples could not understand, and many left Him ; the Twelve remained, bewildered but trusting (John vi, 67–70).

Third scene : The Last Supper. ' With desire I have desired to eat this pasch with you.' After the supper, when He says the words of consecration, the Twelve recognise at once that He is fulfilling the mysterious Promise at Capharnaum. Then He says : ' Do this in commemoration of Me,' and the possibilities of It began to dawn on them.

Fourth scene : To-day : bird's-eye view over the whole world. Our Lord's desire fulfilled. Real Presence multiplied in myriads of small Hosts ; millions of Catholics gathering each morning the Bread from heaven which is their life and food during their journey to the Promised Land. (See also stories 365, 366.)

' Christ has given Himself to us '

Napoleon was an artist in war, and his long succession of victories were the marvel of the world. One day some of his generals were discussing and comparing their master's great battles, and one of them ventured to ask him which was the happiest day of his life. They wondered if he would think of the Bridge of Lodi perhaps, the scene of his early triumph with the Army of Italy, a young general of twenty-six wresting Lombardy from the Austrians. Or more likely of the ' glorious sun ' of Austerlitz, the shattering victory which made him master of Europe.

The Emperor looked thoughtful. ' Ah—the happiest day of my life ? That was the day of my first Communion. I was near to God then.'

' The same also shall live by Me '

This refers to the soul-life of grace, but has sometimes become true even of the life of the body.

There are many cases amongst the saints and mystics of those who took no food whatever except the Blessed Sacrament.

B. Angela of Foligno lived thus for twelve years ; other cases are St. Colette, St. Peter of Alcantara, and a Spanish nun called Sister Louisa of the Resurrection. The historian Matthew of Paris tells of a girl in Norfolk (popularly called Jane the Meatless, fifteenth century) who tasted no food or drink for fifteen years, except her Communion every Sunday. She could not bear even the smell of ordinary food, and she could even distinguish a consecrated Host from unconsecrated ones.

St. Catherine of Siena, too, at the age of twenty gave up eating even the small quantity of bread and herbs which had been her custom, and lived on the Holy Eucharist, with nothing else except water. Sometimes under obedience she took food, only causing such painful sickness that her relatives ceased urging her. Her strength was renewed (as the strength of others by a meal) whenever she received Holy Communion, or sometimes by the mere sight of the Host, or even of a priest who had just said Mass.

St. Rose of Lima, on the way to church, would often stop to take breath, so exhausted was she by her penances. But after receiving Communion she would walk home firmly and easily. When people asked her about her feelings at Communion, words failed her, she could only stammer in confusion: she seemed (she said) to pass entirely into God, and was flooded with such joy that nothing in life could be compared to it. (See also story 102.)

'Food of our souls'

In the middle of a great city (Birmingham) after the war there were thirty or forty thousand of crowded old houses, and the children who lived in them were mostly pale and thin, and much more liable to illness and epidemics than children in other parts of the city. The doctors said this was due to the dirt of the old houses and to lack of air and sun, and the City Council determined to change all this. They built thousands of new houses on the city outskirts, clean and healthy, with a garden for every family, and thousands of families were moved into new homes.

After a few months the doctors and inspectors noticed that in spite of the air and sun, most of the children seemed to be just as pale and thin as before, and just as liable to illness. This was very disappointing, and when they studied the causes they found out that the rents were so high and the bus-fares to work so heavy, that the wage-earners had not enough money left to spend on food. They just weren't getting enough to eat.

CATECHISM STORIES

Fresh air and cleanliness are good, but our bodies must have food. It is the same with our soul. Knowing our religion is not enough : even prayer, even confession are not enough : we need the Food of our soul which Our Lord has provided.

'Yet a great way to go'

Elias had shown the power of the true God on Mount Carmel, but it made no difference to the Israelites in general ; they still followed after Baal and persecuted the worshippers of God. Queen Jezebel sent a messenger to Elias swearing to kill him, and he fled in fear to the desert. Exhausted in body, and utterly discouraged in soul, he lay down and prayed to die.

Read aloud from 3 Kings xix, 2–8 the story of the bread of angels which gave him strength to walk to the mount of God. There he waited till the word of the Lord came to him and told him what to do.

We are not in heaven yet, by a long way. We need again and again the Bread of Life.

The Bread of the Strong

A French army officer recalls how he was taking part in the bitter fighting on the heights of Notre Dame de Lorette, 1915. One of his men was a young soldier from Brittany who showed marvellous courage and nerve. Time after time, when the word was given for another rush forward, he was the first to jump up and plunge into the hail of bullets ; and his example gave heart to all the other men around.

During a pause in the advance he lay next to his lieutenant, who said : ' I wish the company had a few more like you ! How do you do it ? '

' Well, you see, *mon lieutenant*, I was at Communion this morning.'

(See also story 80.)

'He that eateth this Bread . . .'

During the cruel persecution in Tongking, Annam, beginning 1833, the native Christians, when ordered to trample on the crucifix in token of renouncing the Faith, showed superhuman heroism under rackings, scourgings and tearing with red-hot pincers, calling on the name of 'Jesus.' The pagans knew that it was the strength derived from Holy Communion that sustained them. When some martyrs showed special courage, the mandarins would say in wonder : ' Truly he has been eating of the enchanted bread which casts a spell upon the soul.'

One named Xavier, a mere boy, so astonished his judges that they said : ' He has the courage of a lion, yet he is a mere boy ! What would one of their priests be like ! ' As he went to execution the people said : ' Look, he thinks nothing of death ! Indeed the Master of Heaven must have come down to dwell in him ! '

Another young martyr named Michael Mi encouraged his old father, who was afraid, by promising to take the scourging for him. So after his own scourging was over, so that his body was one mass of wounds, he lay down again on the ground and said to the mandarin : ' My father is old and weak, let me be flogged in his place.' His request was granted, and he took the second scourging without uttering a sound. He was condemned at length to be beheaded, with his father and a priest whom they had befriended. The executioner said to Michael : ' Give me some money and I will give you an easier death, I will cut off your head at the first blow.' ' Do it with the Hundred Cuts, if you like,' replied the martyr. ' It matters not, so long as you cut it off somehow. I have plenty of money at home, but I would rather it went to the poor.'

This persecution went on in various forms for fifty years, and there were many thousands of martyrs.

All equal at God's Table

Once in a Vienna church on some great festival, when everybody was crowding up to Communion, a young manservant was just about to take his place at the altar rails when he saw standing in the line just behind him his own master, who was an Archduke of the Imperial Family. The manservant stood aside respectfully, to allow his master to come to the altar rails first. But the Archduke remained where he was, and motioned to the man to go forward. 'Keep your place,' he whispered. 'We are all equal here.'

Any Catholic of high rank would say the same. In the early Church, slaves and nobles knew that social distinctions ceased at the Holy Eucharist, and this was one great reason for the spreading of the Faith. (See also story 201.)

Frequent Communion

The parable of the Great Supper (Luke xiv, 15-24) which comes on the Sunday after Corpus Christi, can be used either about the duty of Easter Communion, or about the invitation to more frequent Communion.

Note that verse 17 indicates that the guests had already *accepted* the invitation.

'With desire I have desired . . .'

God's love for us in the Blessed Sacrament is beyond explanation, and strange things may happen when it finds some real response.

The story of St. Imelda is well known, but there are many such instances recorded of the Sacred Host leaving the priest's hand and flying through the air to the mouth of the saintly communicant.

Once St. Catherine of Siena, filled with desire of Communion, asked her chaplain Father Raymond to offer Mass at once, before the time he intended. After making some difficulties (being tired from a journey) he did so. When he came to give her Communion he saw her face all radiant as an angel's. He spoke inwardly to the Blessed Sacrament : ' Go, Lord, and find your beloved ! ' And immediately the small Host which he was about to take up flew through the air to Catherine. He tells us this himself, and says that many trustworthy persons declared they had seen the same thing happen on other occasions.

A holy nun called Elizabeth of Jesus had been forbidden by her confessor (as a form of mortification) to receive Communion ; while the other sisters were at the altar rails, a host left the hand of the priest and flew to Elizabeth, into her mouth.

Desire for Communion

Desire should be part of our dispositions for Communion, and we may wish that we had the same burning desire as the saints.

St. Juliana of Falconieri (foundress of Servite Tertiaries in Florence, *d.* 1341) lay dying, aged seventy, and was inconsolable because it was not possible for her to receive Viaticum owing to continual vomiting. At last she resigned herself to this deprivation, but earnestly begged that at least she might have the Blessed Sacrament to *see*, otherwise she could not die happy. Father Giacomo agreed to this, and the Sacred Host was brought into her sick-room. Gazing at It with intense love, she tried to kneel in adoration, and after several attempts she managed to throw herself out of bed and stretched herself on the floor in the form of a cross, while colour and youth and beauty came back to her emaciated face. She asked if she might touch the Host with her lips, but this the priest could not allow. Then she begged that he would place It on her breast for a short time, to give her soul some refreshment by Its nearness; and she begged this with so many tears that Fr. Giacomo could not refuse. A veil and then a corporal were placed over her breast and the Sacred Host laid upon it. At the same moment she put all her strength into uttering the words: 'O my sweet Jesus!' and quietly expired. But as she drew her last breath, the Sacred Host disappeared from sight. It had entered into her breast, leaving on it (they discovered) a mark like the cross on the Host itself.

Our Guest

Holman Hunt was once showing some visitors round his studio; they stood before his well-known picture, 'Light of the World.' (Our Lord, with lantern in hand, stands knocking at a door. Show a copy if possible.)

'Surely you forgot something there,' said one visitor. 'Look, there's no handle on the door.'

CATECHISM STORIES

'It was not a mistake,' explained the artist. 'This door represents the human heart, and it opens only from the inside.'

Our Lord stands outside and waits for us to say: 'Come in.' He will never force an entrance. It is for us to invite Him or not, as we choose.

Some Catholics keep Him standing at the door from one Easter duty to another.

Behold I stand at the gate and knock. If any man shall hear My voice and open to Me the door, I will come in to him and will sup with him: and he with Me ' (Apoc. iii, 20).

Spiritual Communions

To Sister Paula Maresca (of Naples) Our Lord appeared carrying two ciboria, one of gold and one of silver. He told her that He preserved in the golden one her sacramental Communions, and in the silver one her Communions of desire.

St. Joanna of the Cross was assured by Our Lord that every time she communicated spiritually, she received a grace equal to that received from her sacramental Communions. 'O my Lord!' she said, 'What a grand way of going to Communion without being noticed, and without troubling anyone but You!' for it was in the days when frequent Communion was unusual and might cause comment, and people had to ask their confessor's permission for it.

> * Is CHRIST RECEIVED WHOLE AND ENTIRE UNDER EITHER KIND ALONE?
>
> *Christ is received whole and entire under either kind alone.*

'Whole and entire under either kind'

FOR the first thousand years or so the Church gave Communion to the laity under both kinds (though sometimes to the sick, etc., under species of bread only). There was always risk of irreverence or spilling, and often a tube was

*BALTIMORE 851
ENGLISH CATECHISM 270

used (as it is in Papal masses to-day). Sometimes the consecrated Hosts were moistened in the consecrated chalice (as in Eastern churches still). Gradually a custom grew up of safeguarding reverence by communicating the laity under species of bread only, and giving them a sip of unconsecrated wine (as in an ordination Mass to-day).

John Wyclif (Oxford scholar and heretical teacher, protected by powerful friends, *d.* 1384) held that the Church had no right to withhold the chalice from the laity, and his view was taken up by the Hussites in Bohemia. They cited Christ's words : ' Unless you eat the flesh of the Son of man *and* drink His blood you shall not have life in you,' and said the chalice was necessary for salvation.

The Church condemned this at the Council of Constance 1420. War broke out in Bohemia, and as a contribution to peace the Council of Basle (1431) allowed the Bohemians to have Communion under both kinds if they would only admit it was not necessary for salvation. Some of the Hussites refused even this compromise, and carried the war on from a mountain headquarters under a fierce leader named Ziska, but were at last defeated in 1453.

At the Reformation the Protestant churches, especially Church of England, adopted Communion under both kinds.

It is not likely that the Catholic Church would ever go back to Communion under both kinds, but it might possibly again be allowed to some reunited schismatic Church.

Christ's Body and Blood inseparable

The bread is changed into Christ's Body as it now is, risen, alive, with His blood in His veins inseparably henceforth. Wherever His Body is, His Blood must be, too, and vice versa.

The point might be illustrated, a little crudely perhaps, from Portia's argument in the *Merchant of Venice*. Antonio was unable to repay his loan to Shylock and was liable to forfeit the security—a pound of his flesh. Portia admits that Shylock may legally cut off the pound of Antonio's flesh, but adds:

> 'Tarry a little, there is something else.
> This bond doth give thee here no drop of blood,
> The words expressly are " a pound of flesh."
> Take then thy bond, take then thy pound of flesh.
> But in the cutting it, if thou dost shed
> One drop of Christian blood, thy land and goods
> Are, by the laws of Venice, confiscate
> Unto the State of Venice.'

Body and Blood of a living person are not separable. The double word of consecration separates Christ's Body and Blood mystically (in sign), but in reality they must ever remain united, and the same is true of His soul, and also of His nature as God.

'Under either kind alone'

Fr. Peter of Cavanelas (Hieronymite monk) had long been tormented with doubts as to the Real Presence. One day saying Mass he came to the words after the Consecration: 'jube haec perferri,' etc., and as he bowed down to kiss the altar a cloud descended on the altar and hid Host and chalice. Then as he gazed in motionless awe the cloud lifted and he saw that the chalice was empty, but the Host was raised above it in mid-air. Still gazing, he saw what seemed like drops of blood falling from the Host into the empty chalice, until it contained exactly the same quantity as there had originally been wine. At the same time his doubts vanished for ever, and his eyes were filled with joyful tears; when he opened them again the Host lay once more on the paten, and he continued the Mass, making the prescribed crosses over Host, chalice, and himself with a fervent devotion.

He never told anyone of this vision during his lifetime, but he wrote it down and the paper was found after his death. The server of the Mass (he noted) had observed nothing but that the Mass was longer than usual and that the priest had shed tears.

CATECHISM STORIES

* IN ORDER TO RECEIVE THE BLESSED
SACRAMENT WORTHILY WHAT IS REQUIRED?
In order to receive the Blessed Sacrament worthily it is required that we be in a state of grace and fasting from midnight.
To be in a state of grace is to be free from mortal sin, and pleasing to God.

'That we be in a state of grace'

A SUITABLE story for this is Our Lord's parable of the wedding garment (Matt. xxii, 1–14). A wedding garment was provided for all the guests; it was just bad manners not to put it on. So baptism and confession are available for all Christians; there is no excuse for a bad Communion.

St. Paul also (Rom. xiii, 14) compares sanctifying grace to a garment: 'Put ye on the Lord Jesus Christ.'

(See also story 382 and others there referred to.)

'Free from mortal sin and pleasing to God'

The King was visiting a mining district and he called at some of the miners' cottages. The honour was greatly appreciated by most, but one woman, when she saw the King coming down her front garden, shut the door and hid herself away. After knocking in vain at the door the royal party tried the next cottage and received a warm welcome.

Afterwards some neighbours asked the woman why she had not wanted the King's visit.

'I *did* want him,' she said in tears of vexation, 'but my house was in such a state, everything so dirty, that I couldn't ask anybody in, let alone the King!'

A state of sin is the only thing that need prevent us receiving our divine Guest, and we can clean up our soul by a good confession. (See also stories 192, 193.)

Confession before Communion

Suppose a boy in confession told a priest he had made a bad Communion: 'Thursday was a holiday of obligation, but I forgot all about it and missed Mass. Next day was the First Friday, and I'm making the nine Fridays, so I went to Holy Communion without going to confession first.' What would the priest say?

(*No sin in forgetting, no need for confession, no bad Communion.*)

Bad Communions

Nothing is so hardening to the heart as a real bad Communion.

Some gangsters in New York, Catholic by descent, were discussing a lad whom they were trying to get into their clutches. He had helped them in two or three frauds, but they felt he was not yet a reliable criminal.

'Get him on gambling and losing and borrowing from his employer's till,' suggested one. Another said: 'Give him a good scare—arrange to have him present next time some guy has to be bumped off.'

But an experienced old ruffian said: 'Take him to church and get him to make a bad Communion. Believe me, he will be ready for anything after that.'

Fasting from midnight

It was the patronal feast of the church and all the school were going to Holy Communion. When the priest came to say Mass he found four boys waiting for him at the church door.

'Please, Father,' said one, 'I forgot and ate a chocolate when I woke up this morning—was it a sin?'

Another said: 'I took a drink of water, then I remembered and spat it out. Can I go to Communion?'

Another: 'I went for a swim first thing this morning and accidentally swallowed a mouthful of water.'

Another: 'I woke up in the night and had a drink and went to sleep again. I don't know what time it was, but I think probably before midnight.'

(*No. 1, no sin, of course, but he cannot go to Communion that day. No. 2 can receive, if he is pretty sure he spat it all out. No. 3 can receive, because what he swallowed was not taken after the manner of food. Same applies to water swallowed while*

CATECHISM STORIES

cleaning teeth. No. 4 can give himself the benefit of the doubt and receive.)

Thanksgiving after Communion

The real Presence of Our Lord lasts, even after Communion, as long as the appearance of bread remains—say ten minutes or so. Hence it is fitting to spend this time in ' thanksgiving.'

St. Philip Neri noticed that a young friend of his was in the habit of receiving Holy Communion and almost immediately getting up and going out. So one morning Fr. Philip fetched from the sacristy two altar-boys with lighted candles and told them to accompany the young man home, one each side of him. Naturally he stopped and asked the boys what in the world they were doing.

' Father Philip sent us to escort you home.'

Going back into church, the young man found Fr. Philip and asked for an explanation.

' When the priest is carrying the Blessed Sacrament,' said the saint, ' he is accompanied by two acolytes with lighted candles, and it seems to me the same escort is due to anyone who is carrying It in his breast.'

The young man stayed and made his thanksgiving.

> * WHAT IS THE HOLY MASS?
>
> *The Holy Mass is the Sacrifice of the Body and Blood of Jesus Christ, really present on the altar under the appearances of bread and wine, and offered to God for the living and the dead.*

The Sacrifice of the New Law

EVERY educated Catholic should have some idea of how and why the simple action of the Last Supper has gradually grown into the fully-developed and sometimes complex ' liturgy ' of the Mass.

This story is briefly indicated in *Twelve and After*, p. 73.

Add that the Last Supper itself came at the end of a long centuries-old ritual which Our Lord and the Twelve had just celebrated—the Pasch.

*BALTIMORE 357
ENGLISH CATECHISM 277

CATECHISM STORIES

Our High Priest

A priest is one who acts as a mediator or link between God and man. This is true above all of the great High Priest of Calvary.

At the crisis of a battle in the War a vital communication between a certain division and Army battle headquarters went dead. Somewhere the wire had been cut by the enemy shells and it was absolutely essential to get it repaired at once. Only one Signals man was available in the divisional staff dug-out at the moment and he went out to find the break and join it. In a few minutes the messages began coming through again. An hour later the man had still not returned and a party went to look for him. He was found lying beside the line, holding together in his hands the two broken ends, with a great shell wound over his heart from which he had bled to death.

(See also stories 56, 455, 458, 461, 507.)

'Under the appearances of bread and wine'

Soon after Abraham settled in Canaan, at Hebron, he heard a piece of bad news. There had been a battle between two leagues of tribes or towns, five kings resisting a raid of four kings; Abraham's kinsman Lot, who lived at Sodom, had been on the losing side and had been carried off captive with his womenfolk, servants, herds, etc.

Immediately Abraham assembled what forces he could —three hundred and eighteen of his own well-armed retainers—and hastened after the army of the raiders. When he caught up with them he divided his men, waited until night, and then attacked from two sides. The enemy were killed in large numbers and the rest were chased northwards, abandoning all their booty. Lot and all his people and belongings were rescued.

As Abraham returned south in triumph a remarkable thing happened. They were passing a rocky hill on which was a fortified city called Salem. It was the city later called Jerusalem : Salem in Hebrew means 'Peace,' and Jerusalem means 'Vision of Peace.' The king of Salem (presumably a local ruler under the Chaldeans) came out and met Abraham and his men in the valley afterwards called

Cedron or Jehosophat, and thanked them for destroying the raiders. No doubt he provided plenty of food and wine to make a feast for them after their marching.

But Melchisedech (his name means 'king of peace') did more than that; we are told that 'he brought forth bread and wine, for he was a priest of the Most High God,' that is to say, he offered a sacrifice of bread and wine in thanksgiving for the victory.

The 'Most High God' means the true God, Creator of all men, not one of the local gods that each tribe or city worshipped as its own, one against another.

'Blessed be Abram,' said Melchisedech, 'by the Most High God who created heaven and earth! And blessed be the Most High God by whose protection the enemies are in thy hands!'

As an act of thanksgiving Abraham gave him tithes (a tenth share) of the battle-spoils; after which the mysterious figure of Melchisedech having appeared suddenly for this one episode only, disappears again from history. (Gen. xiv.)

In those days when sacrifice nearly always meant bloodshed (of animals, or sometimes of human beings in the case of pagan gods), Melchisedech's sacrifice of bread and wine was remarkable.

In Psalm 109 God is represented as saying to His Son the Messias: Thou art a priest for ever according to the order of Melchisedech. That is, going back to the oldest religion of the Most High God, even before the priesthood of Aaron.

Melchisedech, therefore, with his names King of Justice and King of Peace, and his double dignity of King and Priest, and his sacrifice of bread and wine, is a picture beforehand of Our Lord in the Mass.

In the canon after the Consecration we ask God to accept our gift as He accepted 'that which Melchisedech Thy high priest offered up to Thee, a holy sacrifice, a spotless victim.'

The priceless privilege

In penal days an English gentleman was in trouble with the law for having Mass said in his house, and was condemned to pay a fine of five hundred pounds. He went home and carefully picked out five hundred of the best and heaviest gold coins from his treasure-chest, especially Portuguese ones which were marked with a cross. When he counted them out to the judge's officer the latter looked at them in surprise.

'You must have picked out all your best coins to pay this fine!'

'I should have been ashamed to do anything else. No price could be too great to pay for the privilege of attending the Holy Mass!'

The Sunday Mass

Charles and Fred had both been pretty regular at Mass as long as they were at school, though they both often missed at holiday times. After they left school they came for a Sunday or two and then stayed away. Fred stayed away because he wanted to let everybody know he had left school—the same reason why he began smoking cigarettes. Charles stayed away because he always did what Fred did. Secretly Charles wanted to go to Mass, and after a few months he began going to an early one. Fred heard about it and asked him why. 'Well,' said Charles, 'it's a sin not to go, isn't it? The teachers at school always said so.'

'Well, I've finished with school—haven't you?'

'Yes, but it's still true what they said—God commands us to go to Mass.'

'Who said God commands it? It's just a sort of rule Catholics have. I don't see why anybody should go if they don't want to—it can't be a very serious thing—nobody goes to church much, only Catholics.'

Discuss what Charles might answer.

Is Sunday Mass merely a rule of the Church? (*No, it is a practical applying of Our Lord's command: the Church's answer to ' Do this in commemoration of Me.' Our Lord clearly gave us the Holy Eucharist to be the central thing in our religion. He wants us all there with Him to help in His sacrifice. If we care at all about doing His Will we shall be there.*)

(See also stories 264, 265, 363, 364.)

Valuing the Holy Mass

Catholics who do not value the Mass must have forgotten what it really is.

Ambrose Philipps de Lisle was a well-known English Catholic of the nineteenth century and the following story is printed in his life.

When he was a young lieutenant in the Navy his ship happened to be in some South American port alongside a French warship. De Lisle arranged to take his Catholic men to Sunday Mass on the French ship, which carried a priest, and was more convenient than taking them to some church ashore.

The first Sunday he arrived fifteen minutes before time, his men were taken to the place of Mass, and de Lisle was asked into the French officers' mess and made quite at home. After a while he looked at his watch and remembered that it was time for Mass to begin.

' Mass ? Surely you're not going to Mass ? ' said the French officers in astonishment. They, too, were Catholics, but disregarded their religion.

' Yes, I am,' said de Lisle, took his leave and went off and knelt amongst his men before the altar.

About the Sanctus one of the French officers came quietly in. Next Sunday two or three were present, and each Sunday afterwards all the officers came.

Morning Mass

St. Isidore of Madrid worked as a ploughman for a farmer, but had such devotion to the Mass that he managed to be present at it every morning. His master grumbled a good deal about this waste of time, as he considered it, until one morning he went to the field to see if Isidore was at work yet. He was not, but the master found the two oxen working with a shining angel to guide the plough. That is the legend, teaching the truth that a fervent Catholic is also a conscientious worker, and that morning Mass will bring a heavenly blessing on our work throughout the day.

CATECHISM STORIES

* WHAT IS A SACRIFICE?

A sacrifice is the offering of a victim by a priest to God alone, in testimony of His being the Sovereign Lord of all things.

What sacrifice is

EVERYTHING we have, everything we are, comes from God: we must be ready to give it all back to Him—even our dearest possessions—even our life itself.

That is what sacrifice is a sign of; and that is why sacrifice is offered to the Creator only.

All this is contained in the story of Abraham and Isaac, which can be retold to the senior children with full significance.

You can introduce it with several preliminary remarks:
(1) The main point of the story is to teach us that God is Sovereign Lord of all things and we must be *ready* to give everything back to Him. Abraham was not only going to slay his beloved son, but also giving up all prospect of God's promises being fulfilled, that through Isaac he should become a great nation (Gen. xvii, 15–16).

(2) The Canaanites amongst whom Abraham lived no doubt practised human sacrifice and child sacrifice, as their descendants certainly did a few centuries later. In a way it was natural for Abraham and his people to wonder if they ought to do it, too, and a secondary point of the story is to teach that human sacrifice is not according to God's will.

(3) Did God actually command Abraham to slay his son, or did God merely allow Abraham to think He expected it? Perhaps the second supposition raises fewer difficulties, though, of course, God was Lord of Isaac's life, as of all things else.

After some such explanations the story can be read from Genesis xxii, 1–14. When we have a magnificent story told in magnificent language, and hearers of an age to appreciate it, it would surely be a pity to spoil it by 'telling it in our own words.'

Then, if you want to bring home that Isaac is a 'type' of Christ, tell the children that the mountain of Isaac's

*BALTIMORE 358-359
ENGLISH CATECHISM 275

sacrifice was Mount Moriah, part of the ridge where later stood Jerusalem, Solomon's temple and Calvary; it was over the valley where Melchisedech had met Abraham and offered his unbloody sacrifice of bread and wine. Remind them of the words of the canon, where we ask God to receive our gifts as He accepted 'the sacrifice of our father Abraham.' Also of Hebrews xi, 17-19, that Isaac is a 'parable,' or likeness of Christ.

Finally, tell them to bear in mind Abraham representing God the Father, and Isaac God the Son made man, while the story is read through again. (See also stories 659, 660.)

'To God alone'

Sacrifice, especially the sacrifice of the Mass, is the supreme act of adoration. The altar, representing the stone of sacrifice, is the sign of this highest worship.

A good many years ago in the South of England two Catholic college boys were on a cycling holiday and stopped to look at an old village church. The vicar happened to see them and showed them round inside. As they came out he indicated a worn-looking stone in the pavement of the porch.

'There's a bit of real history. That is supposed to be the old altar-stone from the high altar. It must have been put there in the reign of Queen Elizabeth, so that everybody would have to walk on it when they entered the church.'

The boys looked at the stone, and sure enough something of the four crosses in the corners could still be seen.

'Curious to think,' said the vicar, 'that thousands of Masses were said on that stone in this very church.'

'And will be again some day, sir!' said one of the boys.

'Excuse me a moment,' and he knelt down on the pavement and kissed the altar-stone reverently, and his companion did the same.

'Ah, I did not know you were Catholics,' said the clergyman; but he was much impressed and later on had the stone taken up and placed more honourably as a relic in a glass-case in the vestry, where it waits for the conversion of England.

CATECHISM STORIES

* IS THE HOLY MASS ONE AND THE SAME SACRIFICE WITH THAT OF THE CROSS?

The Holy Mass is one and the same sacrifice with that of the Cross, inasmuch as Christ, who offered Himself, a bleeding victim, on the Cross to His Heavenly Father, continues to offer Himself in an unbloody manner on the altar, through the ministry of His priests.

'The same sacrifice with that of the Cross'

ST. COLETTE (recluse and Poor Clare, in fifteenth-century Picardy) one day at the Consecration of the Mass broke out into exclamations: 'O my God! my Jesus! O angels, saints, sinful men! What marvels, what marvels!'

Afterwards the priest (who was also her confessor) asked what had made her thus break the silence. She said: 'When your Reverence lifted the Sacred Host I saw Christ upon His cross, and the blood flowing from His wounds. And I heard Him saying: "Eternal Father, look upon this Body in which I hung upon the cross! Look upon this Blood flowing from my wounds! All this I endured to save sinners, and if they are condemned to hell I have nothing to show for my bitter Passion. For My sake, then, O My Father, save these sinners!"'

(See also stories 72, 660.)

Calvary over again

A certain old lay-brother who could not read was nevertheless fond of using an illuminated prayer book at Mass. 'At the beginning of Mass,' he explained, 'I find a page where the letters are all black, and they remind me of my sins and I try to be sorry for them, until the Offertory. Then while Our Lord renews the sacrifice of Calvary at the Consecration, I look at some red letters, to remind me of the Precious Blood. Finally, when the Communion comes near I look at a golden letter, which makes me think of the happiness of receiving Our Lord and still more of being with Him in heaven for ever.'

*BALTIMORE 360-362
ENGLISH CATECHISM 278

CATECHISM STORIES

'Through the ministry of His priests'

A non-Catholic friend accompanied a Catholic girl to Mass once or twice.

'Well, it seems to me a strange sort of service,' said the friend, after the second time. 'Why does he turn away from the congregation all the time?'

'He is speaking to God, not to the congregation. He turns to the altar, because he is offering the sacrifice on it.'

'I couldn't even tell which of the priests it was this morning. They all look the same in those vestments they wear.'

'That's why they wear them, I suppose; it doesn't make any difference who the priest is, for the time being he is acting for Christ Our Lord. It's Our Lord who really offers the Mass always.'

'Oh, I see—and is that why there is that big cross on the back of the vestment?'

'Yes, and because it is the sacrifice of the Cross being offered again.'

'Oh, well, I shall understand that much about it next time, anyhow.'

Mass-servers and martyrs

Thousands of Japanese were converted by the Jesuit successors of St. Francis Xavier. Severe persecution of Japanese Christians broke out in 1597 (due to imprudent action by some other Spanish missionaries, and Japanese imaginings of Spanish invasion from the Philippines). Twenty-six martyrs were executed together on February 5 —six Franciscan priests and twenty Japanese, including three boys, mass-servers, aged sixteen, thirteen and twelve. The boys had been baptised in the names of Anthony, Thomas and Louis. Great efforts were made to persuade them to give up the Faith, but they said: 'We shall be very glad to die and go to heaven, rather than live and lose our souls.'

On their way to execution Anthony saw his mother weeping, and said: 'You must not cry for me. Think— I am going to see God!'

On the hill of Nagasaki they were all fastened by chains and iron collar to crosses set up in a row. A great crowd looked on, and marvelled to see that the martyrs did not seem terrified but happy and glad ; even the boys. Anthony shouted out : ' Praise the Lord, ye children ! '

Beside each cross stood an executioner with a spear. There was a long roll of muffled drums, then the spears were all lifted together and plunged into the bodies of the martyrs.

This glorious example stirred the other Christians to a great willingness for martyrdom. Guilds of Our Lady were formed, to prepare their members to endure torments and death. Persecution continued for centuries, with thousands—perhaps hundreds of thousands—of martyrs. After a century or two no priests at all were left in Japan, but the Faith still lived on, and when again some missionaries got into the country in 1865, they discovered many thousands of lay Catholics practising their religion as well as they could in secret.

The great devotion they showed to the Mass, while they possessed it, had gained for them the grace of holding fast to Jesus Christ even without Mass and Sacraments.

> * FOR WHAT ENDS IS THE SACRIFICE OF THE MASS OFFERED ?
>
> *The Sacrifice of the Mass is offered for four ends : first, to give supreme honour and glory to God ; secondly, to thank Him for all His benefits ; thirdly, to satisfy God for our sins and to obtain the grace of repentance ; and fourthly, to obtain all other graces and blessings through Jesus Christ.*

' To give supreme honour and glory to God '

THE Mass can do this worthily because Priest and Victim are themselves God.

St. Henry (*d.* 1022) was a Duke of Bavaria who was elected Emperor, gained many victories over the pagan Slavs and other enemies of the Church, and was crowned by the Pope in St. Peter's.

*BALTIMORE 861
ENGLISH CATECHISM 279

When he came first to some city he liked to spend the first night praying alone in some church dedicated to Our Lady, and after arriving in Rome he followed this custom at St. Mary Major. During the night he saw, or dreamed, a great and wonderful vision. Saints and angels beyond counting filled the choir and all the church, and the high altar was made ready for Mass. When the procession came in, he saw that the deacon and subdeacon were St. Laurence and St. Vincent; but the priest who was to sing the Mass was no other than ' the Sovereign and eternal Priest, Christ Himself.'

So the Mass began, and after the Gospel an angel was sent by Our Lady to carry the Missal to the Emperor to kiss. The angel touched him on the thigh, and said: ' Accept this sign of God's love for your chastity and justice.' In the morning he was a little lame in that leg, and remained so ever afterwards. (See also story 122.)

The supreme Act of Adoration

A holy old priest lived in a country district where Catholics were very few. One Sunday morning, after a very deep fall of snow, there was nobody at all in church, and the old priest said Mass with only the housekeeper to answer.

Next day in the village somebody was sympathetic: ' You must have felt sad saying your Mass for an empty church.'

' Empty church?' said the old priest. ' Why, there were thousands there!'

He meant the angels, who assemble in their myriads at every Mass—the Church summons them at the Preface—to adore their Creator present on the altar. (See also story 169.)

The Angels at Mass

In the Preface the Church summons the choirs of angels to join their voices with ours in the Eucharistic thanksgiving.

' One day when a priest was celebrating Mass,' writes St. Bridget of Sweden, ' I saw at the moment of Consecration, all the powers of heaven set in motion. I heard at the

CATECHISM STORIES

same time a heavenly melody most sweet and most harmonious. Numberless angels came down; their chant no human understanding can conceive, nor the tongues of men describe. They surrounded the priest, and looked upon him, bowing towards him in reverential awe.'

'To thank Him for all His benefits'

The very word Eucharist means 'giving thanks.' When He took the bread and wine, Our Lord 'gave thanks' before He uttered the words of consecration.

Later on, when celebrating Mass, the apostles imitated this, and their giving of thanks grew into the Preface: 'Gratias agamus Domino Deo nostro,' etc.

In the Preface we give thanks to God first for His Son and all He has done for us: at the Consecration, to show our thanks, we give Our Lord back to God; at the Communion God gives Him back to us again, to be life and food of our souls. (See also story 171.)

'To satisfy God for our sins'

In ancient Greece a young man was condemned to die for some political crime he had committed. The judge had just passed sentence, and the unhappy prisoner was about to be led out to execution, when his brother, newly returned from the wars, ran into the court. Tearing off his tunic he showed the wounds which he had got fighting for his country, and begged that his guilty brother should be pardoned. Fixing his eyes on the young soldier with admiration, the judge granted his request, and the prisoner was pardoned for the sake of his hero-brother.

So does Our Lord intercede for us at the right hand of God and on the altar at Mass. He begs God to look not on us and our sins, but on His Sacred Wounds, and to forgive us, His adopted brethren, for His sake.

Strength from daily Mass

Towards the close of the great war Marshal Foch, as Generalissimo of the Allied armies, bore upon his shoulders an almost intolerable weight of responsibility. Nearly every day he would rise at six and walk along to the village church for Mass. There he would kneel, following the prayers with his missal, rising at the end refreshed and heartened for his task.

On one occasion (we read) Mordacq came to Bombon with an urgent message from Clemenceau and found that Foch was in church. After a long wait Foch appeared, and explained : ' You see, when I have some free moments —and that does not often happen—I spend them in this abode. Nevertheless, I am a bad Christian, for frequently, instead of praying, I allow myself to slip into meditation, and naturally into meditation on profane matters, on the operations I am preparing, but the Lord, I am sure, will not be angry with me. For always, when I leave His temple, I feel stronger, and above all less uncertain ; it is there very often that I have taken the most grave decisions on the war.'

Foch himself said : ' Once my motto was Knowledge and Faith. I still keep it, but now say, rather, Faith and Knowledge. Yes, Faith first.' He added : ' For this is what matters more.' (See also story 173.)

> * WHAT IS THE SACRAMENT OF PENANCE ?
>
> *Penance is a Sacrament whereby the sins, whether mortal or venial, which we have committed after Baptism are forgiven.*

'This man receiveth sinners'

WE need forgiving, but also God has a need and desire to forgive. Our Lord pictures this in His parables, especially the Shepherd with a hundred sheep, and the corresponding story for women, the Lost Groat (Luke xv, 1–10).

The Prodigal Son (Luke xv, 11–32) teaches the same point, if told from the point of view of the loving, waiting, welcoming father.

The Quality of Mercy

' Never in history has any other ruler, within so short a time, so often granted clemency [as Lincoln during the

CATECHISM STORIES

Civil War]. Most of the offenders were men who had deserted the colours. . . . Every one of these appeals was in fact carefully studied by him, with the result that during the last two years of the conflict there were filed in the War Department hundreds upon hundreds of telegrams, containing the phrase: "Suspend execution of So-and-so."
. . . All these signify that an appeal had been made to him in the last resort after his subordinates, and especially the Secretary for War, had refused aid.

'Some of his excuses were:

"I never felt sure but I might drop my gun and run away if I found myself in line of battle."

"It gives me a restful feeling when, at the close of a hard day's work, I can find some excuse or other for saving a man's life."

"You do not know how hard it is to let a human being die when you feel that a stroke of the pen will save him."'

. . . . . .

An old man whose only son has been sentenced to be shot comes to beg for mercy. Lincoln shows him a wire from General Butler: 'Urgently beg you not interfere with court-martial procedure, for this completely destroys discipline of troops.' The old man having read the telegram sits weeping. Suddenly Lincoln says, out loud: 'To the devil with this Butler,' seizes his pen, and writes: 'Job Smith is not to be shot until further orders from me.' The father remains uneasy—what will happen when further orders are sent? 'I see,' said Lincoln, 'that you are not very well acquainted with me. If your son never looks on death till further orders come from me to shoot him, he will live to be a great deal older than Methuselah.'

. . . . . .

A lad, William Scott by name, having gone to sleep at his post, is under arrest. The President, in the course of an inspection, sees him and says: 'My boy, you are not going to be shot. I believe you when you tell me you couldn't keep awake. But I've been put to a great deal of trouble on your account. What I want to know is, how are you going to pay my bill ? '

The youngster, much perplexed, said in his embarrassment, that it might be possible to raise as much as six hundred dollars on a mortgage.

'No, that won't do. You must pay the debt yourself by doing your duty as a soldier.' (From Emil Ludwig's *Lincoln*.)

If Lincoln felt such a need to forgive, we can understand that God, who is Mercy itself, would feel the same need ; and hence the Sacrament of Penance.

'Sins committed after Baptism'

In the days before steamers or motor-boats, a missionary-priest in the South Seas visited for the first time a small and lonely island inhabited by a few families only. The chief received him favourably, and in a few months the whole island had been instructed and converted. Thereupon the priest took leave of them, with clear directions how to live the Christian life, and promised to visit them again in another year or two.

It was three years, however, before he was able to return. He was received with great joy and preparations were made for Mass and general Communion. But when he suggested that they would want to go to Confession, the chief looked blank.

'I think perhaps you have forgotten the instructions about the Sacrament of Penance ? '

'No, Father, but why should it concern us ? '

'Well, if you are going to receive Holy Communion, you will need to get forgiveness of any sins you may have fallen into since your baptism.'

The old chief stared in amazement, and tears rolled down his cheeks.

'Is that what the white people do ? They sin again after they have been washed in the blood of Christ ? Oh, Father, I would never have believed it ! '

It was the missionary's turn to shed tears now (he said afterwards), tears of joy at the truly Christian spirit of his converts.

The Church still hopes, as in the early days, that Christians will keep their baptismal innocence and never lose their state of grace.

Discuss what the missionary would reply. (*That the Sacrament of Penance can usefully be used—for humility and to get grace—even for venial sins, though not in that case obligatory.*)

(See also stories 439, 440. For a story re distinctions between mortal and venial, see No. 138.)

> * WHEN DID OUR LORD INSTITUTE THE SACRAMENT OF PENANCE?
>
> *Our Lord instituted the Sacrament of Penance when He breathed on His Apostles and gave them power to forgive sins, saying: ' Whose sins you shall forgive, they are forgiven.'*

Christ institutes the Sacrament of Penance

IN the gospels we see Our Lord always kind to ordinary sinners, and using His forgiving-of-sins power at various times (Magdalen, Luke vii, 48; Woman taken in adultery, John viii, 11; Good thief, Luke xxiii, 43).

Then, just as He prepared the apostles' minds for one sacrament by the teaching-miracle of feeding the five thousand, so He prepared them for another by the teaching-miracle of the paralytic (Matt. ix, 1-8), when He claimed in so many words the power of forgiving sins.

It was on Easter night, when the apostles were very much in need of forgiveness themselves, that He handed on the same power to them and the Church. He breathed on them (communicating the Spirit to them), etc. (John xx, 21-23).

Note that the Church is to decide whether the sins are to be forgiven or retained, which implies that they must be made known to the Church, else how could she judge?

For the history of the varying ways in which the Church has used this sacrament, public confession developing into private, etc., see *Twelve and After*, pp. 82-84.

*BALTIMORE 880
ENGLISH CATECHISM 283

CATECHISM STORIES

* How does the priest forgive sins?
  The priest forgives sins by the power of God when he pronounces the words of absolution: ' I absolve thee from thy sins, in the name of the Father, and of the Son, and of the Holy Ghost.'

'The priest forgives sins'

DURING 1937, in Alicante, a young Spaniard of Nationalist sympathies had been caught while trying to board a foreign ship, and lay in prison under sentence of death. Earnestly he was praying, not for release, but to get confession and absolution before he died.

On the night before his execution the cell-door opened and an old man dressed as a pedlar was thrown in.

' Get in here,' said the jailer. ' To-morrow you'll have the cell to yourself.'

The first prisoner lay watching the new-comer take off his shoes and cloak, and prepare himself for the night. Before lying down, however, the old man scratched a small cross on the wall and knelt down to say his prayers.

' Are you a Catholic? ' asked the young man eagerly.

' I am. And you? '

They talked in low tones, and soon the young man told the other of his longing for confession.

' I still think God may grant my prayer.'

' He had granted it already,' said the pedlar, with a smile. ' I am a priest. Ever since the war began I have gone from place to place in this disguise to bring the sacraments to the faithful.'

Next morning the jailer was puzzled to see that the young prisoner, when led out to die, no longer wore a look of fear and strain, but of radiant peace and joy. (See also stories 218, 219, 506, 512, 573.)

The seal of Confession

If you were to visit the Cathedral of Prague you would see a large silver coffin supported by four angels, all made of solid silver, in which are preserved the remains of a priest who faced imprisonment, torture and death itself rather than disclose what he had learnt in the Confessional.

Over five hundred years ago St. John Nepomucene was appointed by King Wenceslaus IV of Bohemia to be

CATECHISM STORIES

Court preacher, and later Queen Johanna, the wife of the King, chose him as her confessor.

One day the King, who was mad with jealousy of his wife, sent for St. John and ordered him to reveal what the Queen had said in her confessions. The priest tried to show him how wicked a thing he was asking. The King promised him honour, riches, a bishopric, and finding this of no avail resorted to threats. Still St. John remained silent. The King then had him imprisoned and tortured with lighted torches on the rack, but all in vain.

For a few days he was set free, but spent the time in preparing for the death he felt sure was near. Soon the King, seeing him from the palace window one day, had him called in, and once more made his unholy demand. With sudden rage at the saint's refusal, he summoned the executioners and gave orders for his death. They waited till nightfall, and then with feet bound back to his neck and a wooden gag in his mouth, the heroic priest was cast into the River Moldau. But, as the body floated down the river, five bright lights shone over his lifeless form so that the inhabitants of the city discovered what had happened, and drew the martyr's body out of the water.

The King fled, fearing the anger of the people, and later he lost his throne and finally died a miserable death.

Three hundred years afterwards, in 1719, the tomb was opened and the body was found only bones and dust, except that in the skull the tongue was found still in a state of preservation, and is honoured to this day as the most precious relic of the Cathedral of Prague, in a splendid reliquary covered with 1200 diamonds.

> *Are any conditions for forgiveness required on the part of the penitent?*
>
> *Three conditions for forgiveness are required on the part of the penitent—Contrition, Confession and Satisfaction.*

God makes His own conditions

God can lay down His own conditions for setting us free from evil of body or soul; and, of course, we must fulfil them.

*BALTIMORE 389, 409, 420
ENGLISH CATECHISM 286

CATECHISM STORIES

The story of Naaman (4 Kings v, 1-15) is suitable for this point. Stress, in connection with verse 13, how easy God has made forgiveness. Perhaps the very easiness makes sinners put off repentance—it will do any Saturday night. Not as if they had to make some great pilgrimage, or something.

Another story on the same point, also about leprosy which is a picture of sin, would be the Ten Lepers (in Luke xvii, 12-19) whom Our Lord required to go and show themselves to the priests as a condition of their cure. And the end of the story reminds us not to forget thanksgiving after confession.

'Three conditions for forgiveness'

Dante with Virgil found himself at the Gate of Purgatory, half-way up the Mount of Purgation. There were three wide steps leading up to it, and an angel with a sword sat at the top and bade them mount. The first step was white marble, so polished that Dante could see himself in it like a mirror. The second step was rugged granite, dark purple-coloured, with great cracks running every way. The third was of porphyry, the colour of blood and flame. The angel took two keys, one gold and one silver, and opened the Gate. 'Both keys are needed,' he told them. 'The gold one is more costly, but the silver one needs more skill in its use. From Peter I have them, and he told me to err rather by opening the Gate than by keeping it locked.'

The first step is sincere *Confession*, by which we see ourselves as we are; the second step is sorrowful *Contrition*, which breaks the hardness of our heart; the third step is *Satisfaction* for sin, done with flaming love and sharing the merits of Christ's passion.

The silver key is the learning and skill of the confessor who judges the penitent's dispositions; the golden key is the sacramental absolution, costly because won by Christ's death.

Note that when the Gate of forgiveness is passed we are still not in heaven, but only at the beginning of Purgatory.

CATECHISM STORIES

* WHAT IS CONTRITION?

Contrition is a hearty sorrow for our sins, because by them we have offended so good a God, together with a firm purpose of amendment.

'A hearty sorrow'

CONTRITION must be of the heart, real and inward.

Pharaoh's conduct towards the Israelites, promising to let them go, and again and again breaking his promise and hardening his heart, is a striking case of false repentance and no real purpose of amendment (Exodus, chapters v to xii and xiv). Many people are like Pharaoh, turning to God in trouble, but with no inward conversion.

Another case often cited as false repentance is that of King Antiochus (2 Mach. ix, 5–28). His repentance was apparently unavailing because his sorrow was not for the offence against God, but only on account of the disease and suffering it had brought on himself.

Contrition must be supernatural

Our sorrow, to be any use in confession, must be somehow on account of God.

A young man had robbed his employers and the day for the accounts to be examined was drawing close. His fraud would probably be discovered, and he was full of fear. 'Oh, how sorry I am I did it! I will never do such a thing again.' Was that contrition? (*No, a purely worldly sorrow.*)

An old Mexican bandit was dying, and a priest was trying to get him into suitable dispositions for receiving the Sacraments, and especially to give up his purpose of killing a mortal enemy whose death he had sworn to ring about.

'You dare not die, my son, with murder in your heart.'

'All right, Father,' he said at last. 'I'll forgive him. But if ever I get better—he'll have to look out!'

'No, that won't do. You must promise not to kill him, even supposing you get better. If you don't promise that, my son, believe me you will go to hell for ever.'

*BALTIMORE 388-397
ENGLISH CATECHISM 287

'Do you mean it, Father? Oh, it would be terrible to go to hell!'"

'Give me your promise, then, and make a good act of contrition.'

'All right, I promise!' He then said the act of contrition with much outward fervour, and ended up with: 'Ah, but what a pity! If only there were no hell!'

Was that contrition, at least attrition? (*No, it arose purely from fear, without any spark of love of God; 'servile fear,' as the theologians call it.*)

St. Thomas More was in the Tower, when his wife (i.e. his second wife, Alice, a widow older than himself, a good housewife but not very intelligent or understanding) came to him and tried to persuade him to give in to the King on the matter of the Oath of Supremacy. The King would forgive him, she said, and he would be able to live the rest of his life with his family in peace and honour.

'How much longer do you think I should live?' asked More.

'Why, a good twenty years yet.'

'Twenty years! And for the sake of another twenty years' comfort in this life you would have me throw away a happiness in the next world that would last for ever and face the prospect of a life of endless misery? Surely that would be a very bad bargain.'

Of course, the saint could rise to higher motives himself, but he was trying to convince a rather matter-of-fact wife.

Would such a motive—concentrating on the saving of one's own soul—be sufficient for contrition? (*Yes, with confession; because we know it is God's desire that our soul should be saved.*)

Sorrow because we have offended God

Examples of contrition in Holy Scripture are: King David (as in 2 Kings xii, 1–10, 13–14). Notice the motives for contrition set before him by the prophet: the meanness of what he had done, the ingratitude he had shown to God, and the punishments which would follow on it.

CATECHISM STORIES

St. Peter after his denial (Luke xxii, 54–62). Tradition says that he wept so constantly that the tears made deep furrows in his cheeks.

St. Paul at his conversion (Acts xi, 1–30). Note especially verse 9, his profound three-day-long act of contrition; and verses 20–30, his immediate, complete and fearless reparation for the past.

In Our Lord's parables we have the contrition of the Publican (Luke xviii, 13), and the Prodigal Son (Luke xv, 17–18, on which see story 174).

See also scriptural examples of perfect contrition under Catechism 293. Also stories 7, 174, 611.

'So good a God'

True story. In a London slum-school a nun-teacher was preparing a class for the Sacraments, and asking them various questions helping towards true sorrow for sin.

'Would you know how to make an act of perfect contrition?' she asked one small boy.

'Oh, Sister, that's easy. I should just look at the crucifix and think as 'ow it was me what done it all!'

Intention of Restitution

Contrition must include, if necessary, a firm will to make restitution, if not already made.

A man accused himself in confession of breaking into a shop four times.

'What did you take from it?' asked the priest

'A dress for my wife.'

'Well, you must send the price of it through the post.'

'Yes, I've done that already, Father.'

'And then, what about the other three times you broke in?'

'Oh well, you see my wife made me take the dress back and change it three times.'

'Firm purpose of amendment'

Margaret of Cortona (*d.* 1297), a beautiful child of working parents, grew up very fond of gaiety and excitement, found pleasure in attracting men. Quarrelled with her stepmother, left home aged eighteen to be maidservant in a nobleman's castle at Montepulciano. Her master fell in love with her, and without being married she lived at the castle as its mistress for nine years. She was generous to the poor, and outwardly gay but inwardly unhappy.

One day her master had been away a few days on a journey; the favourite hound which he had taken with him returned alone and tried to make Margaret come with him. Full of tears she followed the dog out into a wood to a heap of faggots, where the dog stopped, and there beneath them she found her master's body, murdered and hidden, already in decay.

Horror-stricken, filled with terror at the thought of the ruin that might have befallen his soul, and of her own part in it, she left the castle at once, carrying her infant child, and returned on foot to her father's house. He received her back. But her contrition was so deep that she felt she must let it be seen by all. She wore a cord of penance when she went to church, would kneel humbly by the church door, and one Sunday made a public confession of her sinful life. This annoyed her father and stepmother and she was turned out with her child. She was tempted then to return to her old life where many former acquaintances would have welcomed her, but kept to her good resolution.

She went to the Franciscans at Cortona, who decided she was genuine and found her a refuge with two charitable women.

She soon earned her living by nursing, etc., always giving most of her earnings in alms. She became a practical organiser of works of charity and an influence for good in all the district, and died finally aged fifty.

Shortly before her death she was much consoled, she said, by seeing in vision St. Mary Magdalene, 'most faithful of Christ's apostles, clothed in a silvery robe, crowned with precious gems and surrounded by holy angels.' At the same time Margaret heard Our Lord saying to her : ' My Father said to the Baptist, This is My beloved Son. And I say to you of Magdalene : This is My beloved daughter in whom I am well pleased.'

Keeping our good resolutions

In the time of Queen Elizabeth people were made of the same flesh and blood as now, and even some of the martyrs had their weaknesses and falls. The Ven. John Hambly had given up everything for the Faith, becoming first a Catholic and then a priest. But on several occasions, when he was captured and faced with death, he apostatized and agreed to conform to the Protestant religion. In his cowardice he even fell so low as to give information against other Catholics. After repeated falls and repentances he was once more arrested in 1587 and put on trial at Salisbury Assizes. As usual, his courage gave way, and he promised the judge that he would go to the Protestant Church. The trial of other prisoners was then proceeded with, and while Hambly remained waiting in the Court between two warders there happened something that was afterwards regarded by the Catholics as a miracle. ' There came up to him a certain unknown man who, after placing some letters in his hand, at once withdrew. No one preventing him (which in itself was a kind of miracle), Mr. Hambly read and re-read them until at length he broke into tears and gave signs of being strongly moved.' Being asked what had happened, he excused himself and gave no answer at the time. But the next morning, when the judge, as usual, had the prisoners brought into Court again to give their final answer about conforming, Hambly said boldly that his mind was changed ; he expressed his great sorrow for his previous weakness and said he would now accept death most gratefully. So he was executed on the next day and is numbered in the glorious company of English martyrs. No one could ever discover who sent the letter that came to him in Court, and the Catholics of the time said that it must have been brought by his guardian angel. But some think it may have been sent by Mr. Pilchard, a stalwart priest who was in prison at the same time, and also became a martyr himself.

CATECHISM STORIES

* WHAT IS PERFECT CONTRITION?

Perfect contrition is sorrow for sin arising purely from the love of God.
Perfect contrition has this special value: that by it our sins are forgiven immediately, even before we confess them; but nevertheless, if they are mortal, we are strictly bound to confess them afterwards.

Attrition, or imperfect contrition

A LITTLE girl who lived in a large country house was afraid of the dark, and nothing would induce her to go along the passages alone at night. Late one evening her parents were sitting over the fire reading when the little girl appeared in her nightdress and gasped out: 'I'm sure the house is on fire!'

Her mother and father ran upstairs and there, sure enough, smoke was pouring out of a disused room where an electric fuse had started a fire. After putting out the fire they asked the girl what had given her the courage to come through the dark house by herself.

'Oh, I was so afraid of the fire that I forgot about being afraid of the dark.'

Our fear of hell, of losing God or losing His love by offending Him, should be strong enough to drive out our merely selfish fears.

In confession God will accept sorrow arising from fear so long as there is some spark of love in it. (See also story 580.)

'Perfect contrition'

To illustrate perfect contrition in the gospels we have the conversion and subsequent life of Mary Magdalen: 'Many sins are forgiven her,' said Our Lord, 'because she has loved much' (Luke vii, 36-50, viii, 2; John xii, 1-8, xix, 25, xx, 11).

Also the good thief: 'This day thou shalt be with Me in paradise' (Luke xxiii, 39-43).

Legend says that his name was Dismas, that he was born in a robber's cave, the son of the brigand chief; but the baby was a leper. The Holy Family, on flight into

*BALTIMORE 398-404
ENGLISH CATECHISM 293-294

Egypt, sought a night's refuge in the cave. Next day the robber-chief's wife washed her baby in the water which Mary had used for the Holy Child and the leprosy was cured. The baby grew up a brigand like his father and was finally captured, taken to Jerusalem and condemned by Pilate to death. He watched Our Lord carrying his cross and being crucified, drew his own conclusions, surrendered to grace and made his marvellous act of faith and love.

" There is one case in Scripture of deathbed repentance, lest we should despair ; and only one, lest we presume." (St. Augustine.)

Saved through one poor tear

Dante fought in the battle of Campaldino (against the Ghibellines) in 1289. The cavalry leader on the other side was Buonconte of Montefeltro ; after the battle he was missing, and his body was never found.

Years later, when Dante was writing the *Purgatorio*, he describes in it how he found Buonconte in purgatory and asked him what had happened to him in the battle.

' I was mortally wounded in the throat,' replied Buonconte, ' and fled on foot to the bank of a mountain stream called Archiano. There I fell, with strength and sight gone ; I called on Mary's name and died. The angel of God took my soul and the angel of hell complained : " Why do you rob me ? You take the immortal part of him, just for one poor tear of contrition ! But his body at least is mine, to treat as I like ! " So that demon covered the mountains with clouds, the rain poured down and the stream rose and took my corpse, loosening the cross I had made with my arms over my breast and hurled it along till it sank into the muddy depths of the Arno.'

He called on Mary's name and in that moment her intercession gained for him the grace of perfect contrition.

Forgiven even before confession

In 1644 a French nobleman, the Duc de Nemours, fought a duel with a man who had offended him, was run through by his opponent, died in a second or two, without confession, and to all appearance his soul must have been lost, since he was killed in the very act of committing a mortal sin.

But a holy Visitation nun, Sister Mary Martignat, said that God had let her know that the Duke's soul was not in hell, but in the lowest depth of purgatory, perhaps to remain there till Judgement Day, but in the end to be saved. Not for his own sake, but for the sake of others who had prayed for him, he had received in the very moment of dying the grace to make a sincere act of contrition. In spite of a careless life he had not lost the faith, so his soul was ready like tinder to receive the spark that made it blaze up into charity all in a moment.

(On perfect contrition see stories 244, 534, 611.)

> * WHAT IS CONFESSION?
> *Confession is to accuse ourselves of our sins to a priest approved by the Bishop.*
> *If a person wilfully conceal a mortal sin in confession he is guilty of a great sacrilege.*

'To accuse ourselves'

A KING of Prussia once visited a convict prison and, interviewing the prisoners one by one, asked each of them for what crime they had been sentenced. They all declared themselves innocent of any misdeed whatsoever, except one man who owned up to the evil he had done, and said that he deserved what he was getting. The King ordered his immediate release, ' for,' said he, ' this man obviously has no business here among all these innocent people.'

If we want our sins forgiven the first step is to acknowledge that we have committed them and that we deserve to be punished for them.

'To a priest approved by the Bishop'

Some boys from a Midland parish went to camp at the seaside, and one of their priests was with them. When Saturday came round the priest said at tea-time : ' Who's going up to the church for confession ? '

' Can't we go to confession in camp, like we did at the week-end camp at home ? We'd rather go to you, Father.'

*BALTIMORE 408-418
ENGLISH CATECHISM 295-296

'Sorry, I can't hear your confessions here : I'm out of my own diocese.'

The boys were surprised, so the priest had to explain that every priest has the *power* of forgiving sins, but he is not allowed to use it in any place unless the Bishop of that place appoints him to hear confessions.

In the ancient days people told their sins publicly to the whole church ; but later on when private confession became the rule the Bishop appointed certain priests to receive the confessions on behalf of the Church ; and so it is now.

They all walked along the sea-front to the church, and the priest went to confession like anybody else. This, too, surprised one of the little boys, and on the way back he said he never knew priests went to confession themselves.

'Of course they do,' said the priest. 'But they generally go to each other outside the usual confession times, because it's quicker. Our Lord's command applies to all Catholics, even the Pope goes to confession.'

'Look, Father, if you wrote to the Bishop here wouldn't he let you hear our confessions in camp ?'

'I expect he would—perhaps I'll ask him next year.'

Don't put off confession

The best way with confession and Communion is to have a regular time for it, e.g. a certain Sunday in the month.

An old woman had been a long time away from the Sacraments and was always promising to come next Christmas, or next Easter, but never came. At last she was too infirm to come, but refused to make her confession at home, saying she would come when she was able. A mission was held in the parish, and the missioners after several visits got her to promise to make her confession. 'Not to-day though—to-morrow !' she said, and no persuasions could change her. Next morning when the priest came about midday the milkman's milk and the baker's bread were still outside the door, and there was no answer to knocking. One of the neighbours got in round the back, and the old woman was found dead in bed. On the chair at her bedside lay a little diary which she had kept, open at its last entry: 'I am going to confession to-morrow.' (See also stories 140, 578–582.)

We accuse ourselves of sins

Winifred (at a seaside boarding-house, 'liberal table') quite forgot it was Friday, had bacon and sausage for breakfast, beef steak for dinner, and ham and tongue for tea. She wanted to go to Communion on Sunday, so felt obliged to go to confession on Saturday to confess the breaking of Friday abstinence. Was she correct? (*No sin, since she forgot, and therefore no need for confession.*)

James wanted to go to Communion one Sunday for some special reason. It was over a month since he had been to confession, and he was intending to go on the Saturday, but something cropped up to make it inconvenient so he didn't. Next morning he wondered if it would be all right to go to Communion. Since his last confession there was nothing except venial sins, and he made an act of contrition for them, but he still wondered whether he should go to Communion. What should he do? (*It would be right to go. Confession is never obligatory except for grave sin, even at Easter-duty time.*)

When James heard the above principle explained, he said: 'Well, I don't commit mortal sins, so why should I ever go to confession? I could get rid of venial sins with an act of contrition.' (*Regular confession even of venial sins is the general custom of the Church, and is a good thing because (a) it is an act of humility; (b) the absolution gives fresh sacramental grace every time; (c) it is a great safeguard against falling into graver sins.*) (See also story 342.)

Concealing a mortal sin

A man who had been long away from the Sacraments came to confession at Easter and confessed all the mortal sins he had committed except one, which he was too much ashamed of to mention. What would he have to do the next time he went to confession? (*He would have to confess (a) the sin of making a bad confession; (b) the sin he had con-*

cealed at Easter; (c) all the sins he had confessed at Easter, over again; (d) any sins he had committed since his Easter confession.) (See also stories 137, 138.)

Bad confessions

A lad took a couple of shillings from the place where he worked, and was undiscovered. So he did it again, and got into the habit of doing it every week; soon he had stolen and spent nearly £4. Meanwhile he had given up going to confession, but at Easter he went. He felt very sorry for stealing and made his mind up not to take any more money. But when the priest said he must pay the money back, he said he couldn't; at last he promised to pay it back a shilling a week, but he had no intention of doing so, as it would have taken half of his pocket money. Was it a bad confession? (*Yes. His contrition was not genuine. Also he told a lie in confession.*)

A girl took £3 that another girl had saved up for her holidays. The thief kept it hidden somewhere, but after a week or two she felt sorry for taking it, and gave it back to the owner, making up some story about finding it. She went to confession to a priest who knew her, and told all her other sins, but was too ashamed to tell him about the theft, although she felt very contrite about it. Was it a bad confession? (*Yes, confession must include all grave sins. And she could have gone to a priest who did not know her.*)

A girl had done grave harm to another girl's character, by telling lies about her. She felt very sorry for this, went to confession, and promised to do what she could to put the harm right. The priest said: 'Will you make the Stations every night for a week for a penance?' She said: 'Yes, Father,' but in her own mind she determined not to do it, thinking it would be troublesome. Did this make it a bad confession? (*Yes, unless she had ignorance for an excuse. Absolution is given on condition of doing the penance given. If the penitent thinks the penance given is too difficult, he should ask the priest to change it. What if the penitent forgets to say the penance? That does not spoil the confession.*)

(See also story 256.)

Such stuff as dreams

Paul, examining his conscience, remembered a vivid dream he had had, in which he had felt a violent hatred of his brother, and was trying to kill him when he woke up. Paul wondered if he ought to tell it in confession. Should he? (*If he likes, but there is no necessity to. Dreams are not voluntary and we are not to blame for them.*)

N.B.:

'Your wife's not speaking to you—how's that?'

'Because I dreamed I won the penny pool and woke up without giving her half.'

When in doubt ask a Confessor

Peter went to confession and mentioned something he had done, and the priest said: 'What makes you think that is a sin?' Peter said he had read it in a Catholic paper, answers-to-enquirers column. Have such newspaper-opinions any authority? (*None to speak of, unless they are signed, in which case they would have any authority that the name of the author was worth. Such opinions are misleading, because the newspaper-writer cannot have all the circumstances of a case before him. If people are in doubt whether something is sinful they should ask some confessor whose judgement they trust. Why not any confessor? Well, any confessor would do, but obviously some have more experience and knowledge than others.*)

> * HOW MANY THINGS HAVE WE TO DO IN ORDER TO PREPARE FOR CONFESSION?
>
> We have four things to do in order to prepare for confession: first, we must heartily pray for grace to make a good confession; secondly, we must carefully examine our conscience; thirdly, we must take time and care to make a good act of contrition; and fourthly, we must resolve by the help of God to renounce our sins, and to begin a new life for the future.

'In order to prepare for confession'

HILDA went into church for a visit one Saturday morning; it was not the advertised time for confessions, but some-

*BALTIMORE 426
ENGLISH CATECHISM 297

body was just coming out of the confessional. Hilda thought: 'Oh, how lucky, this will save me coming to-night,' and shot straight in without any prayers or preparation whatever. Was it a good confession? (*We'll hope so. If a person goes to confession often, and knows his sins pretty well, and is sorry for them all the time, he is always prepared; though a short special preparation is still desirable.*)

'Time and care to make a good act of contrition'

A certain man came to confession to St. Francis of Sales, and had to accuse himself of very grave sins. He related them rather casually, without showing any feeling of regret. As he went on, the saint began to sigh and groan, as if in pain.

'Is anything the matter, Father? Are you unwell?'

'I am well enough, my son. But I fear you are far from well.'

The penitent continued his confession, and before long St. Francis was openly sobbing with grief.

'Father, whatever is the matter? Why are you shedding tears?'

'Alas, my son, I shed tears because you shed none.'

The man's heart was touched.

'You are right, Father,' he said. 'My heart must indeed be hardened when I do not weep for sins as great as mine. Help me now to make a good confession.'

From that time the man amended his life and became a model Christian. He used to tell this incident himself, saying: 'Many confessors make their penitents cry, but in my case it was the other way round—the confessor was reduced to tears!'

This story perhaps lends itself to discussion. No doubt St. Francis knew the penitent he was dealing with. Our sorrow for sin must be inward and genuine. Still, we must remember that tears and sighs are not real contrition, which is a matter of the will, not of the feelings.

Contrition must cover every mortal sin

A man in a dungeon was fastened to the wall by several fetters and chains, one round each ankle, one round each wrist. He discovered the fetters on his wrists were a little too large, and with painful efforts he got his hands free. He then found he could loosen one of the staples in the wall, and so he set free his left leg. But he was still chained up by the right leg, and nothing he could do was any use to get it free. He remained fastened in his dungeon.

Our contrition and confession must cover every mortal sin, for a single one unrepented of is enough to prevent our being set free.

'A new life for the future'

This includes avoiding the dangerous occasions of sin.

'Now then,' said the greengrocer to a small boy. 'You hop it, quick.'

'What for?'

'I know what you're after—you're trying to pinch one of them apples.'

'You're wrong, then, 'cos I'm trying not to.'

But if he really was trying not to, he ought to go away from the apples. (See also story 71.)

> * WHAT IS SATISFACTION?
>
> *Satisfaction is doing the penance given us by the priest.*
>
> *The penance given by the priest does not always make full satisfaction for our sins. We should therefore add to it other good works and penances, and try to gain Indulgences.*

'The penance given us by the priest'

It may not be a big one, but it is the *sacramental* penance, and, therefore, has extra value from Christ's precious Blood.

A man confessed (let us suppose) that he had got deliberately drunk several times. The priest said: 'Will you promise to keep out of the public-house?'

'Yes, Father.'

'And say the Litany of the Saints for a penance?'

'Yes, Father.'

But at the same time the man said to himself: 'Litany of the Saints! That's too long—I'll never be bothered to say that much.'

He said his act of contrition and received absolution. Afterwards, for his penance, he said the Litany of Our Lady, and said to himself: 'That's quite enough.'

Were his sins forgiven? (*No, because absolution is given on condition of the penance being performed—that is why it is called the Sacrament of Penance.*) Is it a grave obligation to perform the penance? (*Yes, if the penance is given for grave sins, as in this case.*) What if the penitent thinks the priest has given him too difficult a penance? (*He should ask for it to be changed.*)

Two men, Andrew and James, went to confession; both had grave sins to confess. Afterwards, Andrew had to hurry home at once, entirely forgot to say his penance, and never thought of it again. James could not remember what penance the priest had given him; he didn't want to go back and ask, as there was still a queue; so he said some prayers which he reckoned by previous experience would be about right.

Were their sins forgiven? (*Yes. But James should mention the matter in his next confession. And Andrew will still be owing satisfaction for his sins.*)

'Does not always make full satisfaction'

In old days penances were not just a few prayers to be said before the penitent left for church. Sometimes they were hard things like forty days' fast; or wearing sackcloth, or going pilgrimages.

One day when St. Anthony of Padua was preaching he converted a band of robbers who had disguised themselves and come to hear him out of curiosity. After hearing their confessions and giving them absolution, St. Anthony gave them very hard penances because they had committed very grave sins.

One of them, he said, was to go twelve times in pilgrimage to the tomb of St. Peter and St. Paul at Rome. Years and years after, when this robber was an old man, he met a friar on the road, and he told him how when he was young he had heard St. Anthony preach, and how he had told him to go to Rome twelve times. 'And now I am on my way back from Rome for the twelfth time,' he said.

Nowadays lazy penances are the custom even for serious sins, and we can hardly expect that they will make 'full satisfaction.'

The best penances are those God sends us

Sufferings, disappointments, etc., which happen to us can be offered up for our own sins, or for those of others.

While St. Margaret of Scotland lay dying, her husband Malcolm, with two of her sons Edward and Edgar, were besieging the castle of Alnwick which had been seized by the Normans. One day the young Prince Edgar arrived home unexpectedly, and came to his mother's bedside. He brought terrible news, but wished to spare her.

'How is it with your father and brother?' she asked him.

'They are well,' he answered, but she saw the tragedy in his face, and he had to tell the truth. They had both been killed. The Normans had offered to surrender the keys, but only to the King in person; the keys were held out by a soldier on a spear, and when Malcolm advanced to receive them the spear was driven into his eye and brain. Then as the Scots tried to storm the castle, Prince Edward had been slain, too.

It was a crushing disaster to Scotland and still more to Queen Margaret. This is what she said:

'I thank Thee, Almighty God, for sending me so great an affliction in the last hour of my life, to purify me from my sins.' Soon afterwards she passed away.

> * WHAT IS AN INDULGENCE?
>
> *An Indulgence is a remission, granted by the Church, of the temporal punishment which often remains due to sin after its guilt has been forgiven.*

Penance can be remitted to the deserving

THE more intense our love and contrition, the less need there is for the Church to inflict penance on us. This is one idea behind Indulgences.

*BALTIMORE 435-442
ENGLISH CATECHISM 300

CATECHISM STORIES

A man who was ill made his confession once to St. Vincent Ferrer. His sins were many and great, and he expected to get long years of penance. The saint told him to fast every Friday for a year. ' So small a penance for such great crimes ! Oh, Father, it is too little ! '—' It shall be smaller still then,' replied the saint, and he changed it to saying the seven Penitential psalms daily for a week. Again, with tears, the penitent asked for something severe. St. Vincent said : ' Say then, one Pater, Ave and Gloria, once.' At last the penitent understood : pardon is God's free gift, and many sins are forgiven to those who love.

That night the sinner died and St. Vincent Ferrer saw his soul, in a vision, being taken into heaven.

' A remission granted by the Church '

In the early ages of the Church a Christian (let us call him Clement) lay in prison waiting to be thrown to the lions. He had been denounced to the authorities, confessed that he was a Christian, refused to sacrifice to the gods, and was condemned to death.

A former friend named Quintus came to see him in prison. The friend was a Christian, too, but he was in disgrace with the Church. Early in the persecution he had been brought before the magistrates as a Christian, but instead of being a faithful confessor and martyr, he had yielded to threats, burnt a few grains of incense on the altar before the Emperor's statue, and gone home with the little certificate which would protect him from the informers.

For a time he had avoided the Christian gatherings, but the torments of conscience gave him no rest and at last he went to the Bishop. He confessed his crime in full assembly, and became one of the ' penitents ' who, at the Christian meetings, wore a sack-cloth uniform, and knelt apart from the faithful, and would not be admitted to Communion perhaps until their death.

Quintus found where Clement was lying in the dark and crowded prison. He knelt at his feet and kissed his chained hands, full of shame for his own fall. He gave the martyr some fruit and wine which he had in a basket.

CATECHISM STORIES

For a while they talked, then Quintus made the request he had come to make.

'I want to ask you a favour, unworthy as I am. You know what it is.'

'You want me to write an intercession to the Bishop?'

Quintus nodded, too ashamed to speak.

'Well, I will do it gladly for the sake of our old friendship. Give me the parchment.'

Quintus had brought the letter all ready, needing only the signature. It asked that the Church should take the sufferings and death of Clement as expiation for the sin of Quintus his friend, and that Quintus should be set free from penance and restored to Communion.

Clement signed the letter with his fettered hand. The two said farewell, and parted : Clement to wait for his appearance in the arena at the next Games, and Quintus to take his letter to the Bishop, who received it with every respect, and carried out its request by giving Quintus a plenary indulgence from all his penance.

This is a made-up story, but we know that it was an everyday happening during the persecution times. The sufferings of the martyrs, together with those of Christ, made a great ' treasury of merits ' far greater than all the demerits of sinners, and the Church felt justified in using them for the general good.

That was how indulgences became a regular system. For the story of their subsequent history, see *Twelve and After*, pp. 85–86.

(See also story 131.)

> * WHAT IS THE SACRAMENT OF EXTREME UNCTION?
>
> *The Sacrament of Extreme Unction is the anointing of the sick with holy oil, accompanied with prayer.*

'The anointing of the sick'

As in the case of the other Sacraments, the instituting of Extreme Unction was preceded by a promise, or hint, beforehand. In St. Mark's gospel we see how during Our

*BALTIMORE 443
ENGLISH CATECHISM 301

Lord's ministry He not only laid His own hands on the sick to cure them, but also sent out the twelve, two and two, and they preached, cast out devils and 'anointed with oil many that were sick and healed them' (Mark vi, 5, and 13).

Was this already the Christian Sacrament of Extreme Unction, or was it some Jewish custom that Our Lord encouraged them to use?

We know no details of the formal institution of the Sacrament. Perhaps we may imagine Our Lord giving directions about it during His risen life. At any rate, we find it in use by the apostles themselves. Read Ep. James v, 14-15.

Through the gates of death

The following story is told of a Father Capella, who had once been a cavalry officer in the Carlist wars, but became a priest and was in charge of a church in a working-class district of Paris.

He was on his death-bed, and had just been anointed, when he heard from one of his colleagues about a certain parishioner who was also at death's door and was refusing to receive the Sacraments.

'Ah, poor fellow! If only I were on duty—perhaps he would let me hear his confession.'

'I am sure he would—he thinks the world of you.'

'Come on—get me up—put my clothes on!'

They thought his mind was wandering, but he insisted and was obeyed. He had himself carried through the streets to the sick man's house, though so feeble that it seemed every moment must be his last.

At the sick man's bedside he was barely able to speak.

'My friend, we are both going to appear before God—why shouldn't we make the journey together? Come, make your confession to me.'

The dying man kissed the priest's hand to show his consent and the two were left alone. When the confession was finished they had to guide the priest's hand while he did the anointing and gave the last blessing. An hour later priest and penitent were both dead.

CATECHISM STORIES

> * WHAT ARE THE EFFECTS OF THE SACRAMENT OF EXTREME UNCTION?
>
> *The effects of the Sacrament of Extreme Unction are to comfort and strengthen the soul, to remit sin, and even to restore health, when God sees it to be expedient.*

'To comfort and strengthen the soul'

THERE are many true stories of remarkable sick calls, usually to dying people who greatly wished for a priest.

Father C—— of the London Oratory, one day in 1919 was asked to visit a certain Mrs. P—— who was ill at a house in Montpelier Square. He thought she seemed in a critical condition, and arranged to come next morning to administer the last Sacraments; also he gave the nurse the Oratory telephone number and asked her to ring him up if her patient should become worse.

That night as usual the Oratory telephone was switched on to the room of one of the other Fathers. Our Father C—— was wakened out of deep sleep about 3.45 a.m. by his door opening. By the moonlight he could see a figure standing by the door which he took to be the Father-in-charge, who said something, rather indistinctly, about a sick call.

Father C—— told him rather sharply to speak up, on which he said more clearly: 'There is no time to lose—there is a telephone message.' The door closed, and the Father sprang out of bed, taking for granted that the nurse in Montpelier Square had telephoned as he had asked. He got to the house in ten minutes and found lights in the windows, but for twenty minutes could get no answer to his ringing and knocking, which seemed strange since he had been sent for. At last the door was opened, and he went straight up to the sick-room. The nurse was kneeling at the bedside saying some prayers, and looked very surprised to see him, and Mrs. P—— was saying: 'I do wish Father C—— would come!' Afterwards he learned that for the last half-hour she had been expressing

*BALTIMORE 444-446
ENGLISH CATECHISM 303

the same wish, which was the reason why the nurse had suggested saying some prayers.

He gave her all the last Sacraments, and stayed for an hour or two until she became unconscious, when he recited the prayers for the dying. Before leaving he thanked the nurse for telephoning; she said she had not done so, so he said it must have been someone else.

Next morning Father C—— spoke to the Father who had been on duty and said: 'I am sorry I spoke to you so sharply last night.'

'What do you mean?' said the other.

'When you came to call me.'

'But I never did call you last night.'

'Oh, yes you did! You came at a quarter to four to tell me there was a telephone sick call.'

'I never left my room last night. I could not get to sleep, and as it happens I know I was awake at that very time as I had my light on. What is more, there was no telephone call last night.'

Father C—— enquired at the telephone exchange and was informed that there was no record of any call to the Oratory on the night in question. (Summarised from *Lord Halifax's Ghost Book*, page 135.)

'To remit sin'

Two girls were in the house when their father fell downstairs and fractured his skull badly. He was breathing heavily, seemed quite unconscious; some neighbours came in and told the girls to fetch the doctor from up the street. One of the girls said to the other: 'Hadn't I better get the priest as well?' A neighbour said: 'It wouldn't be any good, your father can't hear or speak, so the priest couldn't do anything.' All the same the girl went to both the doctor and priest.

The doctor was in and came in ten minutes, but all he could say was that the patient was already dead. A few minutes afterwards the priest came. They told him the man had expired, but he gave him an absolution and anointed his forehead, and then went through all the anointing as usual with all the prayers from the book.

Discuss : Is it any use calling a priest to a dying person who is quite unconscious ? (*Yes. Extreme Unction forgives sins if God sees in the person sufficient willingness for contrition, even imperfect.*)

Can a person be anointed after death has occurred ? (*Not if it were certain that the soul had altogether left the body— e.g. death by beheading. But ordinarily this may possibly take some time, even an hour perhaps—we know little about it.*)

Why we should pray for the dying

There are psychological phenomena which lead some to hope that at the moment of death a good deal may happen through God's grace even in a very brief time.

Admiral Sir Francis Beaufort describes how as a young man he came near drowning. After ceasing his struggles his senses were pleasurably deadened, but his mind became intensely active and ranged backwards through his life with indescribable rapidity. ' Our last cruise—a former voyage and shipwreck—my school—the progress I had made there, and the time I had misspent—and even all my boyish pursuits and adventures. . . . In short, the whole period of my existence seemed to be placed before me in a sort of panoramic review, and each act of it seemed to be accompanied by a consciousness of right or wrong, or by some reflection on its cause or its consequences. . . . Certainly two minutes could not have elapsed the moment of suffocation to that or my being hauled up.' (H. Martineau, *Biographical Sketches*, 4th ed., p. 229.)

A mountain climber named S. W. Cozzens records the same experience as he was falling from a narrow ledge down hundreds of feet of mountain-side in Arizona. ' Convinced that death was inevitable I became perfectly reconciled to the thought. My mind comprehended in a moment the acts of a lifetime. Transactions of the most trivial character, circumstances the remembrance of which had been buried deep in memory's vault for years, stood before me in bold relief. . . . I seemed to be gliding swiftly and surely out of the world, but felt no fear, experienced no regret at the prospect ; on the contrary rejoiced that I was so soon to see with my own eyes the great mystery concealed behind the veil.' He was caught by a projecting rock and clung to it till the rescuers reached him.

Fr. H. Thurston, S.J., gives these and other instances in the *Month* (Jan. 1935), and remarks that in all such cases the flood of memory, etc., seems to the person concerned so startling that beforehand it would have seemed impossible. None of us (he comments) know all the possibilities of the human mind. Above all, ' none of us know what mysteries may underlie the last moments of human existence, the revelation of truth which may sweep away the mists of years, and the change of heart which may come to those who, not having wholly stifled their better nature, may, like the good thief on the cross, still win pardon from our merciful Saviour by one last act of fervent sorrow.'

All this helps us to understand why Extreme Unction may be given to those who are seemingly unconscious, or even to those who seem dead, if there is some hope that the soul may not altogether be departed.

' To restore health '

An old lady had a touch of bronchial pneumonia and a rather weak heart, and as she was seventy-eight and lived a long way from the church the priest wanted to anoint her. But she said : ' No, what makes you think I'm dying ? Bring me holy Communion if you like, but I don't want to be anointed yet.'

Discuss what the priest would answer.

(*The Anointing is meant to make you better.*)

Must the sick person be in some danger of death to justify anointing ? (*Yes ; all circumstances being taken into consideration.*)

Whose business is it to decide ? (*The priest's.*)

Fortified by the rites of the Church

Some Catholics have a foolish fear of being anointed, but we ought, on the contrary, to desire the help of the sacraments and receive them gladly as soon as the priest suggests it.

When priests were few and scattered, during the persecution times in Scotland, a Bishop was once making a journey on foot over desolate country, and at nightfall decided to seek shelter in a cottage whose light he had seen some distance from his path.

He was made welcome, but as there was no crucifix or other holy sign about the house he thought it better to say nothing of religion. Over a simple meal he could not help noticing an air of sadness about the man and his wife and asked the reason.

'Yes, it is my poor old father who is dying upstairs. It is sad because he will not believe that he is going to die yet, and we cannot get him to prepare for his end.'

'Can I see him?'

The Bishop was taken upstairs and saw at once that the old man's death was a matter of hours, or minutes. He tried to suggest the need of spiritual preparation.

'No, no!' said the old man again and again. 'I'm not going to die—it is impossible.'

'Will you tell me,' asked the Bishop, 'why you say it is impossible?'

The dying man fixed his eyes on the Bishop.

'Tell me first, are you a Catholic?'

'I am.'

'Then I will tell you: I am a Catholic also, and ever since my first Communion I have prayed every day that I should have a priest at the end to give me the last Sacraments. So I know I shall not die till some priest visits me.'

'My son, your prayer is heard! I am a priest, your Bishop in fact. Our Lady made me lose my way to bring me to your side.'

He opened his cloak and showed the episcopal cross on his breast.

'O my dearest Mother Mary, I thank you!' cried the old man with joy. 'Now hear my confession, my lord, for now indeed I know my time has come.'

The Bishop absolved and anointed him, and a few minutes later held him in his arms as he expired.

CATECHISM STORIES

> * WHAT IS THE SACRAMENT OF HOLY ORDER?
> *Holy Order is the Sacrament by which bishops, priests and other ministers of the Church are ordained, and receive power and grace to perform their sacred duties.*

The priesthood of the New Testament

BEFORE Our Lord came it was prophesied that He should be Priest, as well as King and Prophet. 'Thou art a priest for ever, according to the order of Melchisedech' (Ps. cix, 4. See story 50 in Part I).

He came, and exercised His priesthood in the one great Sacrifice, in the Upper Room and on the Cross (read Heb. ix, 11-15).

Then He conferred His priestly powers upon the apostles (look up Luke xxii, 19; John xx, 21; Matt. xxviii, 19), thus ordaining them priests and giving them power to ordain others.

Which they began to do at once (Acts i, 26; vi, 6; xiii, 3).

(See also stories 56, 446, 458.)

Dignity of the priesthood

St. Francis of Assisi resisted all suggestions that he should be ordained priest, and in this way he taught all his followers how lofty and holy a dignity the priesthood is. Only with reluctance did he allow himself to be ordained deacon.

One day he said to the friars: 'If I met an angel and a priest walking together I would salute the priest first and then the angel.'

This puzzled some of the friars, no doubt because they knew priests who were evidently not so holy as angels. So St. Francis explained:

'I would salute the priest first because the angel, although so great, is only Christ's servant, but the priest actually stands for Jesus Christ.'

Sharing Christ's priesthood

In Spain, July 1936, forty priests (of the Claretian order) were being taken off in lorries to execution. They sang

*BALTIMORE 451-455
ENGLISH CATECHISM 305

hymns, shouted in chorus ' Long live Christ the King.' A young man in lay attire stopped one of the lorries and joined himself to the condemned ; he, too, was a priest who preferred to die with his brethren.

At the place of execution one of the firing squad spoke apologetically to one of the martyrs, pointing to the priestly habit he was wearing.

' We have to kill you because you wear these.'

' And we die joyfully,' was the reply, ' because we wear them.'

' Thou art a priest for ever '

Many of the English martyrs suffered death simply for being priests. One of these was Bl. John Southworth, who had spent many years going about Westminster dressed as a layman, but ministering as a priest to the poor Catholic families to whom he was the one link with the Faith. His body has come back to Westminster after lying hidden in France for three hundred years, and visitors to the Cathedral can see it in its glass reliquary.

It was in the middle of the night—June 19th, 1654— that a pursuivant named Jeffries led the official of the law through the dark streets to the house where a tired old man lay peacefully sleeping after a long day of toil. The noise of their entry must have awakened him, and we can picture him lying in his bed, perhaps a little dazed with sleep, but calm and unafraid (for he has long awaited this, and is glad, perhaps, that it has happened in the night, being in that way like his Divine Master's arrest). He sees his room searched ; and soon they drag out his chasuble, rough hands grasp his precious chalice and the other requisites for saying Mass, and they laugh, looking at him in triumph, for here is proof that the man before them is a priest, and therefore worthy of death. They ask him whether he is a priest, and he tells them yes. He has to get up and dress, and is led away, a prisoner, through the streets where he has so long been a familiar and beloved figure—looking his last upon those silent, sleeping houses in which he has helped many a Catholic to make ' a happy death.'

During the next few days he appeared on trial at the Old Bailey. He pleaded 'not guilty' of treason but 'guilty' on the charge of being a priest. There is a striking little account of this trial, written at the time in a letter 'from a gentleman in the City to a gentleman in the Country.' He describes how the judges did their utmost to save Fr. John's life, for many hours suspending the recording of his confession while they tried to persuade him to plead 'not guilty.' 'They pressed him to this in the public court, assuring him that if he would so plead his life should be safe, and that they had no evidence which could prove him to be a priest. And when the old man' (as the letter-writer calls him, for he looked over seventy, though only sixty-two) 'would not be drawn to deny himself to be a priest, taking it to be a denying of his religion, and that the court was compelled to give judgement against him, the magistrate who gave the sentence was so drowned in tears upon that sad occasion that it was long before he could pronounce the sentence, which the law compelled him, as he professed, to give.'

There must have been something about Fr. John Southworth that touched people's hearts; perhaps they had seen him going about his self-sacrificing work among the London poor.

The sentence was the usual one pronounced on prisoners who were to suffer death:

'You shall be taken from the prison from whence you were brought, thence you shall be drawn to the place of execution, and there hanged by the neck until thou art half-dead: your head shall then be cut off and the rest of your members, divided into four parts, shall be fixed up at the usual four points of the city, and may God have mercy upon you.'

After being sentenced he was granted permission to say a few words, and was asked to come nearer, which he did. 'Falling on his knees, he said: "O Lord God, I humbly thank Thee, Who hath made me worthy to suffer for Thy sake." Then, standing up, he spoke to the court and said: "I thank you for what you have done, and for your civilities to me, and I pray God to give you His holy grace, that you and all this nation may be converted to the true Roman, Catholick and Apostolick Faith, and remaine in heaven for ever with Jesus Christ in Glory."

The magistrate answered kindly : " Sir, wee thanke you, and will joyne with you in the latter part." ' (See also story 654.)

A true Father to his flock

St. Ælphege (*d.* 1012) as Bishop of Winchester, spent all his time looking after the poor, denying himself as much as possible to have more to give away. He was Archbishop of Canterbury when the Danes besieged and took the city. They treated the inhabitants with barbarity, despite St. Ælphege's fearless intercessions, and they imprisoned him in one of their boats on the Thames. When plague broke out the Danes asked his prayers, and when he prayed it ceased. But they still refused to release him without ransom, and he refused to ask for the money since it would have to come from the goods of the Church and the poor. So the Danes ill-treated him with stoning and other torments, so badly that one of them in pity split his skull with his battle-axe. ' Jesu, receive me in peace and forgive them ' were his last words.

Priestly zeal for souls

During the French Revolution a certain ruffian in Paris had taken part in the September massacres and other such occasions. Even afterwards he swore that no priest should enter his house and come out alive. Years afterwards he fell sick, and at the request of a relative a priest, fully warned of the danger, came to his bedside.

' What, a priest in my house ! Where are my pistols ? See this arm of mine—it has slaughtered a dozen of your sort ! '

' No, my friend, only eleven. The twelfth one did not die. He was left for dead, but he recovered from the wounds you gave him. Look, here they are.'

And he showed the scars of sabre cuts on head and breast.

' I was the twelfth ! You see, God has preserved me to save your soul.'

The hardened heart of the old man melted at last, and he made a good end.

'His life for His sheep'

During the invasion of Northern China (1938) some Japanese soldiers, out of control, went to a large Catholic school where a number of refugees, etc., had gathered. The priests who were there, several French missionaries and Chinese, refused the soldiers admittance and went outside to ask what they wanted. The soldiers demanded that the women should be handed over to them. After much difficulty and patient persuading under threats the priests got the soldiers to agree to come back the next day for their answer, and they went off. That evening the priests managed to get all the women and girls away to a place of safety. Next day the soldiers came back, and when they found they had been tricked they took out the priests and bayoneted them to death.*

'Their sacred duties'

The duties are all concerned with ministering God's grace to men.

Every bishop and priest night take to himself the title used by the Pope: 'Servant of the servants of God.'

Our Lord taught the apostles this lesson when He washed their feet (see John xiii, 1–17). The Church arranges that every bishop shall re-enact this scene on Maundy Thursday.

St. Oswald (Saxon Bishop of Worcester, and later of York, d. 992) used to wash the feet of twelve poor men and fed them afterwards at his own table. He did this every day. Even on the day of his death he performed the ceremony as usual; he had just kissed the feet of the last poor man, and said the Gloria Patri, when he sank to the ground and gave up his soul to God. (See also stories 675, 676.)

Vocation to the priesthood

A few years ago a Kaffir boy was sitting under a tree lost in thought. A nun passed by and asked: 'What are

* This incident I heard from a well-known English author who travelled in China during the war.—F. H. D.

you thinking about, Paul?' 'Sister, I was thinking I would like to be a priest.'

She watched him after that, and he was a good boy at work and play, and always at Mass every morning. His school-days came to an end, but the seminary at Marianhill could not take him unless he had the necessary £60. 'I must work and get it, then,' he said.

He worked on a farm, but the pay was very small. So like many other natives he decided to work in the Johannesburg gold-mines, so deadly to the health of the body and often of the soul. He served a three years' contract, enduring the terrible heat and damp far underground, and the brutal treatment of the overseers, and resisting the city temptations to which his companions gave way in their free time. Three years of hell, but he had saved the £60.

He went to Marianhill, showed the money to the priest-superior. 'Father, I want to be a priest.' But even as he spoke the tell-tale hollow cough racked his frame.

'Well done,' said the priest. 'But you must see a doctor first.'

Alas, the young man was already in the grip of miner's tuberculosis, and the doctor's report gave him only a year or two to live.

The priest broke the news to him; at first he broke down, sobbing and coughing with his hand pressed to his mouth. Then he recovered himself. 'Yes, I was afraid of that.'

'Nobody knows how God works in these things,' said the priest. 'He does not call you to be a priest. Keep your money, buy a little plot of ground here and live happily close to the mission.'

'No, Father, that isn't what I worked for. I wanted to be a priest. If I can't be one myself perhaps some other boy can be one for me. You will find some boy who will make a good priest. Take the money, I don't want it, give it to him. I'm going back to the mines. It doesn't matter when I die. If I live another few years I might save enough for another boy, too.'

Paul went back to the mines. In 1935 (according to a Catholic paper of that year) he was still working there, and praying God to keep him alive a little longer to get another few pounds for his second priest.

Fostering vocations

St. Brigid, even when Abbess of Kildare, used often to tend the flocks of sheep on the Curragh, which was also used as a training ground for sports.

One day she saw a lad there training for a race. His name was Nennidh.

'Where are you running to so fast?' she said.

He saw she was a nun and answered impertinently:

'I'm in a hurry to get to the Kingdom of Heaven!'

'He is happy who makes that journey. Pray for me that I, too, may reach the blissful kingdom.'

Nennidh felt ashamed he had been disrespectful.

'Perhaps I shall miss the way somehow myself; you must pray for *me*, please.'

'I will,' said Brigid. Then suddenly God let her see a little into the future.

'Don't be afraid, Nennidh. I can see you are going to be a priest, and some day before I die your hand will give me the holy Viaticum.'

After that she always prayed for Nennidh, and he remembered her kindness and her strange words about the future. Before long he took to study, became a priest and went for years to Britain as a missionary. When St. Brigid was near her death sure enough Nennidh came back from his travels and was in time to give her the Viaticum.

> * WHAT IS THE SACRAMENT OF MATRIMONY?
>
> *Matrimony is the Sacrament which sanctifies the contract of a Christian marriage and gives a special grace to those who receive it worthily.*

The plain gold ring

POPE PIUS X was the son of simple, hard-working parents in a little Italian village. He returned there to say his first Mass. When, later on, he was consecrated Bishop, he

*BALTIMORE 457
ENGLISH CATECHISM 306

paid a flying visit to his cottage home before taking possession of his diocese. We are told his mother gazed proudly at his ring and then said with a smile : 'Yes, Beppi, it is very beautiful, but you would never have worn it if it had not been for this one,' and she held up her own toil-worn hand with its plain gold ring.

The next Pope Pius (eleventh) granted an indulgence of 100 days (diocese of Westminster) to husband and wives who should kiss the wife's wedding-ring and say : 'Grant us, O Lord, that loving Thee we may love each other, and live according to Thy holy law.'

The Sacrament sanctifies the natural contract

The Church warns us of the danger of mixed marriages, but if the faith and good example of the Catholic party are strong enough the non-Catholic is often led into the Church, sometimes before marriage but sometimes after.

A case in point is the highly romantic story told about the parents of St. Thomas of Canterbury. It is usually regarded as mere legend, but there is nothing impossible about it in itself; we know that the obscurity of his birth was often a subject of comment, and just at that time, when the Christian kingdoms of Jerusalem, etc., were being consolidated under Baldwin I, there was much coming and going between East and West

A young Englishman named Gilbert with a servant, or perhaps a friend, named Richard, went to Palestine to serve against the infidels. At some skirmish or siege they were both captured by a Saracen leader (the story calls him a prince) and became his well-treated slaves.

Gilbert attracted the favourable attentions of his master's daughter, the 'princess,' and the two had many secret conversations, in which she questioned him often about his country and religion, which she could see he held very dear.

'Tell me,' she said one day, 'you say this Jesus Christ is more worthy to be loved and served than all else—would you then be willing even to give your life for Him ? '

' It would be the greatest joy that could happen to any Christian,' he answered, and his faith and charity were so contagious that she inwardly determined that she, too, would become a Christian if ever she was able.

Meanwhile some of the Christian slaves had made a plan to escape; Gilbert and Richard joined them, the attempt was successful, and after many adventures the two friends found themselves back in England.

The Saracen girl wept bitterly when she knew that Gilbert was gone, but soon tears gave way to generous resolution; she fled secretly from her father's house and embarked somehow on a vessel that was sailing to England.

In due course the ship arrived at London, and she found herself wandering in the streets of the city, destitute, friendless, unable to make herself understood, and with no idea how to set about finding the friend she had come to seek. By a miracle of good luck she saw amongst the crowd a familiar face—it was Richard, who had been a fellow-slave of Gilbert. She ran to him and implored him to take her to his master. Richard could not do this at once, but he found a lodging for her in a good lady's house.

Next day when Gilbert came to see her she threw herself at his feet and asked him with many tears to tell her how she, too, might become a friend and disciple of Jesus Christ. Such desire for the Faith and such confidence in himself naturally touched his affection, and he not only promised to instruct her in the Christian religion, but also then and there asked her to be his wife, to which she agreed with much happiness. Soon she was baptised, taking the name of Matilda, and they were married. Gilbert had still to complete his crusading vow, and returned to the Holy Land, while the faithful Richard remained at home to serve and protect the young wife. After three and a half years Gilbert returned safely amid great rejoicings and they lived happy ever after, and were blessed with the son who afterwards became the great Archbishop of Canterbury.

'The contract of a Christian marriage'

The important words are 'I will.' There can be no valid marriage without free consent.

'A certain girl had promised her virginity to God, but

her father had compelled her to take a husband. On the night of the wedding, with everything prepared for the banquet, she ran away from her home and parents and fled to St. Brigid. Next morning her father came after her. But St. Brigid saw him in the distance riding with his troop ; she faced him and made the sign of the Cross in the air against him : and the whole troop was fixed to the ground. When he saw this he repented at once and he and his men were released. And so the girl was set free from her worldly spouse and betrothed to Christ, as she had vowed in her heart.' (*Vita prima*, C. 17.)

(See also story 305—St. Bathilde.)

God must come first

SS. Marcian and Nicander were two young soldiers in the Roman army who refused to offer incense to the idols and were brought before the judge. He urged them to take time for consideration, but they declined it. They were left in prison for twenty days, and then as they were of the same mind still the judge ordered them to be beheaded without further suffering. They thanked him and wished him peace.

Each had a young wife and a baby. The wife of Marcian met him on the way to his execution. She carried her child in her arms and implored Marcian to yield and save his life. He embraced her and the child, and then told her to leave him for God's sake.

The wife of Nicander behaved in more Christian fashion. She came to his trial and encouraged him : ' Look up to heaven, and keep faith with Jesus Christ.' And she went with him to his execution, carrying her child. ' You were away from me ten years on foreign service and every hour I prayed to see you again. Now I see you and rejoice. I can be proud that I am the wife of a martyr.'

Married out of the Church

(N.B. The following story could easily be retold about a Catholic boy, from the boy's point of view.)

Jessie, aged eighteen, the best Catholic out of a rather careless family, went to a dance with a girl-friend and met

CATECHISM STORIES

a boy whom she seemed to get on well with. He asked her to meet him again, and they began to go out regularly together, and after a while visited each other's home. Neither of them ever made any reference to church or religion. After twelve months or so Jessie happened to mention that she was a Catholic, but the young man showed no interest and evidently thought it made no difference one way or the other.

When Jessie was nearly twenty they decided to get married in a month's time as there was a chance of getting a house. Jessie went to see the priest, but he happened to be out; her fiancé (who was shy and disliked the idea of a church marriage) got annoyed and said: 'Oh, let's have it at the Registrar's.' So they were married at the Registry Office and went to live in another district.

For a few weeks Jessie forgot about church; then one day she noticed a Catholic church and went inside. After that she went to Mass occasionally. When Lent came round she went to confession, but when she told the priest she was married in the Registry Office he said she must not come to Communion till the marriage was put right. He told her what to do, and she said she would do it, but afterwards it seemed too much trouble. She soon stopped going to Mass altogether. When she had a baby she would have liked to take it to the Catholic church but did not know whether the priest would baptise it.

For discussion:

Would the priest baptise the baby? (*Yes, if the mother would try to bring the child up Catholic.*)

What about Jessie's marriage? (*She is properly married by the law of England, but not properly married according to the law of the Church at the present time, the year 1939. She can come to Mass but not to Holy Communion.*)

What should Jessie do to put it right? (*Get her husband to agree to go through the religious part of the ceremony, not publicly in church, but privately. He would have to sign the usual promises, about the children being brought up Catholic, etc.*)

How should she have acted before the marriage? (*She should have spoken of her religion earlier, encouraged the young man to come to church with her, should have gone earlier to the priest, if possible, should have been quite firm about being married in the Catholic church, however ' quiet ' the marriage might be.)*

(See also stories 306, 307.)

Married as a Catholic

Commissar Wesselinsky, bachelor chief of the Leningrad police, fell in love recently with a beautiful Italian girl who was on a visit to Leningrad.

He wanted to marry her—in the Soviet way. The girl said she would marry him, but it must be a Catholic ceremony.

Commissar Wesselinsky went to his chief, the Minister of Police, in Moscow.

The Minister replied : ' If you marry in a Catholic church you will have to resign your position in the police and your membership of the Communist Party.'

Commissar Wesselinsky pleaded with his sweetheart again. She was as firm as ever.

The marriage has just taken place in the only Roman Catholic church left in Moscow.

Two hours after the ceremony the bridegroom was dismissed from his post. ·Wesselinsky is a husband but no longer a police officer. (*Daily Express*, July 2, 1935.)

> * WHAT SPECIAL GRACE DOES THE SACRAMENT OF MATRIMONY GIVE TO THOSE WHO RECEIVE IT WORTHILY ?
>
> *The Sacrament of Matrimony gives to those who receive it worthily a special grace, to enable them to bear the difficulties of their state, to love and be faithful to one another, and to bring up their children in the fear of God.*

Marriage is a true vocation

ST. MARGARET (of Scotland) was a Saxon princess who had spent the first nine years of her life as an exile at the court of St. Stephen, King of Hungary. After that she was at Westminster, with King Edward the Confessor, and taught by the great Lanfranc and his monks.

*BALTIMORE 458, 466
ENGLISH CATECHISM 307

CATECHISM STORIES 375

She was about twenty-one when the Norman invasion and the battle of Hastings shattered her little world. With her brother Edgar (who had been elected King after Hastings) and her sister she escaped by sea, meaning to return to Hungary ; but storms blew their ship to a wild unknown coast, which turned out to be Scotland. There they met with uncouth, terrifying warriors, who took them to their King Malcolm.

This was the young Malcolm who figures in Shakespeare's *Macbeth* and who had overcome the murderous usurper by the help of King Edward the Confessor. He was now perhaps forty, and had been king for nine years ; but his kingdom was still very much the half-savage realm pictured in Shakespeare : religion neglected, murder and violence common, good manners, morals and learning all forgotten.

Out of gratitude to Edward the Confessor, Malcolm received the Saxon prince and princess kindly and kept them at his court. Without delay, probably at first sight, he fell in love with Princess Margaret, beautiful, refined, intelligent, seeming like a miracle from heaven in such rough surroundings. When William the Conqueror demanded that Edgar and the princesses should be handed over to him, and sent his armies to fetch them by force, Malcolm cheerfully went to war rather than surrender them. He held his own, and defeated three Norman forces, one after another, in Northumberland (it was in this war that the Normans built Newcastle-on-Tyne), and at last a treaty was made, fixing frontiers and promising the Norman King's friendship for Edgar.

Malcolm made no secret of his love for the fair refugee, and soon he was asking her to marry him. She answered, however, that she had always intended to be a nun and still hoped to return to England to take the veil as soon as she safely could. But Malcolm, though careful not to force her consent, was also persevering in his persuasions, never tiring of pointing out to her how much they could do together for the spiritual good of Scotland. At last this argument, and her own affection for the big rough-tempered soldier who had proved such a true friend, changed her mind. Marriage was evidently to be her vocation. They were married about 1070, three or four years after her arrival.

Then began the wonderful life-work which St. Margaret did for her adopted country. She sent to Lanfranc for an adviser, and he sent her Turgot, Prior of Durham, who guided her work and has written her life for us.

At first Malcolm did not always understand her ideas, but was influenced more and more by her goodness. He was as ignorant as his nobles were, could not read a word himself; but ' he used to turn over and examine her books and kiss those she liked best.' He learned to join in her long prayers at night in Lent (in her little Norman chapel still to be seen at Edinburgh Castle) and in her personal service of the poor. When Margaret gathered a big meeting of the Highland priests, to instruct them better in the Catholic religion, Malcolm acted as interpreter into Gaelic.

(For St. Margaret and her children see story 278 in Part III. Other details of her life in *Stories in School*, page 80.)

After twenty-three years of married life, happy for themselves and the Scottish people, Malcolm and Margaret died —as many husbands and wives have wished to die—at the same time.

Malcolm, with several of his tall sons, was at war again with the English, who had taken the castle of Alnwick in a surprise raid. Malcolm besieged the English raiders, who offered to surrender; they presented the keys on the point of a spear, which when the King advanced to receive them was treacherously driven into his eye and killed him. His eldest son Edward then led an assault on the castle, but he, too, was killed.

Meanwhile Margaret, now aged forty-seven, was lying at home in her last illness. On the day when (as they knew later) Malcolm was killed she seemed very sad and said: ' Perhaps this day a greater evil hath befallen Scotland than any this long time.' Four days later her second son, Edgar, arrived from the army. She asked him for news of his father and brother. Not to alarm her he said they were well. ' I know how it is,' she said. Then, lifting her hands to heaven, she praised God : ' I thank thee, Almighty God, for sending me so great an affliction in the last hour of my life, to purify me from my sins as I hope by Thy mercy,' and shortly after departed this life.

Margaret and Malcolm were buried together at Dunfermline, and during the disturbance of the Reformation the relics of both found refuge in the Escorial palace in Spain, but in the course of time seem to have been lost. The whole Catholic Church keeps St. Margaret's feast on June 10. (On care of children see stories 277–279.)

'The difficulties of their state'

Sometimes these arise from becoming too much accustomed to each other ; the attentions and consideration of courtship days should be carried on into married life.

Shop Manager (to Assistant) : ' Simpkins, are you mad ? Whatever do you mean by being so rude to that customer ! '

' Oh, that wasn't a customer—that was my wife.'

'For better or for worse'

A young man came to St. Brigid and lamented that he had lost the love of his wife who despised him and would have nothing to do with him. The saint gave him some holy water and told him to get the priest to sprinkle it all through the house, on bed and board and everywhere. No sooner was this done than, by St. Brigid's prayers, the affection of the wife turned strongly to her husband. So much so that when he got up early one morning before dawn to sail his boat on the sea she woke up panic-stricken to find him gone, searched everywhere, saw him at last from the shore, and rushed into the sea to reach him. The waves were running so high that she was drowning, but another boatman fished her out and restored her wet but happy to her husband.

(This quaint story is told in flowery Latin verse at considerable length in the *Vita Tertia*, ch. 6. It seems a little lacking in point, unless perhaps it is subtle propaganda for the religious life as a more peaceful existence than marriage ! At any rate, it indicates that St. Brigid should not be counted with those who regard matrimony as 'rather a wicked sacrament.')

Mixed marriages and their difficulties

True story. A Catholic girl, after considerable hesitations on grounds of religion, got engaged and married to a non-Catholic who promised often and fervently that he would never interfere with her practice of the Faith.

Soon after marriage, however, she found that he seemed quite without any idea of the meaning of religion, and soon he was grumbling and putting every obstacle in the way of her attendance at Mass.

She was unhappy about it but firm. He passed from jeers to threats, and the climax came one Sunday morning when in a great rage he picked up an iron bar and said if she attempted to go out he would strike her down with it.

With beating heart and a prayer for courage she calmly put her coat and hat on, and walked past her husband to the door.

He gazed after her, with astonishment first, and then with deep shame. He put the bar down and sat for a long time thinking.

When his wife got back she found him laying the table for their meal, and by several other little actions he showed his sorrow for what had occurred, but it was not until the evening that he spoke of it.

'Did you really think I'd hit you, lass?'

'I didn't know, Jim,' she said, 'but what I did know was that I was more afraid of offending God than I was of anything an iron bar could do to me.'

Never again did he try to hinder her from Mass; and gradually he learned to admire the Faith which inspired such courage and devotion, and the happy day arrived when he became a good Catholic himself.

'To love and be faithful'

A notable example of wifely devotion was a certain Lady Amabel Herbert of the seventeenth century. She was a daughter of Sir Walter Aston, known for her rare beauty as 'the Rose of England.' At Madrid, where her father was Ambassador, she met young Sir Edward Herbert (who came there with his friend the Prince of Wales, afterwards Charles I), and they were married in a few months.

They had twenty years of happiness and a large family of children. Then the Civil War broke out. Sir Edward, of course, fought for the King, and Lady Herbert followed the Royal army about as well as she could.

On the fatal summer day of Naseby she was waiting for news in Northampton, a few miles off. Conflicting reports came ; finally definite news of disaster, but no word of her husband. He must be dead, or lying wounded on the field. At midnight she determined to go in search of him, ignoring the difficulties raised by friends, and set out with one trusty servant.

She reached the battlefield and it was a fearful sight, for there was no Red Cross in those days. A thousand lay dead and hundreds of wounded and dying scattered in heaps, for whom she could do nothing when they besought her in agonising tones. There were women engaged in looting the corpses of cavaliers whom they had seen a few hours before (they said) ' as fine as peacocks.'

After a time the hope to find her husband, alive or dead, seemed all in vain. Then, ' she felt a light cold touch on her hand and looking round beheld a small dog.' It was Sir Edward's greyhound.

When, guided by that faithful creature, they found the body, it was cold and stiff. ' Alas,' said the servant to Lady Herbert, ' 'tis a lost labour. All we can do now is to procure a Christian burial.' He was mistaken. Some hours later when they had entered a deserted cottage some miles away they restored the apparently dead man to life. After that the problem was how to hide what they had done.

Sir Edward, after being moved from place to place, was hidden in a cottage in Gloucestershire, where for fear of discovery he could only occasionally be visited by his wife. And at last she went one night to find the cottage empty. Sir Edward was a prisoner, already on his way to the Tower.

CATECHISM STORIES

She followed, but soon her husband, still a sick man, was tried and condemned to die. Then she made her supreme effort to save him. Cromwell's daughter had intervened in vain. Lady Herbert was allowed to visit her husband, and one night she exchanged clothes with him and he escaped to France.

They could scarcely hang *her*. She had committed no treason. ' I had no design but to save my husband. . . . Which of you . . . would have done less? ' she asked her enemies. She herself was allowed to ' escape ' and joined her husband, whom she discovered, however, to be a dying man. Shortly afterwards he died in her arms.

She lost her eldest son at the battle of Worcester, but it was her own bravery that won the last historic campaign connected with her name. Charles II ignored the claims of her eldest surviving son until she herself went to court. ' You see,' she said, ' a family who . . . by their loyalty have lost all, save honour ; who now seek but their own, which it is in your Majesty's power to restore.' It was enough, and Charles was not allowed by some of his own courtiers afterwards to forget his good intentions.— (Acknowledgments to J. E. J. in the *Birmingham Post*.)

* CAN ANY HUMAN POWER DISSOLVE THE BOND OF MARRIAGE ?

No human power can dissolve the bond of marriage, because Christ has said : ' *What God hath joined together let no man put asunder*.'

' No human power can dissolve marriage '

THE question of divorce was settled beyond argument by Our Lord Himself. Divorce had always been permitted under the Law, but in the time of Christ there was controversy between two parties of scribes about the reasons for which divorce could be allowed. Some would allow it for any trivial reason, some only for grave reasons like unfaithfulness.

Hence the questions of the Pharisees in Matthew xix, 3-9 and Our Lord's answers. He disallows divorce

*BALTIMORE 459
ENGLISH CATECHISM 312

altogether, and admits separation only for the gravest reasons.

Marriage is broken only by death

Father Fouquet, in West Africa, baptised during the winter an old native man and an old woman, and after their baptism they were married and returned to their distant village.

In the springtime, when the Christians came back to visit the mission, the old couple were among the first, and the missionary could see from their faces that the joy of the honeymoon was indeed a thing of the past.

'Father,' said the old man, 'I am very pleased to see you. We have had a long and weary winter, and the old woman you married me to is quite unbearable. Instead of marrying her I ought to have got rid of her long ago. Please, Father, can you unmarry us?'

'Yes, Father, do unmarry us!' the old woman broke in with a torrent of indignant complaints against the husband, so that Father Fouquet had time to think things over.

'Well, my children,' he said at last, 'you *can* be unmarried, but it is a long and difficult business.'

They both insisted that they must be unmarried.

'Very well, let us begin at once. Go and wait for me in the church.'

He followed them in, taking with him his breviary and a holy water sprinkler. He made the couple sit close together in the front bench, then he knelt before the altar and began saying his office. At the end of each psalm he got up, made a big Sign of the Cross over the couple, and gave a rap with the sprinkler first on the head of the man, then on the woman. When this had gone on for nearly an hour his office was finished and no visible effect had been made on the couple, except they rubbed their rather sore heads occasionally.

'Wait a moment,' he said, 'I must fetch another book, and then I will come back and go on unmarrying you.'

He returned with a large book of spiritual reading, and after reading a paragraph he got up as before and grasped the sprinkler. But the old man took hold of his arm.

'Father, is this ceremony going to last much longer?'

'Well, it depends on the hardness of your heads. You know you were married "till death do us part," so I have to go on until one or the other of you falls to the ground and expires. But I'm not tired—let us go on.'

'Father, I think we might stay as we are—what do you think, wife?'

'Yes, it would be better. I told you so just now, when the Father went out. We had better stay married.'

So they went away happy, and nobody else has ever asked Father Fouquet to unmarry them. (*A.P.F. Annals*, October 1932.)

'Till death do us part'

If people know that marriage is 'for better or for worse' they are more likely to try to make a success of it.

Once when St. Columba was staying on an island near the Irish coast a woman came to him and said she couldn't stand her husband, who had some kind of deformity. She wanted to leave him and enter a convent, and thought Columba would help her in this devout purpose. But he said: 'It would be wicked to put asunder those whom God has joined. You are bound by the law to your husband as long as he lives. Come now, let the three of us join this day in prayer and fasting.'

So they went away and Columba prayed for them all that day and all through the night. Next morning the woman came with her husband, and Columba asked her in his presence if she still wanted to enter a convent.

'I know now, O Columba, that your prayer was heard, for during the night in a strange way my heart changed from hatred to love. This man whom I hated yesterday I love to-day.'

The saint sent them away with his blessing.

(See also stories 305, 308.)

VIRTUES AND VICES
WITH
APPENDIX

THE SEVEN VIRTUES

'One God above all, and through all, and in us all'

IF we love God, we have found the secret of the Universe; in Him the whole world lives and moves and has its being.

Guthlac (d. 714) was son of a Saxon earl, but at fifteen became leader of a roving company of bandits. After nine years of reckless violence he found himself one night filled with self-disgust and contrition at so empty a life. In the morning he told his companions to choose another leader, as he intended to take service under Christ; then turning away from their entreaties, he went to Repton Abbey where he did penance for two years. Then (aged twenty-six) he became a hermit on a remote and dreary island in the Lincolnshire fens, called Crowland. Here he lived his life of prayer, was ordained priest, and was sought by rich and poor from all over Mercia as a spiritual guide. 'Nothing stayed in his mind but charity, pity, peace and forgiveness. No one ever saw him angry, excited or sorrowful.'

We read that the wild birds and fishes would come and eat out of his hand, and the swallows perched on his head and shoulders and let him help to build their nests. An abbot-visitor wondered to see this, and St. Guthlac answered: 'Have you not read that all created things unite themselves with him who unites himself with God?'

'One Faith'

A remote pagan village in Africa was ruled by an old chieftain who had heard of the Christian religion and was anxious to hear more. One day a Catholic catechist arrived; the chief readily gave him leave to teach and took some instructions himself. But he heard of a Church of England mission being started in a neighbouring village, and when he realised that Catholic and C. of E. each claimed to be the true Christian Church he said he must study both before making up his mind. He made a journey to the nearest big town and there his difficulties were increased as he discovered the existence of a third Christian religion, a Methodist mission which had no bishops and told the chief that if he wanted to please God he must learn to read the Bible. Considerably discouraged, he went back to his village and tried to work it all out for himself; but it was too much for him and in the end he died still a pagan.

(See also story 114.)

Two Testaments

In the days before the Boer War the Jews in Pretoria came to President Kruger and asked if they, like the other 'denominations,' could receive a grant of land on which to build their synagogue. This was promised without any difficulty. But when the grant was made the Jews discovered that their site was only half the size of the sites allotted to the other religions. They went to old Kruger again and asked the reason.

'Well,' he said, 'you Jews only accept half the Bible, and not the best half of it either. If you agree to accept the whole Bible I will give you the whole block.'—*Tablet*, February 4, 1939.

We should return God's love. (Two Great Precepts)

A CATHOLIC lad was living away from home in London, and got very careless about his religion. Every morning going to work he passed a Protestant chapel, where there was usually a printed placard outside. One day a new placard said:

'*If God loved you as much as you love God, where would you be?*'

CATECHISM STORIES 387

The first morning he read it without reflecting. On the second morning he said to himself : ' Well, it certainly would be awkward ! '

On the third he made a resolution to keep to Sunday Mass and monthly communion.

' Let us therefore love God : because God hath first loved us ' (1 John iv, 19).

An instance of pure love of God is the story of St. Thomas Aquinas to whom Our Lord on the Crucifix spoke :

' You have written well about Me, Thomas. What will you have for reward ? '

' Nothing but Thyself, Lord ! '

(See also stories 7, 8, 24, 45, 229 and 244.) and 244.)

Love of God inseparable from love of man

These two precepts of Charity were given by Our Lord Himself when a scribe asked Him a stock question often debated by the scribes : which (out of the 613 commandments in the Law) was the most important commandment of all ? Our Lord took two (from Deut. vi, 4, and Lev. xix, 19) and joined them into one great commandment of Love. All else depends on that, He says. Read the incident from Mark xii, 28–34, and cf. Matt. xxii, 40.

What loving our neighbour means

Our Lord's own story, expressly on this topic, is the Good Samaritan, Luke x, 30–37.

Two main points taught :

1. That our neighbour means not merely those near to us in blood or sympathy ; but everybody, even strangers, especially anybody who *needs* our love.
2. That loving anybody means standing by them *when* they need us.

Recall great sayings of Our Lord on this topic from Matthew vii, 12 and Luke vi, 31 ; and note the advance on previous moral teaching (e.g. Confucius, or scribes) which said merely negatively : Do not do to others what you would not wish them to do to you.

(See also stories 45, 54, 57, 245-249, 293, 643, 651, 658, 659, 661.)

'Who is my neighbour ?'

St. Vincent of Paul, child of simple countryfolk in the Landes, as a small boy used to work with the shepherds. When he was twelve years old (it was 1588, year of Spanish Armada) he was sent to do some work for a neighbouring farmer, and started back home the proud possessor of thirty sous, the first money he had ever earned. He was thinking that he would not spend them, but lay them aside to begin some savings. But on the road he met with a poor man, whose rags and misery moved him to such pity that he took out the thirty sous and gave him the lot. Then he went on, lighter in pocket and still lighter in heart.

Faith, Hope and Charity. (Three Theological Virtues)

OF Faith, notable Scriptural examples are Abraham, who at God's word went out from his kindred (Gen. xii, 1-4) and believed God's promise that Sara should have a son (Gen. xvii, 19) ; the widow of Sarephta, who believed the prophets' promise that the meal and oil would not waste (3 Kings xvii, 8-16) ; the man born blind, who confessed his faith so boldly (John ix, 1-38).

Of Hope : Moses, who encouraged the terrified Israelites when they were pursued by Pharaoh (Exod. xiv, 8-14) ; Judas Machabeus, in 1 Mach. iii, 13-26.

Of Charity : Abraham, who loved God with sovereign love (Gen. xxii, 12) ; Joseph, who loved his brethren (Gen. xiv) ; the mother of the Maccabees, who loved her sons with a true charity that put God first (2 Mach. vii).

On these Theological Virtues see also stories 17 to 24, and 231 to 249.

Religious Vocation. (Three Evangelical Counsels)

A GLORIOUS episode of the early Jesuits was the martyrdom of the Portuguese Fr. Ignatius Azevedo and thirty-nine

CATECHISM STORIES 389

other fathers, novices and lay-brothers on their way to reinforce the missions in Brazil (1570). Their ship, separated from the rest of the squadron, was attacked off the Canary Isles by several vessels commanded by the Huguenot pirate Jacques Sourie. There was a sharp fight on the deck of the Portuguese ship, but its crew was soon overcome by the well-armed pirates.

Fr. Azevedo's head was cleft open, and the novices were stabbed and thrown overboard as they were helping the wounded. Some of the youngest were set to work on the pumps, but when they refused to eat some meat (for it was an abstinence day) they too were thrown into the sea. One young novice, named Simon de Aeosta, still in lay attire, was taken to the pirate-chief's ship in the hope that he might give valuable information. 'Are you a Jesuit, too ?' asked the chief. 'Yes, I am the brother in religion of those who are killed : we all belong to the same Company.' He was immediately beheaded and thrown overboard.

Commandments and Counsels

The story of the rich young man in whom Our Lord's sudden love was disappointed, and the subsequent discussion about the incident, is told in Mark x, 17-31. It is about poverty, but still more about religious vocation in general ; and illustrates clearly the distinction between Commandments and Counsels.

Faithfulness to the Vows

St. Jerome tells us the strange story of the monk Malchus, who had entered on the religious life when still a youth, and in spite of his rich father's opposition. For years he had lived happily as a monk. But when his father died, and he found himself heir to the estate, he was tempted to go back to the world. The abbot knelt before him and implored him not to abandon the life which he had begun so well ; but all in vain. Malchus left the monastery and joined a caravan going in the direction of his home in Syria.

But on the way the caravan was attacked by pagan tribesmen, and Malchus was carried off and sold into slavery, together with a young Christian woman attached to the caravan.

In captivity his mind turned back to God and his vows; and the Christian woman, too, moved by his example, made a vow to live a single life. Both held to their religion, in spite of threats of death from their pagan master.

One day Malchus sat down wearily and watched a colony of ants working with such industry and co-operation that it made him think of the peaceful orderly life of the monastery which he had deserted. There and then he made up his mind to risk everything to get back.

Soon an opportunity occurred. He made his escape into the desert, accompanied by his Christian fellow-slave. Seeing from afar their master with an attendant pursuing them on dromedaries, the two fugitives hid in a cave. The master tracked their footprints over the sand, and was about to enter the cave when he, and the attendant with him, were killed by a lioness which was crouching there as if to guard the entrance.

Malchus and his companion made their escape on the waiting dromedaries. He reached his monastery safely, lived faithfully as a monk for many years, and in his old age told his story himself to St. Jerome.

Following vocation under difficulties

' The daughter of a pagan from Baudoinville (Belgian Congo) told her father she wanted to become a nun. Stubborn refusal—and no wonder! He had disposed of her long before, and had eaten the goats received in payment over and above. The brave girl made no fuss, but slipped quietly away and engaged herself as a carrier of loads, which in reality far exceeded her strength, so as to earn sufficient money to make restitution to the would-be husband. This was supplementary work, besides her share of service at home, which she never shirked. When she finally found herself in possession of the right amount she went to her father and said: " Here is the price you once paid for me. Now I am free. God is calling me, I must go."

Again : at Bembeke (Br. Nyasaland), of five aspirants to the religious life only four presented themselves one morning. What could have become of the fervent Euphrasia ? On her way home the previous evening she had been presented with a new house and . . . a husband ! All had been prearranged by her pagan parents. Though taken by surprise, Euphrasia refused firmly. Animals had already been killed, and an amount of native beer brewed for the marriage feast. Five other girls were married in Euphrasia's village that day, and she was to have been the sixth, but all her relatives' coaxing proved vain. The poor girl had a hard and long fight for her liberty, but finally managed to resume her training for the Sisterhood.' (From *The White Sister*, Sept. 1938.)

The joy of being poor

Of all men who have become poor for the love of God, St. Francis of Assisi is the most famous. Here is the story of how he and his two first brothers received their command from God to go out penniless along the roads and preach.

A rich citizen of Assisi called Bernard de Quintavalle (town councillor, middle-aged, much respected) had watched Francis's strange behaviour for two years and been impressed by his preaching. To study him more closely he invited him to his house (see story 548). At last he told St. Francis that he wished to give up his wealth, his house, and his position and follow him in his poverty for the love of God. It must have seemed a big responsibility to St. Francis, still only a young man. So he suggested that they better go to the church and see if they could find in the Gospel some words of Christ which would guide them what to do ; as, once, the Gospel for the day had guided St. Francis himself to go forth completely poor —even without shoes. So they set out. And on the way they called for another friend of theirs—a learned man called Peter Cathanii, who also wanted to serve God perfectly, and had been trying humbly to learn how from St. Francis.

In the church St. Francis prayed that he might come on the right place, and then he went to the big book of Gospels which was there for all to read, and opened it. This is what he read out : ' If thou wouldst be perfect, go, sell that thou hast, and give to the poor, and thou shalt have treasure in heaven ; and come, follow Me.' (Matt. xix, 21.)

That seemed just right ! But perhaps Our Lord had still another message. So he shut the big book and opened it again, just anywhere, and it said : ' Take nothing for your journey, neither staff, nor scrip, nor bread, nor money ; neither have two coats ' (Luke ix, 3).

The third time they came on something very hard to follow, which was really the explanation of all the others :

' If any man will come after Me, let him deny himself, and take up his cross, and follow me ' (Matt. xvi, 24).

So the three friends left the church very happy, and Bernard sold his house and his land and all his rich stuffs ; and Peter sold all his precious books ; and they carried all the gold and silver to a square in front of the old Church of St. George, and St. Francis sat on the steps with his lap full of money ; and gave away great glittering handfuls to all the poor people who crowded round. It was a glorious orgy of giving and of contempt for money. A priest named Silvester came up ; he had sold Francis some materials for repairing the church of San Damiano, and now thought he had not been paid enough and came prepared to haggle. ' You want some more money ? ' cried Francis cheerfully. ' Certainly—here you are ! ' And he shovelled piles of coins into Silvester's arms. The priest went home, thought very hard, and later on joined St. Francis himself.

When the last coin had been distributed Francis and Bernard and Peter, smiling with delight at being really poor and truly free to follow Christ, went down the hill to the little chapel in the woods and began their life as comrades in holy Poverty.

Francis never forgot that day of grand largesse. When he lay dying he sent for Bernard (to come and share a special dish that was prepared for him), and placed his hand on his head to give him the blessing of the first-born. 'Write this,' he said to his secretary Leo : ' The first brother God gave me was Brother Bernard, who began with me to fulfil entirely the holy Gospel and distributed all his goods to the poor. For that and many other reasons I am more bound to love him than any other brother. Let the ministers and all the brothers look on him as they would on me.'

When Francis was dead Brother Elias set all the friars collecting money to build the Basilica at Assisi, over the saint's body, and put up a marble vase there to receive money offerings. Brother Leo smashed the vase and was scourged and banished. Bernard made strong protests, too, and after some years had to escape to Mount Sefro, where he lived as a hermit till Elias was deposed.

In 1241 he was living in Siena, venerable and kind and full of stories of Francis for the younger friars. When his time came to die he made a celebration of it, and invited all the brothers from round about to a great feast of cherries. 'I beg that you will all eat with me my last supper.' After they had eaten he said his last words to them, ending : ' For a thousand worlds I would not have been other than a servant of Christ. Hear my prayer, that you love one another.'

So with face joyful and shining he leaned back and died. (See also stories 617 and 644.)

The Vow of Chastity

St. Brigid, who was the daughter of a king and one of his bond-women, was wonderfully beautiful and on that account was sought in marriage by rich suitors ; but she had vowed herself to God. Her father, however, was anxious to get her married to a certain nobleman and cared nothing about her vow. So Brigid prayed that she might become ugly instead of beautiful so that the nobleman would not want to marry her. God answered her prayer by a dreadful ulcer that broke out on her eye. All her beauty was gone, and her father allowed her to receive the veil of the religious life from St. Maccaile. As she knelt with her seven companions on the altar steps and made her vow (says the story) her eye was suddenly healed and she rose up more beautiful than ever. People always said that she bore the likeness of Our Lady herself, and she was called ' the Mary of the Gael.'

(See also stories 266, St. Lucy ; and 310, St. Edmund.)

The power in Obedience

Two noblemen admiring the holiness and learning of St. Benedict each sent their son to be educated by him.

Maurus was a boy of twelve and the younger one, Placid, was only five. Benedict watched over them and cared for them till they learnt not only to obey him but to love him as their own father.

It was a healthy, happy life for two boys, and when lesson time was over they could clamber over the rocks or wander on the sunny mountain-side looking for wild flowers, nuts and berries.

Sometimes in a dry season the mountain springs would fail, and then Placid and Maurus would take turns to fetch water from the lake near by.

One day as St. Benedict knelt at prayer he suddenly saw a vision of the younger child stooping to fill his pitcher at the water's edge. As he watched the boy slipped, and before he could utter a cry for help the water closed over his curly head. Calling Maurus to him St. Benedict told him to run to the lake to rescue the little boy from drowning.

Although unable to swim Maurus ran to do the saint's bidding. Arriving at the lake side, and seeing Placid struggling in the water, Maurus ran forward on to the lake's surface, and as he ran the water became firm under his feet so that he reached the drowning boy and was enabled to drag him to safety. Thus did Almighty God reward by a miracle a boy's unhesitating obedience to his superior.

Obedience is fruitful

In one of the Egyptian monasteries a man came and asked to be admitted. The abbot told him that the chief rule was obedience, and the man promised to be patient on all occasions, even under excessive provocation. It chanced that the abbot was holding a dried-up willow-wand in his hand; he forthwith fixed the dead stick into the earth and told the newcomer that he was to water it until, against all the rules of nature, it should once again become green.

Obediently the new monk walked every day two miles to the River Nile to bring back a vessel of water on his shoulders and water the dry stick. A year passed by, and he was still faithful to his task, though very weary. Another year, and still he toiled on. Well into the third year he was still trudging to the river and back, still watering the stick, when suddenly one day it burst into life.

This story is related in the *Dialogues* of Sulpicius Severus, on the authority of an acquaintance named Postumianus who had travelled in the East. ' I myself,' said the latter, ' have beheld the green bush—the former dead stick—which flourishes to this day in the atrium of the monastery. Its waving green foliage is a living witness to the mighty virtues of obedience and faith.'

The treasures that cannot be taken away. (Three Eminent Good Works)

IN the story of Tobias we read that the younger Tobias returned home with his unknown companion, and the old father thanked the latter for all he had done, and asked him to accept half the money that had been recovered. But the young man refused, and told them the secret of who he really was:

' Bless ye the God of heaven, because He hath shown His mercy to you. It is good to hide the secret of the King, but honourable to reveal and confess the works of God. *Prayer is good with fasting and alms; more than to lay up treasures of gold.* When thou didst pray with tears and didst bury the dead I offered thy prayer to the Lord.

And now the Lord hath sent me to thee. For I am the Angel Raphael, one of the seven who stand before the Lord.' They fell on their faces with awe, and he wished them peace and was taken from their sight.

These three good works represent our complete offering to God : by prayer we offer our soul to Him, by fasting our body, and by alms-deeds whatever else we have.

Our Lord speaks of the same three good works in Matthew vi, and speaks of them also as true ' treasures ' that cannot be lost (Matt. vi, 1–21).

Rejoicing in the Living God

Bernard de Quintavalle, wealthy and influential citizen of Assisi, had for two years watched with interest the seemingly crazy conduct of young Francis Bernardone. He was aware himself of a desire for God and a gift for prayer that had never had full exercise : could it be that this much ridiculed play-acting dandy-turned-beggar had the secret of it ? Wishing to study Francis more closely and judge his sincerity, he asked him to supper and stay the night. He made up a bed for him in his own room.

They retired, and Francis pretended to be asleep at once. Bernard kept still, too, but watched by the dim light of a tiny lamp. Soon he saw his guest rise from bed, kneel up, and spend the rest of the night in prayer. From time to time words came from him like a great sigh of delight : always the same words—' Deus meus et omnia ! ' ' My God and my all ! ' Francis, who had left all earthly possessions, was enjoying the one Treasure worth having.

Next morning Quintavalle told Francis he was ready to join him and begin life anew. For the rest of the episode see story 543.

Later, as one of the friars, he gave himself to humble nursing and begging, and his leisure to contemplation. St. Francis, while he lived, ' right willingly spake with him by day and night ; and so they were sometimes found together rapt in God the whole night long in the wood, where the two of them had met to speak of God together.'

In after years ecstasy came easily to Brother Bernard,

CATECHISM STORIES 397

sometimes even when he was walking with another friar, and he would cling to a tree for support. But he preferred to cease labours for times of contemplative refreshment, and eight days without such a break seemed to him like eight years.

(See also stories 161 and 167-170.)

The quality of prayer

Two friends arranged to go a bicycle ride after school. It is a glorious summer afternoon ; a particularly dull lesson ; how anxiously they keep looking at the clock ! At last they are free. Soon they are out in the country, lying for hours perhaps by some river bank, eating or reading, talking or silent, happy, wishing the sun would never set, content just to be together.

Our prayer-time, truly speaking, should be like that : rest and refreshment. If we say our prayers as an unwilling task, anxious to get them over, it is not true prayer. Instead, settle down to enjoy them—to enjoy a little time with our God, the fulness of all joy.

(See stories 163-166 and 594.)

Daily actions can be made into prayer

A certain Brother Bonaventura was the monastery cook, and a very good one. When he had finished work he would retire to prayer, in which he enjoyed heavenly consolations. To get more time for this he begged the superior to relieve him of his work in the kitchen. He got his request and was able to pray for longer hours ; but he found that the sweet consolations had vanished and instead he was tormented with dryness and distractions. Seeing his mistake, he humbly begged his superior to let him go back to the kitchen, and again his prayers became a time of spiritual delight.

Self-denial as a form of prayer

A priest (it is told of the late Fr. Petit, S.J.) had tried everything to get an old man dying in hospital to make his peace with God. All in vain. The more he tried the more the old man blasphemed. The priest paced his room : 'What can I do to save this poor soul?' At last he smiled, an idea struck him : 'Ah, yes—that cup of coffee ! '

At the end of his lunch the housekeeper arrived as usual with the cup of black coffee.

'No thank you, Mary—not to-day.'

'Father, what's the matter? Are you ill?'

'Ill? No, what makes you think that?'

'Well, Father, you've never refused your coffee after lunch before. In fact if it wasn't ready you always rang for it. You must be ill not to want it when you've taken it so regularly all these years.'

Just then the door-bell rang. It was a message from the hospital—the poor old sinner had asked for the priest to come, and Fr. Petit had the joy of assisting him to make a holy death.

(See also story 554.)

Fasting as penance

The great forty days' fast proclaimed in Ninive (Jonas iii, 1-10) shows one purpose of fasting, namely penance for sin.

The pleasures of renunciation

St. Macarius, hermit, once received a city visitor who brought him a large fresh bunch of grapes : an acceptable present in the torrid desert, especially for one whose diet was nothing but herbs. But to the saint the wonderful grapes seemed not so much an opportunity for eating but rather an opportunity for self-denial and for an act of kindness. He sent the grapes with a message of greeting to the nearest hermit in the desert.

A few days later, when he had forgotten all about it, a messenger arrived from another hermit, bringing a message of greeting and a bunch of grapes—yes, it was the very same bunch, not a grape missing !

A brief enquiry revealed what had happened. The

CATECHISM STORIES

first hermit had had the same holy idea as St. Macarius and had passed on the grapes to another; and that one to another, and so on, till they had gone the round of all the hermits in the district and returned to their starting place.

The saint fell on his knees and thanked God that such graces of self-denial and charity had blossomed in the desert.

(See also stories 79, 568.)

Suffering can help prayer

All pain and suffering comes under the name of 'Fasting,' if willingly accepted. When thus kneaded into our prayers it greatly increases their power.

This again is one of the things we can learn from the ' Little Flower.'

She was dying of consumption, and the doctor who attended her remarked: ' If only you knew what this young nun is suffering ! Never have I seen such suffering borne with such supernatural joy.'

' Oh, my Mother ! ' she said to the superior, ' what does it signify to write eloquently [as she had often written herself] about suffering ? That means nothing—nothing ! One must be *in* it ! '

One night the infirmarian found her awake.

' What are you doing ? You ought to try to get some sleep.'

' I cannot, Sister, I'm in too much pain. So I'm praying.'

' What do you say to Our Lord ? '

' I'm not saying anything. I'm just loving Him.'

(See also stories 78, 79.)

The minor trials of life

At the Jesuit College of Majorca in 1604 the Forty Hours was being celebrated, and the chairs from all the rooms of the community were borrowed for use in the church. When they were returned afterwards the chair of lay-brother Alphonsus (Rodriguez) was somehow forgotten. The holy old man (aged seventy-three at the time) made no complaint or remark, and for a whole year he managed with no chair to sit upon or put his clothes on at night. He would have been thus content for the rest of his life, but next year when the Forty Hours had ended a chair was brought back to his room.

(See also stories 199 and 564.)

Christian care for the poor

In A.D. 258 the Emperor Valerian issued an edict that all bishops, priests and deacons should at once be arrested and put on trial. The Pope (Sixtus II) was one of the first to be seized. He had entrusted the treasury of the Church to the deacon Laurence, with instructions to distribute everything to the widows and orphans, which Laurence did, even selling the sacred vessels.

As the Pope was being taken to execution Laurence followed him in tears.

'Where are you hurrying to, holy Father? And what have I done—why are you going to the sacrifice without your deacon? I have done your command with the treasures of the Church.'

'I am not leaving you, my son. You will follow me in three days.'

Laurence was soon arrested. The Prefect demanded that he should produce the treasures of the Church.

'The Church is indeed rich,' said Laurence. 'I will show you the treasures, but give me a little time to gather them.' Time was given, and Laurence went over the city seeking the widows and orphans and lame and aged whom the Church supported. He gathered them all together in rows in front of the church, then went and brought the Prefect. 'Here are the Church's treasures!'

The enraged Prefect promised Laurence a slow and painful death, and he was chained to a gridiron over a slow fire. So great was his desire of God that he seemed not to feel the torment. After some time he said to the Prefect: 'Let my body be turned now, one side is roasted enough.' He was turned by the Prefect's order, and soon he said:

'Now it's done enough—all ready to be served.' He then prayed for the conversion of Rome, that through Rome the world might come to the Faith ; and lifting his eyes to heaven gave up his spirit.

(See also stories 202, 557, 596–600.)

The open hand

One Easter King Oswald of Northumbria was sitting down to dine with a number of important guests, including St. Aidan, the monk from Iona who christianised many parts of the North of England. The King and his guests were hungry for they had fasted late to receive Communion at the Easter High Mass. A great silver dish of different kinds of roasted meats was placed before the King, that he might take the first portion before his guests were served. At that moment one of his servants came to him and said that a large number of poor people, hungry and destitute, were at the gate, hoping for an Easter meal. Stretching forth his hand to the steaming dish, St. Oswald called two servitors and said : 'Bear this to my poor people, and when they have eaten, cause the dish to be hewn in pieces, that each one may have some silver as his Easter alms.'

The hungry guests watched the dish being borne away, and waited—perhaps impatiently—for more food to be brought for them. One guest was not impatient, but delighted at what he had seen. St. Aidan, taking the hand of the King that had given the Easter alms so generously, said : 'This hand will never see corruption.'

His prophecy was fulfilled, for when St. Oswald fell in battle his followers took his hand as a relic, and it was preserved in Bamborough Church (and later at Peterborough), and from a chronicle of six hundred years afterwards we know that it was then still incorrupt.

Alms-giving at the expense of others

There was once a boy scout who after going to bed remembered that he had not done his 'good deed' during the day. So he got up out of bed, took his white mouse of which he was very fond, and gave it to the cat to eat.

This was kindness to the cat, no doubt, but at the expense of the white mouse.

It is like people who show a misguided generosity in alms-giving while they don't pay their debts or a proper wage to their employees.

The Four Gospels

The writing of the four Gospels can be told in narrative form ; some points will be found in *Twelve and After*, p. 39.

Here is a story showing how the Gospels were valued by one of the saints.

' Margaret was very fond of her precious books. Most beloved of all was a little book of the Gospels. Malcolm could not read, and did not know what it was ; but he knew it was the book she loved best. One day she did not find it in its usual place and was searching for it in great distress. Just then the King entered, and after asking what she was looking for, and pretending to think she was over-distressed at the loss, suddenly drew his hand from beneath his tunic and she saw that he had her little book, but now resplendent in a binding of gold and precious stones. After that he asked her to read to him from it, and he grew to love the story of Our Lord's life nearly as much as she did herself. You can see the very book now if you go to the Bodleian Library at Oxford.' (*Stories in School*, p. 82.)

Prudence. (Four Cardinal Virtues)

PRUDENCE (or we might say Forethought) is the virtue which makes the right use of means towards the End.

The parable of the Wise Virgins (Matt. xxv, 1–13) can be read as it stands ; our lighted lamp is the life of grace, needing to be fed with the oil of the Sacraments.

If we may judge from Our Lord's parables this virtue of Prudence, of practical common sense in our salvation, being *ready* at all times, is a thing He wishes to put in the front of His teaching.

Various aspects of Prudence are pictured in the Talents (Matt. xxv, 14-30), the Unjust Steward (Luke xvi, 1-9), Hidden Treasure (Matt. xiii, 44), Pearl of Great Price (Matt. xiii. 45).

(See also stories 11-16.)

Justice for all

St. Margaret of Scotland was full of charity to the poor; but this would not have sufficed if she had not also shown them *justice*. At first there were no courts where a poor man could plead his case and have his wrongs redressed. So St. Margaret, the Queen, went out herself, and, sitting on the rock where she had first rested when arriving in Scotland, let her poor subjects gather round and explain their grievances, and she herself settled their disputes. This, however, was only the start. Gradually she got the King to appoint judges and to have courts established all through Scotland, where the poor and weak could get equal justice with the rich and strong.

(See also stories 322, 329, 349, etc.)

Fortitude means courage

Fortitude means the courage of attack as well as the courage of endurance. Here is the story of a boy's rising to the occasion in the course of duty.

In the days when the British Navy was occupied in suppressing the slave trade, the *Black Joke* brig, under Lieut. William Ramsay, lay at anchor at Fernando Po, April 22, 1831. From a passing vessel the commander heard that in the Old Calabar River was a large armed Spanish slaver brig, ' the finest slaver that had been on the coast for some years.' Its officers when on shore had made no secret of their intention to fight if necessary. With one large pivot and four broadside guns, and a complement of over seventy men, they reckoned themselves more than a match for the *Black Joke*, which carried only one long pivot gun and one carronade, and forty-four officers and men.

The *Black Joke* at once proceeded to Old Calabar and waited some days outside the river-mouth until one morning early the slaver emerged under all sail. There was a long chase and a running fight until after midnight, in which the slaver would no doubt have escaped if the wind had not fallen so light that both vessels had to use their sweeps (oars).

'At about 1.30 a.m. of the 26th the *Black Joke* was so near that it became evident a close action must ensue, upon which the Spaniard hauled up his lower sails, and with his sweeps so managed his vessel as to keep up a determined fire—almost every shot telling upon the spars, rigging and sails of the *Black Joke*. Lieut. Ramsay, in consideration of the heavier weight of metal of his adversary, and actuated by a desire to spare as much as possible the lives of the wretched slaves, resolved upon boarding, and a light air fortunately favoured his intentions. Meanwhile the men were ordered to lie down and shelter themselves from the enemy's fire. Two steady men were appointed to lash the vessels together, the two guns were loaded with grape, and their captains ordered to fire directly the word "Board" was given. All being prepared, the *Black Joke* ran alongside the Spaniard, the preconcerted order was given, the guns fired, and Lieut. Ramsay, with the mate and ten men, simultaneously leaped on board; but from the force with which the two vessels met they separated again before the rest of the boarders could follow. The position of the little band on the hostile deck, opposed to more than seventy antagonists, was extremely critical, when Mr. Hinde, a midshipman not fifteen years of age, who was the only officer left on board the *Black Joke*, with extraordinary presence of mind ordered all hands to the sweeps, pulled alongside, got the vessels lashed, and then boarded, leaving only one or two wounded men behind in their own vessel. With this reinforcement the combat was speedily decided; those who continued to offer resistance were cut down and the rest ran below and begged for quarter.

The prize proved to be a brig of 300 tons, one of the most beautiful vessels ever seen afloat, mounting five 18-pounders, with a complement of seventy-seven officers and men, of whom fifteen were killed or drowned, four desperately wounded, and several others severely and slightly. The *Black Joke* lost only one man killed, and Lieut. Ramsay, Mr. Bosanquet, the mate, and five men were wounded. Over the sufferings of the unfortunate 496 slaves on board we will draw a veil : suffice it to say that, from the necessity of confining them below during the chase and subsequent action, 26 were suffocated, and of the remainder 107 were found in a deplorable state from their confinement and want of air, and of them 60 died after they were landed at Fernando Po.' (*Deeds of Naval Daring*—Gifford.)

(See also stories 22 and 592.)

The courage of endurance

Early in the thirteenth century the lord of Viscaya was at war with Alonzo King of Leon, and one of the key fortresses was the impregnable castle of Gujar. A knight named Marco Gutierez was in command there. Alonzo hoped to gain possession of it without fighting, but Gutierez was proof against all his bribes and threats. Then Alonzo laid seige to the castle, a long and terrible siege that went on for seven years. At last the brave defenders, worn out and starving, died one after the other. Gutierez alone remained alive, still refusing to open the gates. With all his strength gone, he put the keys round his neck, lay down inside the inner gate and awaited death with calmness.

Meanwhile the besiegers had planned a new assault. Scaling the walls with long ladders, they found no resistance ; but in the courtyard below they came upon Gutierez, helpless but without fear, still refusing to surrender.

King Alonzo was moved to tears of compassion at the sight, and instead of carrying out his threats he cared for the heroic knight and set him at liberty.

Accepting trials gladly

To welcome suffering along with Christ is the best kind of self-denial.

At Salamanca in the early days St. Ignatius was put in prison on suspicion of heresy. Somebody came and expressed sympathy with him in this misfortune. 'Misfortune!' said Ignatius. 'You must have little love for Christ in your heart if you think it a misfortune to wear chains for his sake. I tell you in all Salamanca there are not as many chains and fetters as I long to wear for the love of Jesus Christ.'

(See also stories 80, 497, 655, 665.)

Thanking God for hardships

John Rigby was a Lancashire layman, a manservant, who suffered for the Faith under the Act of Uniformity. In prison an order was made to put an iron chain on him. When the keeper brought it Rigby said: 'Put it on in God's name,' and when it was fixed 'I would not change my chain for my Lord Mayor's great chain,' and he gave the keeper sixpence for his trouble.

When the jury gave their verdict, the foreman spoke softly. 'Speak up and be not afraid,' said Rigby. The verdict was Guilty, and Rigby said in a loud voice: 'Laus tibi Domine, rex aeternae gloriae!' The judge said: 'Good Rigby, think not that I seek your death. Will you yet go to church?' 'No, my lord.' 'Why then, judgement must pass.' 'With a good will, my lord.'

After being sentenced to be hanged, drawn and quartered he said: 'Deo gratias! all is but one death, and a flea-bite in comparison of that which it pleased my sweet saviour Jesus to suffer for my salvation.'

There is a cross for each one

A legend. An Egyptian desert hermit visited the great city. It was market-day, and one merchant had a stall offering nothing but little gold crosses. The hermit asked their price.

'I do not sell them. Those who love the cross can take one for nothing.'

'Ah then, if there is nothing to pay I can take this one. I thank you!'

'My brother,' said the strange merchant with a smile, 'it is good to hear thanks for a cross.'.

The hermit returned to his desert home and soon fell ill with a fever. He recovered, but the attacks returned again and again, and his health failed more and more.

He had forgotten the little gold cross, but one day he felt it in his pocket and pulled it out and examined it carefully. On the back in small letters he saw, what he had not noticed before, the one word, '*Fever.*'

Then he realised that the strange merchant was Christ. Already he had endured the fever with patience, but henceforward he accepted it with joy as the cross given to him by Our Lord Himself.

(See also story 79.)

A schoolboy wrote home : 'Send me two shillings for Lent. I haven't got any money, and I'm giving up sweets, but there wouldn't be any merit in it unless I had the money to buy them.' He would have done better if he had accepted willingly his lack of money ; the best 'mortifications' are those that just happen. (See also story 497.)

Taking God's part

Notable examples of Fortitude in Scripture are David against Goliath (1 Kings xvii, 1–54), Elias before Achab (3 Kings xviii, 1–20), and the mother of the Machabees (2 Mach. vii, 1–42, but it is better to shorten the narrative and stress the mother's counsel to the seventh son, verses 25–29). In the New Testament, besides the supreme example in the Passion we might take the Apostles before the Council (Acts iv, 1–23 ; v, 25–42), and the martyrdom of St. Stephen (Acts vi, 8 ; vii, 59).

(See also stories 250, 252.)

Control of appetite

B. Henry Suso (Dominican mystic of Constance, fourteenth century), when meal-time came, was accustomed to kneel in spirit at Our Lord's feet and ask Him to be his guest at table. He pictured Our Lord to be sitting in the place opposite and would often give a friendly glance towards his imaginary Guest. He would offer his food and cup to be blessed by Our Lord, and would ask Him to eat or drink a share of it. It was his custom to drink only five draughts, in honour of the Five Wounds. Being specially fond of fruit, for two years he never touched it; but afterwards he took it moderately so as not to seem singular.

(See also stories 344 and 628-633.)

Right use of money

The virtue of temperance is concerned with many other things besides eating and drinking, e.g. money.

' They say money talks. What does it say to you ? '
' Generally good-bye ! '

The eternal facts. (Four Last Things)

THREE explorers in South America were captured by a remote tribe of Indians. At last they managed to escape, with enough food to last some time. For fear of being seen they hid themselves all day and travelled by night; they had no maps or compass, but guided themselves by the stars. This worked all right at first, but then they had to go through a vast forest in which were narrow tracks often branching in all directions. The trees were so close and over-arching that the stars were mostly hidden, and this part of their journey was the most difficult and perilous. But whenever there was a tiny clear space of sky they studied the heavens carefully and so managed to keep direction, reached the great river they were making for, and were picked up by a passing steamer and taken to civilisation.

The truths of Faith—God, our heavenly destiny, the four last things, Our Lord and His grace, etc.—these are the stars on which we need to keep our eyes fixed, but the outward shows of the world crowd upon us (like the trees in the forest) and hide the eternal facts.

(See also stories 11-16 and 192.)

We must all die some day

Dr. William P. Rothwell, known as a 'good fellow' to his friends because he always paid the bill at social gatherings, and whose booming comment, 'This is on me,' was a local byword, was buried at Pawtucket, Rhode Island. yesterday, under a large stone he had set up in a cemetery bearing his self-chosen epitaph : 'THIS IS ON ME.' (*Daily Express*, July 1, 1939.)

(See also stories 11 and 12.)

Calm preparation for death

St. Phocas was a Christian gardener who lived near what is now called the Black Sea. He grew flowers and fruit, and was hospitable to all comers. One evening three soldiers came by, looking tired after a long journey, and Phocas asked them in and gave them supper. They confided to him that they were looking for a Christian of the name of Phocas, with orders to behead him when found.

'He lives hereabouts—perhaps you can tell us where.'

'Yes, I know him well. But it is late now. Sleep in my house to-night, and to-morrow I will point him out to you.'

The soldiers accepted his hospitality gratefully and went to rest. Then Phocas took a spade and set to work to dig a hole in the garden. All night he worked and prayed, and in the morning the task was finished. When the soldiers got up they found their host standing by a newly-dug grave.

'I promised to show you Phocas. You need go no farther, I am he.'

The three soldiers were aghast at the idea of killing the man who had been so kind to them.

'Don't be afraid. You see I am prepared—here is my grave all ready. You have only to carry out your orders. Otherwise you will be afraid to go back.'

It was true, they dared not disobey their orders. One of them drew his sword and stepped forward, Phocas knelt with bowed head, and in a moment his head was struck off and his soul was with God in the everlasting garden of heaven.

Ready for the last crossing

Following is from the reminiscences of Fr. Finnegan, O.M.I., Electric Chair Chaplain at Huntsville, Texas. He had (by 1939) attended one hundred and sixty-one condemned convicts, of whom eighty became Catholics before execution.

'George Brown, the assassin of an entire Texas family, has left with me an indelible memory. As he stepped out of his cell to walk to the chair, Brown turned to me: "You have been very kind to me. I don't mind the electric chair now. When I shall get to the other side, I shall pray God to keep you here long and help many other poor devils like me." "Brown," said the prison Governor, "have you any message to give to those here present, before we bind you?" "Yes," he replied, "one word. Fellow prisoners, prepare, as I have done, for the last crossing. Thank God, Father Hugh has helped me to settle my accounts. Cheerio, everybody." He kissed the crucifix as I held it to his lips, sat down without any fuss, and six minutes later was dead. . . .'

A good conscience need not fear death

At a favourite execution ground in the Casa de Campo, Madrid, at the beginning of the civil war, 1936, a priest was brought along in a car and put up against the wall to be shot. He pulled out a gold watch.

'This is all I have,' he said to the firing squad. 'I give it to the one who proves himself the best shot.'

Impressed by his courage in the face of death, the militiamen lowered their rifles and told him to get away. (*Birmingham Gazette* in August, 1936. See also story no. 2.)

Death is the gateway to Heaven

Siena and Perugia were at war, and a young Perugian in Siena, Niccolo di Toldi, had been condemned to be

CATECHISM STORIES 411

beheaded for speaking against the Government. Frantic at the injustice, he refused the Sacraments, and St. Catherine undertook to do what she could with him. Her visit melted his heart; he prepared for death, and made her promise she would be with him at the hour of his execution next morning.

She kept her promise and was with him at Mass and Communion. His only fear now was that he would not be brave at the last moment; he laid his head on her breast and implored her to stay with him. She promised that she would be waiting for him at the scaffold.

'I waited for him, therefore,' she wrote to her director, 'at the place of execution, with continual prayer, and in the presence of Mary, and of Catherine, virgin and martyr. I besought and implored Mary for this grace: that he might have light and peace of heart at the last moment, and that I might see him return to God. Then he came, as quiet as a lamb, and seeing me he laughed and asked me to make the Sign of the Cross over him. I did so, and said: " Up to the wedding feast, my sweet brother, for soon you shall be in everlasting life." He knelt down with great meekness, and I stretched out his neck and bent over him, reminding him of the blood of the Lamb. His lips said nought but Jesus and Catherine. And as he said it, I received his head into my hands.'

She seemed to see his soul entering the glory of God, and turning first to bow in grateful farewell to Catherine herself, as a bride bows to her friends who have escorted her to her new home. 'Then was my soul at rest. . . . I could not bear to have removed from my garments the blood that had fallen on them.'

The certainty of death and judgement

A young man came into the confessional and the priest gave him the blessing.

'Excuse me, Father, but I haven't come in to make a confession really. I've only come to win a bet.'

'Whatever do you mean, my son?'

'My friends dared me to come, and one of them bet

me a round of drinks that I wouldn't, and I took it on. They're all in church now to watch me do it.'

The priest was appalled at the sacrilege.

'Don't you know that confession is a holy sacrament, and you are profaning it?'

'I'm not worrying about that, Father.'

'Aren't you afraid that God will punish you?'

'I'm not worrying about that either, Father.'

Before such a brazen face the priest felt helpless and remained silent a while. Then he said:

'Well, you've carried out your programme and now I'll carry out my duty. I can't give you absolution, but I will give you a penance. For the next month, every night you will repeat these words: There is a just God, but I'm not worrying about that. I shall die some day, perhaps to-night, but I'm not worrying about that. There is a hell for the unrepentant, but I'm not worrying about that.'

The young man left the confessional, rejoined his friends, and told them everything the priest had said. They had a good laugh and said that he must perform the penance before he could rightly claim to have won the bet. So he promised to do it, and actually did so. But as he repeated the words night after night they sank into his mind and heart, and in a week he went back to the church and made a genuine confession.

(On Judgement, see also stories 91–97 and 595.)

No appeal from God's Judgement

It is possible to deceive ourselves and our confessor, even on our deathbed; but before the Judgement Seat of God all pretence is ended at last.

The Socialist leader Wallisch, idol of the workingmen of Vienna, was about to be hanged for his part in the fighting of 1934 between the Socialist Party and the Catholic government.

Somebody asked him if he would like to see a priest.

'There is no need, thank you. I shall soon be seeing the priest's Boss.'

CATECHISM STORIES 413

He was a brave man, honest in his unbelief, a worker for social justice. The men who ordered his death were themselves overthrown by the Nazis soon afterwards and many of them executed.

May the just Judge have mercy on us all!

We may lose our soul

This is taught incidentally by several of Our Lord's parables, even though the main point of them is something else; e.g. the Wedding Garment (Matt. xxii, 1-13), the Ten Virgins (Matt. xxv, 1-12), and the Sheep and Goats (Matt. xxv, 31-46). And especially Lazarus and the Rich Man (Luke xvi, 19-31), in which we can point out that the picturesque details of heaven and hell are in the Jewish language of the time.

It is possible to lose our soul for ever

Perhaps we usually think of hell as a danger for others, but it is a danger for every one of us.

A German missionary in Africa went home on leave and came back with a fine set of large coloured pictures to illustrate his sermons. They were a great success. Every Sunday after the sermon the natives rushed to the picture and discussed it with excitement.

One day the sermon was on Hell. The natives seemed very impressed, and the priest went off to breakfast hoping that the picture of the lost souls would fix the impression. Before he got inside his house he heard screams of delight and laughter, and turned round to see his congregation dancing with glee in front of the picture of hell. Very indignant, he strode back to the crowd.

'Silence! What do you mean by all this noise? Hell is not a laughing matter!'

One of the natives took him by the arm up to the picture.

'Don't you see, Father? Look—all the people in hell are *white!*'

(On Hell, see also stories 140-142 and 479.)

'Because they deserve Thy dreadful punishments'

There was once in the old days in the Abruzzi a dangerous brigand named Maltivoglio. He was captured, but not enough evidence could be gathered of his many crimes, so he was put on the rack to make him confess.

But he had made his preparations for this beforehand. On his right foot was tattooed a small picture of the gallows, and every time he felt himself about to confess he would look at the picture and say to himself: 'Maltivoglio, that is what you will get if you give in!' And so he managed to endure all the pains.

In the same way the Christian should have in reserve the thought of hell to keep him from sin if higher motives fail.

No repentance in the next life

The Mission Father was asking the children some questions to see if they had understood his instruction.

'Now, supposing you died in a state of mortal sin, where would you go, Johnny?'

'Hell, Father.'

'Yes! and whatever would you do then?'

'Go to confession, Father.'

'Go to confession? And who would you go to confession to?'

'You, Father!'

* * *

We must either save our soul or lose it for ever.

'Ah, well, there's a good many worse than I am,' people say sometimes.

But if we lose our soul there will be little consolation in finding sinners in hell more wicked than ourselves.

'Well, did you pass your exam, son?'

'No, Dad, but I'm top of those who didn't.'

Hell is complete and final Failure.

Our choice at death is final

St. Martin's biographer tells us that the saint once tried to convert the devil. Some of the monks (he says) heard the devil insulting Martin and accusing him of receiving ns monks who in earlier life had committed crimes. The devil mentioned the monks and their crimes. 'They have repented,' said Martin, 'and the Mercy of God has pardoned their sins.'

'There is no pardon for criminals,' replied the devil. 'When one has fallen from grace, he can expect no mercy.'

'Not so,' exclaimed Martin. 'Even you, unhappy one, if you would cease to pursue mankind, if you would repent to-day now that the judgement day is near, I am so sure of the mercy of the Lord Jesus Christ that I would promise you pardon and peace!'

If the damned would repent they would be pardoned; but they would rather stay damned than repent.

The choice our will makes as we leave this life (theologians say) cannot change once we enter the spirit-world.

What is hell like?

The main thing about hell is the final loss of God. Beyond that we must admit we know very little about it. What is meant by the 'fire' of hell? How many souls go to hell? The answer to such questions is—we just don't know.

'A Galway man who admired realistic oratory, speaking of a favourite preacher said : " He preached a sermon on hell, and you'd think he was bred, born and reared in it." ' (*Irish Humour*, by M. O'Mahony.)

Desire of heaven

If we realised what the 'beatific vision' of God is, we should long for it as the saints do.

Frederick Myers was asked by a churchwarden : 'What do you really think will happen to you when you die?'

'I suppose I shall go to everlasting bliss, but I wish you would not talk about such disagreeable subjects.'

(On Heaven see also stories 149 to 154.)

Our true home-country

St. Pamphilus was a priest of Cæsarea in Palestine, martyred under Diocletian in 309. He had conducted a school of religious teaching, and was especially busy in copying and diffusing the scriptures, continuing this work even in prison.

A number of his disciples had become martyrs before their master. We are told that it was the thought of heaven and its joys which not only sustained them through fearful torments, but filled them with a manifest happiness that staggered the pagan onlookers.

Whenever a Christian was brought before the Governor the first question was : ' What country do you belong to ? ' The answer given by the martyrs of Cæsarea was always the same.

' My country is heaven. Our God and Saviour lives there now, since He rose from the dead. He has prepared a place for us. Heaven is my home and I shall soon be there.'

And the pagans, with nothing to hope for after death, watched the Christians so full of faith and joy, and many rushed to become converts on purpose to share the same martyrdom and the same hope.

' The Spirit of the Lord.' (Seven Gifts)

THE Seven Gifts were first spoken of as such by the prophet Isaias, who saw the future Messias with the Spirit of the Lord resting upon Him, in the Seven Gifts (read Isa. xi, 2–3).

So of course the whole of Our Lord's life is a story illustrating the Seven Gifts in example or teaching. For instance :

Wisdom :	Luke ii, 47–49 ; x, 38–42.
Understanding :	Mark viii, 33 ; Matthew ix, 13 ; xii, 7 ; Luke xxiv, 25.
Counsel :	Matthew xxi, 1–5 ; Luke ix, 53–56 ; Luke vi, 12–17.
Fortitude :	Matthew xvi, 21 ; xx, 17 ; xxi, 12 ; xxvi, 42 ; xxvii, 12, 34 ; Luke vi, 7–11.
Knowledge :	Luke iv, 17–22 ; John vi, 6 ; vi, 15.
Piety :	Luke ii, 49 ; iii, 22 ; x, 21 ; xxii, 42 ; xxiii, 46 ; John xx, 17.
Fear of the Lord :	Matthew x, 28 ; John iv, 23–24.

CATECHISM STORIES

Remembering our final end. (Wisdom)

Wisdom is the virtue by which we keep our eyes fixed on the End for which we exist, and judge all earthly things accordingly.

Jewish legend says that Solomon, the wisest of all men (see story in 3 Kings iii, 5-15, of his dream-prayer for an understanding heart), was once visited by a king from afar who asked a favour.

'Give me,' he said, 'a sentence to remember, one which will help me both in times of trouble and in times of prosperity.'

The sentence Solomon gave him was : '*This too shall pass away.*'

In after life, when that king was crushed by adversities, he would say to himself : 'This too shall pass away,' and patience and courage would return. When he was prospering and all men spoke well of him he would say : 'This too shall pass away,' remembering not to be too much lifted up, since all earthly joys will fade.

(See also stories 7, 8, 9, 11, 230, 570, 578.)

'The foolishness of God is wiser than men.' (Wisdom)

When the Oberammergau Passion play was performed in 1922 (it is done only every tenth year) an American film magnate offered the villagers a million dollars if they would make a cinema version for him. They regarded this as a temptation, because it seemed incompatible with their real object in performing the play, which has always been purely for the glory of God. They refused the offer firmly. To make quite sure that there should be no change of mind some of the performers cut off their long hair which had been allowed to grow for their parts in the play. In a worldly sense their refusal was foolish, but doubtless true wisdom in the eyes of God.

'Lord, that I may see.' (Understanding)

Pius XI one day was passing along the rows of pilgrims at an audience when his eyes fell on a blind boy. He stopped and lifted his ring to the lips of the lad, who began to tremble with emotion, whilst tears streamed from his vacant eyes. '*Caro*,' said the Pope consolingly, 'we are all blind.' That is, until God enlightens us. We are not able to see what the great facts of our Faith mean, except in so far as the Holy Spirit inwardly shows us by the gift of Understanding.

' O guide our minds with Thy blest light.' (Counsel)

For stories on the Gift of Counsel (i.e. grace of prudent foresight and decision in practical affairs) we need not go outside Our Lord's parables, which constantly stress the point.

Building a tower, etc. (Luke xiv, 25–33).
Ten Virgins (Matt. xxv, 1–12).
Talents (Matt. xxv, 13–30).
Treasure and Pearl (Matt. xiii, 44–46).

Also perhaps the incident of Martha and Mary in Luke x, 38–42.

Crosses need to be grasped firmly. (Fortitude)

A certain holy nun had many afflictions and began to sink into discouragement. She felt that God had deserted her. One night God sent her a dream. Our Lord came to her, wounded, crowned with thorns, bearing a huge cross. As He came nearer she saw that He had a second cross too, but a smaller and lighter one. He held it out for her.

"Take up your cross, My daughter, and follow Me.'

She followed Him up a steep hill, often forcing a way through thorns and briers. Her feet were soon bleeding, and the cross seemed heavier and heavier; in desperation she called to Our Lord for help.

He did not come back to her but turned round and spoke.

' The right way to carry your cross is to clasp it firmly, and place your feet in My footsteps.'

She clasped her cross firmly and at once it grew lighter. She carefully observed wherever Our Lord's feet trod, and saw that in those places the thorns disappeared and

CATECHISM STORIES 419

flowers sprang up immediately in their place. The rest of the journey to the top of the hill seemed easy, and as Our Lord turned to congratulate her she awoke with a heart full of new courage and even eagerness to share in His Passion.

(See also stories 78, 497.)

The conquest of Fear. (Fortitude)

Fr. Isaac Jogues, French Jesuit apostle of Canada, was ordained priest aged twenty-eight in 1635, and landed at Quebec the following year. With a fellow Jesuit he travelled and preached among the Indians around the great lakes, and reached places on Lake Superior where no white man had been seen before. After six years of constant perils, he and his party were attacked by some Iroquois of the Mohawk tribe. Fr. Jogues was struck down unconscious, and as he came to his senses two Indians were biting off his fingers with their teeth.

He was taken captive, with his two companions, and for two months was carried round the Indian villages and constantly tortured; beaten till covered with blood; pegged down to the ground and live coals put on their bodies; fingers burned by slow fire.

On one occasion one of Fr. Jogues' thumbs was sawn off. Having already lost his forefinger, he thought he could never say Mass again. He picked up the severed thumb, and said: 'I offer it to Thee, O God, in remembrances of the holy sacrifices I have offered for seven years, and in atonement for my want of love when I touched Thy sacred Body.'

For thirteen months he then lived as a slave, under the most degraded conditions, in the village of Ossernenon (now called Auriesville), not far from the Dutch Protestant settlement of New Amsterdam, now New York. Meanwhile the story of his adventures and sufferings had reached France and made his name famous. At last, when he was about to be burned alive, the Dutch traders persuaded him to escape in one of their trading-boats, and they sent him across the ocean to France.

He landed on the coast of Brittany and made his way to the Jesuit College at Rennes, where the lay-brother at the door took him for a wretched beggar. He insisted on seeing the Rector, and said he had news from Canada.

'From Canada?' said the Rector. 'Do you know Fr. Jogues?'

'I know him well.'

'Is he alive or dead?'

'He is living—I am he.'

He was received with great honour at the royal Court of Versailles. The Pope granted him a special privilege of celebrating Mass, even with his mutilated hands. 'He is a martyr of Christ,' said the Pope. 'It would be strange if he were forbidden to drink the Blood of Christ.'

In France Fr. Jogues was treated as a hero and a saint, but he took the first ship he could back to Canada. He returned to Ossernenon where he had been a slave, but this time it was to arrange a treaty of peace between the French and the Iroquois. In the autumn he came again on a preaching-mission to the Mohawks. The crops had failed, and some of the Indians said it was on account of the evil spirit of Fr. Jogues.

The Iroquois dug up the hatchet and sent out a war party to capture him. His escort of friendly Hurons fled, but Fr. Jogues continued on his way to Ossernenon. The Iroquois warriors met him near Lake George, stripped him and slashed him with knives, beat him and dragged him to the village. There, a few days later, he was struck down with a tomahawk and his head was cut off. He was canonized, with seven other martyrs of Canada, in 1930.

(See also stories 78–80 and 620, St. Agatha; and various English martyrs, 114, 118, 154, 234, 286, etc.; 469, St. John Nepomucene.)

The science of life. (Knowledge)

When St. Dominic was still a young student in Palencia, there was a famine.

He spent all his money to relieve the poor, and sold his furniture, too. He had nothing left but his books, and

CATECHISM STORIES

when the famine continued these, too, went in the same way.

A friend came in and was aghast to see the empty shelves.

'What sort of knowledge should I get out of dead books,' said Dominic, 'while living men, brethren of mine, were dying of hunger?'

True knowledge is knowledge of God's Will, and other knowledge is useless unless it helps in that.

The essence of prayer. (Piety)

St. Teresa of Lisieux, motherless from the age of four, was devoted through her childhood to her earthly father, enjoying her companionship with him, and seeking to rejoice his heart with her love.

As she grew older this love became the pattern of her love for her Father in heaven. For her, all religion was summed up in her 'little way,' which meant simply loving God as her Father.

As a child she had much pleasure in praying, especially at Holy Communion. 'Tears of happiness welled up and overflowed,' she said, describing her first Communion (age eleven). 'All the joy of heaven had come down into one heart.'

But when she entered the convent these consolations came rarely; for the most part she was dry and drowsy at prayer-time, feeling no attraction towards the things of God. She was glad of this, because it meant that her *will* could be directed to God all the more clearly. Nothing for herself; 'all, all shall be for Him.'

'Sometimes when I am in such a state of spiritual dryness that not a single good thought occurs to me, I say very slowly the Our Father.'

Her whole idea of praying was to rejoice the heart of God her Father by giving Him as much love as possible. 'From the age of three I have not refused the good God anything.' She would not have any special desires in her prayers but only a general desire to be united to His Will in every least thing.

'It has pleased Almighty God to reveal to me that the only way to perfection is the way of the little child who sleeps without fear in its father's arms.'

Her last words as she was dying were : ' Oh, I love Him ! My God . . . I love Thee ! '

(See also stories 2, 17, 24, 183, 184.)

God our Judge. (Fear of the Lord)

When St. Chad was Abbot of Lastingham, he received into the monastery a nobleman named Owini, who tells us how the saint, watching the various moods of Nature across the great sky of the Fen country, was reminded of the eternal truths of God. Sunshine no doubt put him in mind of God's love for us ; but what Owini noticed more was St. Chad's reaction to bad weather. When the wind began to blow threateningly, he thought of God's warnings, and he would say : ' God have mercy on all poor sinners.' When the wind rose to gale force he would close his books and kneel in prayer. And sometimes, when the whole sky was darkened and lightning and thunder rent the air, he would go to the church and pray till the storm was over. Owini asked him why he did this.

' Because, my son, it is the Lord who moves the air, and sends the thunder and lightning. He sends it to put us in mind of that Day when He will come in His majesty to judge the living and the dead. So in the storm we should fear and adore God and repent of our sins.'

No doubt he thought of Our Lord's words : ' As the lightning cometh out of the east and appeareth even unto the west, so shall the coming of the Son of Man be.'

(On fearing to offend God, see also stories 134, 137, 479.)

Our Judgement will be decided on what ? (Seven Corporal Works of Mercy)

THE original story about the corporal works of mercy is Our Lord's parable in Matt. xxv, 31–46, in which the whole list occurs except the burying of the dead.

If we are to believe Our Lord, these ' corporal works of

CATECHISM STORIES 423

mercy' are the main point on which our judgement is to depend.

Why? Because they are the practical test of whether we love our neighbour, and the love of our neighbour is the practical test of whether we love God.

For 'burying the dead,' the Scriptural examples are Tobias i, 18–25 (add xii, 12) ; and also Joseph of Arimathea and Nicodemus.

'You did it unto Me'

The saints often have experiences which enact these words of Our Lord.

St. John of God (d. 1550) was a Portuguese boy who ran away from home for adventure at the age of nine, worked as a shepherd in Spain, fought as a soldier against French and Turks, tried to ransom Christian slaves from the Moors, and lived at Gibraltar and tried to help God's cause by selling holy books and pictures round the countryside.

Then in his forties he was 'converted' by a sermon, and showed his contrition by lamenting his past loudly through the streets of the city, beating his breast. He seemed off his head, and was put into an asylum. There he gave himself to the care of the sick and suffering, and thus found his true vocation.

He came out and began to gather poor men who were homeless, put them in a house which he rented, and supported them by work and begging. After a time others joined his efforts, and they became an order of nursing brothers.

He used to search the streets for the sick and the homeless. One night he found a destitute man who seemed to be dying. He picked him up in his arms (as his usual custom was), carried him to the hospital, laid him on a bed and washed him. After washing his feet he knelt to kiss them, and was startled to see them appear as if pierced with nails, the head of each nail glowing with light. From the bed a voice spoke to him :

'John, to Me is done all you are doing to the poor in My name. It is My hand that is held out to receive the alms you give. Me you clothe, Mine are the feet you wash.' Then (the story ends) John looked up full of consolation, and the vision had vanished from sight.

Christ comes disguised

A Portuguese romance tells the story of a young man who travelled to the Indies to seek his fortune, and in a few years returned to Lisbon with several ships laden with wealth.

'Now,' he thought, 'I will play a trick on my relations.' He put on some worn-out clothes and went to see his cousin Pedro.

'Here I am, your cousin John: after some years in India, I have come back home. You see how I am fixed —can I stay in your house for a time?'

'Ah, my dear John, how I wish I could put you up! Alas, there isn't a room free in the house.'

John went round to another friend, and another, and everywhere found the door closed against him. Then he returned to his ships, put on some expensive attire, sallied into the town with a fine retinue of servants, and purchased a large mansion in the main street. In a day or two his fabulous wealth was the talk of the city.

'Who could have imagined it!' said the relatives and friends who had received him so coldly. 'If only we had known! How differently we should have acted! But it's no good now—we have spoilt our chance with him for ever.'

Our Lord Himself comes to us under the guise of all who need our help.

The duty of social justice

Old people often have a bad time, but not many years ago (say 1900) things were far worse for them. In the olden days, when most people had a house, a bit of land, rights on the common, etc., people were able and willing to support their old parents. But in the eighteenth and nineteenth centuries people were driven from the land into towns and factories; their wages were so low and uncertain that they could not keep themselves and their children, let alone old parents. Old people no longer able to work usually had to go into the 'workhouse' as paupers. Workhouses were much like prisons; and in the workhouse the old couples were separated into different buildings for men and women.

Many people thought that this was right and reasonable, most thought it unfortunate but unavoidable. A few people said it ought to be changed, and they formed a society to urge Parliament to grant Old Age Pensions. Naturally they were called all sorts of names, and people said it would be the ruin of England and the Empire; such things ought to be done by charity (they said), not out of the public funds. But the society kept on with their writing and speaking, others joined them, and in a very few years everybody began to say they were right, and all the political parties began to put Old Age Pensions on their programme. Then the Act was passed (1904) and gave old people five shillings a week at seventy; not enough, but it made all the difference to a good many.

The best way of performing the corporal works of Mercy in these days is to change the bad laws that make people poor. Private charity will always be needed, but it can never take the place of social justice.

(See also stories 201, 360, 649.)

True love for the poor

St. Elizabeth of Hungary (for whom see story No. 306), in the spirit of her model, St. Francis of Assisi, was a shining example of the corporal works of mercy.

As a child she had learned from her parents to love the poor. When she came to live at the Wartburg she would give all her pocket-money to the beggars at the castle gate, and go round the kitchens and pantries to find what food she could for them.

After her marriage with Louis her charities had full scope, though they were a sore point with the officials. One legend tells how she was one day going down the rocky path loaded with a basket of food for some hungry family, when she ran unescapably into her husband with all his hunting-party. He jumped down from his horse to greet her, and shyly she tried to conceal her burden with her mantle. But he drew the mantle aside, teasingly, and there instead of the expected food was a basketful of beautiful out-of-season roses ! He took one to keep, and as he rode on he was full of awe at the miracle wrought by God to glorify the charity of his beloved Elizabeth.

Louis was away at the Emperor's court when a great famine afflicted the country-side. Elizabeth took charge, and gave away all the corn in the royal granaries and all the money in the royal treasury. Every day she fed nine hundred poor people who lived near the castle. When Louis came back he agreed with everything she had done.

Many of the poor people had no clothes to go even to work in ; so when the famine was over she distributed a shirt and new shoes to all able to work, and clothing and money to the others. Then she divided her own rich silk robes and veils amongst some of the poor women, ' not to wear but to sell.'

For the sick she always had a great tenderness, especially for lepers, whom (in imitation, no doubt, of St. Francis) she loved to attend to with her own hands.

'One day she found a poor man—a leper—suffering terribly. Perhaps he was a wandering beggar ; anyhow, he had no bed to lie on and rest after she had dressed his wounds, so she took him back to the castle, and laid him on her own bed ! Her mother-in-law was very angry, and when Louis came in she said, "See, someone she loves much better than you. See, your wife lays lepers upon your bed, and it will give you the leprosy." This time Louis really felt a little bit annoyed. He snatched off the covering, and then stood still, full of wonder and awe ; for, as the old book says, "The Lord opened the eyes of his soul," and he saw lying upon his bed the form of Jesus Christ, with pierced hands and feet, and wounded side.

All stood speechless for some time, until the vision faded ; and then Louis, with the tears running down his face because of what he had seen, told Elizabeth to do all she liked in her charity, and let no one trouble her.' (*Stories in School*, p. 41.)

She established a hospital with twenty-eight beds at the foot of the Wartburg, and went every day to tend the sick there. There was a children's ward there, too, for sick, or orphaned, or deserted children. They used to crowd round Elizabeth crying ' Mother ! ' One day she was bringing some toys for them, little trinkets of glass and earthenware ; her carriage was somehow upset on the rough road, she was thrown out and the toys were spilled and rolled all down the hill, and everybody said it was a miracle, because not one of the toys was broken.

' How can I thank Thee enough, Lord, for letting me gather here these dearest friends of Thine, and serving them myself! ' Somebody heard her pray this aloud, while working in the hospital.

Let us add two other points which complete her seven corporal works of mercy.

When still a child princess at the Wartburg she would sometimes visit the unhappy prisoners in the dungeons, and take them what comforts she could.

When she had to leave the Wartburg as a widow, and her children were taken from her, she was sent to stay with her uncle, the Bishop of Bamberg. He was bent on finding another husband for her, for she was still only twenty, but while Louis was living she had taken a vow not to marry again in the case of his death. While she was at Bamberg her husband's followers brought his body back from Italy, and she was able to bury her beloved dead. This she did, weeping floods of tears, in the family burying-place of her people in the monastery of Reinhardsbrunn.

When her friends had recovered her dower-money for her, she used it to build a Franciscan hospital at Marburg, and spent her whole time tending the sick there, wearing the habit of the Third Order of St. Francis. She was still only twenty-four when she died in 1231.

Giving drink to the thirsty

If something special is desired for 'giving drink to the thirsty,' a good example is St. Giles (France, about A.D. 700). In his younger days he served the king and had no lack of money, but was always giving it to the poor. If a stranger enquired where he dwelt, he would be told: 'Go into such a street, and look for a crowd of poor people—that will be the house.' Every day he entertained some poor people in his house, serving them before he took his own meal. It is particularly mentioned that he gave them wine to drink, although he never drank wine himself.

Passions must be under control. (Seven Capital Sins)

TRUE story. A party of young English officers went big-game shooting in East Africa. One of them shot a lioness, and afterwards, finding her cubs, took them back to his Norfolk home.

He fed them by hand until they could feed themselves, and every day used to romp and play with them. As they grew their play sometimes got a little rough, but still the young man amused himself with his unusual pets.

Then the time came when it was considered wise to have the animals confined in a cage with iron bars, but their owner persisted in going into their cage to play with them as before.

He disregarded the warnings of those who feared the lions' strength, till one evening, when the animals were almost full grown, the young man went to visit them as usual. Dusk was falling, and as their owner closed the barred door of the cage behind him, one of the beasts made a spring at him. Before help could reach him the young man was dead, killed by the pets he had pampered.

If we do not gain the mastery over our passions and keep them under control, one day they will master and destroy us.

(See also stories 10, 146, 209-212, 304, 344, 406, 429, 477, 568.)

The seven weaknesses of human nature

The school clock turned unreliable. The caretaker wound it regularly, the head-teacher kept putting the hands right, but it would not keep time; it was always slow, or fast, or stopped altogether. The life of the school, lessons, and play alike, was upset owing to the clock.

At last the man who supplied the clock was called in, and listened to the head-teacher describing the symptoms.

'It's no use regulating the hands,' said he. 'There must be some dirt in the works that is causing all the trouble.'

He cleaned out the inside, and the clock once more kept good time.

It is much the same with our souls. When we fail to do right, and develop sinful habits, the real trouble is something inside us, some 'predominant passion' that is a source of sin.

Different people have different tendencies, but the main sources from which all temptations arise have long been classified into seven—the Seven Capital Sins. It is our business to become aware which of these is our own special danger, and to cleanse our soul from its effects as far as possible by confession and self-denial.

(On this subject see also story 128, The seven terraces of the Purgatorio.)

Spiritual pride

The Pharisees represented Jewish religion at its best and most spiritual (at least in their teaching, which was in many respects akin to Our Lord's), and for that very reason they were specially liable to the sin of self-righteousness.

Our Lord pictures it in the parable of the Pharisee and publican (Luke xviii, 10).

I should not compare myself with other people, but with myself as I ought to be, or better still with the holiness of God.

Another parable ('Friend, move up higher,' Luke xiv, 7-11) teaches a similar lesson, and can easily be told in story form.

Arrogance

Some examples of pride given in Sacred Scripture are:

Pharaoh, who hardened his heart against the will of God (Exodus v to x, and xiv).

Goliath, who gloried in his own strength (1 Kings xvii, 1–52).

Roboam, whose display of arrogance led to the division of Israel from Juda (3 Kings xii, 1–24).

King Ozias, whose heart was lifted up by prosperity, and he tried to usurp the priestly office (2 Para. xxvi).

Aman, who was the ambitious favourite of Xerxes, and whose anti-Semitic plans were foiled by Queen Esther (Esther, iii to vii).

Herod Agrippa, who allowed himself to be acclaimed as a god (Acts xii, 18–23).

The achievements of Man

Pride means making oneself the centre of everything, instead of God. Not only individuals do this, but also men collectively, when they try to build empires and civilisations apart from God.

In Genesis xi, 1–9 we have a teaching story about the very earliest city-civilisation in Mesopotamia.

Miles of earth-mounds still remain by the banks of the Euphrates to show where the city of Babylon arose in the dawn of history. There remain also the bases of the vast Ziggurats, or pyramidical towers used as temples, but not for the true God.

The Chaldean and other empires rose and fell for thousands of years, but always defeated by the disunity of tribes and nations. Only through God and His Church can the human race truly come together and be truly civilised.

Vainglory

Vanity is a lesser sin than Pride, and is a weakness of smaller minds.

Penitent : I have been very vain of my good looks, Father.

Confessor : That wasn't a sin, my child, it was only a mistake.

(See also stories 312 and 313.)

CATECHISM STORIES 431

'Quia mitis sum et humilis Corde'

Our Lord was at pains to teach the disciples vividly the lesson of true humility: amongst His followers he is greatest that is most willing to be servant of all.

So the incident of the child in the midst (Mark ix, 32-36; Luke ix, 46-48).

Then in the Upper Room Our Lord gave the apostles (and us) a supreme picture of His humility when He knelt before each of the disciples to wash their feet. (Story in John xiii, 1-17.)

'Learn of Me'

In America a party of men in charge of a corporal were hard at work unloading a wagon of wood. There were not enough men for the job, and when presently a passer-by stopped and spoke to the corporal the latter grumbled about the difficulty of six men being expected to do the work of ten.

'Why don't you lend a hand yourself, then?' the stranger enquired.

'Me?' said the corporal indignantly. 'I'm the *corporal!*'

The stranger said no more, but took off his coat and set to work to help with the unloading; when it was done he put on his coat and went on his way.

Later the corporal learnt that his voluntary assistant had been none other than Washington, President of the American Republic.

So do the truly great follow the example of Our Blessed Lord and do tasks that little men think beneath their dignity.

The charm of humility

The natural result of knowing one's right place towards one's Creator and one's fellow-men is an unassuming demeanour, of which numberless examples are told in the lives of the saints.

St. Bathilde (see story 305), after handing over the

government to her eldest son, founded a Benedictine convent at Chelles, near Paris, and retired there to end her days as a nun. She was not the only queen there—there was also St. Hereswith, sister of St. Hilda and queen of the East Angles The two queens took the lowest place amongst the novices, and were only happy when their rank was entirely forgotten and they were put to menial duties. Once Bathilde was asked how she could enjoy such a lowly life after her years of power and wide influence for good. She said : ' When I think of my Lord and Saviour Jesus Christ, King of kings, and Lord of the Universe, who came not to be waited on but to serve, and when I see Him washing the feet even of a traitor, I know not where to put myself, and I could not imagine a greater happiness than to be trodden under foot by all.'

.   .   .   .   .   .

St. Bonaventure, the great Franciscan saint and theologian, heard that the Pope intended to make him a Cardinal. He fled from Italy, but the Pope summoned him back and sent two messengers to meet him with the Cardinal's hat. They found him at a friary near Florence. He was washing up after dinner, and they held out to him the hat there and then. ' You must excuse me, my hands are dirty,' he said. ' Please hang it there ' (he pointed to the branch of a tree close by) ' and take a walk in the garden till I have finished my work.' When the dishes were all washed he picked up the hat with much sorrow and went to thank the messengers.

.   .   .   .   .   .

St. Thomas Aquinas, at the height of his fame, was lecturing at Bologna and staying in the Dominican priory there. One day one of the friars was sent on some errand into the city and told to take with him some other friar, the first he saw. The first he saw happened to be a visitor unknown to him, walking up and down the cloister deep in thought. Summoned without ceremony, St. Thomas (for he it was) obeyed and followed the friar at once.

But he was not a fast walker, being considerably on the stout side, and could not help lagging behind his energetic leader. 'Come along, come along!' said the friar impatiently. But as they went on he noticed that his stout and perspiring companion was being observed by all and saluted with great respect. Finally one passer-by stopped him and asked: 'Isn't that the Angelic Doctor, Thomas Aquinas, that you have with you?'

The friar was overwhelmed and poured out his apologies; St. Thomas said: 'Not at all, not at all! Only I am so sorry I could not walk as fast as you wanted.'

. . . . . .

Fr. Vincent McNabb has related the following anecdote of the great Scriptural scholar, Père Lagrange, O.P.

'I always remember one incident that was told to me. A group of young priests wanted to make a pilgrimage to the Holy Land and, incidentally, they longed to have speech with Père Lagrange.

'They travelled by a French boat where they had the privilege of an altar for saying Mass. After going on the boat, a rather poorly-dressed friar from the steerage came along and asked them if he might say Mass the next morning.

'Rather unwillingly they agreed, telling him that he might say Mass after they had said theirs. Morning after morning he came to say his Mass and then went back to the steerage.

'When the young priests arrived at St. Etienne to call on the great master it was the grubby little friar from the steerage that they found to be Lagrange.'

(See also stories 592—Fr. Jogues arriving at Rennes—and 637.)

Humility is not pushful

St. Anthony of Padua, specially gifted by God from his youth, was already becoming greatly valued for his knowledge and eloquence in the great abbey where he was a Canon, when he felt God's call to become a poor Franciscan friar.

The minister who took charge of him did not realise that he was a gifted scholar and sent him to a humble friary on the top of a rocky mountain. There were only a few simple friars there. One of them had hewed out a little cave in the rock. This he gave to St. Anthony, who made it his cell. There he spent most of his day in prayer. But one job he specially made his own—washing up the plates and dishes.

He didn't tell the friars anything about himself and, of course, they never guessed that their new brother, who always chose the meanest jobs, was a nobleman's son and a scholar of one of the greatest monasteries in Portugal.

For a year St. Anthony lived like this. But God meant His faithful servant to be made known.

In the town near by there was one day a meeting of Franciscan and Dominican friars for an important ceremony. After the service the Superior asked the Dominicans to preach a sermon. But they all said they were not prepared, and so did the Franciscans. So the Superior turned to St. Anthony, who had come as a companion of his minister, and ordered him to preach. St. Anthony tried to get out of it, but finding he must obey, he walked slowly up into the pulpit.

The friars did not expect much of a sermon. This was only poor Brother Anthony, whose chief job was washing dishes.

Soon the friars sat up and stared. The young unknown friar was pouring forth a wonderful flood of eloquence. Only a scholar could preach like that, and only a scholar who was full of the fire of the Holy Ghost could move the hearts of his hearers as this man did! They quite forgot the preacher, and were carried away by his words into a greater love of God. When at last he ceased, and walked quietly down from the pulpit, his eyes on the ground, deep humility in his heart, his hearers turned to each other in wonder and delight, and all said they had never yet heard such a preacher.

When St. Francis was told what had happened he was delighted to hear he had such a wonderful man among his friars. It ended in his sending St. Anthony to do what

CATECHISM STORIES

many years ago he had longed to do—that is, preach to the heretics who were opposing the Catholic Faith.

(For other anecdotes of St. Anthony see stories 38 and 653.)

'Be merciful to me a sinner!'

One element in our humility is remembering our own faults.

A famous Father of the Desert was Moses the Ethiopian. He had originally been an escaped slave, and then captain of a robber band. At the age of forty God's grace came to him. He went to a monastery, made a public confession to the monks of all his crimes and secret sins, and asked in tears to be admitted. The rest of his life he spent in penance and prayer, till he was martyred by some barbarian soldiers.

One day there was a meeting of the hermits to decide what to do about one of them who had committed a serious fault. Moses did not attend until a second summons was sent to him. When at last he arrived amongst the waiting hermits he was staggering under a heavy basket, carried on his back. Everybody could see it was filled with sand. 'What is the basket of sand for?' somebody asked. 'These are my numberless sins,' he replied. 'I still have to carry them, though they are behind me—and yet I am sent for to judge the sins of others!'

The brethren were so impressed that they decided to pardon the delinquent.

Avarice

Judas is always regarded as a melancholy instance of this. The common purse of Our Lord and the apostles was in his keeping, and perhaps he allowed avarice to take possession of him (John xii, 4-6; xiii, 29; Matt. xxvi, 14-15).

The passion for security

Our Lord's parable of the rich man and his well-filled barns (Luke xii, 13-31) teaches the futility of covetousness.

Greed takes us to hell

A rich and respectable woman died and was very indignant to find herself in hell. She made such a noise that St. Peter heard and asked one of the angels what it was about.

'Somebody in hell thinks she ought not to be there—she says there must be some mistake.'

'That's not likely.' But the clamour continued and St. Peter sent the angel to investigate. He returned. 'She says she has always been *very* respectable and *deeply* respected, and evidently some blunder has been made.'

'Well, ask her if she ever did anything kind to anybody.'

The angel went back and asked the question. The woman thought a long time, and then began to say all over again that she had always been so respectable.

'Yes, but have you ever done anything *kind?*' More thought, and then : yes, she had once given an onion to a tramp ! The angel went back to report.

'Well, an onion is something. Take that onion and hold it out to her, tell her to hold on to it and you will draw her up to heaven.'

So the angel did so and the woman held on and was drawn up out of hell. But the other people in hell saw her rising, and ran and held on to her skirts, and others held on to *them*, and soon the angel was lifting the whole population of hell towards heaven. When the woman saw that she was indignant :

'Let go ! ' she said. ' Let go, all of you ! It's *my onion !* '

As soon as she said that word the onion broke and she fell back into hell with all the others ; and after that St. Peter doesn't take any notice, however much noise she makes.

(This is from Miss M. Royden, who attributes it to some Russian short story writer.)

Greed does not pay

Two boys sat on the bank of a pool fishing. They used a simple rod and line with a worm, no hook. Soon their glass jar had several tiddlers in it. A few yards away a man was catching roach and perch.

'Why don't we ever catch a big fish instead of these tiddlers?' asked Johnny. 'Our worms are as good as his!'

Tom, who was older and more experienced, gave the reason.

'His worms are on a hook, and ours aren't. Sometimes a big fish goes for our worm, but when he feels himself being pulled he lets go, and there is no hook to hold him.'

'Why can we catch tiddlers then?'

'Because the tiddlers are so greedy they won't let go, even when they feel themselves being pulled. It's the greediest ones that get caught.'

'Oh look! I've got another bite!' cried Johnny. 'Oh —lost him after all! Well, what about *that* tiddler—he couldn't have been so greedy, could he?'

'It was you that was greedy that time—you snatched the line and snatched the worm out of his mouth.'

Travel light to heaven

During a set-back in the conquest of Mexico, 1520, Cortez and his little army of a few hundred Spaniards, with some friendly Indians, planned to escape from the city unobserved by a night march across a causeway which crossed the lake. The vast treasure of gold which had been gathered was abandoned.

'Take what you will of it,' said Cortez to his men. 'But be careful not to overload yourselves. He travels safest in the dark night who travels lightest.'

Some of the soldiers took ornaments which were small but valuable. 'But the troops of Narvaez' (says Prescott's history, referring to some reinforcements which had only recently joined Cortez) 'showed no such discretion. To them it seemed as if the very mines of Mexico were turned up before them, and rushing on the treacherous spoil, they greedily loaded themselves with as much as they could carry or stow away in wallets and boxes.'

The night march began, in darkness and rain. But some Aztec sentries observed them and gave the alarm in the city. The priests sounded their shell-trumpets, the ominous beating was heard of the huge war-drum in the temple of the war god. The causeway was soon beset by Aztec warriors in their war canoes, showers of arrows fell among the Spaniards out of the darkness.

Two gaps were known to exist in the causeway, and a portable bridge had been brought along to cross with. But in the darkness and confusion something went wrong, and at the second gap the retreat was held up till corpses and wagons and boxes of gold made a sort of bridge to pass over. Worst of all, a third breach was found further on, and here the cavaliers had to swim their horses across as best they could, with the infantry men holding on.

Only a comparative few of the Spaniards escaped from the carnage and reached the safety of the friendly Indian tribe. ' Those fared best who travelled lightest ; and many were the unfortunate wretches who, weighed down by the fatal gold which they loved so well, were buried with it in the salt waters of the lake. Few of the rearguard escaped. It was formed chiefly of the soldiers of Narvaez, who fell the victims in some measure of their cupidity.' (Prescott, *Conquest of Mexico*, Book V, c. 3.)

(For other stories on Covetousness and its opposite, see under Seventh Commandment, stories 317–320 ; and Tenth Commandment, stories 347–358. Also story 588 in this volume.)

Money is a danger to salvation

The aircraft-carrier *Courageous* was torpedoed in September 1939, with the loss of nearly half the twelve hundred men on board. She began to heel over almost at once, the lifeboats could not be launched, and the men were ordered to get into the water. They undressed hurriedly, and on all sides men were going through their money, keeping the notes and throwing away the coins.

' In my belt,' said one survivor, ' I had fifteen shillings

CATECHISM STORIES 439

and ninepence. If a man's going to be in the sea for any length of time, even fifteen shillings and ninepence begins to drag. So I took the money out of the belt and flung it into the sea. Suddenly the ship took a dive still lower into the water. I had a momentary glimpse of the captain with his hand raised in salute to the colours, and then we were in the sea. . . . I saw a Carley raft and swam to it, and was quickly joined by a lot of other chaps.'

The Christian looks on money as likely to be a hindrance in the saving of his soul.

You can't take it with you

At a secondary school they had an occasional examination paper on general knowledge and current events. One question, soon after the famous oil-king died, was : ' How much did Rockefeller leave ? ' One boy answered : ' Every farthing.' It was not the expected answer, but the examiner gave him full marks.

(On meanness or generosity towards religion, see stories 373–376 ; towards the poor, 556–558.)

Surrender to unchastity is failure

In Tennyson's poem, ' The Holy Grail,'* Sir Percivale tells how the knights of the Round Table were at banquet when the Holy Grail miraculously passed through the hall, covered with a luminous cloud. Many of them swore to spend twelve months in quest of it. At the end of the year the survivors reassembled, and told their story.

The mightiest knight of them all, Lancelot, told how he had sought the Holy Grail in hope to free himself from the toils of his secret sin with the Queen, but it was the sin itself which prevented him from finding it. He fell into a madness, and wandering over wastes and seas he came to the enchanted towers of Carbonek, a castle on a sea-girt rock, guarded by lions ; he heard a sweet voice singing

* *Poems of Tennyson:* Oxford University Press, p. 646.

in the topmost tower, and climbed a thousand steps, and forced a door :

> ' It gave, and thro' a stormy glare, a heat
> As from a seventimes-heated furnace, I,
> Blasted and burnt, and blinded as I was,
> With such a fierceness that I swooned away—
> O, yet methought I saw the Holy Grail,
> All pall'd in crimson samite, and around
> Great angels, awful shapes, and wings and eyes.
> And but for all my madness and my sin,
> And then my swooning, I had sworn I saw
> That which I saw ; but what I saw was veiled
> And covered : and this Quest was not for me.'

He had sought out the Grail, but could not behold it, because of his state of sin.

Sir Percivale tells how he met Sir Galahad, the youngest knight, and saw him cross the dark sea and enter the spiritual city, the city of the Grail, to be crowned king there.

Lust ends in cruelty

St. Agatha, the first of the virgin-martyrs mentioned in Mass and Litany of the Saints, was a noble maiden in Sicily, about A.D. 250. The Governor Quintianus was taken with her beauty and tried every way of seducing her, in vain. Then he had her denounced to his own tribunal as a Christian, and remanded her in the care of an evil woman named Aphrodisia, in order to overcome her chastity. After a month Aphrodisia reported that she was wasting her time on Agatha Quintianus therefore had her brought before him again.

' Are you not ashamed, being of so noble a family, to lead the life of a Christian just like any slave ? '

' To be a lowly Christian slave is a much finer thing,' she replied, ' than all the riches and pride of kings.'

This made the Governor, who had himself been consul in Rome, very angry.

' Sacrifice to the gods, or else get ready for the torturers.'

She was beaten and put in a dungeon, and the next day stretched on a rack, and red-hot plates applied to her sides, not to mention other torments.

CATECHISM STORIES 441

'Merciless tyrant!' she exclaimed. 'You should be ashamed to be so cruel to a woman—remember you were once an infant at your mother's breast.'

Back in prison, she had a vision of St. Peter, who healed her wounds. After a few days she was again before the Governor, and again tortured by being rolled on hot coals and broken pottery. An earthquake now shook the city, and the people attributed this to the anger of the Christian God at the Governor's conduct. So he hurried Agatha back to prison, in a dying condition. 'Lord, Thou hast guarded me as a child, Thou hast taken away from me the love of this world, Thou hast given me to overcome the torturers! Now receive my soul!' Then she passed to her heavenly reward.

(For other stories bearing on Unchastity and its opposite, see Nos. 8, 211, 212, and all under Sixth and Ninth Commandments.)

Dangerous companions

We may well think that St. Teresa (of Avila) exaggerates the significance of her own early faults, or perhaps she is tending to merge morals with ascetics, or the commandments with the counsels; but maybe there are some girls who might benefit from what she tells us.

She was brought up very piously (as the anecdotes of her childhood show), but her mother died when she was thirteen. She was already a tall girl of delicate beauty, with big dark eyes, full of gaiety and charm, the centre of an admiring circle of friends and relatives. For a time her favourite occupation was the reading (unknown to her father) of 'romances'—tales of knights and ladies in which love-making was treated as the only real end of life— corresponding to one kind of cinema-product to-day. 'I was so enchanted with the extreme pleasure I took in these, that I could never be happy unless I had some new romance in my hands.' She even wrote a romance herself, which seems to have been quite a success amongst her friends. Meanwhile her piety was forgotten, and worldly occupations took its place. 'I began to copy the fashions, to take delight in fine dresses, to take great care of my hands' (they were small and beautiful hands) 'and to use all the vain ornaments and perfumes I could.'

Then she describes how she came under the influence of some worldly cousins who often came to her father's house. ' He was careful to forbid entrance to any except them, and would to God he had forbidden them also ; for I see now the danger there is, when one is at an age to receive the first seeds of virtue, in mixing much with persons who know the foolishness of the world and entice others to take part in it.' She laments (says Alban Butler) that the familiarity she had with a vain female cousin, and one other person who lived in the same folly, so changed her as to leave no sign of her former impressions of virtue.

She was then in her sixteenth year, and her father, noticing that for three months she had lost her fervour, sent her to finish her schooling at a convent in Avila. For a week she was very bored with it, but soon forgot her frivolous companions and recovered her interest in the things of God.

At the time her two or three years of worldliness had seemed nothing worse than harmless amusement, with some venial sin at the worst. But in after-life she always reckoned that her soul had been in very great danger. She used to say that she could see the very place in hell which would have been hers if she had continued along the path she had been following during those few years.

N.B.—About dangerous reading : Père Lacordaire was once asked by a lady if there was any harm in reading novels. ' It's for you to tell me that,' he replied. People must be honest with themselves and give up what they feel to be dangerous in their own case.

(See also stories 312, 313, 314, 346.)

Indecent conversation

People who have an itch for unbecoming talk and stories which have no point except indecency, might learn from this one :

One morning a boy, knowing that the family washing

CATECHISM STORIES 443

bill was a serious consideration, was wondering whether he should put on a clean collar, or whether yesterday's would do again. He looked at it carefully. ' I think it might pass,' he said to his mother.

' No,' she said. ' If it's doubtful, son, it's dirty.'

It is the same with the dirty stories ; not necessarily sinful, but dirty.

' The spirit against the flesh '

Work is one of the surest remedies for temptations against chastity. The great St. Jerome was much liable to these, and had acquired a habit of sinning against the Sixth Commandment in his boyhood. He was not baptised until his teens, and then he began a long fight against his temptations. Fasting, disciplines, and other austerities seemed to make little difference. What he found most helpful was study. Finally he had the idea of learning Hebrew, with an old Jewish rabbi for teacher. It was very hard work, but at last he knew the language so well that he translated the whole of the Old Testament from Hebrew into Latin, for which Catholics have been very grateful to him ever since. He found himself working at this enormous task with such interest and energy that his bodily desires, though not disappearing of course, no longer dominated his imagination or filled his leisured thoughts.

(See also story 345.)

' Mater castissima '

St. Anthony of Padua was another saint who was subject by nature to frequent temptations of this kind. It was not his way on these occasions to feel upset or afraid. He would merely lift up the eyes of his mind to Our Lady in heaven, and say : ' My Queen and my Mother, watch over me,' and go on calmly with whatever he was doing. It is said that Our Lady appeared to him shortly before his death, and told him of the great reward that awaited him in heaven for his faithfulness.

(See also stories 310 and 343.)

Quarrelling

Two old desert hermits had lived quietly next to each other for many years. At last one said :

' This is rather a slow life : let us have a quarrel, as other men do.' The other said : ' How does one begin a quarrel ? '

' See,' said the first, ' I will place this stone between us. Then I will say : That stone is mine. Then you must say : That is not true—it's *my* stone. Now let us begin.'

He placed the stone in the middle.

' Keep away from this stone—it belongs to me.'

' No, you are wrong, it is my stone.'

' I tell you it is mine ! '

' Oh, well, if it is really yours, you must take it.'

They had lived peacefully in Christ so long that they did not know how to quarrel or to covet. (From Rufinus.)

(See also story 298.)

Nursing a grievance

Two sisters lived together in Edinburgh, in one large room with two beds. One day they had an argument about whose turn it was to wind the clock. There were sharp remarks and sharp answers, and they stopped speaking to each other. For fifty years they lived in that room without speaking. They divided the room into two by a chalk line, halving the fireplace and the door. Neither of them ever crossed the line or spoke to the other, much less did anything to help the other. (Told by R. L. Stevenson as a fact.)

This is only an extreme instance of the way many relatives and neighbours live, but what a thing to come to !

Impatience can be checked

Blessed Peter Faber once came to the door of a monastery and rang the bell for admittance. For some reason or other the door was not answered, and while he was kept waiting in the street the saint employed his time in praying for the souls in purgatory, who like himself had to wait.

After a while he rang the bell again, but nobody came; so he prayed for the poor who wait at the doors of the rich, that God might give them the grace to bear their hard lot with patience and so to gain the joys of heaven.

Again he rang, and nobody came; and he prayed for all those in prison waiting for the day of release, that they might repent of their sins and escape condemnation in God's judgement.

Again he rang. Nobody came. Then he prayed with more fervour still in union with the Good Shepherd, lovingly and patiently waiting for the return of many a lost sheep. So when at last the porter came to the door, Blessed Peter did not regret that he had been so long.

(See also stories 199, 555 and 587.)

Gluttony ruins health and fitness

A middle-aged millionaire, head of some large business in U.S.A., was too fond of eating and drinking, and suffered much from gastric troubles and gout. While engaged on a ten-course dinner by himself one evening, some gangsters entered and took him off to a lonely wooden house in the mountains. There they held him to ransom, and when he refused to write the necessary letters they kept him on bread and water.

This went on for several weeks. Then one day, when there was only one rather careless guard left to watch him, the millionaire got away, hid in the woods till night, then managed to reach a road and stopped a passing car.

When the police reached the hut, of course the kidnappers had disappeared. But the millionaire did not mind much, for his gout and gastric ulcers had entirely disappeared, too. After this experience, though he did not go back to bread and water, he was much more careful about his diet.

(See also stories 344 and 568.)

We should know when to stop

Even as children we ought to learn moderation in food:

FATHER: What's 'e crying for now?

MOTHER: That kid's never satisfied. 'E's 'ad a stick o' rock, fish and chips, 'arf a pound of chocolate creams, two ginger beers, winkles, and five cornets, and yet he don't seem 'appy.

Enough is as good as a feast

' Mrs. Churchill's sister, Miss Nellie Hozier, and her friend, Miss Angela Manners, had gone out as nurses on the first opportunity in 1914, and somehow or other got taken captive on the retreat from Mons. Dissatisfied with the conditions of their confinement, Miss Hozier demanded an interview with the German commandant. " In prison," she told him, " there are two things that I always insist upon : one is Bread, and the other is Water." ' (From *The Observer.*)

The temperate are the trustworthy

A scriptural example of temperance is Gedeon's battle as related in Judges vii, 1–23. His three hundred picked men were those who had showed self-control when thirsty, kneeling and drinking from their hands, not lying down by the waters and drinking like dogs.

The Drink habit

Young people who take to drinking are foolish, for it may become a wretched slavery.

VICAR'S WIFE: I was sorry I saw you coming out of the public-house yesterday, William.

VILLAGE TOPER: Yes, mum, so was I. But I *must* come out sometimes.

What Drink can do

' Terrorised into silence a seventy-seven-year-old widow kept secret for three months an amazing attack on her by her son, who tore her wedding-ring from her finger in order to sell it for drink.

' This was disclosed at Liverpool Police Court when ——

(33), unemployed seaman, of —— Street, Liverpool, pleaded " Guilty " to stealing a gold wedding-ring, a roll of linoleum, a blanket and a bed-sheet from his mother.

'He was sentenced to six months' hard labour. The police said —— had been out of work for fourteen months, and since he separated from his wife six months ago had been living with his mother and two sisters.

'Instead of paying for his keep he was continually demanding money from them, and he had been living in such a state of terror that they were afraid to disclose his cowardly attack on his widowed mother which took place last December.

'He pawned the ring and threw the pawn ticket in his mother's face, saying: "You can get it out of pledge if you want." The old woman and her two daughters were terrified of him, and this cowardly theft would never have come to light but for the fact that detectives heard of it when inquiring about the other thefts.

'When Mrs. —— refused to part with the ring her son got hold of her and pulled it from her finger by force. Her flesh was torn and her hand and arm were blue from his violence for weeks afterwards.' (*Reynolds' News*.)

The envious mind

Envy is a bitter sadness about the superior qualities or good fortune of another.

In Genesis iv, 2–4, envy is represented as the motive which leads Cain to murder his brother.

The whole conduct of the Jewish scribes and chief priests towards Our Lord as described in the gospels, is a terrible example of envy, as even Pilate could see (Matt. xxvii, 18).

Our Lord Himself has given us a picture of how envy works (even in otherwise good people) in the behaviour of the elder son in the parable of the Prodigal (Luke xv, 25–32). The elder son envied the prodigal's warm welcome, and perhaps, too, he envied him his riotous living, though he professed to be shocked at it.

Note the father's remark in verse 32 about being *glad* ; this is the opposite of envy which is a sadness.

Another instance of envy and jealousy in the parables is that of the workers in the Vineyard (Matt. xx, 1-16).

The envious tongue

Envy is the parent of most evil-speaking against the character of others.

The artist Giotto painted the Seven Deadly Sins in a chapel at Padua. Envy is represented as a female, with wide ears spread out to catch every bit of gossip, and a poisonous tongue like a serpent; and this tongue coils back and stings the eyes of Envy herself, so that she is blind to the truth.

The poet Spenser represented the same vice as a ' Blatant Beast,' a monster coming out from dark and foul places, having a thousand poisonous tongues, working havoc and shame through all mankind.

Too much class-consciousness

There is sometimes a good deal of envy, as well as zeal for justice, in the socialist or communist mind.

' Glorious weather to-day, mate ! '

' Yes, it is.'

' Well, why do you look so glum then ? '

' Because the capitalist class are enjoying it too ! '

The generous mind

The opposite of envy is the glad recognising of the good qualities or good fortune of others. Of such generosity of mind the Dominican St. Thomas Aquinas and the Franciscan St. Bonaventure were both examples.

They were both commanded by the Pope to compose an Office and Mass for the new festival of Corpus Christi. The better one of the two was to be chosen, and both saints arrived to read their manuscripts to the Pope. It was St. Thomas's turn first. When he had finished the Pope asked St. Bonaventure to read his, but Bonaventure replied ' *Non est* '—' There isn't one.' While St. Thomas was reading his beautiful Office and Mass (which the

CATECHISM STORIES 449

Church uses now) St. Bonaventure, full of admiration, had been quietly tearing up his own effort.

On another occasion St. Thomas called to see St. Bonaventure, and asked the lay-brother at the door whether Bonaventure was busy at the time.

' He is writing the life of our holy patriàrch St. Francis,' said the lay-brother.

' Then I will go away,' said Aquinas. ' It would not be right to disturb one saint when he is writing the life of another.'

The poison of jealousy

Jealousy is much the same as envy; we want to keep something for ourselves, and are sad at the possibility of others having any share in it.

From their own experiences, inward or observed, children in their teens can often recognise that jealousy is a disease of love and leads to tragedy.

Shakespeare's *Othello* is a terrible picture of the sixth Deadly Sin, in more than one of its aspects.

Beginning with sketches of a mild case of parental possessiveness (Brabantio) and of a rejected suitor's spitefulness (Roderigo), it shows the black-hearted Iago envious of Cassio's promotion and of Othello's happiness. Othello listens to him, and gives way to fatal jealousy.

The essential story, from this point of view, is told in one long scene, Act III, Scene 3.

The sin of Acedia

The seventh Deadly Sin is not so much laziness, but rather the inactivity that is due to cowardice or cynicism or lack of interest or want of confidence in God; in short the lack of love. Sloth says: ' Oh, what's the use ? ' e.g. Our Lord's parable of the Slothful Servant, who hid his talent out of fear (Matt. xxv, 14–30).

The slothful person loses interest and hope and is found unready at the critical moment: hence the parable of the Foolish Virgins (Matt. xxv, 1–13).

Similarly several parables of Servants Watchful and

Unwatchful (Luke xii, 35-48). The bad servants were not merely lazy, but had no interest in their job and no faith in their master's return.

(See also stories 302, 345 and 434.)

Facing up to difficulties

A little mountain village : all the carts laden with butter, cheese, eggs, honey and vegetables start off for market, along the narrow road—a steep cliff on one side, a precipice on the other. Suddenly all are held up ; the road is blocked by a great fall of stones and earth from the mountain-side.

All gather round ; everyone says it's not his job to clear the road ; they quarrel and blame each other. No one will help, or work unpaid ; many go home.

A boy named Julian thinks it's a pity all the carts are held up because no one will do a good turn. Consults his poor old grandfather, with whom he lives in a cottage near by. They fetch their old barrow and two shovels and start work.

All day they toil in the hot sun ; the people think they're fools. At last late in the evening only one barrowful is left to cart away. Julian suddenly calls out : he has unearthed a leather bag ! All crowd round. Julian cuts the cord and pulls out a handful of *glittering gold pieces !*

The people start clamouring that it belongs to all the village since it was found among the mountain stones.

All unseen, the lord of the village has ridden up. 'No, good people,' he says, ' the gold is the unexpected reward of those who freely served their fellows. I caused that pile of earth to fall on the road ; I placed the gold beneath. It was to test my people.'

Even so God allows difficulties in the world to give His children the chance to overcome them. He, too, hides a golden reward.

' Be you also ready '

Of St. Charles Borromeo the story is told that he was once playing cards with friends when conversation turned on what they would do if they were told they must die for certain in an hour's time. One said he would make his will, another that he would hasten to confession, another that he would spend the time in prayer. Somebody asked St. Charles what he would do.

'I should go on playing cards,' he said.

Christians who are ever on the watch, living every day as if it were their last, and doing every action for God in the spirit of the 'morning offering,' are ready at all times for anything.

(See also story 550.)

No hurry!

The Devil summoned his demons to a council of war, how best to get mankind to do his will.

'Send me,' said one. 'I will tell them there is no God.'

'They know there is,' was the answer. 'They would never believe you.'

'Send me,' said another. 'I will tell them there is no Hell.'

'Even if they believed you, they will still hope for Heaven.'

'Send me,' said a third. 'I will tell them there is no hurry.'

That was greeted as a grand idea. The third demon was sent out into the world and has laboured with great success ever since. (Acknowledgments to *Torches for Teachers*.)

Lost opportunities

'" While we have time, let us work good to all men. . . ." Titus, son of Vespasian, who to avenge the blood of the Lord destroyed Jerusalem and entered Rome in triumph, is said to have been so good-hearted that one night at supper he remembered he had done no kind action that day, and he said : " Friends, to-day I have lost a day ! "

'We, meanwhile, do not realise that hours, days, moments, ages are being lost to us when we talk with idle words for which we must render account in the day of judgement.' (St. Jerome, Comm. on Galatians, book 3, c. 6.)

The Poor in spirit

What really matters is to be ' poor in spirit ' (Our Lord tells us) ; and some of those noble and princely saints who lived amongst outward riches managed to be among the most truly ' poor ' for the love of Christ.

St. Francis of Assisi lived in actual poverty; St. Elizabeth of Hungary lived in a rich palace, and yet she had the same spirit. When about thirteen years old St. Elizabeth became a member of St. Francis's Third Order. Cardinal Ugolino, the friend of St. Francis, was also a friend of Elizabeth's, and she must have asked him to get her some little thing belonging to the holy Founder, for Ugolino asked St. Francis to do as Elias had done for his disciple and leave her his cloak—' as she is full of your spirit,' he said. St. Francis, delighted to hear of this dear little Lady Poverty, sent her his cloak. It remained St. Elizabeth's greatest treasure. When she was dying she left it to one of her friends, saying : ' Despise it not because it is old and patched and worn : it is the most precious jewel that I ever possessed,' and she told how she always put it on when she wished to pray for some special grace, and how she was always heard.

(On Poverty as a virtue see also stories 350, 540, 543.)

The Meek bear no grudges

St. James, son of Zebedee, was not very meek when he first joined Our Lord. He wanted to call fire down on a Samaritan city (story in Luke ix, 51–56). But by the time of his martyrdom (he was beheaded by Herod to please the Jews, Acts xii, 1–2) he had learned the lesson. A tradition reported by Eusebius tells us that the man who denounced him before the tribunal, seeing his fearless confession of Christ crucified, repented and declared himself a Christian. He was sentenced to be beheaded along with St. James. On the way to execution he asked St. James

CATECHISM STORIES 453

to forgive him, and after a moment of hesitation the saint gave him the kiss of peace (as if at the Holy Eucharist), saying ' Peace be with thee.' Then they knelt side by side to receive the sword of the executioner.

Christian revenge

There was a cholera epidemic in Paris during 1832. A Sister of Charity who was going to the hospital one day was rudely insulted by a working-man ; he followed her, shouting bad language, and would have struck her if not prevented by the bystanders, but she went quietly on to her duty.

A few days later a new patient was brought to the hospital, already crowded with hundreds, with deaths every few minutes. ' No room—not for one more ! ' said the officials at the door. The new patient was being turned away when Sister M—— happened to pass and recognised him ; it was the man who had so insulted her.

' Oh, don't send him away ! I will find a corner for him somewhere—I will look after him myself.'

He was taken in, and the Sister tended him unceasingly, in addition to all her other patients.

He did not recognise the Sister as one of those he had insulted for, alas, he had insulted many.

On the eighth day he was out of danger, but found a new nurse looking after him.

' Where is Sister M—— ? ' he asked.

' She took the cholera herself and died during the night.'

In that way Sister M—— had taken her revenge in the Christian fashion and the man's hatred of religion was changed to repentance and faith.

(See also story 71.)

Christian martyrdom

In the great Japanese persecution, a list of Christians to be put to death was being drawn up in the town of Bungo.

Andrew Usugamara, a prominent citizen, went to the authorities. 'Put my name at the top of the list. I was the first to become a Christian.'

He went to his eighty-year-old father to encourage him for martyrdom. But the old man, a former Samurai warrior who had only been converted six months before, though quite willing to die for the Faith, could not see why he should die unresisting.

'No, no—I still have my sword! I shall die fighting—it would be a disgrace to be killed without defending myself.'

Usugamara saw it was useless to explain the Christian idea of martyrdom.

'Well then,' he said, 'if you will not die as the martyrs die, will you go into the country and take my child with you, to save his life and bring him up a Christian?'

The old man was very indignant.

'What, run away like a coward? No, I shall stay here and be martyred with the rest of you. Only I must defend myself and kill one or two of my attackers first, and then I shall be martyred with great joy.'

Usugamara gave up the argument and fell back on prayer, which was soon answered. His young wife was busy embroidering a magnificent kimono, and the old man, who was very fond of her, asked her what it was for.

'I want to look my best,' she said, 'when they come to fix me to the cross.'

The old man looked round, and he saw all the rest of the household similarly engaged, preparing the sacred ornaments and rosaries, etc., which they intended to wear on the day of martyrdom. All at once he changed, threw away his sword, took up his rosary and said: 'I will die the same way as you. We will all go to Heaven together.'

There was great rejoicing, and he kept his word till the end.

'Beati qui lugent'

In our mourning we should imitate Our Lord, whose tears were for the *sorrows* of mankind, especially of His own friends (death of Lazarus, John xi, 32–36), and for the *sins* of the world, especially of His own people (Luke xix, 41–44).

(See also St. Joan of Arc, story 214; and for mourning for sins, story 492.)

The hunger and thirst after justice

Less than a hundred years ago, with the Industrial Revolution in full swing, child-labour, or rather child-slavery, in England went on in conditions indescribable. The country folk had been driven into towns by the Enclosure Acts, and, often workless themselves, were forced to send their children to the factories.

In the pin-making, children commenced as early as five years old (usually to pay off money that their parents borrowed) and worked from 6 a.m. to 8 p.m. After fifteen they were useless for this or any other work.

In the Yorkshire worsted-spinning mills children began aged eight, working at busy times from 3 a.m. to 10 p.m. Deformity and loss of use of limbs was frequent in the teens or before, owing to the positions necessary at the spindle.

Pauper children were sent from London to Lancashire by canal in boat-loads, called apprentices, but really to become slaves in the cotton-mills and work fourteen hours a day.

In coal-mines children of six, or even younger, were used as 'trappers,' sitting alone in the dark in a small recess by the ventilation-doors. Babies were used to frighten the rats from their father's food. In some parts women and little girls, bent double, pushed coal-trucks along the mine-galleries, or pulled them by chains on all fours, like animals. In the mines, too, workhouse apprentices were used; boys of eight bound apprentice for twelve years, forced to work in the dangerous places where miners would not send their own boys; and in case of refusal taken before magistrates and sent to prison.

Thousands of little 'climbing boys,' of six or thereabouts, were used by chimney-sweeps and forced and beaten into climbing up narrow chimneys to clean them. At first they would come down with their arms and knees streaming with blood. They would have to do several chimneys a day perhaps. Fairly often they got wedged inside and died suffocated by soot.*

* For these facts and many others, see J. L. and Barbara Hammond's *Lord Shaftesbury*.

The man who, more than any other, put a stop to these cruelties, was Lord Shaftesbury. His own childhood, both at home and at his early school, was miserable; but an old servant of the family, Maria Millis, loved the small boy and from her he caught a deep religious spirit (though very Evangelical Protestant) which inspired his whole life. At Harrow he was happier, and there one day he met a pauper's funeral and was so shocked by the coarse levity of it that he made up his mind to work for the neglected poor. As the son of a great family he went into Parliament as a matter of course at the age of twenty-five. He was a strong Tory and always remained so in all matters except where his pity was aroused for the victims of cruelty.

Very soon he became the leader of those who were fighting the battle of the child-workers. For over fifty years he worked and wore himself out, speaking in Parliament and at meetings, visiting industrial districts, seeking out witnesses for Govenment enquiries, writing endless letters, burdening himself with debt for his good causes.

Everything was against him and his helpers: the influence of the employers, the obstruction of politicians, the resistance of the House of Lords, the apathy of the public. The reformers were ridiculed as 'humanity-mongers,' and accused of ruining British trade.

But gradually progress was made. In 1847, by the help of a conscientious mill-owner named Fielden, the Ten Hours Act was passed and put an end to the worst factory abuses.

In 1842 the Mines Act began to put some limit on the employment of children underground.

As for the climbing-boys, they were protected in theory by Acts of 1840 and 1864, which were evaded by sweeps or not enforced by magistrates. It was not until 1875 that Shaftesbury was able to get them enforced, using two recent cases as an argument. Christopher Drummond, aged seven and a half, had been sent up a flue near Gateshead and taken out dead fifteen minutes later; and George Brewster, aged fourteen, died after sweeping a chimney near Cambridge. Shaftesbury got an Act passed

CATECHISM STORIES

making it obligatory for chimney-sweeps to have a licence, which could be withdrawn if they sent the boys up chimneys.

Shaftesbury also worked hard for the reform of the lunacy laws and private asylums, and in improving health and housing, especially for the agricultural labourers on his own estates, which he received from his father in very bad condition. Unfortunately, here he wrecked his own plans by leaving affairs too much in the hands of an agent who proved untrustworthy and brought him almost to ruin.

Shaftesbury was a strong anti-Popery Protestant, but when he died Cardinal Manning said of his life : ' It was a noble and unique Christian manhood. What a retrospect of work done. It makes me feel that my life has been wasted. . . . He took human suffering and human sorrow, and the helplessness of childhood and the poor, as the end of which to live. He spent and was spent for it, and his own life was a suffering life like the Man of Sorrows going about doing good.'

(See also stories 137, 322, 329, 561, 598.)

' Beati misericordes '

When St. Brigid first started life as a handmaid of the Lord seven other noble maidens joined her, and Bishop Maccaille received their vows, gave them the white habit and veil that for centuries remained the dress of Irish nuns, and helped them found the first convent ever established in Ireland. The holy bishop suggested that as there were eight of them, each should choose one of the Beatitudes from Our Lord's Sermon on the Mount as her own motto. They read over the eight blessed virtues that Christ had praised so specially, and the other sisters asked Brigid to choose first. The one Brigid chose was ' Blessed are the merciful.'

In those days when people had less natural sympathy towards suffering, there was much needless cruelty. St. Brigid by her tender care for the poor, and her well-known kindness to animals, gave an example of Christian mercy which was much needed; and her choice of a motto shows that she was fully aware of this.

(See also stories 465, 596–600.)

Mercy to one's enemy

During the revolutionary wars, one of the French commanders in the Army of the Alps was General Dumas, father of the great novelist. He rode into a village square one day and found that the political commission had erected a guillotine there, and was about to execute four ragged Italians. He asked what their crime was.

'They had plotted to assassinate you, General, as you arrived.'

'I would rather you released them,' said Dumas.

'Pardon, General, but you have no power to interfere with the sentence of the republican tribunal.'

It was true—Paris would break him for it.

'All right,' he said, 'but I have power to requisition fuel for the army.'

He turned to the soldiers who were guarding the prisoners. 'Take down that guillotine. Chop it up for firewood.'

To the prisoners, now left unguarded, he said: 'Now, then, run for it while you can!'

They escaped, and there was one more story to tell of the General's notoriously kind heart.

(See also stories 71 and 646.)

Mercy to animals

The saints love and respect all animals because God is their Creator, and cares for them (Matt. vi, 26; x, 29). Sometimes, like St. Francis or St. Brigid, they have special power over animals, or strange fore-knowledge about them.

Here is the remarkable story of St. Columba and the crane that came from Ireland.

'And another time it befell, while the saint was living on Iona, that he called one of the brethren to him, to speak

CATECHISM STORIES

to him. Go thou, he said, three days from now to the west of this island at dawn, and sit above the shore and wait: for when the third hour before sunset is past, there shall come flying from the northern coasts of Ireland a stranger guest, a crane, wind-tossed and driven far from her course in the air: tired out and weary she will fall on the beach at thy feet and lie there, her strength nigh gone: tenderly lift her and carry her to the steading near by: make her welcome there and cherish her with all care for three days and nights; and when the three days are ended, refreshed and loth to tarry longer with us in our exile, she shall take flight again towards that old sweet land of Ireland whence she came, in pride of strength once more: and if I commend her so earnestly to thy charge, it is that in that country-side where thou and I were reared, she too was nested.

'The brother obeyed: and on the third day, when the third hour before sunset was past, stood as he was bidden, in wait for the coming of the promised guest: and when she had come and lay fallen on the beach, he lifted her and carried her ailing to the steading, and fed her, famished as she was. And on his return that evening to the monastery the Saint spoke to him, not as one questioning but as one speaks of a thing past. May God bless thee, my son, said he, for thy kind tending of this pilgrim guest: that shall make no long stay in her exile, but when three suns have set shall turn back to her own land.

'And the thing fell out even as the saint had foretold. For when her three days' housing was ended, and as her host stood by, she rose in first flight from the earth into high heaven, and after a while at gaze to spy out her aerial way, took her straight flight above the quiet sea, and so to Ireland through the tranquil weather.'

(See also story 5—St. Kevin and St. Malo.)

We should have kindness for animals, but not let it run away with us so far that we forget to be kind to human beings.

Like the little girl who cried when she was shown a

picture of the early Christians being martyred in the amphitheatre:

'What are you crying for?'

'That poor little lion at the back—he isn't getting any!'

'Beati mundo corde'

'Clean of heart' means a heart free from every kind of self-seeking.

Of few men could this be said more truly than of St. Anthony of Padua.

From earliest life he put God first, and became a priest (Augustinian Canon) in his native Lisbon. But it seemed too easy a life when he heard of the first Franciscans; and especially when the bodies of five of them, martyred in Morocco, were brought to Lisbon. He joined the Franciscans himself (changing his name of Ferdinand to Anthony) and went to Morocco. But instead of martyrdom he endured a long and severe illness, and was sent back useless in a ship bound for Portugal, but it was driven by storms to Sicily. From there he begged his way to Assisi, where St. Francis was holding the Chapter of 1221.

Anthony looked so ill and weak that no superior would take him, but at last a Provincial sent him to say Mass for some friars at a mountain hermitage near Bologna, where he spent his time working in the kitchen, carefully concealing the fact that he was a wonderfully gifted orator, one of the greatest the Church had seen. For how this gift became known, see story 610 in this volume.

The usual selfish motives which sway men's hearts—riches, fame, power, ambition, success—carnal desire, too, see story 624—none of them could adulterate his single-minded purpose of doing the divine Will.

'They shall see God.' St. Anthony went to the Beatific Vision at the early age of thirty-six; but even in life he was rewarded by seeing God in human form. Not long before his death he was staying in a man's house at Camposanpiero, near Padua. At night the man saw a marvellous light streaming on to the garden from Anthony's window;

CATECHISM STORIES 461

he went to it and looked, and saw the Holy Child standing on an open book upon the table, with His arms around the neck of the saint who was caressing Him lovingly. Afterwards Anthony asked his friend to keep silence about the vision, and he did so until he gave evidence of it before the Pope for the canonisation, a few months after the saint's death.

(See also stories 137, 197, 214, 340.)

'Beati pacifici'

Archbishop Affré of Paris was murdered during the Revolution of 1848. Horror-stricken by the slaughter which for three days had been going on, he resolved to try whether it would be possible to reconcile the contending parties. Dressed in his pontifical robes, carrying the Cross, and attended by two chaplains, he set out for the Place de la Bastille. The people, knowing his danger, fell on their knees and begged him to turn back. He answered quietly, ' It is my duty. A good shepherd giveth his life for the sheep.' He was mortally wounded near the Bastille by a shot fired from a window. The insurgents, horror-stric', carried him to a neighbouring hospital. When told he had only a few minutes to live, he said: ' God be praised ! May He accept my life as an expiation for my omissions during my episcopate, and as an offering for this misguided people.' Then, repeating once more ' A good shepherd giveth his life for his flock,' he added, ' and may my blood be the last that is shed.' With those words on his lips he passed away.

(Lewis C. Price: *Archbishop Darboy and some French tragedies*, p. 68.)

Persecution is a privilege

B. Thomas Sherwood was a young lay Catholic of London, in his twenties. His mother, one of those Cornwall Tregians who helped B. Cuthbert Mayne, spent fourteen years in prison and died there. Young Mr. Sherwood was short in stature, healthy of body and very temperate in diet, with a special charm in his conversation. He was enthusiastic about the Faith, reading what books he could get and conversing often with priests; and ' was able to give good counsel to any of the more ignorant sort.' He desired in fact to study for the priesthood. But one morning he was met in Chancery Lane by a young man from Dorsetshire, whose mother, Lady Tregonwell, was a Catholic; and he suspected Sherwood of arranging for priests to visit her house and say Mass secretly. This young man, in his hatred for Sherwood, called the constable and had him arrested.

After severe treatment in prison he was executed at Tyburn. Amidst all his torments his exclamation was: ' Lord Jesus, I am not worthy to suffer this for Thee; much less to receive those rewards which Thou hast promised to those that confess Thee.'

(See also stories 80, St. Ignatius of Antioch, and 564, St. Ignatius Loyola.)

APPENDIX

(This section consists of stories which rightly
belong to the earlier volumes.)

The Catechism is to be lived

SOME years ago the Chinese authorities decided to introduce football into China, and the schoolmasters in one district were told to teach their boys the game. They sent for a book containing all the rules of Association Football. Then they translated it into Chinese. Then they set their unhappy scholars to copy out all the pages and pages of rules and learn them by heart.

When they could all repeat the rules correctly, the masters arranged to have lectures on the rules to make sure they were understood. The lectures were followed by test-papers, the results of which were rather discouraging.

Just then an Englishman happened to visit the town, and some of the boys told him of their desire to become footballers and of the many hours of study they had devoted to it.

'Good heavens!' he said, 'you'll never learn the game like that! The only way to learn to play is by *playing*.'

He got a ball and took them to a field, and in half an hour they knew more about football than six weeks of study had taught them.

Some boys adopt 'Chinese methods' with the Catechism. The Catechism is (so to speak) the book of Rules for living a Christian life; but it is not much use learning up the answers unless we actually live them in our lives.

(See also stories 115, 164.)

The Creed is an act of Faith *

In 1882 Lieut. le Long led a brave company of Arctic explorers from the United States. They all perished in the

*For Baltimore Catechism answer 6-7
English Catechism 14

desolate ice and snow; with awful sufferings. But their bodies were found, and with their bodies a pencilled diary. How the world was moved when the diary was published! It told how they had looked day after day for rescue, and had died one after the other, and all the time were brave and kind to one another. 'And, then, when they are too weak to do more, they stand under that open sky, on that cold and terrible waste, and recite together as an act of loving faith the Creed that reminds them of God's fatherhood, His almightiness and His love, and they breathe together the prayer which Christ's own lips have taught us to use in all our needs.' (Walker Gwynn: *Five Hundred Stories*, quoted by Rev. P. Dearmer.)

God has revealed the facts that matter most. They are in the Creed: a solid rock to stand on in the face of the worst that life can do to us.

(See also stories 25 and 570.)

'Who is Jesus Christ?' *

IF legend is true, one of the saints once received a startling answer to this very question.

It was St. Pedro Pascual, bishop of Jaen, who went to Granada as a missionary, and by his example and his teaching converted many Mohammedans to Christianity. This enraged the authorities, who seized him and cast him into prison and treated him with cruelty and neglect. After a time St. Pedro's friends heard of his plight and collected his ransom-money. Instead of purchasing his own freedom St. Pedro used the money to release a number of his poor converts who were also prisoners.

Our Lord rewarded him in a wonderful way. One day a lovely boy presented himself to serve Pedro's Mass. It was Pedro's custom to catechise the altar server after Mass and he was much struck by the perfect way the boy who had served at the altar answered his questions. Presently he asked the question, 'Who is Jesus Christ?' 'I am He,' said the Boy, showing him nail prints in hands and feet. 'You have endured imprisonment for My sake so I have done this for *your* sake, to show how

*For Baltimore Catechism answer 77-79
English Catechism 32

CATECHISM STORIES 465

pleasing to Me are the sacrifices you have made for the prisoners.'

The holy bishop died a martyr in a Moorish prison, A.D. 1300.

(See also story 58.)

' His life for His friends ' *

'WE went on through the long narrow street, and just as we were in sight of the end the figure of a man dashed out from a farm-house on the right. Immediately the rifles began to crack in front, and the poor chap fell dead before he reached us. He was one of our men, a private of the Royal Irish Regiment. We learned that he had been captured the previous day by a marauding party of German cavalry, and had been held a prisoner at the farm where the Germans were in ambush for us. He tumbled to their game, and though he knew that if he made the slightest sound they would kill him, he decided to make a dash to warn us of what was in store. He had more than a dozen bullets in him. We carried him into a house until the fight was over, and then we buried him next day with military honours. His identification disc and everything else was missing, so that we could only put over his grave the tribute that was paid to a greater : He saved others ; himself he could not save.' (Told by a corporal of the West Yorks, in *Westminster Gazette* of October 1, 1914.)

The spirit of sacrifice *

IN the summer of 1914 Alfred Victor Smith was a young police-constable on duty in Blackpool. When war broke out he joined the 5th East Lancs, and in 1915 was in Gallipoli. Two days before Christmas he had pulled out the pin from a hand-grenade and was throwing it when somehow it fell from his hand. He shouted to the others along the trench but saw that they could not get to safety quick enough. In a second the grenade would explode, and he saw only one way to save them. He dropped flat upon the grenade and smothered the explosion, of course at the cost of his own life.

* For Baltimore Catechism answer 90-94
English Catechism 55

The Victoria Cross was awarded to him, and the French Croix de Guerre, and his heroic example of self-sacrifice was cited in the orders of the French Tenth Army.

' He was such a lovable lad,' wrote the Chief Constable of Blackpool upon hearing of his death. ' All the men are upset. His gentleness endeared him to us all.'

(See also stories 72, 73, 74.)

Dying for his mates * (at. answer 55)

SELF-SACRIFICING heroism happens every day amongst the workers in mines or other industries.

At Miles Platting in July, 1938, some men were working in a sewer-shaft, but came up because the air was bad, and the air-compressor could not be got to work to clear it.

Patrick Murphy, the foreman, aged fifty-four, and John Robert Byrnes, a labourer, went down by ladders to investigate. The air was still bad. Coming up again, Murphy saw that young Byrnes had fallen over, and went back to help him. He picked Byrnes up, but then himself collapsed on him.

John Henry Mears, a miner aged forty-nine, then tied a wet handkerchief over his face and had himself let down in a ' skip.' He picked up Murphy, put him down, signalled to be pulled up, but fell out of the ' skip ' as soon as it left the bottom of the shaft and did not move again.

' No man could have done a braver deed,' said the Coroner to Mrs. Mears at the inquest, ' than your husband did in going down the shaft to help the two men at the bottom.' (From *Daily Herald*, August 3, 1938.)

The Church of all ages and all nations **

IN the National Museum of Ireland is a small bell of earliest Celtic times, which tradition says belonged to St. Patrick. At the Dublin Eucharistic Congress of 1932 it was brought out in cotton-wool and used for the High Mass in Phœnix Park, which was broadcast by the B.B.C.

The bell had to be rung by its Museum guardian, who

* For Baltimore Catechism answer 90-94
English Catechism 55
** For Baltimore Catechism answer 158
English Catechism 97

CATECHISM STORIES

knew how to strike the hoarse note safely from its age-weakened sides.

'Suddenly across the dead silence of a million men and women, who kneel on the grass in unshakable belief that they kneel in the actual presence of God, comes a strange and indescribable sound. At first I think it is like something muffled and rung in a cave by the sea. It is a hollow sound. It is an old sound. It is the sound of St. Patrick's Mass bell telling Irishmen, after its centuries of silence, that Christ has come among them.

'The sound comes three times. It is the very sound that so long ago, in that lovely April of faith when Patrick flung down the heathen gods, drew Irishmen to his little chapel. It is the bell that, as legend says, the saint took with him to Croagh Patrick when he wrestled with demons. It was the bell that was buried with him in the year 461. It is the sound of the bell that the saint whom the West adores, Columcille or Columba, took years afterwards to St. Patrick's tomb. And now it is ringing for Mass again, not only in Dublin, not only in Ireland, but all over the world.

'The sound of the little bell is made to grow mighty, and it goes in the waves of the air throughout the earth. Men in distant lands can hear it. It crosses the sea with the speed of thought. It reaches the Holy Father in Rome. It rings across continents, and the message it gives to the world to-day is the message it gave to Ireland fourteen hundred years ago At the sound of it, the armed men round the altar spring to attention; trumpeters blow a fanfare. The officers lift their drawn swords in salute, holding them towards the Host. The square mile of humanity on its knees covers its eyes and bends in prayer. There is no Catholic in the immense crowd who does not believe that he is in the presence of God. A movement like a ripple runs across the crowd. It is the Sign of the Cross. In the hush I can hear a bird singing, and I hope that the sound of its voice went out over the world with the sound of St. Patrick's bell.' (Acknowledgements to H. V. Morton, in the *Daily Herald*.)

'You are my friends.' *

ST. LOUIS IX, on his way to the Crusade in 1248, turned aside at Perugia to visit Brother Giles, the third of the original companions of St. Francis. St. Francis had called him 'knight of my Round Table,' perhaps because in the early days he was a great wanderer; later he preferred solitude and contemplation. He was now growing elderly; St. Louis was in his thirties. There was excitement among the friars, who expected an interesting conversation, for Giles was famous for his wise and holy sayings.

The King and the friar met, and embraced; they looked long at each other, embraced again and parted, without a word.

'That was the King of France!' cried the friars, 'and you said nothing to him!'

'Our spirits spoke,' said Giles. 'They understood each other like old friends.'

By prayer we call on God's grace. **

WE cannot win our battle without God's help, and God's help comes in answer to our prayer.

Charlemagne is returning with his army from Spain after seven years' war. He must go through the pass of Roncesvalles into France, and he leaves a rearguard of twenty thousand men. Roland, his nephew, the famous captain, commands the rearguard. With him is Oliver, his boyhood friend and comrade-in-arms; and the warrior-archbishop Turpin of Rheims; and the rest of the twelve peers who ride ever with Roland.

Charlemagne is far up in the pass. King Marsilius of Saragossa has had word by the traitor Ganelon, and has sent a hundred thousand Saracens to attack the rearguard. The blast of their thousand clarions is heard from far. Oliver from a hillock sees the vast army approaching; they cover all the valleys and the plain.

'The pagans are many,' he tells Roland, 'and meseems our Franks are few. Comrade Roland, sound your horn! Charles will hear it, and he will turn the army back.'

*For Baltimore Catechism answer 170-174
English Catechism 102
** For Baltimore Catechism answer 475, 477-485
English Catechism 141

CATECHISM STORIES

'May it not please God! Never shall it be said by living man that I sounded my horn on account of pagans! Rather will I strike hard with Durendal my sword, and you will see it all blood up to the hilt. The Franks are strong and valiant, and the pagans are come to their death.'

Three times Oliver urges Roland to sound his horn, and three times Roland refuses.

'French valour shall not fail through me! I would rather death than dishonour. Strike on, and gain the Emperor's love!'

Roland is daring and Oliver is wise. The archbishop absolves the French army, and they go into the fray shouting the battle-cry of Charlemagne: 'Monjoie!'

All day they fight. At last all the Saracens are slain, and the surviving French go over the field searching for their dead friends.

Then suddenly King Marsilius himself appears on the field with another great host, and seven thousand trumpets sound the charge. The French know they must die, but they will fight valiantly to the end.

After many famous deeds done, Roland sees the great slaughter of his men. He calls to Oliver: 'I will sound the horn, and Charles will hear it and return.'

'No,' said Oliver. 'It would be no act of valour to sound it now. When I told you to you would not.'

'Why are you angry with me?'

'Comrade Roland, the fault is yours, and the French are dead. If Charles had been here, this battle would have been won. Now here we shall die, and our comradeship will have its end before the fall of night.'

The archbishop rode up and heard them disputing. 'Enough of blaming each other! Sounding the horn cannot save you now. Better to sound it, however; then Charles will return to avenge us and bear our bodies to burial.'

Roland has put his ivory horn to his mouth, he grasps it firmly and sounds it with all his might. High are the hills, and the sound carries far—thirty leagues away the echo was heard. Charles heard it and all his companies.

'I hear the horn of Roland! He would never sound it unless he were fighting!'

The French army turns back, riding with haste, praying they may be in time.

Roland and Oliver have turned to battle again. Their Franks are as bold as lions, and they put to flight the troops of Marsilius, who rides away wounded.

But now comes the Algalif of Cartagena to the attack, with a great fresh army of blacks from Africa. Oliver kills their leader, but is himself wounded to death. The Franks lie dead on the field. Roland, wounded and spent, sounds his horn again feebly. Charles hears it, and orders all the trumpets in the army to sound in reply.

The pagans, warned by the sound, prepare to flee, but as they go they gather round Roland and the brave Archbishop, hurling their spears and arrows. The Archbishop is dead, and Roland feels his own death near. He speaks words of thanks to his fair and holy sword Durendal which has won so many provinces for Charles. Then he lies down on a hillock with his face to Spain; he remembers the Emperor and the sweet country of France. He confesses his sins, and holds up his right glove to God for forgiveness. The angels take his soul to Paradise.

Charlemagne comes and sees the plain covered with dead. He rides after the pagans and destroys them. Then he comes back and makes search amongst the slain.

When he finds the body of Roland he falls upon it in a swoon. Then he takes up the bodies of Roland and Oliver and the Archbishop, and bears them away to France with great honour.

Always something to thank God for. *

A LITTLE boy was made to finish his rice pudding.

'Now say your grace.'

'What, for that horrid rice pudding?'

'You must thank God, and you can't go and play till you do.'

An interval of silence, then—

'All right. Thank God that I wasn't sick after it.'

Every cloud has a silver lining if we look for it.

*For Baltimore Catechism answer 476
English Catechism 142

CATECHISM STORIES

Spreading the Faith. *

IN some remote parts of the Soudan the negroes regard dying persons as already dead, and bury them while still breathing.

A mission-sister on her travels one day heard a faint wail apparently coming from the ground, and saw a movement of the soil. Digging rapidly with her hands, she soon uncovered the body of a baby girl, still alive. Taken to the mission-house, the baby survived, was baptised by the name of Martha, and grew up a lively and intelligent little Christian ; the only ill-effect of the burial-alive was that she was quite blind.

This was in 1921. Arrived at the age of twelve, Martha made up her mind to leave the mission and go back to her native village and make her home with her own family who had buried her alive. Her idea was to be an apostle to them, and so it happened. One by one she brought her numerous brothers and sisters to the mission to be instructed and baptised, then her mother and father ; and now (1939) at the age of eighteen she has turned her efforts to the conversion of the other villagers and is bringing them also to Christ.

Answers to prayer. **

DURING the revolt of Mohammedan tribes in the Soudan in the 'nineties, a mission-group consisting of one mission-father and three sisters of the Pie Madri remained at their post in spite of official warning, and were taken by the rebels. For months they were in captivity, and often tortured to make them renounce the Christian faith.

At last a friendly Arab got word to them from outside, offering to contrive their escape by night ; and finally definite arrangements were made that on a certain night he would be waiting for them with four camels at a spot outside the village.

On the last day a message came that only three camels could be procured, and the captives were faced with a terrible dilemma. One camel would of necessity have to carry the priest, because he alone knew the way across the

*For Baltimore Catechism answer 493
English Catechism 151
**For Baltimore Catechism answer 496
English Catechism 154

desert. Must one of the sisters be left behind to bear alone the savage fury of the tribesmen? Or should one camel be loaded with two riders, thus reducing the speed of the whole party, and rendering very unlikely their escape from the swift camels of the pursuers?

The captives could not make up their minds what to do. Meanwhile it was absolutely necessary that they should get some sleep before the long and perilous journey, so they lay down after earnestly praying to God that by some means or other He would arrange that nobody need be left behind.

Their prayer was answered. Two hours before dawn their messenger came to say that the camels—three camels —were waiting. When the party arose it was found that God had taken to Himself one of the sisters—the youngest and strongest in fact—who had died peacefully in her sleep. (Acknowledgements to Sister Francesca Kirby.)

Mary is ' our Mother also.' *

IN 1531 Mexico had been conquered for ten years, Cortes was absent in Spain, and the Spanish settlers were ill-treating and enslaving the Indians ; many said the Indians were mere animals without human souls, and it was wrong to baptise them. Bishop Zumarraga (who had been sent from Spain as Protector of the Indians) with his Franciscans made thousands of Indian converts, but could do little to save them from their white masters.

On December 9 a poor Indian convert, baptised Juan Diego, a peasant aged fifty-eight, was coming down to Mass and instruction at a mission church near Mexico City. Suddenly the desolate track was bathed in supernatural light, and on a rock above him he saw a maiden of Indian appearance, magnificently dressed, about fifteen years old, who called him to her : ' Come here, son.' She told him she was Mary the Mother of the true God, and she wished him to tell the Bishop to have a church built on the spot where she stood.

He went, but Bishop Zumarraga asked many questions and was not encouraging. On the way home Diego saw the

*For Baltimore Catechism answer 85
English Catechism 167

CATECHISM STORIES

Lady again and told her she should send someone more important; but she insisted, both that day and the next, that he should get an answer from the Bishop. The Bishop at a second interview said that the Lady should be asked for a sign.

Meanwhile, two days after, Juan's uncle took a fever and seemed to be dying. Juan went to the mission-church for a priest, but took another path lest he should be delayed by the apparition. But the Lady crossed the mountain-side and met him : ' What road is this you are taking, son ? ' He told her about his uncle, but she said he would get well (and in fact she appeared to the uncle at the same time and cured him). Juan must go to the Bishop, she said.

Juan asked for the sign, and she told him to go up amongst the rocks and gather the roses he would find there. Roses amongst the rocks, in midwinter !—sure enough, there they were, and he filled the lap of his blanket (Indian cloak) with them. The Lady arranged them, and told him to keep them hidden till he saw the Bishop, and sent him off.

He came to the Bishop and unfolded the blanket. The roses fell out, and the Bishop and his attendants fell on their knees ; for there on the blanket was a life-size picture of the Lady herself, just as Juan had described her, painted in glowing red and blue and gold with the rays of the sun around her and the moon beneath her feet.

This is the painting still honoured at the great shrine of Our Lady of Guadalupe. The blanket is made of thin woven stuff like poor sacking, and the colours seem to be of no known oil or other material.

The church was begun immediately and the picture was solemnly enthroned there in 1532 : and everyone, Spaniards, too, paid honour to the Holy Mother who had appeared to an Indian, herself in the likeness of an Indian. Henceforth the poor Indians felt they were just as good in the eyes of God as the white men, and many more Indians became Christian. In 1537 a bull of Pope Paul III declared that Indians were capable of receiving the Faith and the Sacraments, and ought to have equal rights with white men.

'Their prayers have great power with God.' *

ST. COLETTE, second foundress of Poor Clares, was once approached by a young man of worldly and sinful life, who said in jest : ' If you really are a saint, work a miracle now, and make me holy ! ' The saint did not lift her eyes to look at him, but simply prayed aloud : ' Hear his words, Lord, and make them true ! ' The young man stared ; the mockery died from his face ; he went hastily away, turned into a church, asked for a priest, and made a good confession. From that time he led a good life, and not long afterwards died a good death.

Even when the saints are still on earth, their prayers have great power ; much more when they are in glory.

(See also no. 123.)

The sin of Presumption. ** 179)

A C.E.G. speaker was talking to the crowd about heaven.

' Look here,' said a facetious heckler, ' what worries me is how I am going to get my shirt on over my wings.'

' Don't you worry, my friend, your particular trouble will be getting your trousers on over your tail.'

Christ and Cæsar. *** 98)

WHEN Napoleon was excommunicated by Pius VII in 1809 (Cardinal Pacca tells us in his *Memoirs*) he made light of it and said : ' Does he think it will make the muskets drop from the hands of my soldiers ? '

All the same he felt uneasy, and told one of his ministers to draw up a list of all the monarchs that had been excommunicated. The minister thought he was not serious, and did nothing about it, but Napoleon insisted, and the list was actually presented to him by M. de Champagny. There were eighty-five cases, not counting the case of Napoleon himself which was tactfully omitted. In all the cases, the excommunication seemed to have had some kind of effect.

Three years afterwards, Napoleon's decline began with

---

*For Baltimore Catechism answer 171, 172, 215-218
  English Catechism 158
* For Baltimore Catechism answer 207-209
  English Catechism 179
** For Baltimore Catechism answer 246-249
  English Catechism 198

CATECHISM STORIES 475

the disastrous retreat from Moscow; and a strange circumstance was noticed by Catholics, that the muskets did actually fall from the hands of thousands of Napoleon's soldiers, owing to the intense cold and the disorganised retreat.

Atrocity stories. *

How facts may be distorted and falsified when passions run high may be illustrated by the following extracts, all purporting to describe the same incidents. The first is from a German newspaper, the *Kolnische Zeitung*, and simply tells how, in 1914, when the news of the capture of Antwerp became known, the church bells of Cologne and other German towns were rung as a sign of rejoicing.

'When the fall of Antwerp got known the church bells were rung.'

The French paper, *Le Matin*, reported it as follows:

'According to the *Kolnische Zeitung* the clergy of Antwerp were compelled to ring the church bells when the fortress was taken.'

The English paper, *The Times*, took up the tale:

'According to what *Le Matin* has heard from Cologne, the Belgian priests who refused to ring the church bells when Antwerp was taken have been driven from their places.'

The Italian paper *Corriere della Sera* went one better:

'According to what *The Times* has heard from Cologne, via Paris, the unfortunate Belgian priests who refused to ring the church bells when Antwerp was taken have been sentenced to hard labour.'

Finally the incident was twisted by *Le Matin* into this:

'According to information to the *Corriere della Sera* from Cologne, via London, it is confirmed that the barbaric conquerors of Antwerp punished the unfortunate Belgian priests for their heroic refusal to ring the church bells by hanging them as living clappers to the bells with their heads down.'

(These quotations are taken from Lord Ponsonby: *Falsehood in War Time*. Quoted by F. C. Happold, in *This Modern Age*.)

*For Baltimore Catechism answer 265-267, 270
English Catechism 220

Reverence in genuflecting. *

When we have to genuflect we can remember St. Antony of Padua's first miracle, and try to genuflect with at least as much reverence as Bonvillo's horse did. It is not a mere legend, but a fairly well-attested story.

Antony was preaching to the heretics in North Italy, and a leading heretic named Bonvillo refused to acknowledge Christ's real presence in the Eucharist, because no change was to be seen in the bread. He was sitting on his horse at the edge of the audience, no doubt, heckling the saint from the saddle.

'I only believe the evidence of my own eyes.'

'Supposing your own eyes saw your horse adore the Blessed Sacrament,' asked Antony, 'would you believe then that Christ was present?'

'Yes, I would.'

'Will you arrange a test then?' said Antony, full of faith that God would take compassion on the heretic. Bonvillo now began to get careful.

'Wait a minute—will you agree to this? I will keep the horse unfed for two days. Then on the third day we will meet in the public square, you carrying the Sacrament and I carrying a feed of oats, and we shall see what the horse does.'

Now it was Antony's turn to be careful, but his faith was still firm.

'I agree to that, but even if the horse goes to the oats it will not disprove the Real Presence—it will merely be due to my sins.'

Everybody heard about the challenge and on the third day the square was crowded. Bonvillo stood on one side with his oats, on the other stood Antony reverently holding a consecrated host over a ciborium. The horse was led out. As soon as it was left to itself the animal slowly walked up to the saint, knelt before him, and remained so until Antony told it to rise. The miracle was obvious to all, and Bonvillo was converted.

*For Baltimore Catechism answer 343
English Catechism 266

'I am the Living Bread.' *

RACHEL L—— was a Jewish girl who knew nothing of Christianity, but disliked everything Christian by instinct. One day at dusk she was passing the open door of a church, and out of curiosity went in. Benediction was just beginning, and Rachel, feeling very much a stranger, sat down timidly on a chair near the door. As the ceremony proceeded a strange fascination held her, and when the priest blessed the people with the Host she was filled with an overwhelming emotion, of which she could give no account afterwards except that she suddenly felt absolutely certain that Our Lord was really in the Host.

Next day she sought a priest for instruction; he made many difficulties, but at last, seeing she was in earnest, he received her into the Church. As a convert she had many tribulations to endure in her Jewish surroundings, and sacrifice became her daily bread. She is now a very active social worker, strengthened in her trials and good works by the Eucharistic King who had so wonderfully made Himself known to her. (From *Our Lady of Sion*, summer number, 1939.)

Once a priest, always a priest. **

In the Great War about 20,000 priests (called up from many foreign missions as well as from parishes and monasteries at home) had to serve in the fighting ranks of the French Army. In the first five weeks of the War over 200 won the Legion of Honour and 400 were recommended for the Military Medal.

On one occasion a part of the line was being badly hammered by German guns, and a battery of French 75's was sent to its aid. It was commanded by an enormous captain who, being clean-shaven, seemed a little out of his element. But he knew his business. Climbing a tree, he directed such an accurate fire on the two German batteries causing the trouble that they were practically wiped out.

That artillery captain was a priest, and after the engagement he celebrated Mass in a ruined barn near by, first

*For Baltimore Catechism answer 343
English Catechism 266
**For Baltimore Catechism answer 451-455
English Catechism 305

exhorting his gunners to pray especially for the Germans they had just exterminated, and while the guns still boomed, leading them in the De Profundis.

* * *

Nor were the French priests alone in their courage. An English lieutenant entering a trench from which the enemy had just been driven heard someone talking in a low voice. Creeping forward, he saw a man supporting the head of another. He thought it a doctor until, on challenging, the man held up a crucifix and he knew it was a priest giving absolution to a dying Bavarian.

The priest could speak no English or French, the Englishman no German, so they carried on a halting conversation in Latin, in which the lieutenant learnt that the priest had deliberately remained behind, risking death, to minister to his dying countryman. The Englishman thought this the bravest thing he had encountered in the War and allowed the priest to return to his own lines. (In the *Universe*, Nov. 10, 1939.)

God creates through Love. *

Dame Juliana, the medieval mystic of Norwich, once in vision saw lying in the palm of her hand something very tiny and round, the size of a hazel-nut. She was wondering what it was, and the answer came: 'It is all Creation: it is all that is made.' Then she wondered that a thing so little and fragile could possibly last, for it seemed every moment as if it would fall to nothing. 'And I was answered: It lasteth and ever shall: for God loveth it. And so hath all thing being, by the love of God.'

'In this little thing I saw three properties. The first is that God made it. The second is that God loveth it. The third is that God keepeth it. But what beheld I therein? Truly the Maker, the Keeper, the Lover.' (*Revelations of Divine Love*, c. 5.)

*For Baltimore Catechism answer 35-37
English Catechism 19

No Race-distinctions in the Church. *

On the feast of Christ the King, 1939, Pope Pius XI consecrated in St. Peter's twelve new bishops and sent them forth like the twelve apostles to teach all nations. They came from Switzerland, Italy, Spain, Germany, Denmark, Mexico ; there was also a Chinese, a Hindu, and two negroes, one from Uganda and one from Madagascar. (These were not the first black bishops—there had been one in the nineteenth century and another in the sixteenth.)

It was the second month of the second Great War. Many nations of the world were fighting each other because they had thought too much about nation and Race, and not enough about being one Family.

The Holy Father spoke to the new bishops, white and brown and yellow and black.

' Christ took His title of King in the darkest days, when He stood a prisoner before Pilate. Happy are those nations which accept the reign of Christ and make their laws according to the Gospel, and live in justice and freedom.

' The present events will pass. The Catholic Church is not afraid of time. Mankind is divided by greed and hatred and jealousy, but the Church of God is for all peoples without distinction of race.

' Go out and conquer the whole world (said the Pope), not with armaments but with the power of truth and love.'

The one Ark of Salvation. *

A ship was hopelessly wrecked on the rocks not far from the shore. The lifeboat went out to rescue the sailors and reached the ship just as it was breaking up. The men were taken off the wreckage and the rocks ; soon the boat was quite full, and the skipper gave the order to make for the shore. Some of the shipwrecked crew were still in the sea. They swam to the crowded boat and managed to hold on to the sides and were thus carried safely to land.

This is a picture of the different ways in which souls

*For Baltimore Catechism answer 158
English Catechism 97

may be saved. Those inside the boat are the members of the visible Church on earth. The others are pagans who have only the baptism of desire, or baptised Christians who remain outside the true Church, and are saved because they are in good faith.

www.ingramcontent.com/pod-product-compliance
Lightning Source LLC
Chambersburg PA
CBHW032012230426
43671CB00005B/60